NETSCAPE COMMUNICATOR™

VISUAL SOLUTIONS

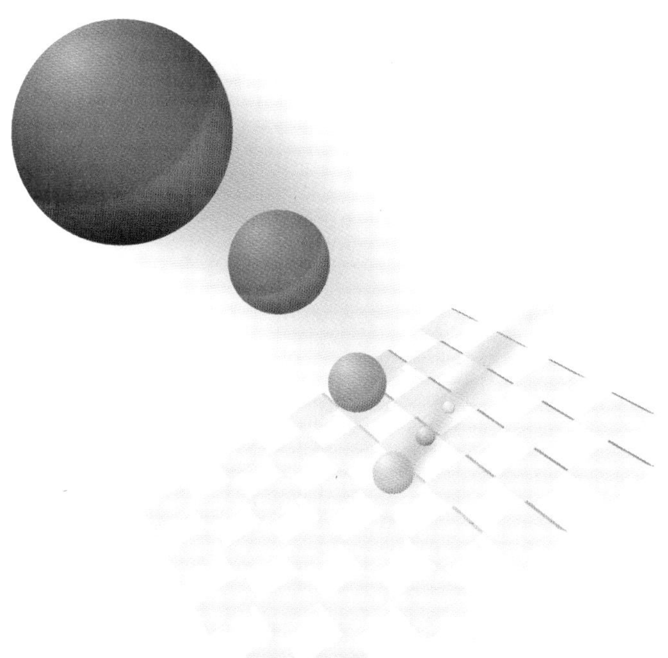

by: maranGraphics' Development Group

Corporate Sales

Contact maranGraphics
Phone: (905) 890-3300
(800) 469-6616
Fax: (905) 890-9434

Canadian Trade Sales

Contact Prentice Hall Canada
Phone: (416) 293-3621
(800) 567-3800
Fax: (416) 299-2529

Visit our Web site at:
http://www.maran.com

Netscape Communicator™ Visual Solutions

Canadian Cataloguing in Publication Data

Maran, Ruth, 1970-
Netscape Communicator : visual solutions

(Visual solutions)
Written by Ruth Maran.
Includes index.
ISBN 1-896283-32-2

1. Netscape Communicator. 2. Internet (Computer network) - Computer programs. 2. World Wide Web (Information retrieval system) - Computer programs. I. MaranGraphics Inc. II. Title. III. Series.

TK5105.883.N48M37 1997 005.7'13769 C97-932107-7

Printed in the United States of America

10 9 8 7 6 5 4 3 2 1

Trademark Acknowledgments

The 3-D illustrations are the copyright of maranGraphics, Inc.

Screen Shot Permissions

maranGraphics™

Every maranGraphics book represents
the extraordinary vision and commitment of a unique family:
the Maran family of Toronto, Canada.

Back Row (from left to right): *Sherry Maran, Rob Maran, Richard Maran, Maxine Maran, Jill Maran.*

Front Row (from left to right): *Judy Maran, Ruth Maran.*

Richard Maran is the company founder and its inspirational leader. He developed maranGraphics' proprietary communication technology called "visual grammar." This book is built on that technology—empowering readers with the easiest and quickest way to learn about computers.

Ruth Maran is the Author and Architect—a role Richard established that now bears Ruth's distinctive touch. She creates the words and visual structure that are the basis for the books.

Judy Maran is the Project Coordinator. She works with Ruth, Richard and the highly talented maranGraphics illustrators, designers and editors to transform Ruth's material into its final form.

Rob Maran is the Technical and Production Specialist. He makes sure the state-of-the-art technology used to create these books always performs as it should.

Sherry Maran manages the Reception, Order Desk and any number of areas that require immediate attention and a helping hand.

Jill Maran is a jack-of-all-trades and dynamo who fills in anywhere she's needed anytime she's back from university.

Maxine Maran is the Business Manager and family sage. She maintains order in the business and family—and keeps everything running smoothly.

CREDITS

Author:
Ruth Maran

Copy Development:
Wanda Lawrie
Kelleigh Wing

Technical Consultant:
Paul Whitehead

Project Coordinator:
Judy Maran

Editors:
Brad Hilderley
Peter Lejcar
Carol Barclay
Raquel Scott
Jason M. Brown

Layout Designer:
Treena Lees

Illustrators:
Chris K.C. Leung
Russ Marini
Ben Lee
Jamie Bell

Screen Artist & Illustrator:
Jeff Jones

Screen Captures & Editing:
Tina Veltri
Roxanne Van Damme

Indexer:
Kelleigh Wing

Screen Captures & Post Production:
Robert Maran

ACKNOWLEDGMENTS

Thanks to the dedicated staff of maranGraphics, including Carol Barclay, Jamie Bell, Jason M. Brown, Francisco Ferreira, Brad Hilderley, Jeff Jones, Wanda Lawrie, Ben Lee, Treena Lees, Peter Lejcar, Chris K.C. Leung, Michael W. M[ac]Donald, Jill Maran, Judy Maran, Maxine Maran, Robert Maran, Russell C. Marini, Raquel Scott, Roxanne Van Damme, Tina Veltri, Paul Whitehead and Kelleigh Wing.

Finally, to Richard Maran who originated the easy-to-use graphic format of this guide. Thank you for your inspiration and guidance.

TABLE OF CONTENTS

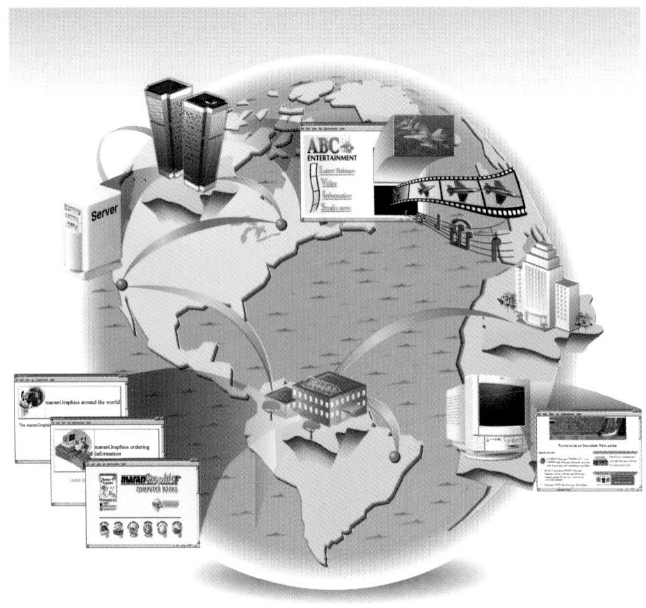

CHAPTER 1 Introduction

CHAPTER 2 Browsing the Web

CHAPTER 3 More Browsing

CHAPTER 4 Using Bookmarks

CHAPTER 5 Work with E-Mail Messages

TABLE OF CONTENTS

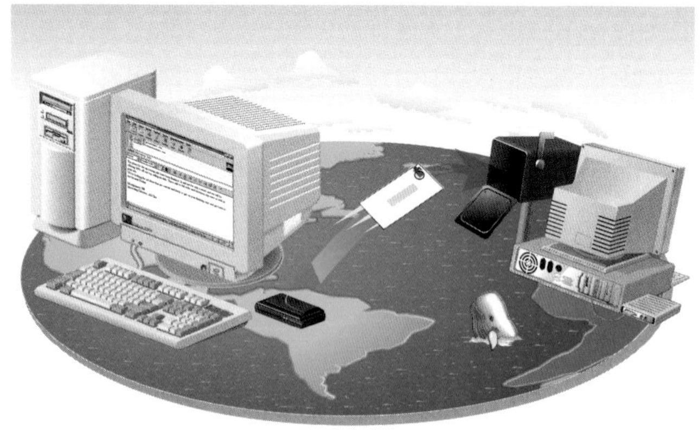

CHAPTER 6 Send E-Mail Messages

CHAPTER 7 Work with Discussion Groups

CHAPTER 8 Using Netcaster

CHAPTER 9 Create Your Own Web Pages

CHAPTER 10 Using Conference

CHAPTER 11 Cool Web Sites

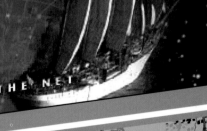

WELCOME TO

NETSCAPE

YOUR GUIDE TO NAVIGATING THE NET

CHAPTER 1

Introduction

What can I do with Netscape Communicator? How do I start and set up Netscape Communicator? Find out in this chapter.

INTRODUCTION TO THE INTERNET

THE INTERNET IS THE LARGEST COMPUTER SYSTEM IN THE WORLD

The Internet consists of thousands of connected networks. A network is a collection of computers that are connected to share information. Each government, company and organization is responsible for maintaining its own network.

HISTORY OF THE INTERNET

In the late 1960s, the U.S. Defense Department began the Internet as a military research project. The government created a network that covered a large geographic area and could withstand a nuclear attack. If part of the network failed, information could find a new route around the disabled computers.

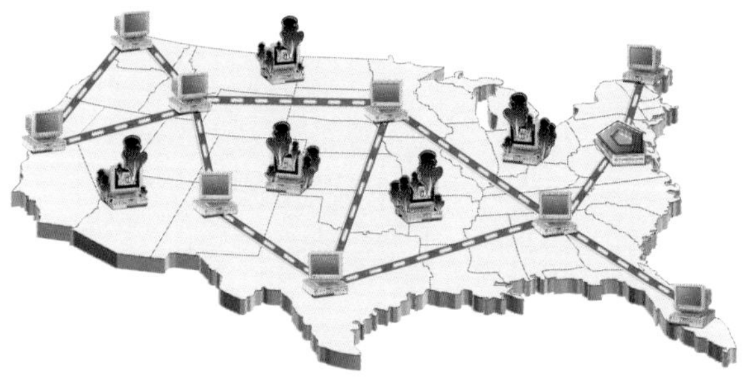

The network quickly grew to include scientists and researchers across the United States. Eventually, schools, businesses and libraries around the world were on the Internet.

WHAT THE INTERNET OFFERS

The Internet gives you access to a vast amount of information and allows you to contact people around the world with similar interests. You can exchange electronic mail (e-mail), find research material, view video clips, listen to music, get programs, join discussion groups, shop and much more.

CONNECTING TO THE INTERNET

Most people use an Internet Service Provider (ISP) to connect to the Internet. A modem transfers information between your computer and the ISP. Once you pay for your connection to the Internet, you can exchange information on the Internet free of charge. Organizations pay for the information that passes through their networks, which allows you to avoid long-distance charges.

INTRANETS

An intranet is a small version of the Internet within a company. Employees can use the intranet to exchange e-mail, read documents and join discussion groups that deal with company issues.

HOW INFORMATION TRANSFERS

All the computers on the Internet work together to transfer information back and forth around the world.

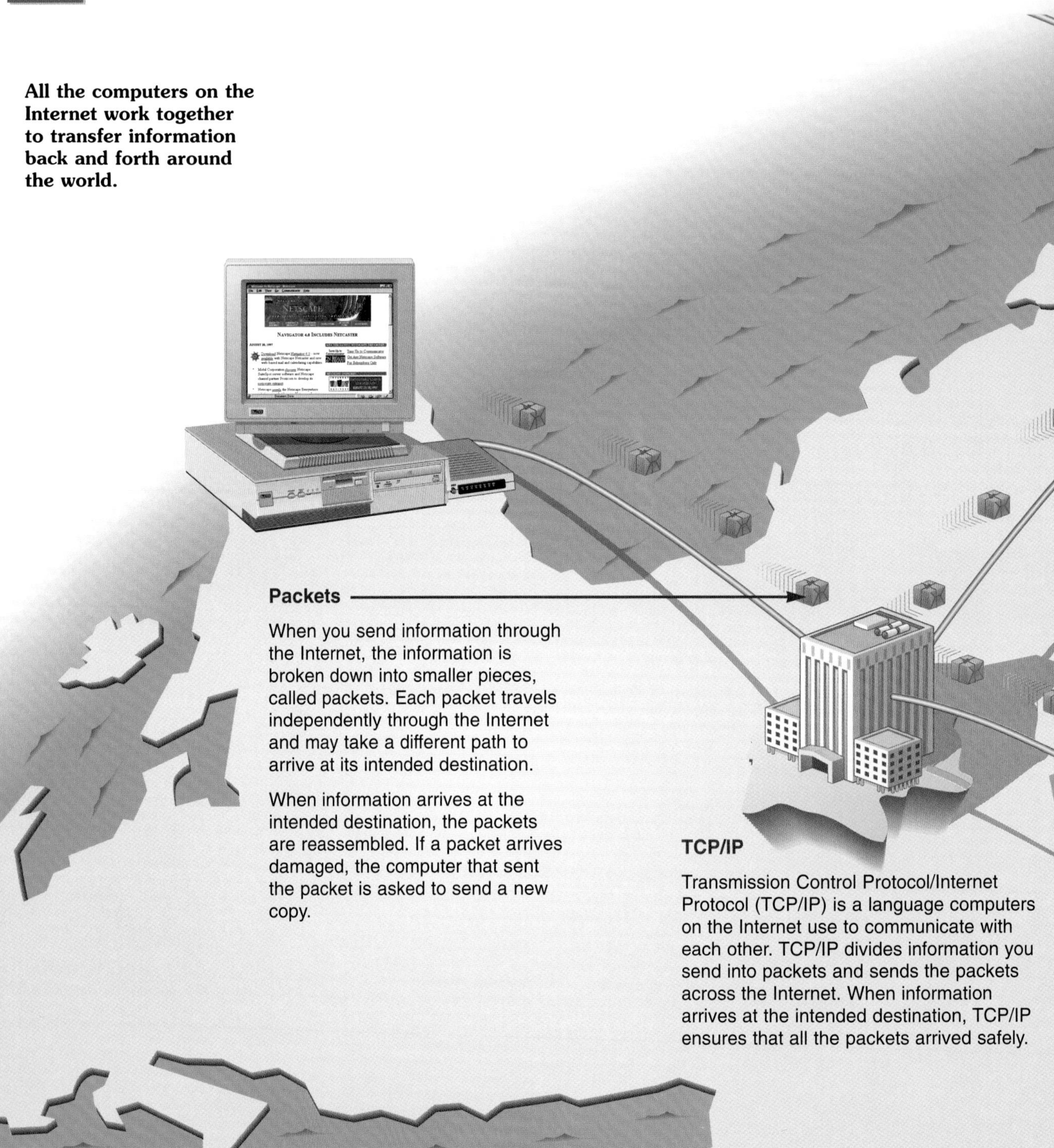

Packets

When you send information through the Internet, the information is broken down into smaller pieces, called packets. Each packet travels independently through the Internet and may take a different path to arrive at its intended destination.

When information arrives at the intended destination, the packets are reassembled. If a packet arrives damaged, the computer that sent the packet is asked to send a new copy.

TCP/IP

Transmission Control Protocol/Internet Protocol (TCP/IP) is a language computers on the Internet use to communicate with each other. TCP/IP divides information you send into packets and sends the packets across the Internet. When information arrives at the intended destination, TCP/IP ensures that all the packets arrived safely.

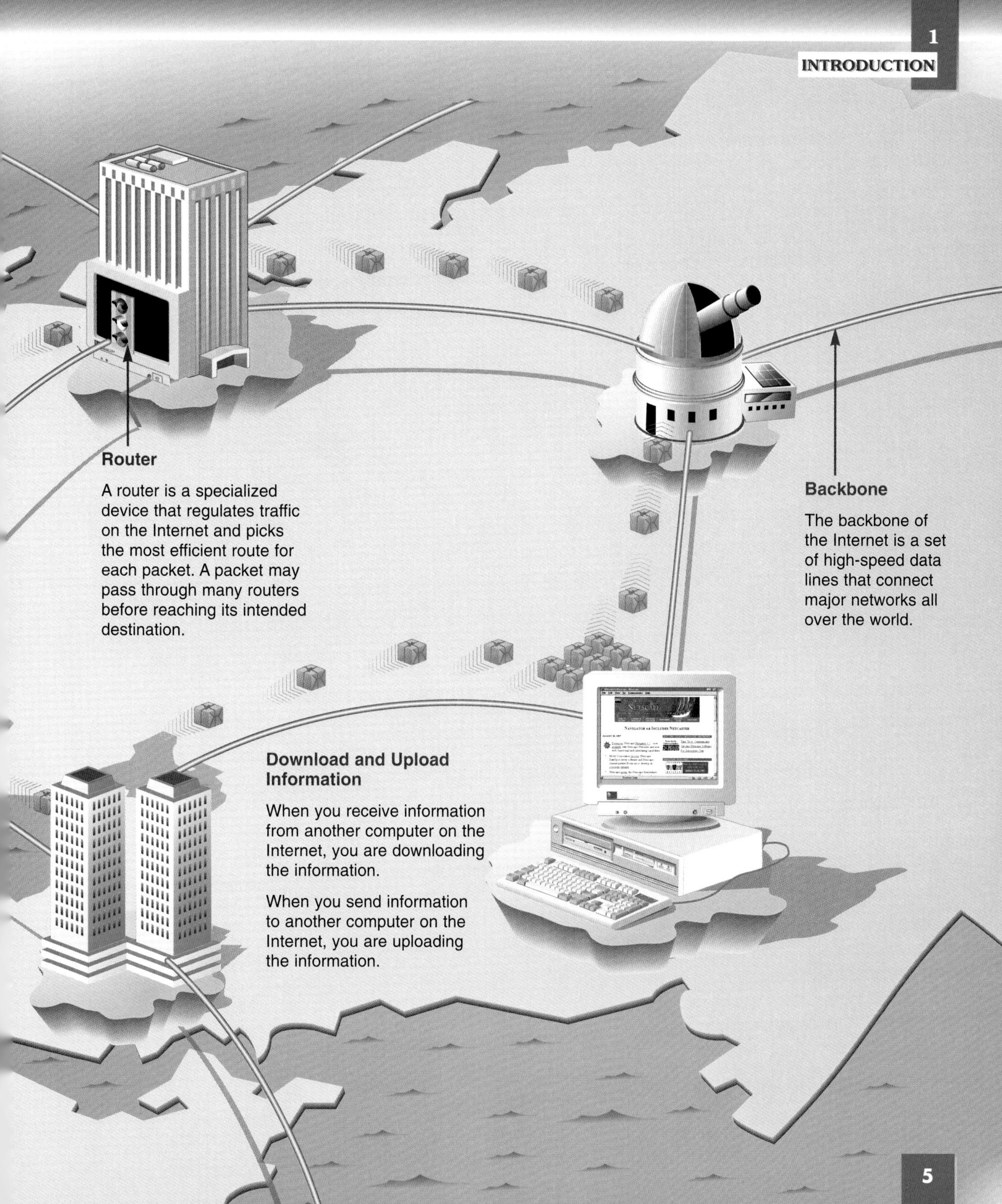
Router
A router is a specialized device that regulates traffic on the Internet and picks the most efficient route for each packet. A packet may pass through many routers before reaching its intended destination.
Backbone
The backbone of the Internet is a set of high-speed data lines that connect major networks all over the world.
Download and Upload Information
When you receive information from another computer on the Internet, you are downloading the information.
When you send information to another computer on the Internet, you are uploading the information.

INTRODUCTION TO THE WEB

The World Wide Web is part of the Internet. The Web consists of a huge collection of documents stored on computers around the world.

The World Wide Web is also called the Web.

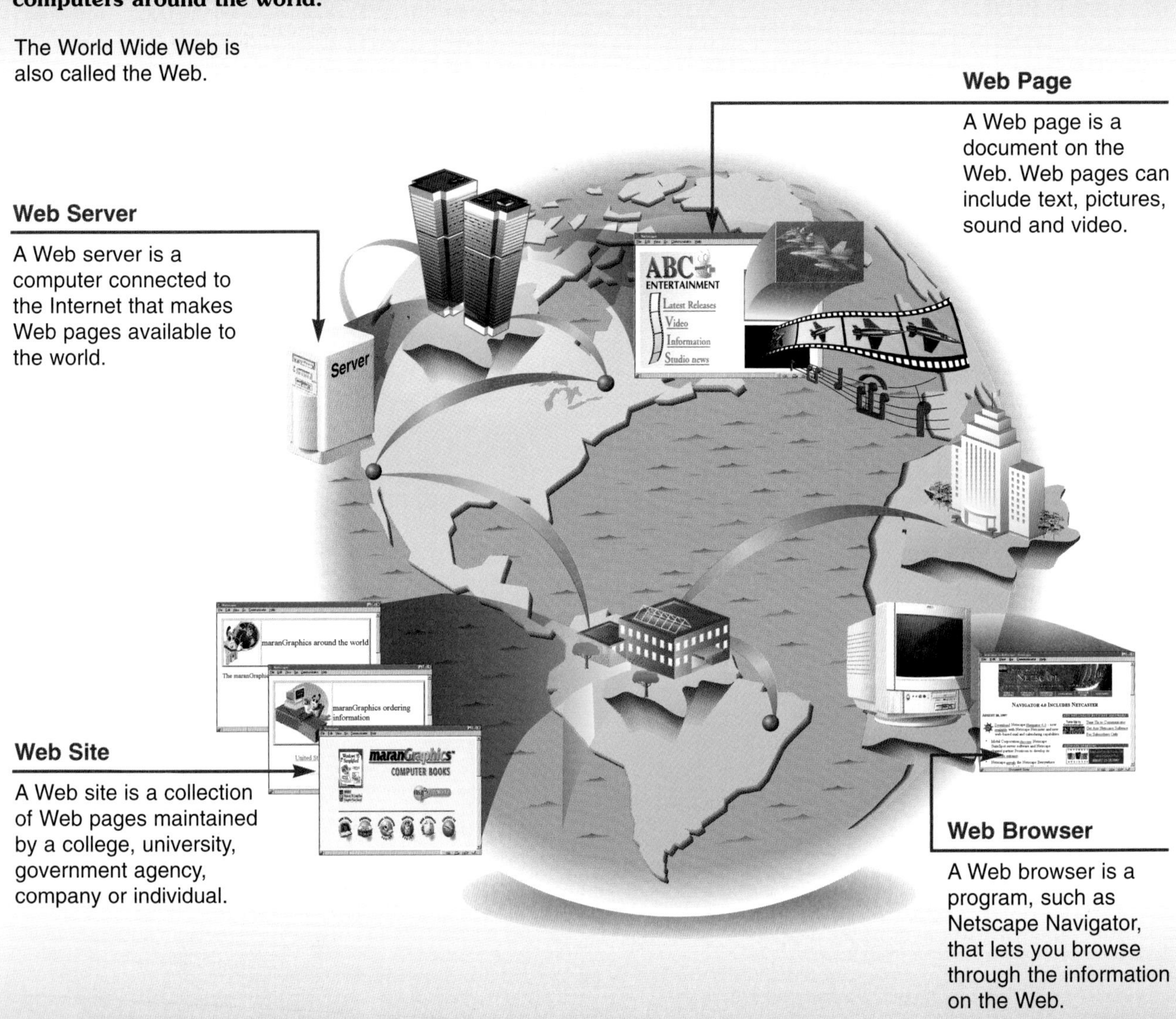

Web Page

A Web page is a document on the Web. Web pages can include text, pictures, sound and video.

Web Server

A Web server is a computer connected to the Internet that makes Web pages available to the world.

Web Site

A Web site is a collection of Web pages maintained by a college, university, government agency, company or individual.

Web Browser

A Web browser is a program, such as Netscape Navigator, that lets you browse through the information on the Web.

HTML

HyperText Markup Language (HTML) is a computer language used to create Web pages.

HTML consists of plain text with codes, called tags, that define how text and graphics will appear on a page.

URL

Each Web page has a unique address, called the Uniform Resource Locator (URL). You can instantly display any Web page if you know its URL.

All Web page URLs start with **http** (HyperText Transfer Protocol).

Links

Web pages contain highlighted text or images, called links, that connect to other pages on the Web. You can select links on a Web page to display a page located on the same computer or a computer across the city, country or world.

Links allow you to easily move through a vast amount of information by jumping from one Web page to another. This is known as "browsing the Web".

WHAT YOU CAN DO WITH NETSCAPE COMMUNICATOR

The Netscape Communicator Standard Edition allows you to perform many tasks.

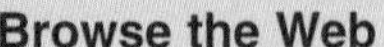

Browse the Web

Netscape Navigator lets you easily browse through the information on the World Wide Web.

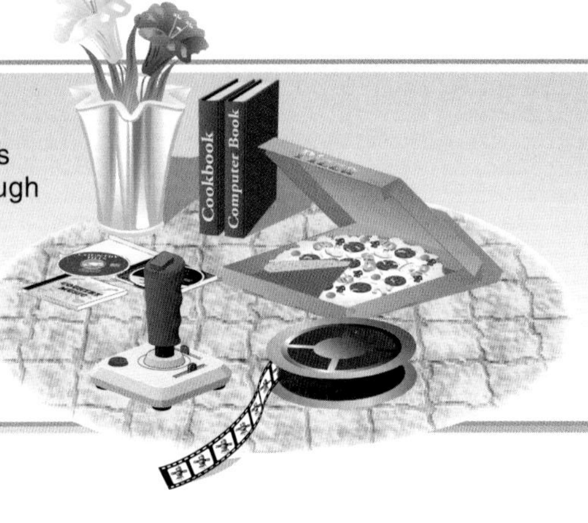

You can find information on every subject imaginable, play games, listen to music, watch video clips, purchase products and much more.

Exchange Electronic Mail

Netscape Messenger lets you exchange electronic mail with people around the world. You can exchange messages with friends, colleagues, family members, customers and even people you meet on the Internet. Exchanging electronic mail is fast, easy, inexpensive and saves paper.

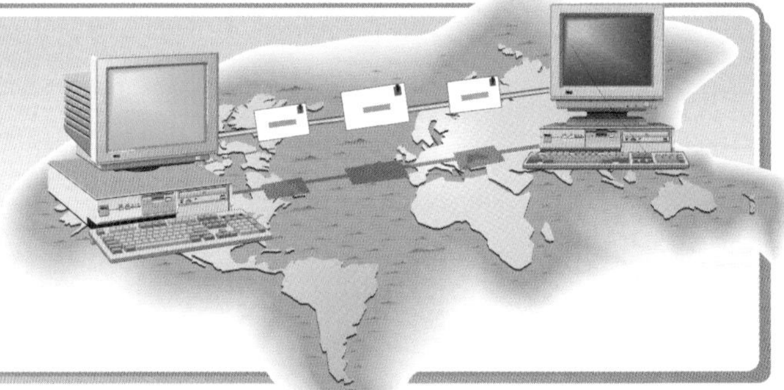

Join Discussion Groups

Netscape Collabra lets you join discussion groups to meet people around the world with similar interests. You can ask questions, discuss problems and read interesting stories.

There are thousands of discussion groups on topics such as the environment, food, humor, music, pets, photography, politics, religion, sports and television.

Create Web Pages

Netscape Composer allows you to create and edit your own Web pages.

You can place pages you create on the Web so people around the world can view your information.

Participate in Conferences

Netscape Conference lets you easily communicate with other people on the Internet. You can chat with a colleague, exchange files, browse the Web together and work on the same document.

You can also use Conference to talk to another person over the Internet and avoid long-distance telephone charges.

View Channels

Netscape Netcaster allows you to view channels of information. A channel is a Web site that Netcaster automatically delivers to your computer at times you specify.

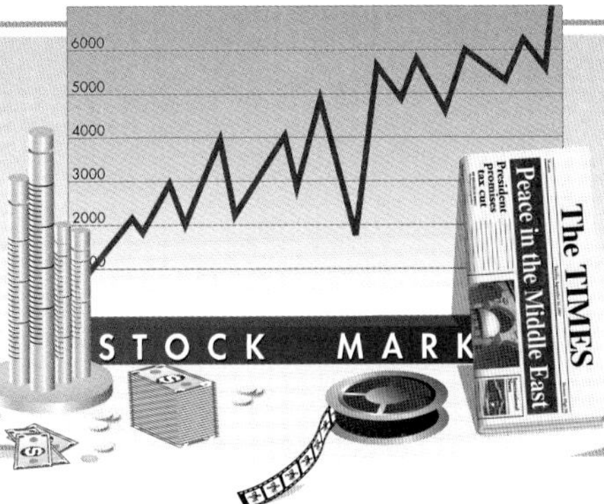

Any Web site can be a channel. You can have channels that cover topics such as home decorations, movies, music, news, stocks or travel.

START AND SET UP NETSCAPE COMMUNICATOR

The first time you start Netscape Communicator, you must provide information, such as your name and e-mail address. Communicator stores the information you provide in a profile.

■ START AND SET UP NETSCAPE COMMUNICATOR

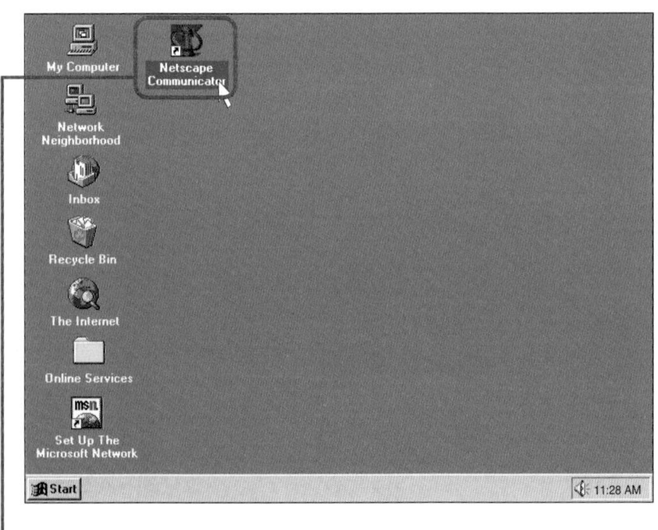

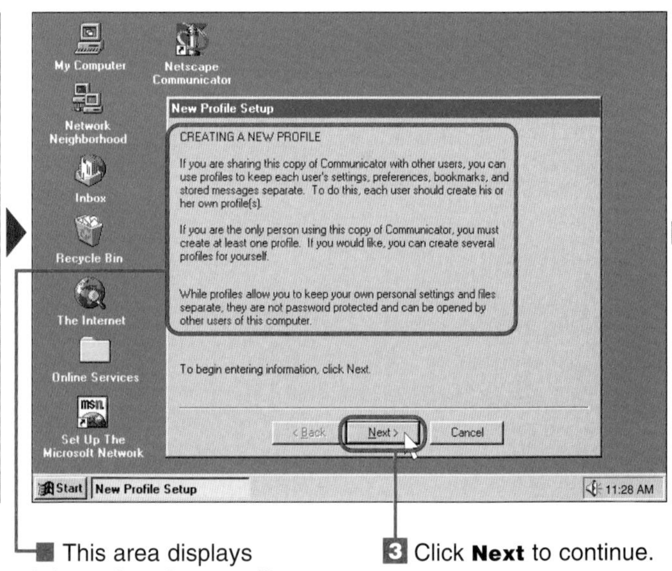

1 Connect to your Internet service provider using a program such as Microsoft Dial-Up Networking.

2 Double-click the **Netscape Communicator** icon on your desktop.

■ The New Profile Setup dialog box appears the first time you start Communicator.

■ This area displays information about profiles.

3 Click **Next** to continue.

How can I find the information I need to set up Communicator?

You can ask your network administrator or Internet service provider for the information. You will need the following information to set up Communicator:

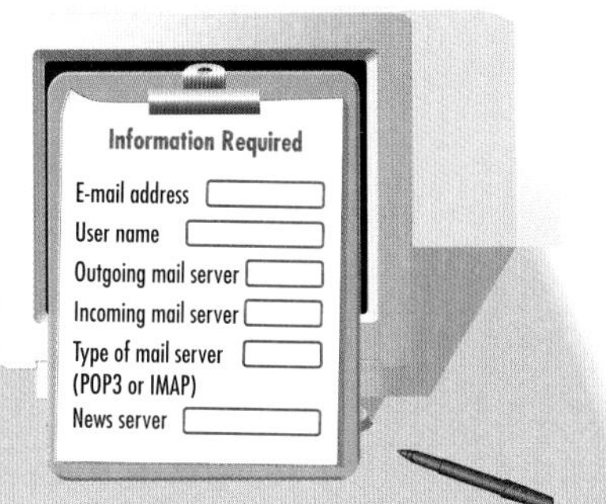

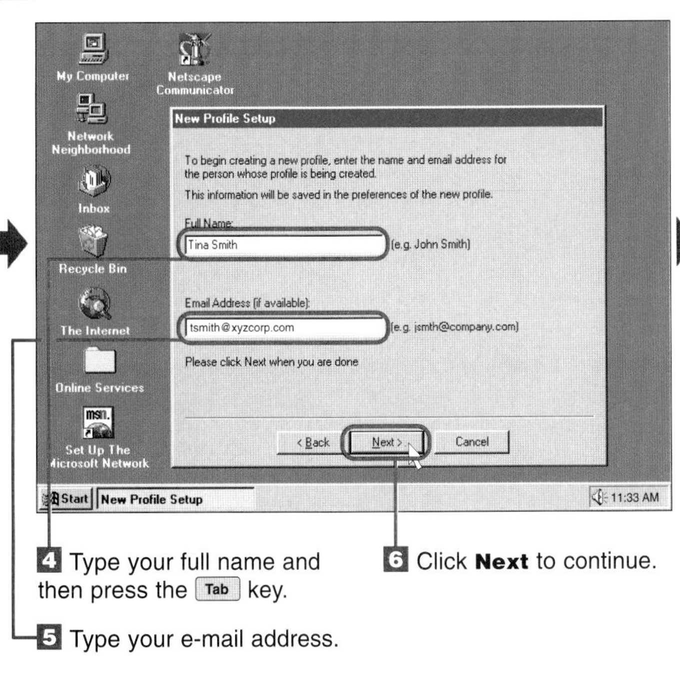

4 Type your full name and then press the Tab key.

5 Type your e-mail address.

6 Click **Next** to continue.

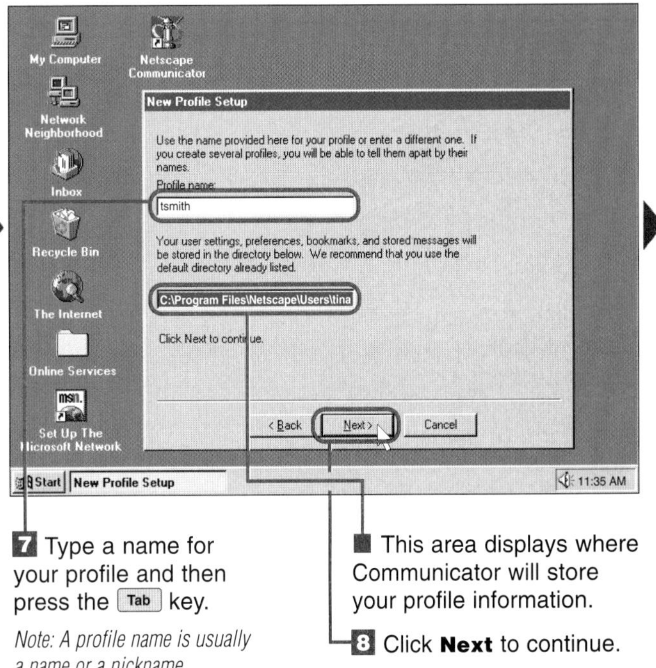

7 Type a name for your profile and then press the Tab key.

Note: A profile name is usually a name or a nickname.

■ This area displays where Communicator will store your profile information.

8 Click **Next** to continue.

CONTINUED

START AND SET UP NETSCAPE COMMUNICATOR

When setting up Netscape Communicator, you will be asked for the information needed to send and receive your e-mail messages.

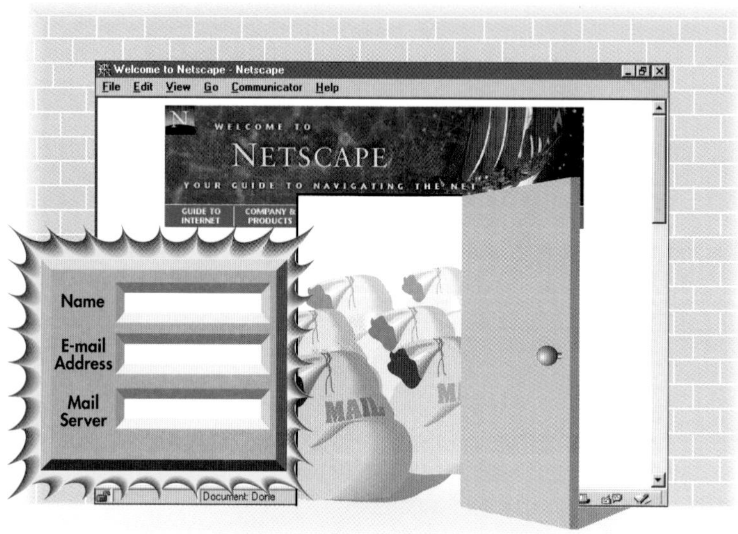

START AND SET UP NETSCAPE COMMUNICATOR (CONTINUED)

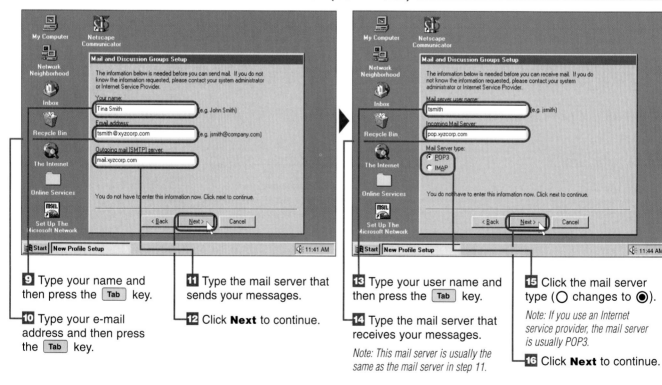

9 Type your name and then press the Tab key.

10 Type your e-mail address and then press the Tab key.

11 Type the mail server that sends your messages.

12 Click **Next** to continue.

13 Type your user name and then press the Tab key.

14 Type the mail server that receives your messages.

Note: This mail server is usually the same as the mail server in step 11.

15 Click the mail server type (○ changes to ◉).

Note: If you use an Internet service provider, the mail server is usually POP3.

16 Click **Next** to continue.

?

Will I have to create a profile each time I start Communicator?

You only have to create a profile the first time you start Communicator. The next time you double-click the Netscape Communicator icon on your desktop, the Netscape Navigator window will appear so you can immediately begin browsing through the information on the Web.

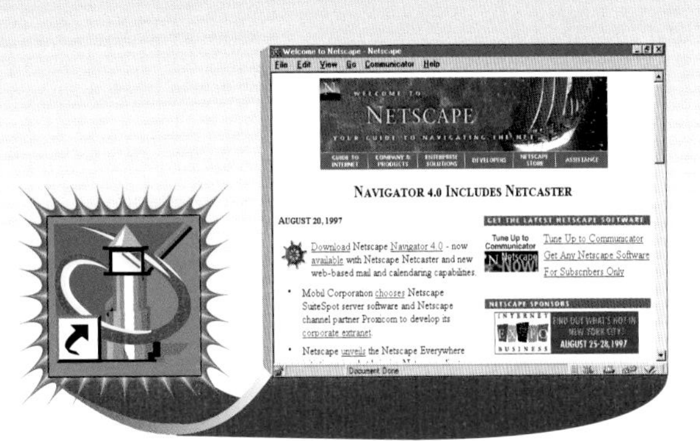

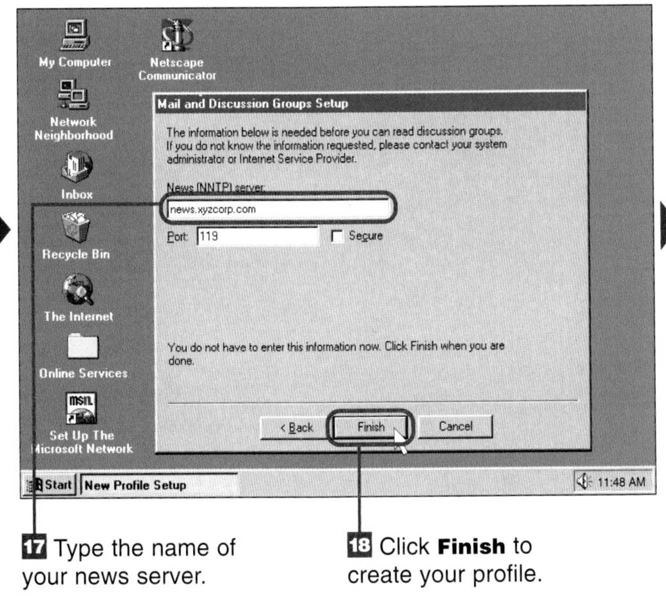

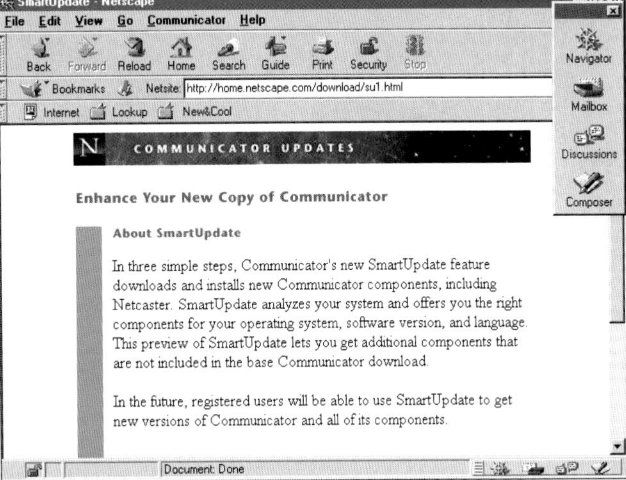

17 Type the name of your news server.

Note: The name of the news server usually begins with the word news.

18 Click **Finish** to create your profile.

■ The Netscape Navigator window appears, which allows you to browse through the information on the Web.

USING THE COMPONENT BAR

The Component Bar gives you quick access to the various parts of Netscape Communicator.

USING THE COMPONENT BAR

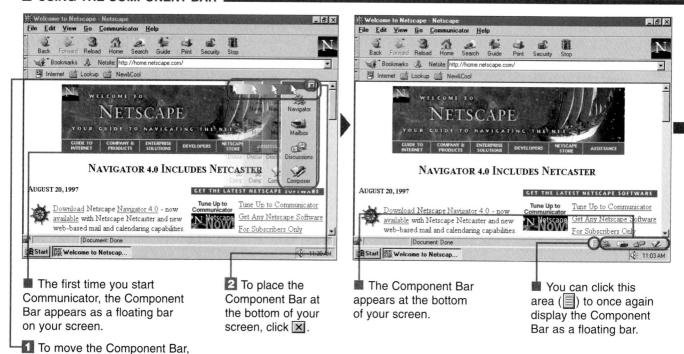

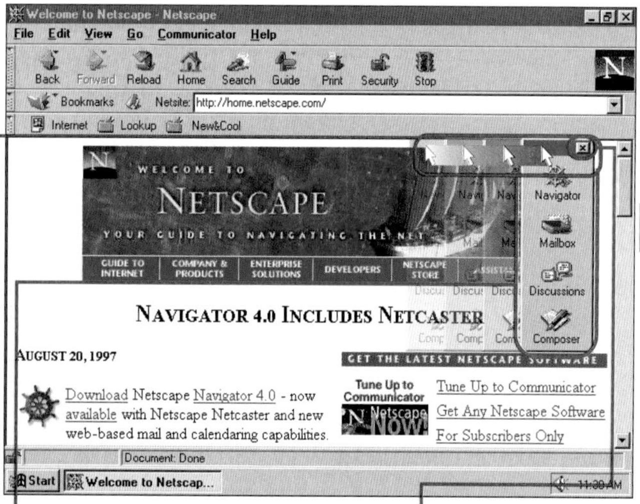

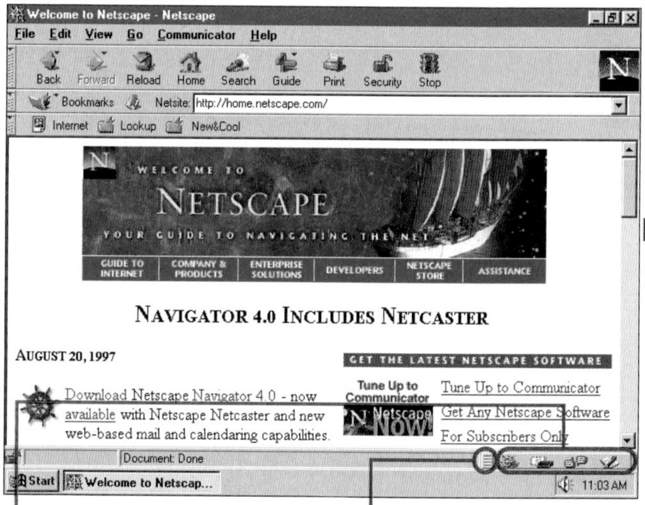

■ The first time you start Communicator, the Component Bar appears as a floating bar on your screen.

1 To move the Component Bar, position the mouse over the title bar and then drag the bar to a new location.

2 To place the Component Bar at the bottom of your screen, click ☒.

■ The Component Bar appears at the bottom of your screen.

■ You can click this area (▤) to once again display the Component Bar as a floating bar.

? What does each component allow me to do?

Navigator

Browse through the information on the Web.

Mailbox

Read and send electronic mail.

Discussions

Read and send discussion group messages.

Composer

Create your own Web pages.

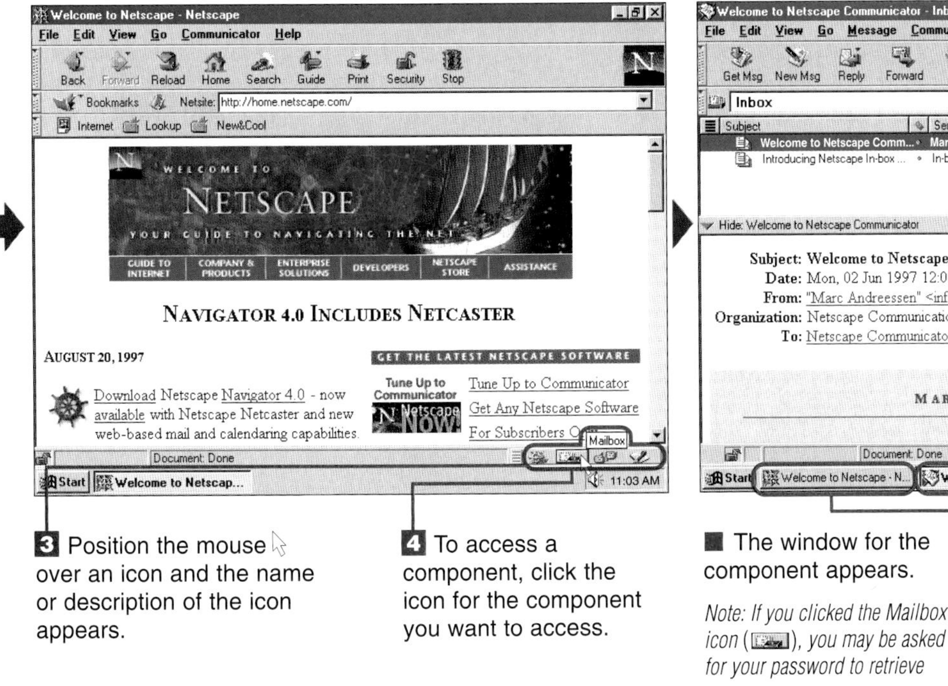

3 Position the mouse over an icon and the name or description of the icon appears.

4 To access a component, click the icon for the component you want to access.

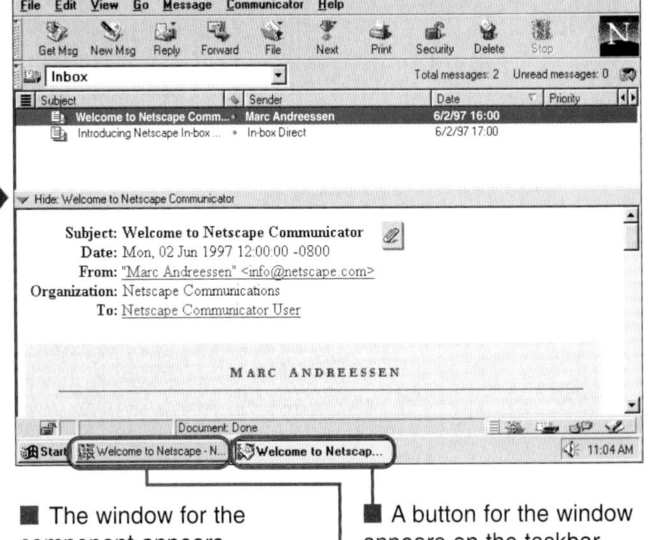

■ The window for the component appears.

Note: If you clicked the Mailbox icon (), you may be asked for your password to retrieve your messages.

■ A button for the window appears on the taskbar.

■ You can switch between windows by clicking the appropriate button on the taskbar.

WORK WITH TOOLBARS

Netscape Communicator provides toolbars to help you quickly select commonly used features. You can easily hide or display these toolbars at any time.

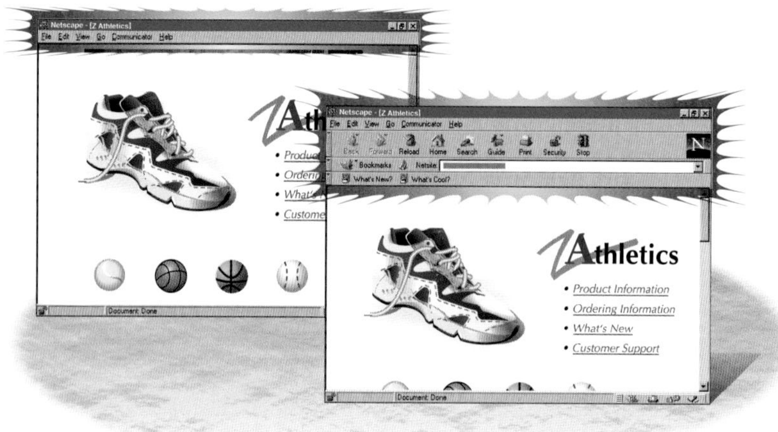

Toolbars take up space on your screen. If you do not often use a toolbar, you can temporarily hide the toolbar to provide a larger viewing area.

WORK WITH TOOLBARS

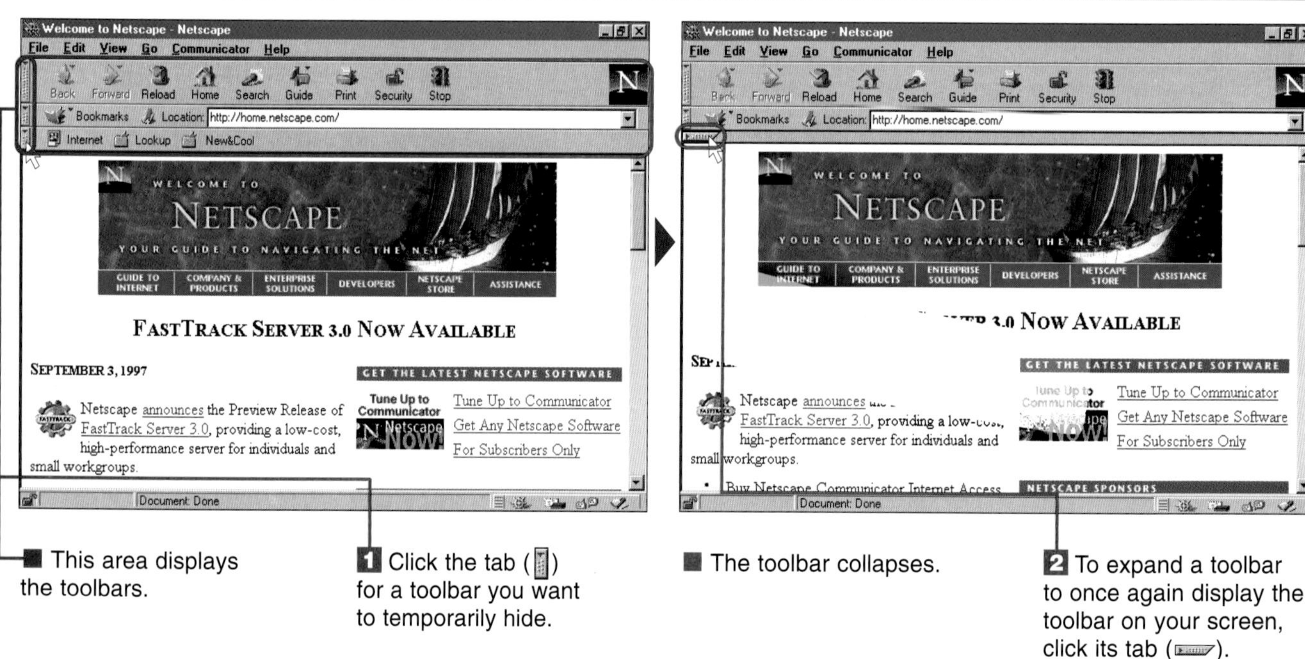

■ This area displays the toolbars.

1 Click the tab ( ) for a toolbar you want to temporarily hide.

■ The toolbar collapses.

2 To expand a toolbar to once again display the toolbar on your screen, click its tab ( ).

EXIT NETSCAPE COMMUNICATOR

When you finish using Netscape Communicator, you can exit the program.

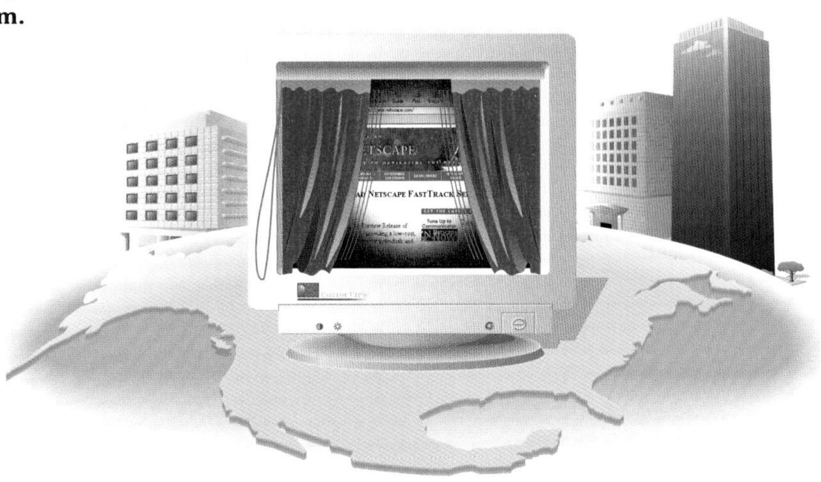

EXIT NETSCAPE COMMUNICATOR

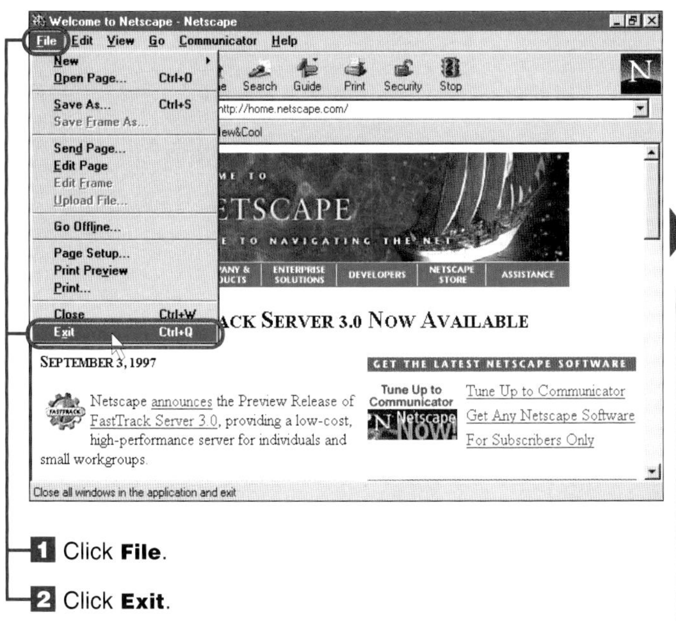

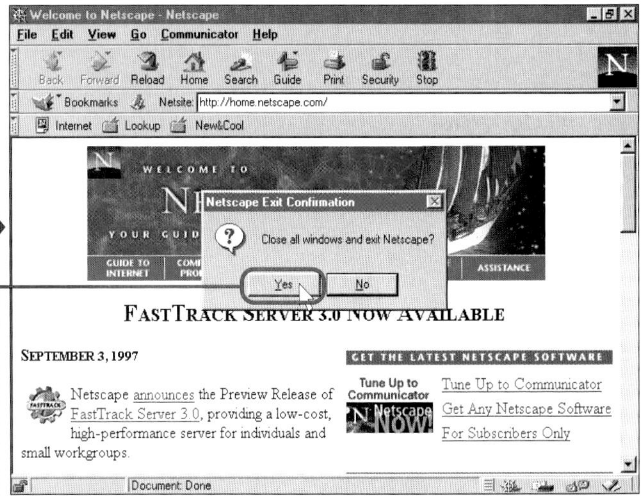

1 Click **File**.

2 Click **Exit**.

■ A dialog box appears if you have more than one window open.

3 Click **Yes** to close all the windows and exit Netscape Communicator.

4 Disconnect from your service provider.

The Netscape Communicator Professional Edition includes the same components as the Standard Edition, as well as three additional programs. These programs help you work more efficiently on your company network or intranet.

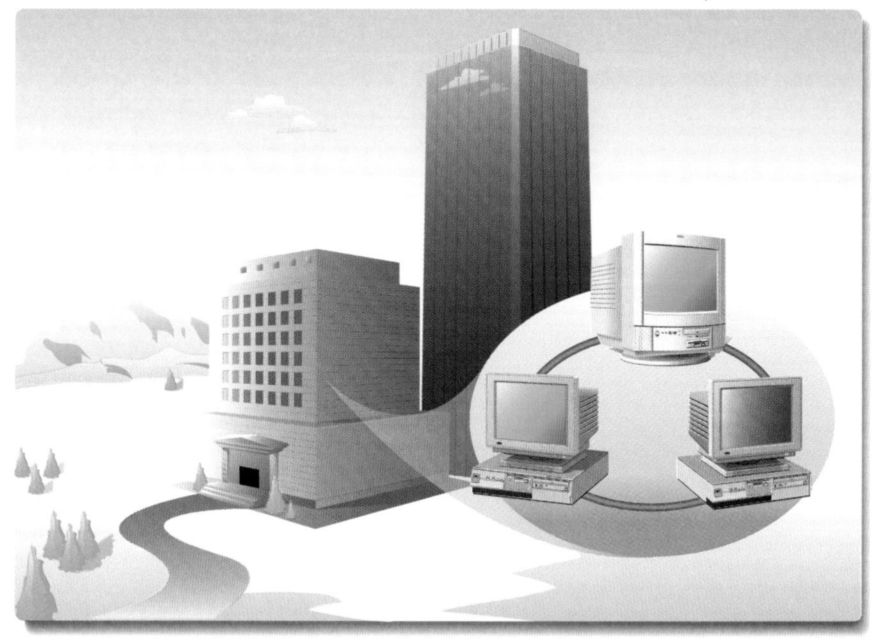

Calendar

Calendar helps you plan and schedule meetings with your co-workers. When you select a date and time for your meeting, Calendar checks the schedules of each person you want to attend the meeting to make sure they can attend. Calendar lets you send an e-mail message to each person to let them know you added the meeting to their calendars.

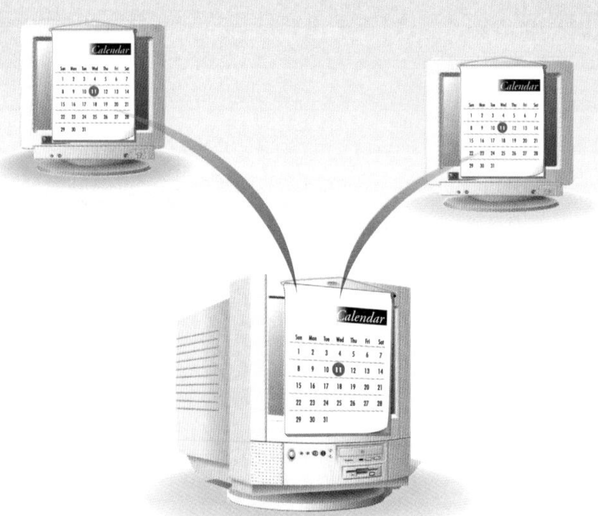

Calendar also allows you to keep track of events on your own calendar and add tasks to a to-do list.

Calendar can support up to 100,000 users. Your company network or intranet must have a Calendar Server to use Netscape Calendar.

IBM Host-On-Demand

IBM Host-On-Demand lets you use simple text commands to run programs and access information on a mainframe computer on your company network.

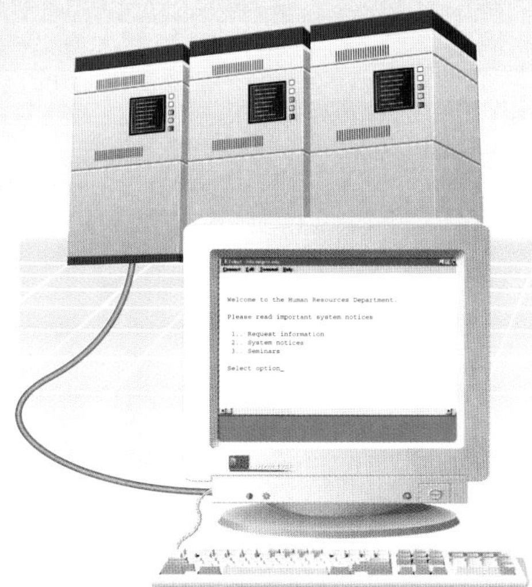

IBM Host-On-Demand also lets you use telnet to connect to computers on the Internet, such as the Library of Congress. Many government agencies and universities make the information stored on their computers available by using telnet.

AutoAdmin

AutoAdmin allows your system administrator to manage and set up Netscape Communicator preferences for everyone on the company network or intranet.

The system administrator can use AutoAdmin to automatically install and upgrade Netscape Communicator features and plug-ins, as well as change a server or home page address on every computer on the network.

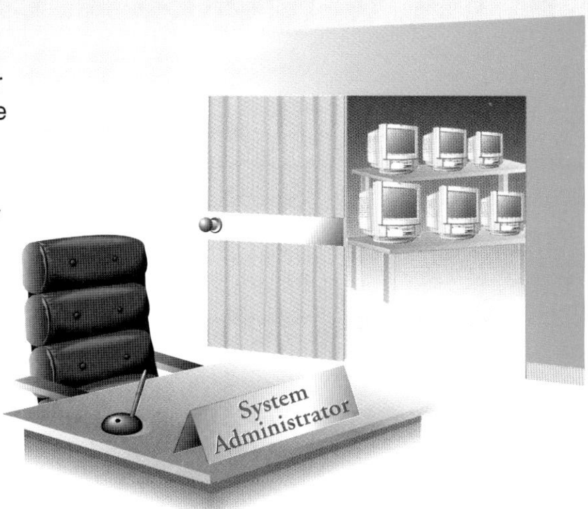

The system administrator needs the Netscape Mission Control feature to set up and use AutoAdmin. For information on Netscape Mission Control, see the home.netscape.com Web site.

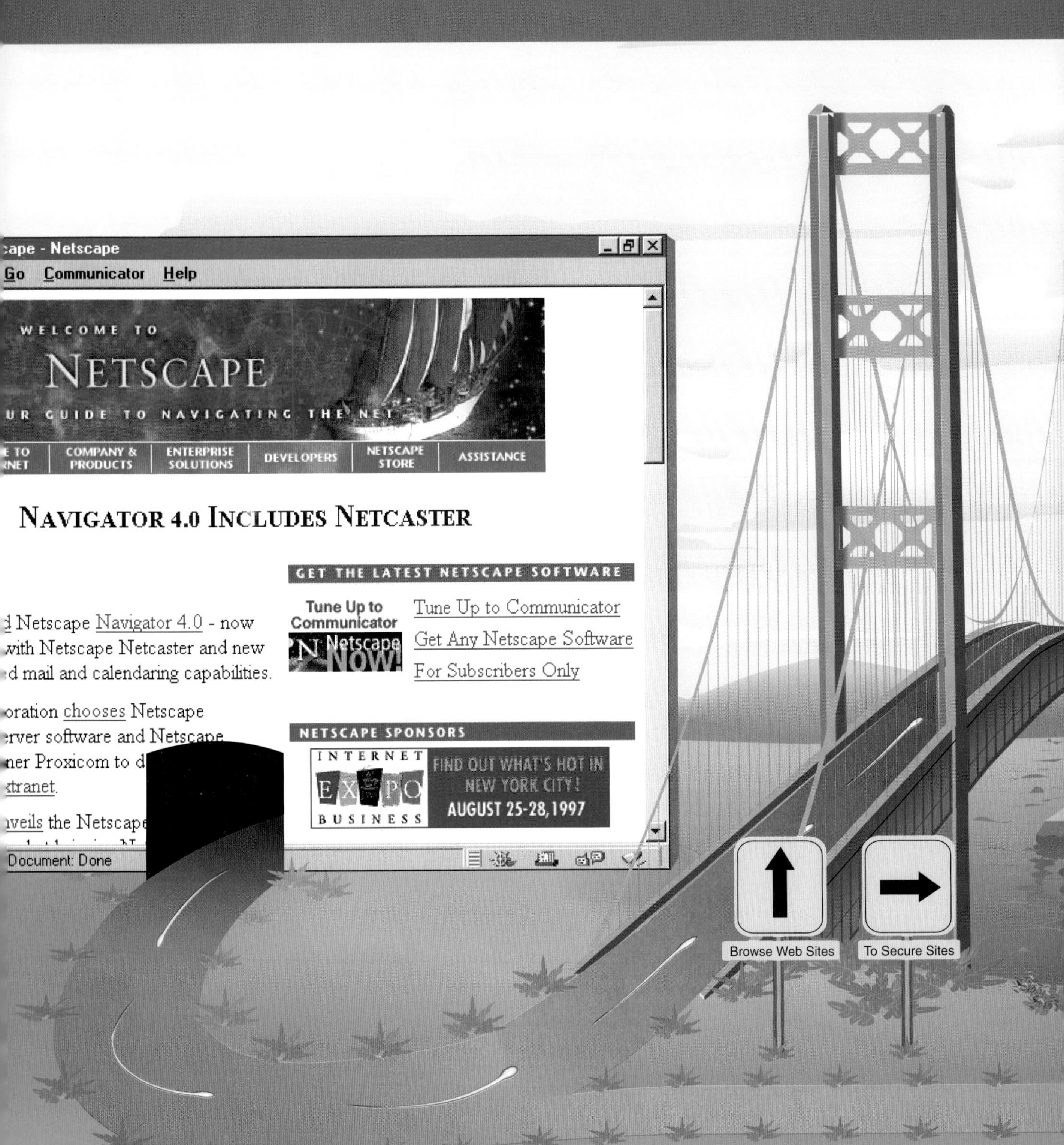

cape - Netscape
Go Communicator Help
WELCOME TO
NETSCAPE
UR GUIDE TO NAVIGATING THE NET
COMPANY & PRODUCTS
ENTERPRISE SOLUTIONS
DEVELOPERS
NETSCAPE STORE
ASSISTANCE
NAVIGATOR 4.0 INCLUDES NETCASTER
GET THE LATEST NETSCAPE SOFTWARE
Tune Up to Communicator
Netscape Now!
Tune Up to Communicator
Get Any Netscape Software
For Subscribers Only
d Netscape Navigator 4.0 - now
with Netscape Netcaster and new
d mail and calendaring capabilities.
oration chooses Netscape
erver software and Netscape
ner Proxicom to d
xtranet.
veils the Netscape
NETSCAPE SPONSORS
INTERNET EXPO BUSINESS
FIND OUT WHAT'S HOT IN NEW YORK CITY!
AUGUST 25-28, 1997
Document: Done
Browse Web Sites
To Secure Sites

CHAPTER 2

Browsing the Web

Would you like to begin browsing the Web? This chapter teaches you how to display Web pages, select links, search the Web and much more.

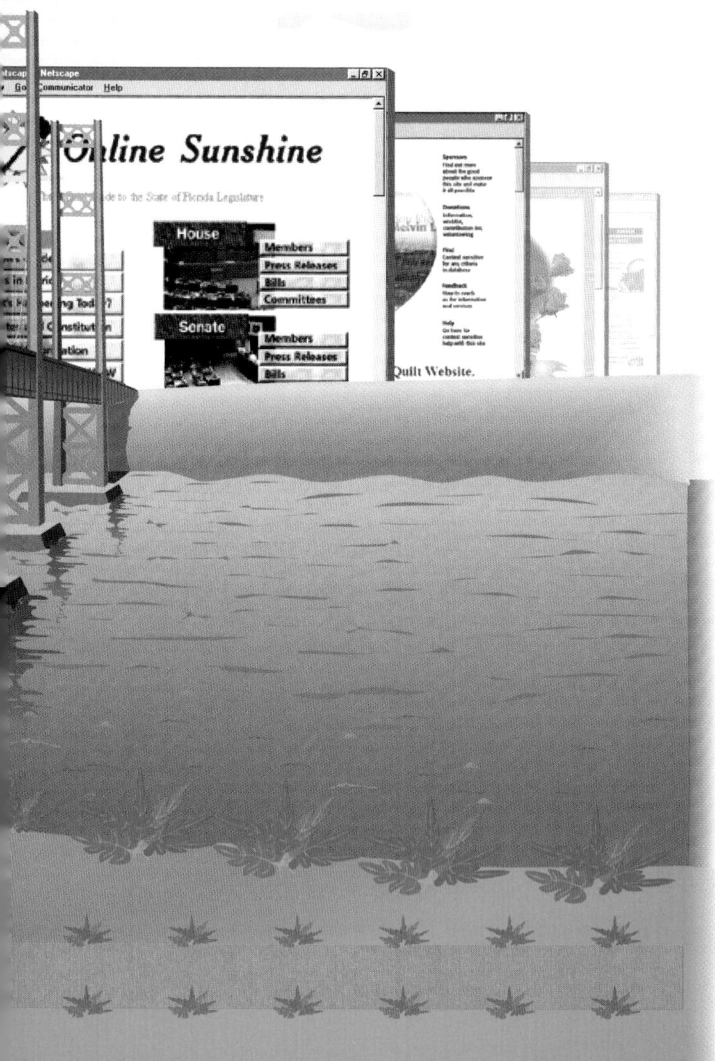

DISPLAY A SPECIFIC WEB PAGE

You can easily display a page on the Web that you have heard or read about.

You need to know the address of the Web page you want to view. Each page on the Web has a unique address, called a URL.

DISPLAY A SPECIFIC WEB PAGE

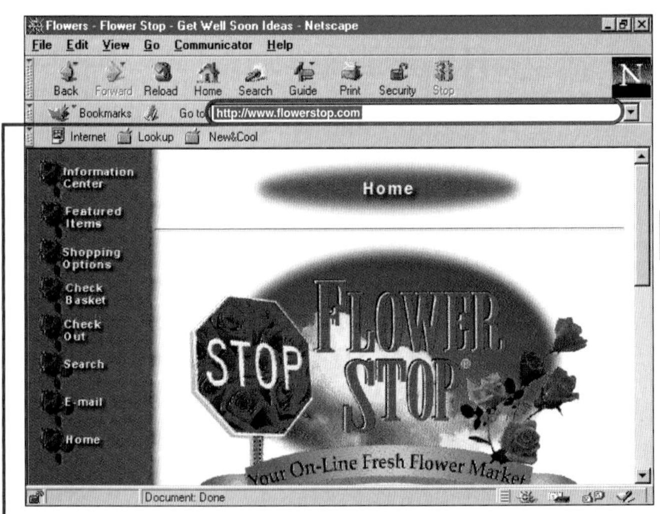

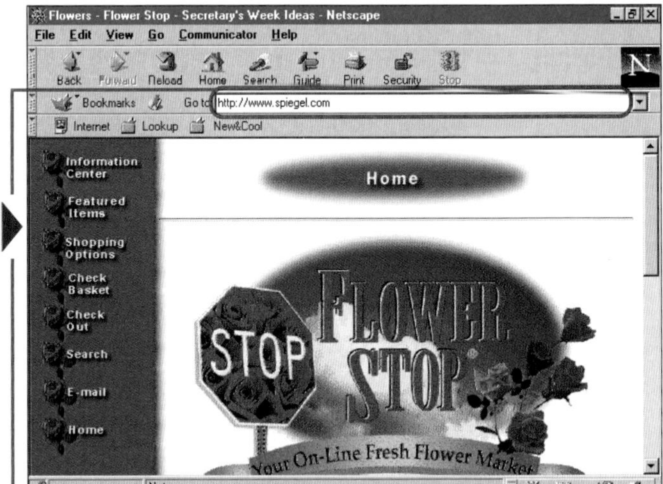

1 Click this area to highlight the current Web page address.

2 Type the address of the Web page you want to view and then press the Enter key.

■ Addresses can be case-sensitive. Make sure you enter upper and lower case letters exactly.

Note: When you start typing the address of a Web page you have previously visited, Navigator completes the address for you.

How can I save time when typing Web page addresses?

You can leave off **http://** and **www.** when typing a Web page address. For example, you could type **http://www.maran.com**, **www.maran.com** or **maran.com** to display the maranGraphics Web page.

■ The Web page appears on your screen.

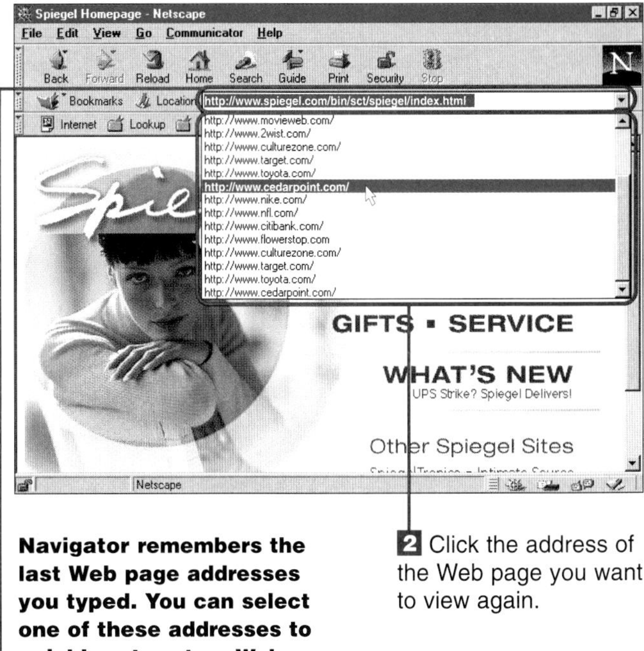

Navigator remembers the last Web page addresses you typed. You can select one of these addresses to quickly return to a Web page.

1 Click ▼ in this area.

2 Click the address of the Web page you want to view again.

SELECT A LINK

A link connects text or a picture on one Web page to another Web page. When you select the text or picture, the other Web page appears.

Text links are usually underlined and blue in color. If you have previously selected a text link, the text will usually be red in color.

SELECT A LINK

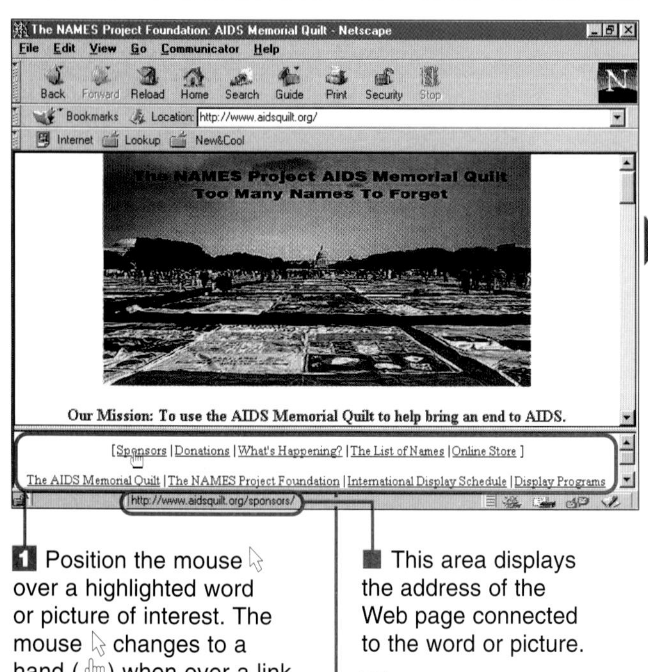

Tenth Year Sponsors - Netscape

We gratefully acknowledge our Tenth Year sponsors:

Major Sponsors:

American Express is a long-time supporter of the NAMES Project Foundation. In 1996, American Express was a major sponsor of the historic display of the AIDS Memorial Quilt in Washington, D.C.

Connect: Host www.aidsquilt.org/sponsors contacted. Waiting for reply...

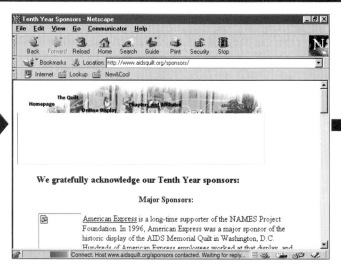

1 Position the mouse over a highlighted word or picture of interest. The mouse changes to a hand ( ) when over a link.

■ This area displays the address of the Web page connected to the word or picture.

2 To display the Web page, click the word or picture.

■ Navigator displays the page connected to the word or picture.

■ Text transfers quickly to your computer so you can start reading the text on a page right away. Images transfer more slowly. You may have to wait a moment to clearly view the images.

Where can a link take me?

A link can take you to another part of the current Web page, another Web page on the same computer or a Web page in another city or around the world.

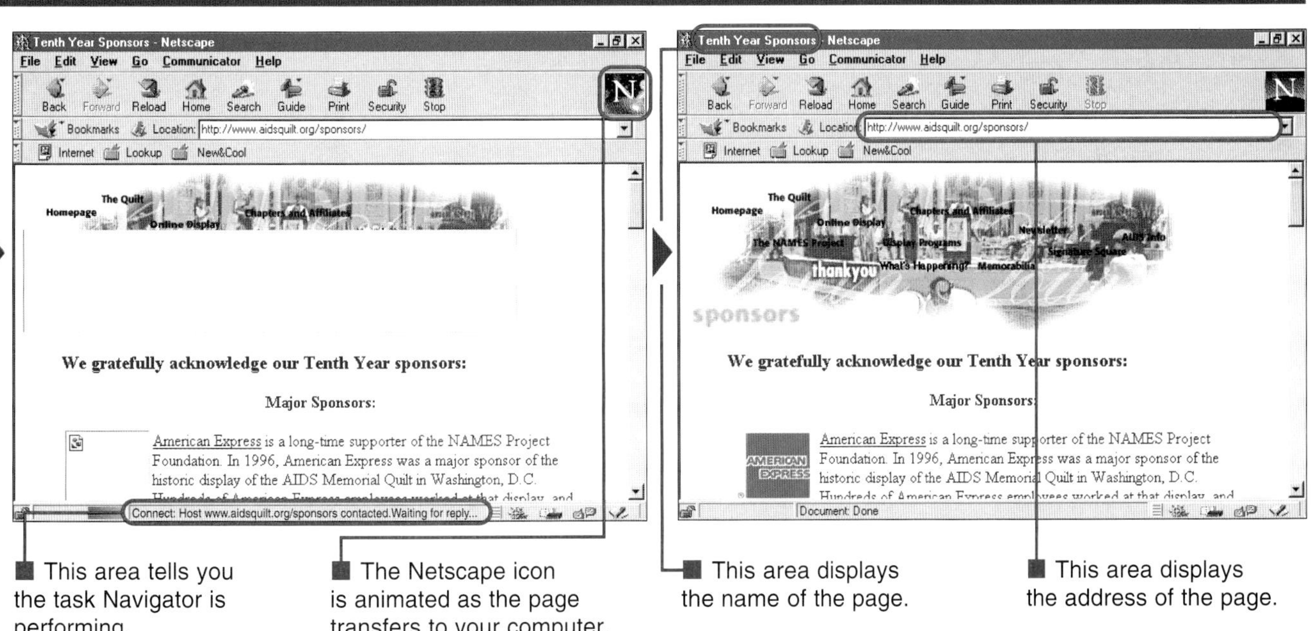

■ This area tells you the task Navigator is performing.

■ The Netscape icon is animated as the page transfers to your computer.

■ This area displays the name of the page.

■ This area displays the address of the page.

STOP TRANSFERRING INFORMATION

If a Web page is taking a long time to display, you can stop transferring the page and try connecting again later.

The best time to try connecting to a Web site is during off-peak hours, such as nights and weekends, when fewer people are using the Internet.

STOP TRANSFERRING INFORMATION

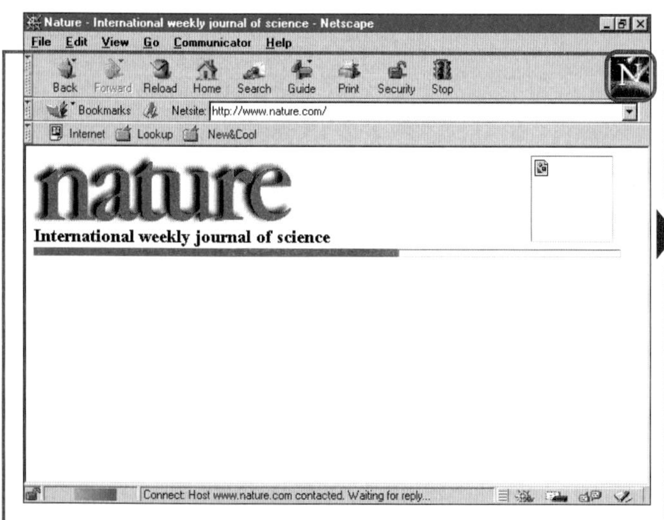

■ The Netscape icon appears animated when information is transferring to your computer.

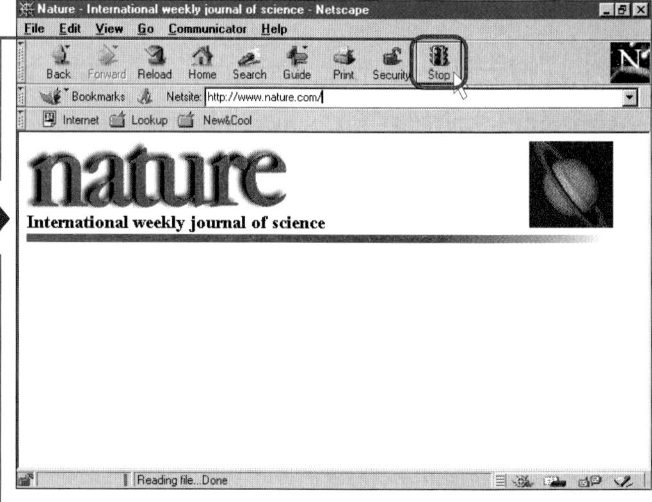

1 Click **Stop** to stop the transfer of information.

■ Navigator stops transferring the information.

■ You may also want to stop the transfer of information when you realize a Web page is of no interest to you.

RELOAD A WEB PAGE

You can reload a Web page if you want to update the displayed information, such as the current news. Navigator will transfer a fresh copy of the page to your computer.

You may also want to reload a Web page if the page appears distorted.

RELOAD A WEB PAGE

1 Click **Reload** to transfer a fresh copy of the displayed Web page to your computer.

■ A fresh copy of the Web page appears on your screen.

MOVE THROUGH WEB PAGES

You can easily move back and forth between Web pages you have viewed since you started Navigator.

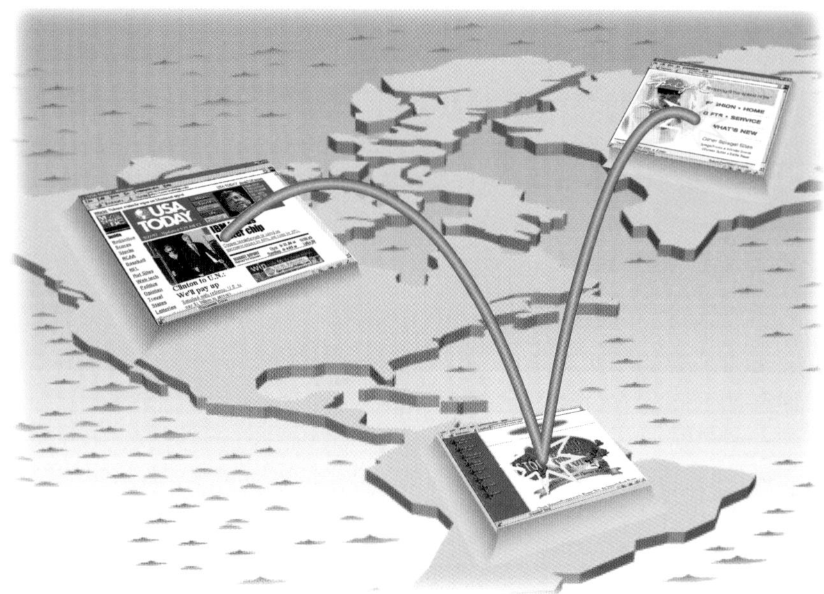

MOVE THROUGH WEB PAGES

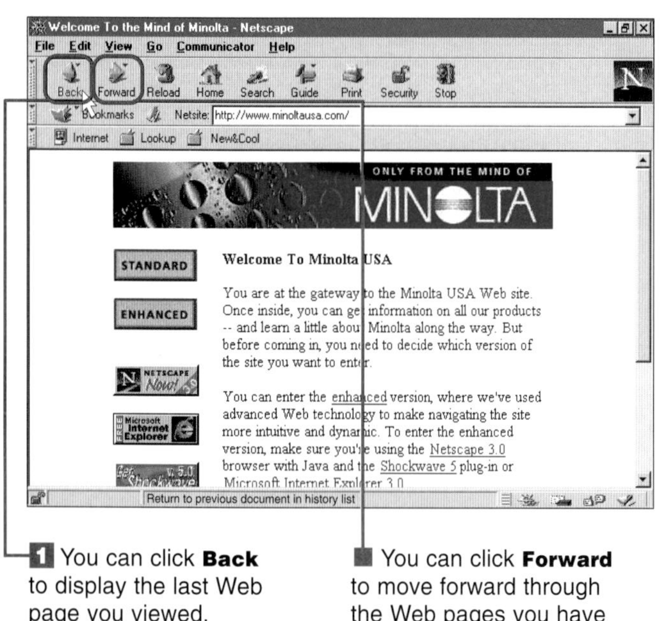

1 You can click **Back** to display the last Web page you viewed.

■ You can click **Forward** to move forward through the Web pages you have viewed.

You can display a list of Web pages you can quickly return to.

1 To display a list of Web pages, position the mouse over **Back** or **Forward** and then hold down the left mouse button. A menu appears.

2 Click the Web page you want to view.

PRINT A WEB PAGE

You can produce a paper copy of a Web page displayed on your screen.

PRINT A WEB PAGE

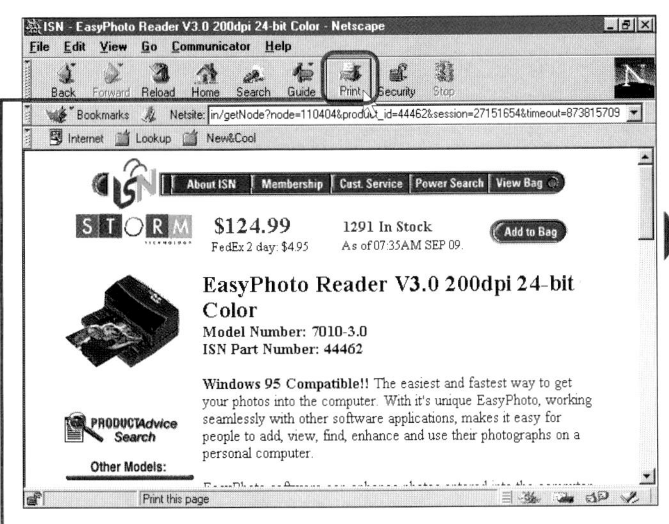

1 Click **Print** to print the Web page displayed on your screen.

■ The Print dialog box appears.

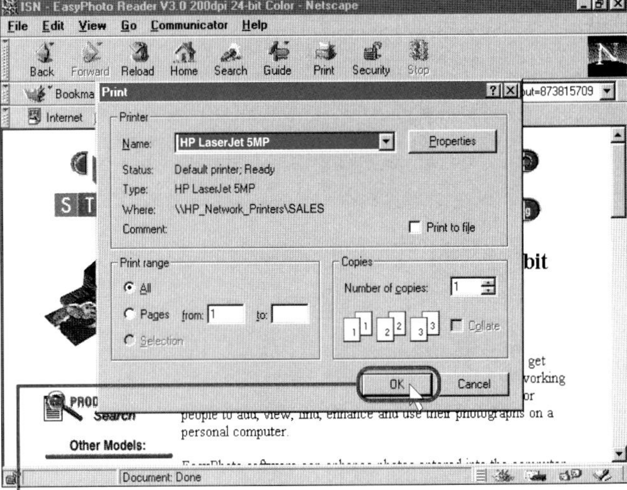

2 Click **OK** to print the Web page.

PREVIEW A WEB PAGE

You can see on your screen how a Web page will look when printed.

PREVIEW A WEB PAGE

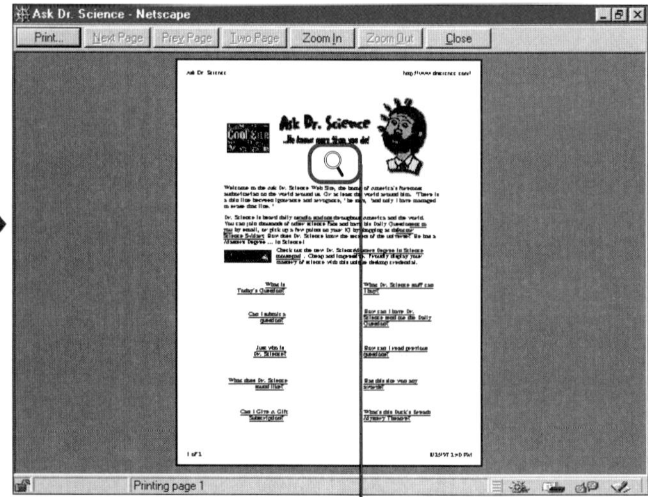

1 Click **File** to preview the Web page displayed on your screen.

2 Click **Print Preview**.

■ The Web page appears in the preview window.

Note: Navigator may need a few moments to display the page.

3 To magnify an area of the page, click the area of the page.

Does Navigator include additional information on each printed page?

Navigator prints the Web page title and address at the top of each page.

The page number, total number of pages and current date and time print at the bottom of each page.

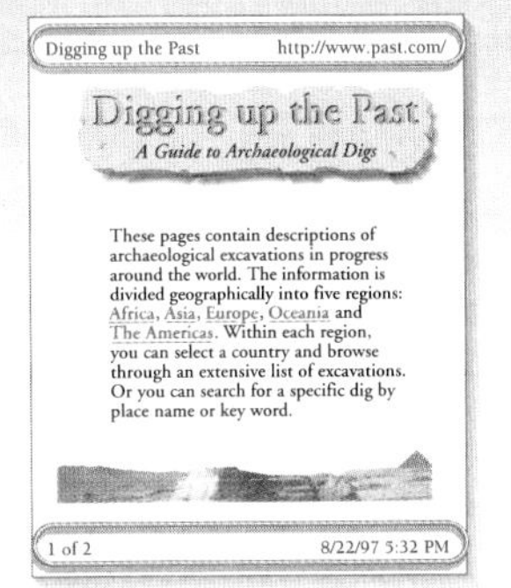

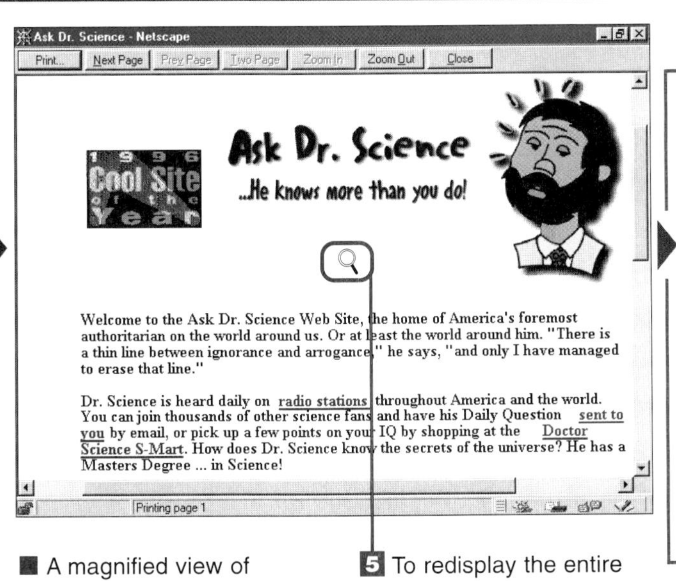

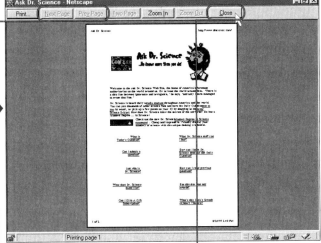

■ A magnified view of the page appears.

4 To further magnify the page, repeat step **3**.

5 To redisplay the entire page, click anywhere on the page.

6 If the information will print on more than one page, you can click one of these options to display the next or previous page.

7 Click **Close** to close the preview window.

DISPLAY AND CHANGE YOUR HOME PAGE

You can specify which Web page you want to appear each time you start Navigator. This page is called your home page.

DISPLAY YOUR HOME PAGE

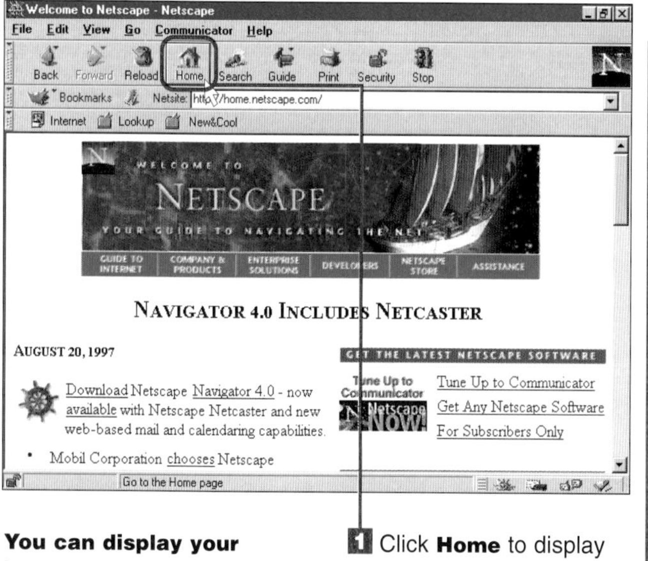

You can display your home page at any time.

1 Click **Home** to display your home page.

CHANGE YOUR HOME PAGE

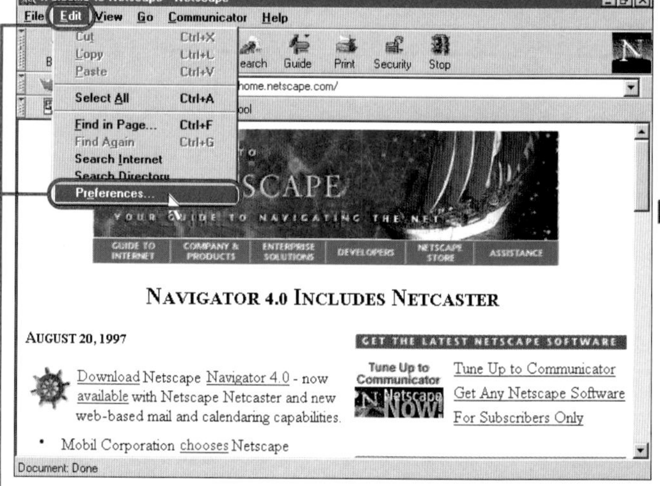

1 Click **Edit**.

2 Click **Preferences**.

■ The Preferences dialog box appears.

?

Which Web page should I use as my home page?

You can choose any page on the Web as your home page. You may want to choose a home page that provides a good starting point for exploring the Web. Your home page can also be a favorite Web page. Navigator initially sets the Welcome to Netscape page (home.netscape.com) as your home page.

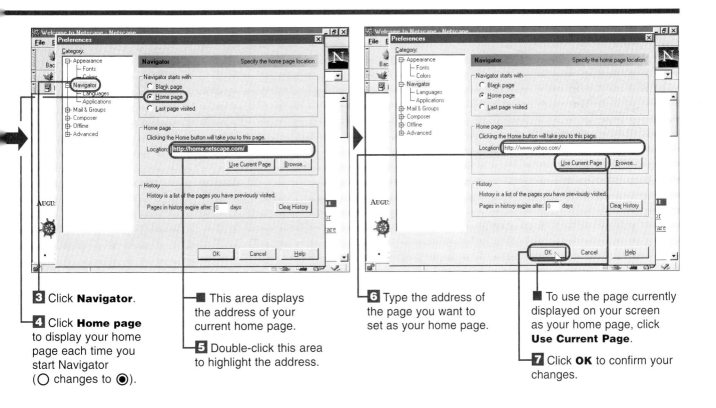

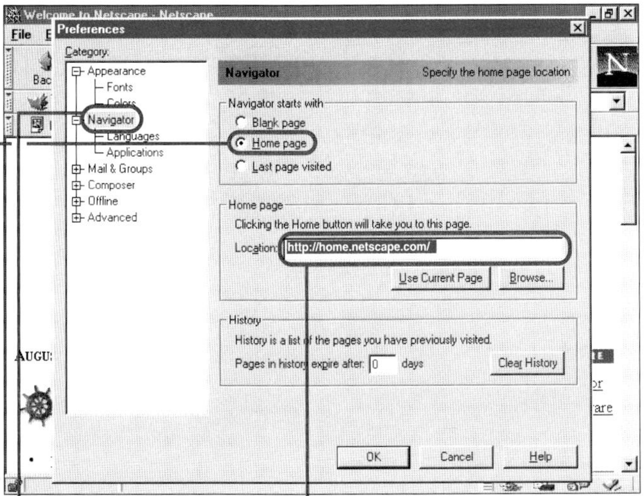

3 Click **Navigator**.

4 Click **Home page** to display your home page each time you start Navigator (○ changes to ◉).

■ This area displays the address of your current home page.

5 Double-click this area to highlight the address.

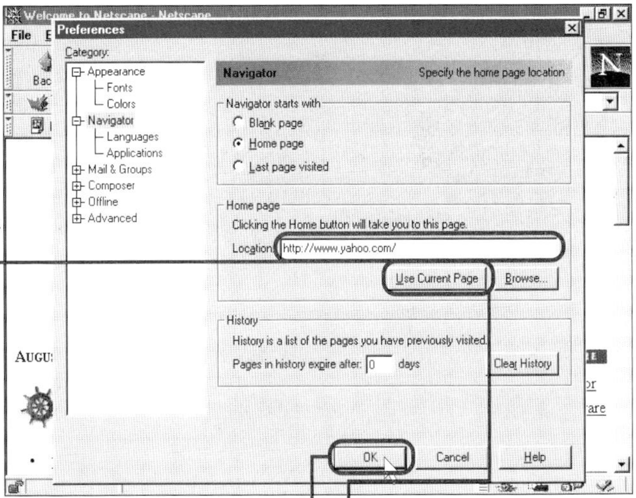

6 Type the address of the page you want to set as your home page.

■ To use the page currently displayed on your screen as your home page, click **Use Current Page**.

7 Click **OK** to confirm your changes.

You can find pages on the Web that discuss topics of interest to you. Navigator gives you quick access to popular search tools such as Yahoo!, Excite, Infoseek and Lycos.

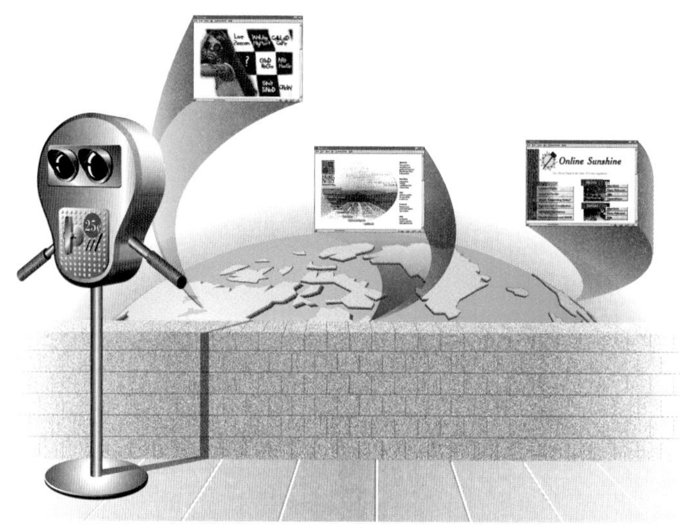

Searching for information will not find every page on the Web that discusses a topic, but it will give you a good starting point.

PERFORM A QUICK SEARCH

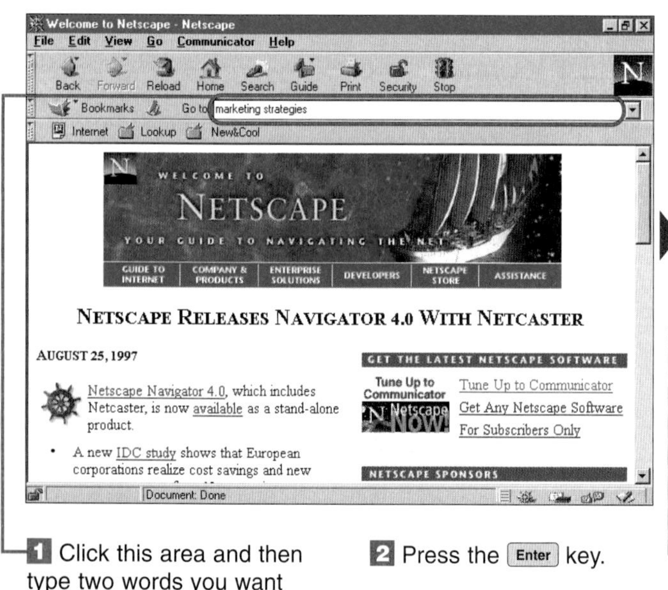

1 Click this area and then type two words you want to search for, separated by a blank space.

Note: If you type only one word, Navigator will think you typed a Web page address.

2 Press the Enter key.

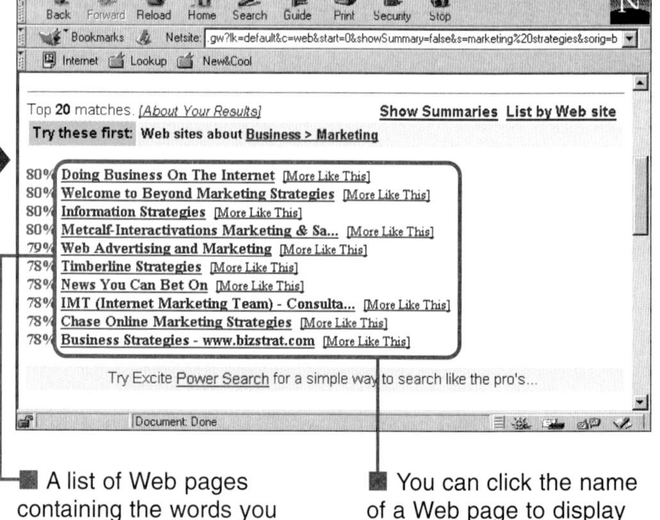

■ A list of Web pages containing the words you specified appears.

■ You can click the name of a Web page to display the page.

? How can I search for a Web page?

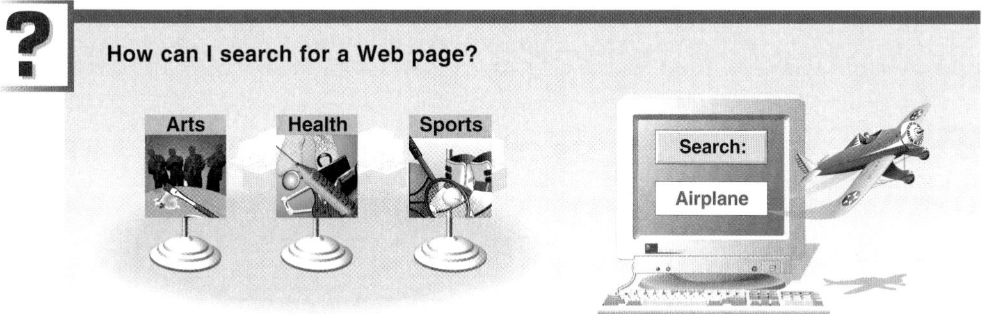

Search by Category

You can browse through categories such as arts, health and sports to find information that interests you.

Search by Topic

You can specify a word or phrase to find a specific topic of interest. Navigator will display Web pages that contain the word or phrase.

USING THE SEARCH PAGE

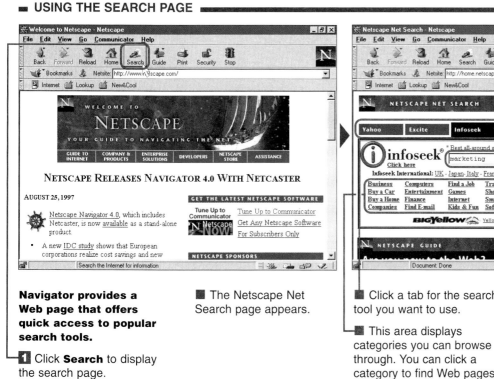

Navigator provides a Web page that offers quick access to popular search tools.

1 Click **Search** to display the search page.

■ The Netscape Net Search page appears.

■ Click a tab for the search tool you want to use.

■ This area displays categories you can browse through. You can click a category to find Web pages within a category of interest.

■ You can click this area and type a word you want to search for. Press the Enter key to search for the word.

AltaVista

AltaVista lets you search for a specific topic of interest. You can choose to search Web pages or Usenet discussion groups.

You can access AltaVista at the www.altavista.digital.com Web site.

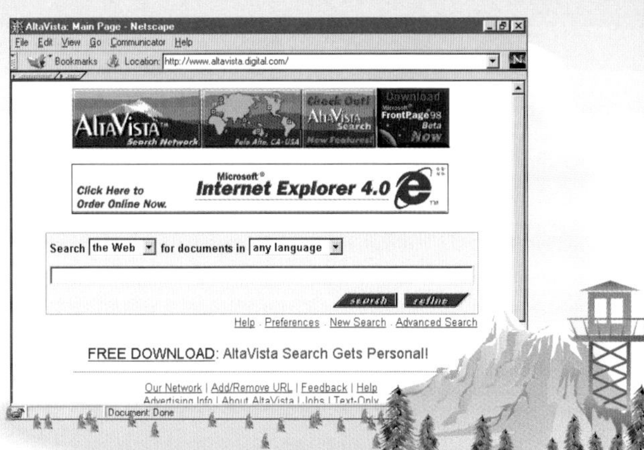

With a listing of over 30 million Web pages, AltaVista is one of the largest and most popular search tools on the Web.

Like most search tools, AltaVista allows you to add your personal or corporate Web page to its database.

HotBot

HotBot is a site maintained by Wired magazine that lets you search for a specific topic of interest. You can search Web pages, Usenet discussion groups or top news sites. Try to use at least two or three search words, separated by spaces, for the best results.

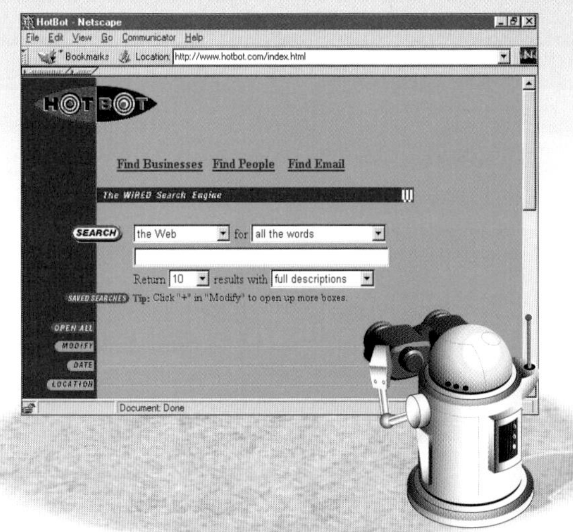

HotBot also lists sites it considers to be the best sources on the Web. These sites are organized into categories such as maps, careers and games.

You can access HotBot at the www.hotbot.com Web site.

Infoseek

Infoseek lets you search for a specific topic of interest or browse through categories, such as education or politics. You can search the Web, Usenet discussion groups, e-mail addresses and more.

You can access Infoseek at the www.infoseek.com Web site.

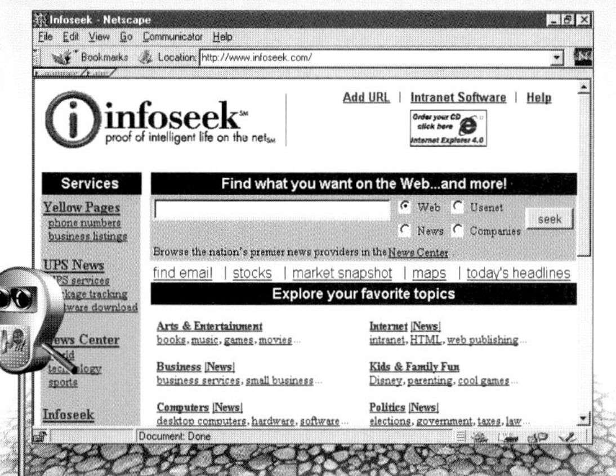

Infoseek offers a feature that allows you to track your UPS packages.

Infoseek also offers a link to the BigYellow search page where you can find businesses, people and e-mail addresses.

Yahoo!

Yahoo! was started by two students as a way to keep track of their favorite Web pages. The list quickly grew into one of the best search tools on the Web.

Yahoo! lets you search for a specific topic of interest or browse through categories, such as education or science.

You can access Yahoo! at the www.yahoo.com Web site.

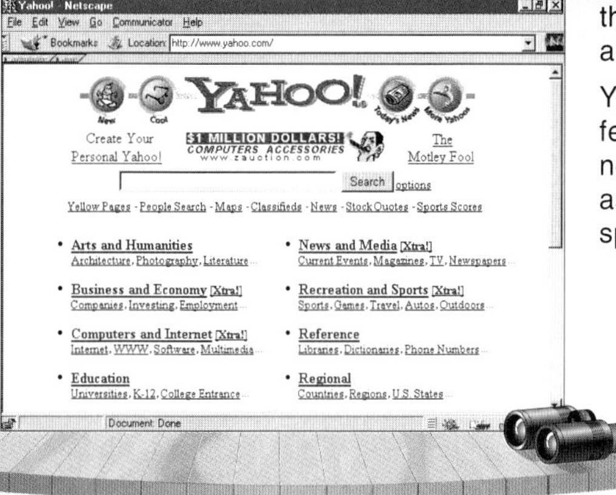

Yahoo! offers a **Cool** feature that takes you to a list of Web pages that Yahoo! considers innovative and interesting.

Yahoo! also offers a **Today's News** feature that gives you up-to-date news for various categories such as entertainment, politics and sports.

USING THE GUIDE BUTTON

Netscape offers five Web sites that give you quick access to useful and interesting information on the Web.

USING THE GUIDE BUTTON

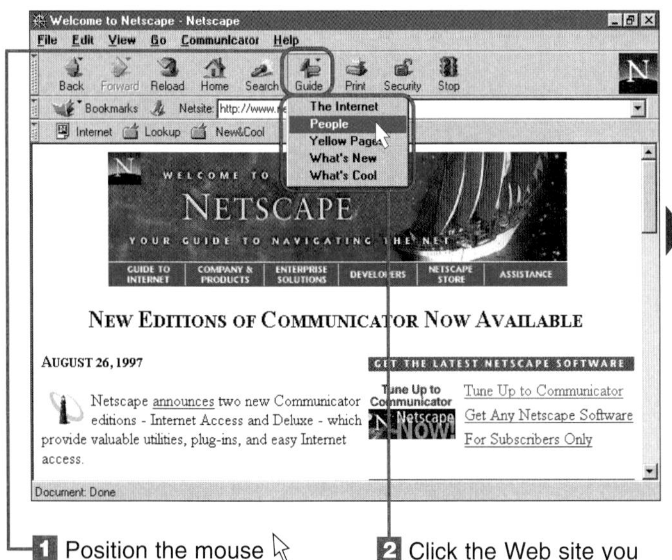

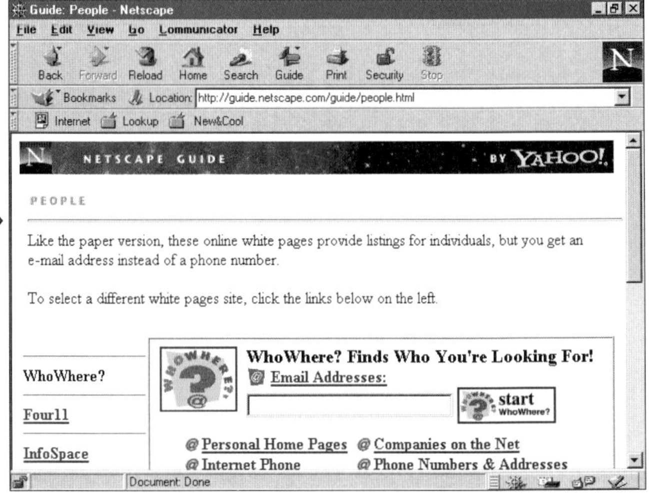

1 Position the mouse over the **Guide** button and then hold down the left mouse button. A menu appears.

2 Click the Web site you want to display.

■ The site you selected appears.

THE GUIDE BUTTON MENU

The Internet

You can search for information on the Web by browsing through categories such as business, computers, entertainment and travel.

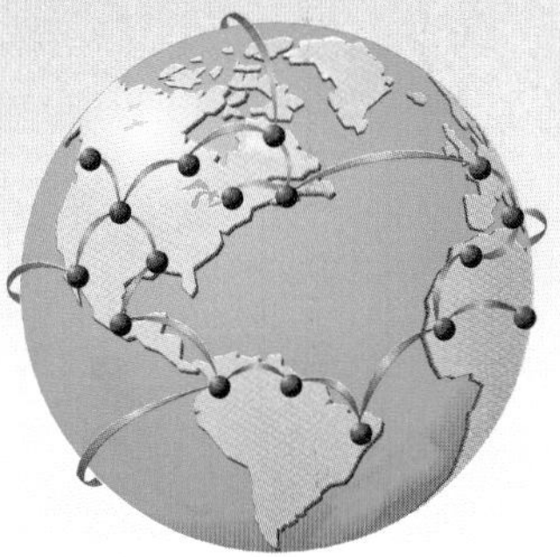

Select a category to find today's headlines, Web events and Web pages that deal with topics that interest you.

People

You can search for the e-mail address, phone number or mailing address of a friend or colleague.

Finding an address is helpful if you lost an address or you want to surprise someone with a message.

Yellow Pages

You can find the mailing address and phone number for businesses around the world.

You can search for companies in specific categories such as auto repair, florists and restaurants.

What's New and What's Cool

You can see a list of new Web sites and sites that Netscape considers innovative and interesting.

DISPLAY HISTORY OF VIEWED WEB PAGES

Navigator keeps track of all the Web pages you have recently viewed. You can easily return to any of these pages.

DISPLAY HISTORY OF VIEWED WEB PAGES

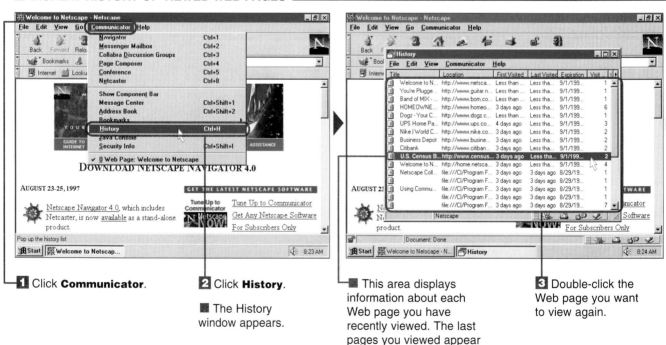

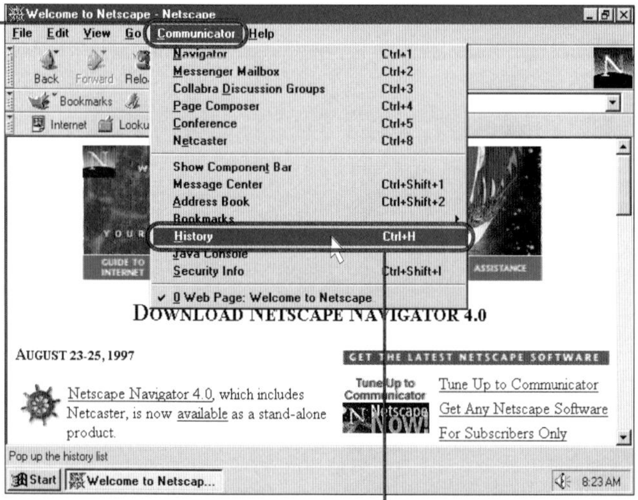

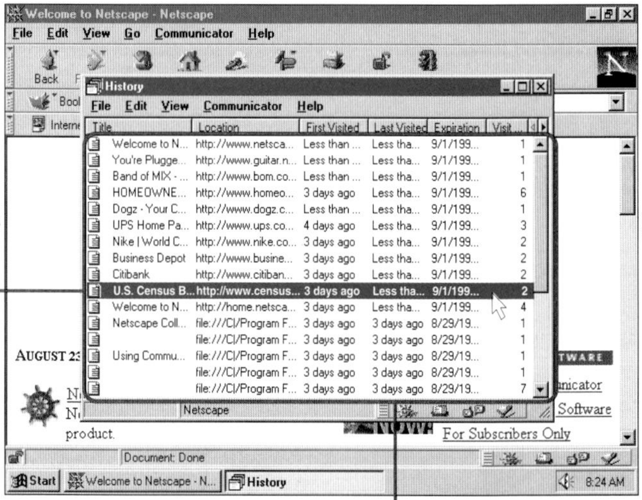

1 Click **Communicator**.

2 Click **History**.

■ The History window appears.

■ This area displays information about each Web page you have recently viewed. The last pages you viewed appear at the top of the list.

3 Double-click the Web page you want to view again.

?

What is the difference between the History window and the Go menu?

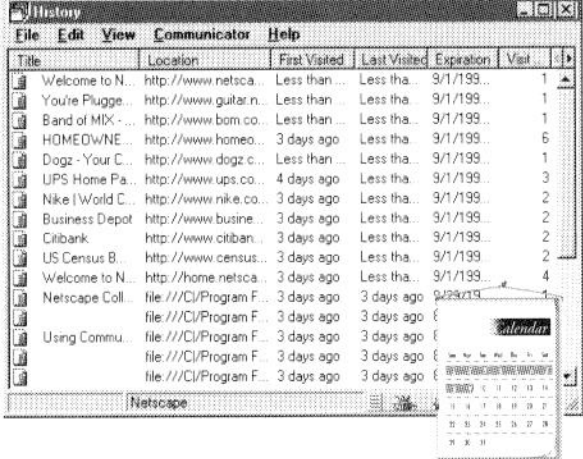

The History window displays the Web pages you have viewed over the last nine days, even if you close the program.

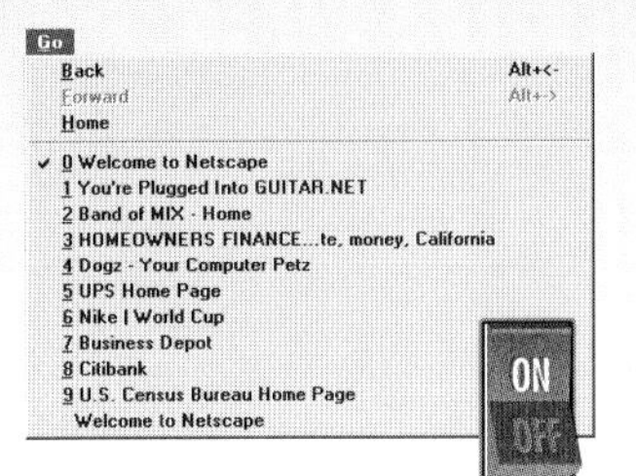

The Go menu displays the Web pages you have viewed since you last started Navigator.

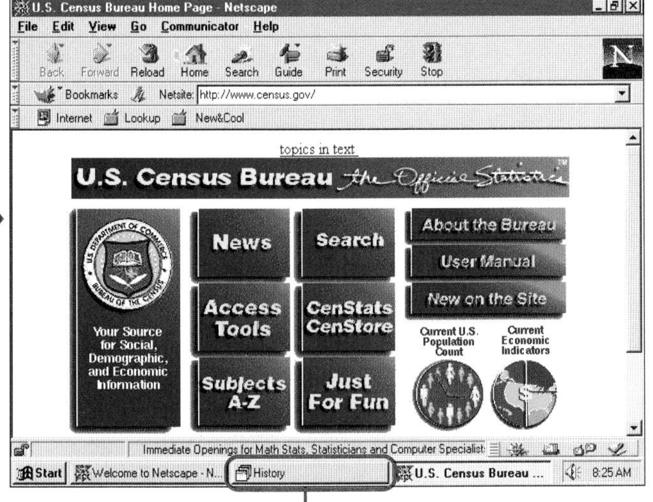

■ Navigator displays the page you selected.

■ The History window disappears from your screen. The taskbar displays a button for the window.

■ To redisplay the History window, click its button on the taskbar.

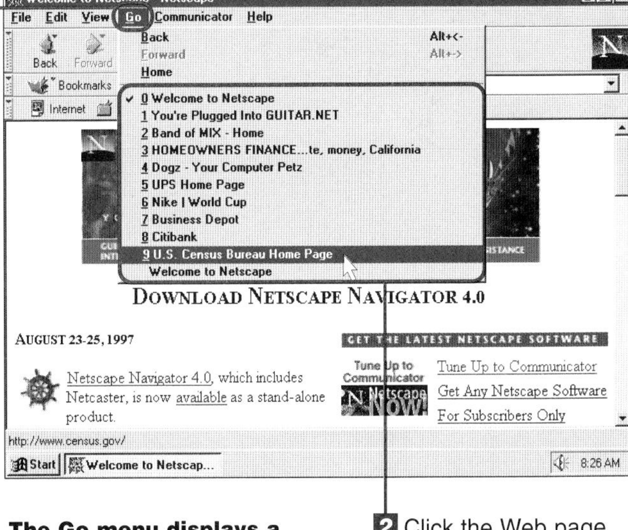

The Go menu displays a short list of Web pages you have recently viewed. You can easily return to any of these pages.

1 Click **Go** to display a list of Web pages you have recently viewed.

2 Click the Web page you want to view.

CHANGE WHEN HISTORY EXPIRES

You can change how long Navigator keeps track of Web pages you visit. If you view many Web pages in a short period of time, you may want to reduce the number of days that Navigator keeps track of pages.

You can also clear the History window. This is useful when the window displays so many Web pages that it is difficult to locate the pages you want to view.

CHANGE WHEN HISTORY EXPIRES

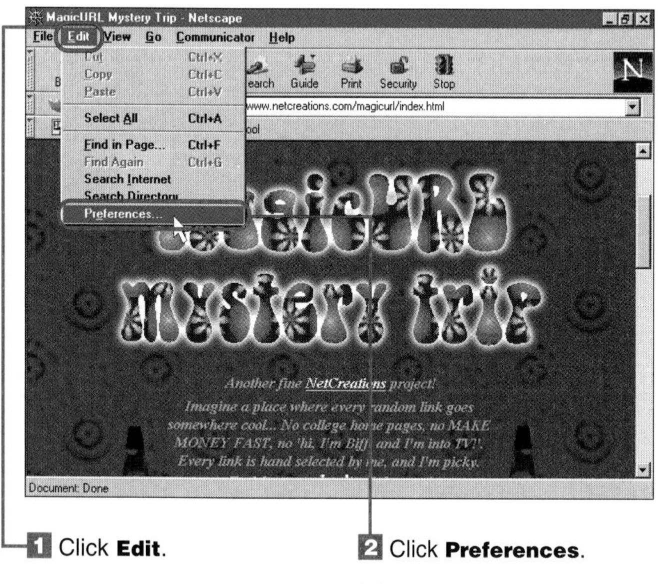

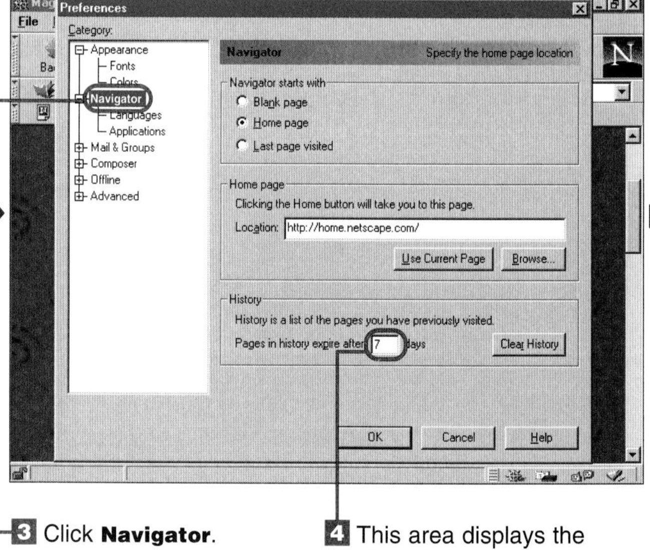

1 Click **Edit**.

2 Click **Preferences**.

■ The Preferences dialog box appears.

3 Click **Navigator**.

4 This area displays the number of days Navigator keeps track of Web pages you visit before clearing the pages. You can double-click this area and type a new number of days.

After clearing the History window, how can I return to a page I recently viewed?

You can use the Go menu to display a list of Web pages you have viewed since you last started Navigator. Clearing the History window does not affect the Go menu. If you want to clear the Go menu, you need to exit Navigator.

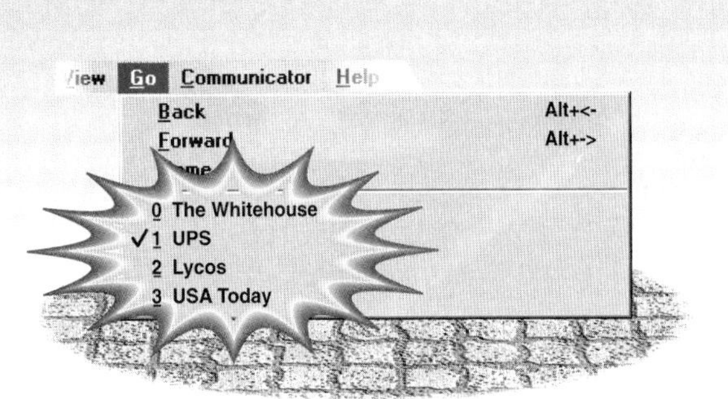

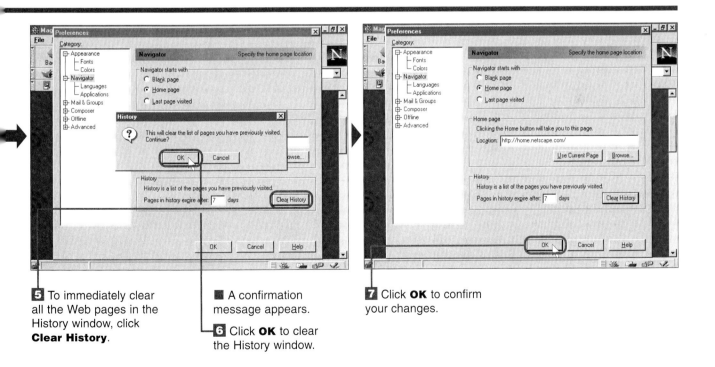

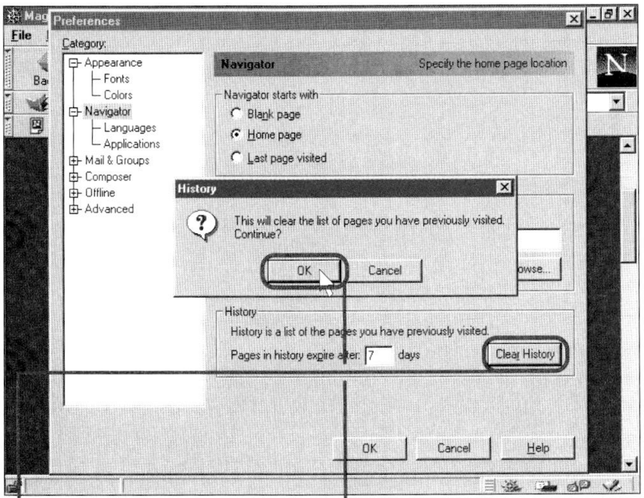

5 To immediately clear all the Web pages in the History window, click **Clear History**.

■ A confirmation message appears.

6 Click **OK** to clear the History window.

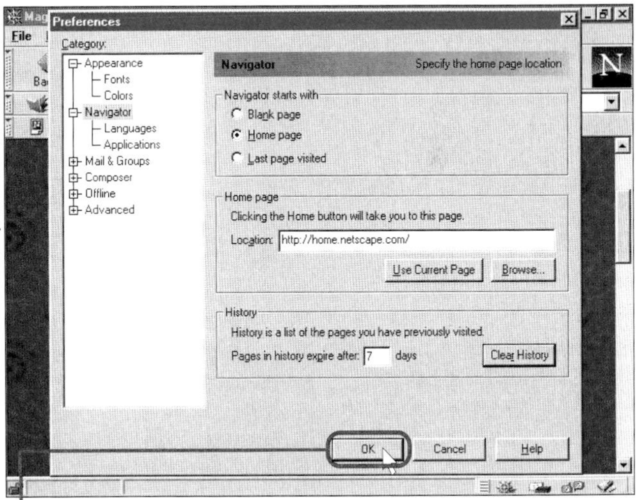

7 Click **OK** to confirm your changes.

FIND TEXT ON A WEB PAGE

If you are viewing a Web page that contains a lot of text, you can use the Find feature to quickly locate a word of interest.

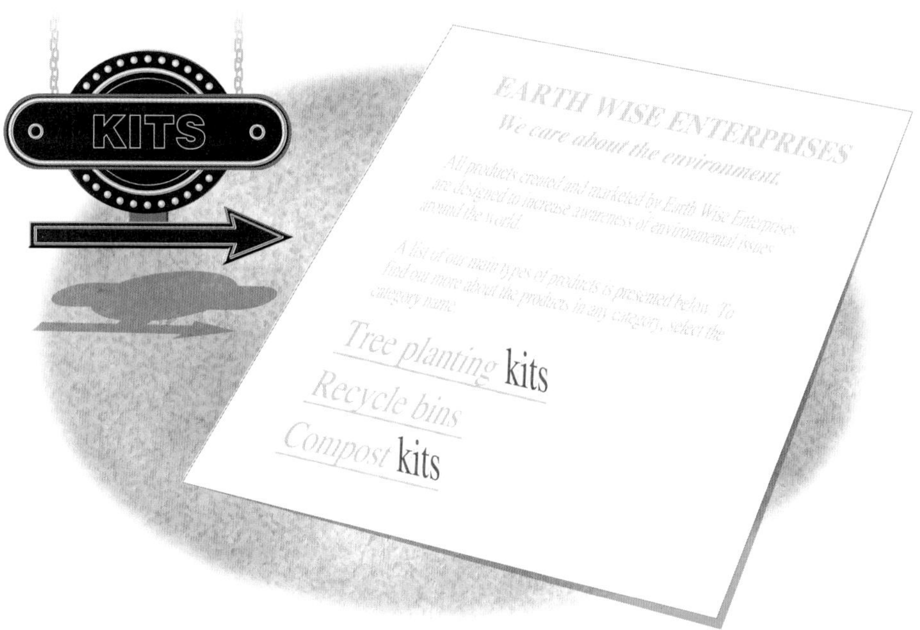

FIND TEXT ON A WEB PAGE

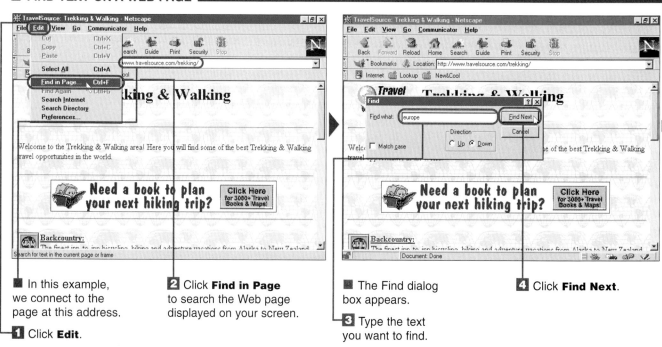

■ In this example, we connect to the page at this address.

1 Click **Edit**.

2 Click **Find in Page** to search the Web page displayed on your screen.

■ The Find dialog box appears.

3 Type the text you want to find.

4 Click **Find Next**.

Will Navigator find words that are part of larger words?

When you search for a word on a Web page, Navigator will find the word even if it is part of a larger word. For example, if you search for **place**, Navigator will also find **place**s, **place**ment and common**place**.

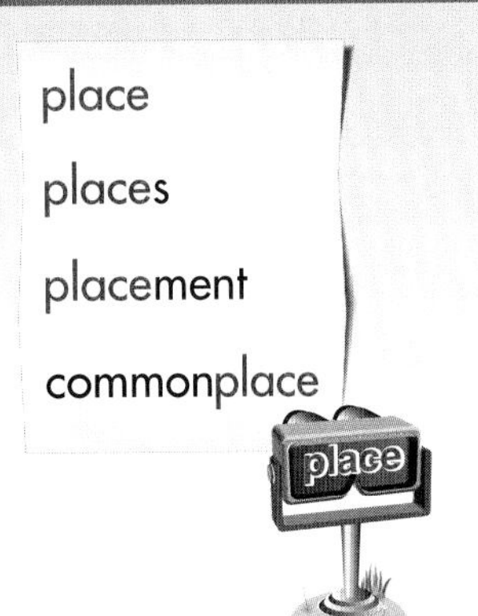

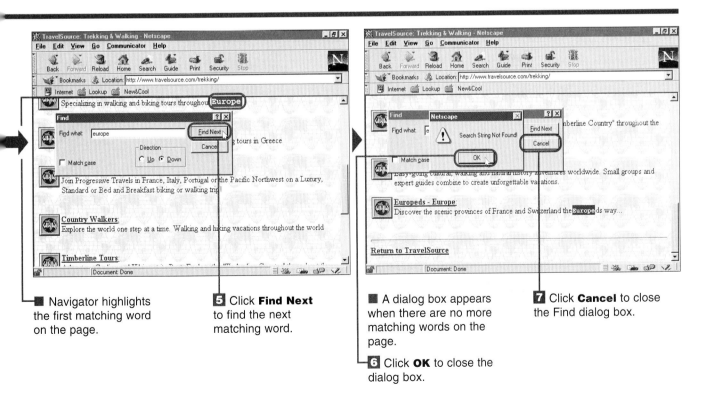

■ Navigator highlights the first matching word on the page.

5 Click **Find Next** to find the next matching word.

■ A dialog box appears when there are no more matching words on the page.

6 Click **OK** to close the dialog box.

7 Click **Cancel** to close the Find dialog box.

SAVE AN IMAGE

You can save an image displayed on a Web page. Saving an image allows you to view the image when you are not connected to the Internet.

If you plan to use an image from a Web page, make sure the image does not have any copyright restrictions.

SAVE AN IMAGE

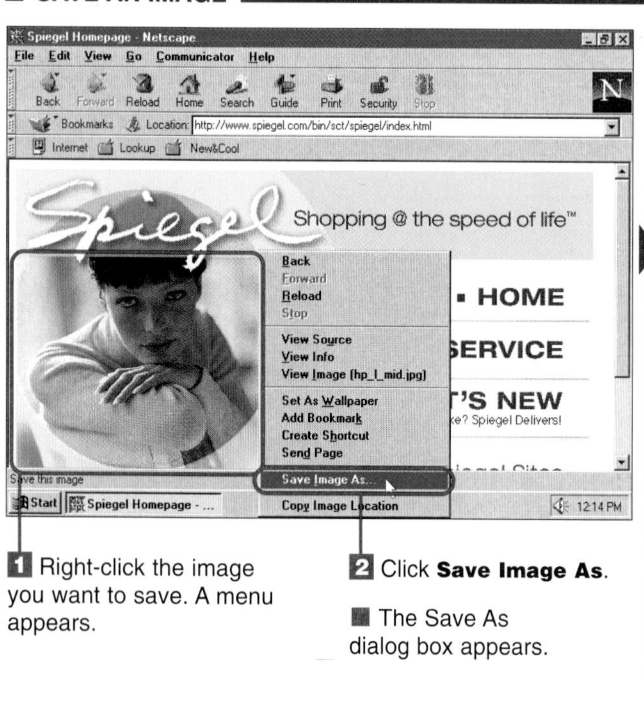

1 Right-click the image you want to save. A menu appears.

2 Click **Save Image As**.

■ The Save As dialog box appears.

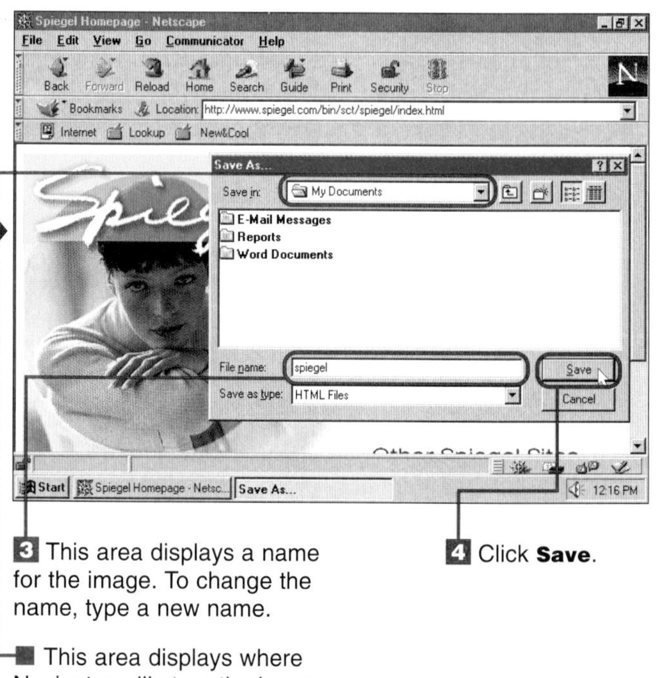

3 This area displays a name for the image. To change the name, type a new name.

■ This area displays where Navigator will store the image. You can click this area to change the location.

4 Click **Save**.

SET AN IMAGE AS WALLPAPER

You can use an image you like on a Web page to decorate your desktop.

SET AN IMAGE AS WALLPAPER

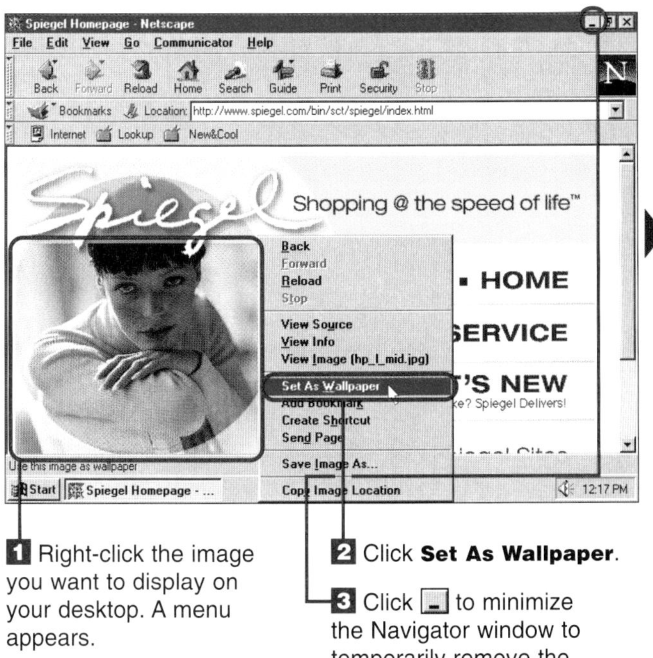

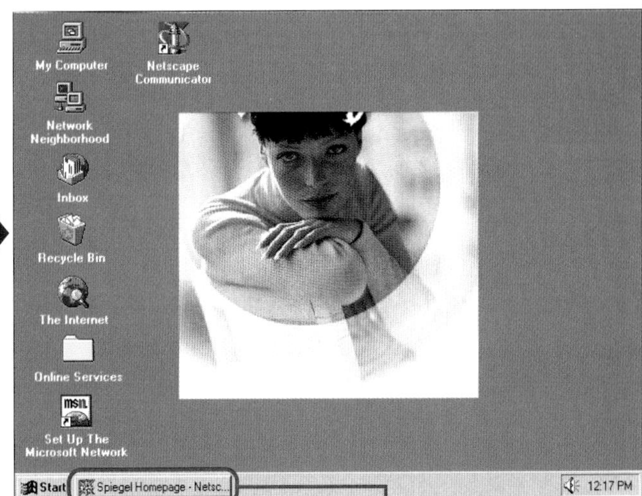

1 Right-click the image you want to display on your desktop. A menu appears.

2 Click **Set As Wallpaper**.

3 Click ▁ to minimize the Navigator window to temporarily remove the window from your screen.

■ The image you selected appears on your desktop.

Note: To remove the image from your desktop, refer to your Windows manual.

■ Click the button on the taskbar to redisplay the Navigator window.

SAVE A WEB PAGE

You can save a Web page displayed on your screen. Saving a Web page allows you to view the page when you are not connected to the Internet.

If you plan to use text from a Web page, make sure the text does not have any copyright restrictions.

SAVE A WEB PAGE

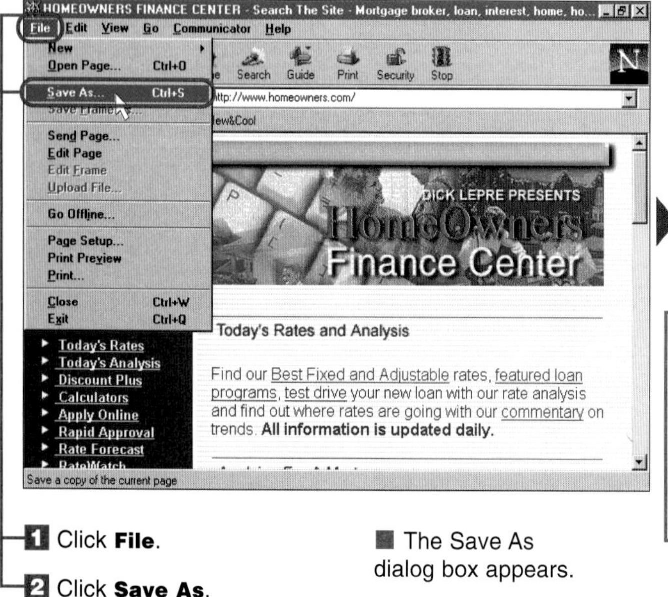

1 Click **File**.

2 Click **Save As**.

■ The Save As dialog box appears.

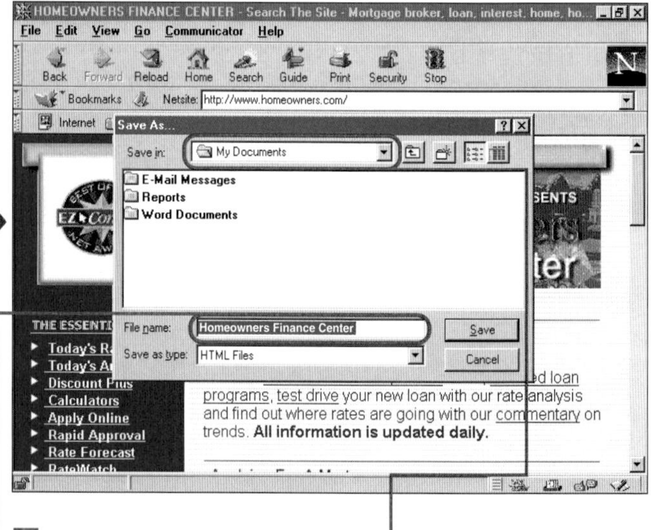

3 This area displays a name for the Web page. To change the name, type a new name.

■ This area displays where Navigator will store the Web page. You can click this area to change the location.

When I save a Web page, does Navigator save the images displayed on the Web page?

No, when you save a Web page, Navigator saves only the text. The images will not appear when you open a saved page. You must save any images on a Web page separately if you want to keep the images and view them at a later time. To save an image, refer to page 46.

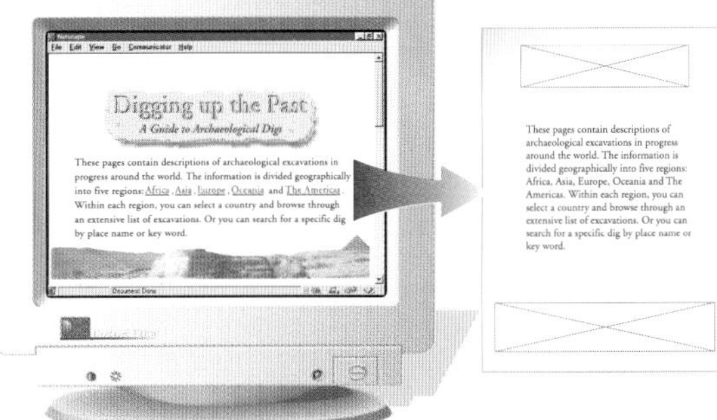

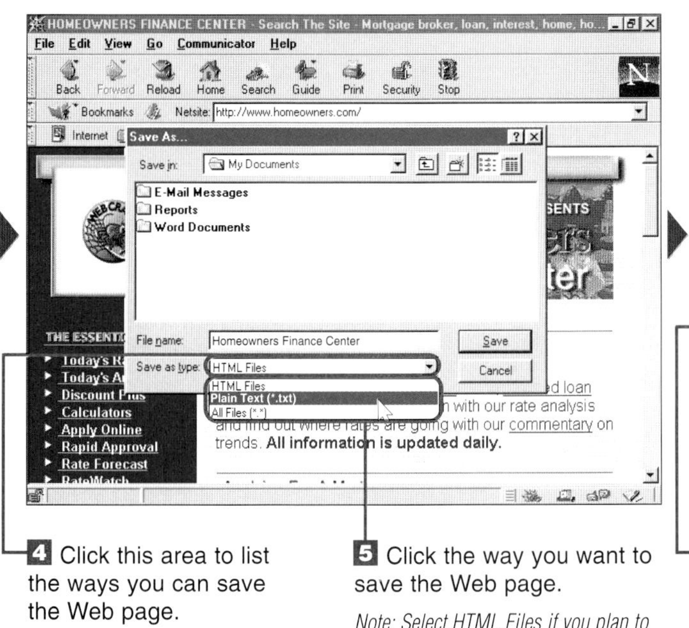

4 Click this area to list the ways you can save the Web page.

5 Click the way you want to save the Web page.

Note: Select HTML Files if you plan to display the page in Navigator. Select Plain Text if you plan to display the page in a word processor.

6 Click **Save** to save the Web page.

OPEN A SAVED WEB PAGE OR IMAGE

You can open and view a saved Web page or image even if you are not connected to the Internet. This allows you to take your time when reading a Web page or viewing an image.

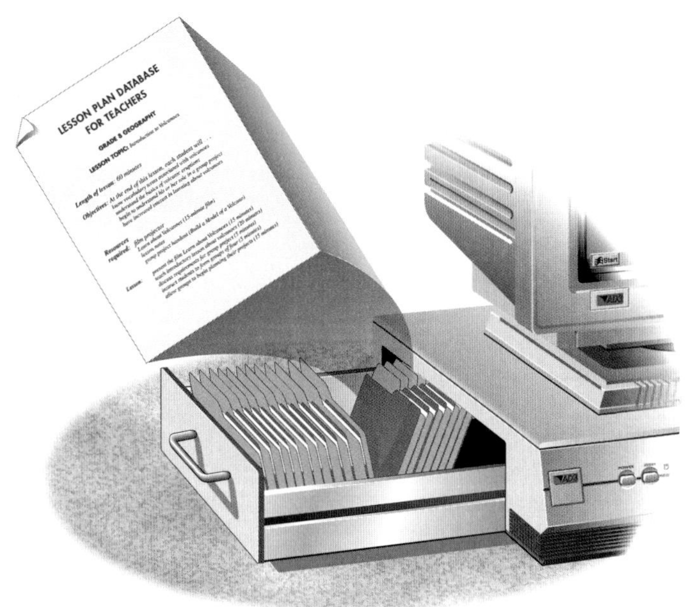

OPEN A SAVED WEB PAGE OR IMAGE

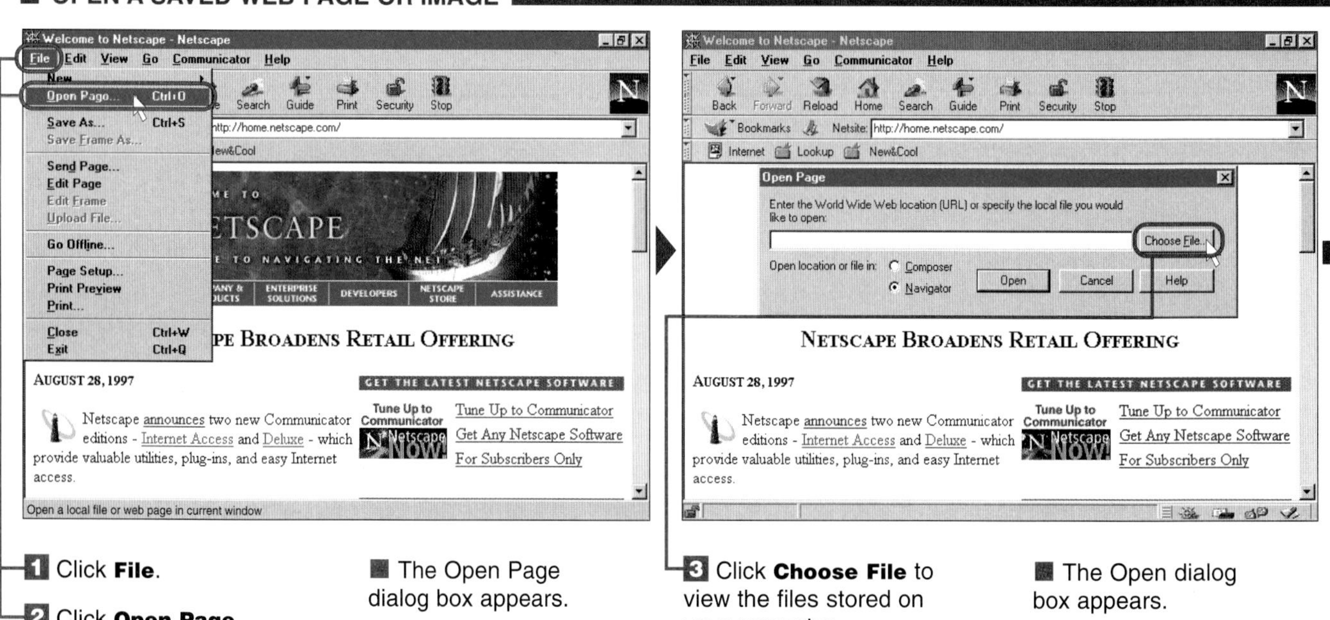

1 Click **File**.

2 Click **Open Page**.

■ The Open Page dialog box appears.

3 Click **Choose File** to view the files stored on your computer.

■ The Open dialog box appears.

?

Do I need to return to pages on the Web that I saved?

Make sure you occasionally return to pages on the Web you saved to review any updated information. Companies and individuals may change their Web pages to add additional information or make the pages more attractive.

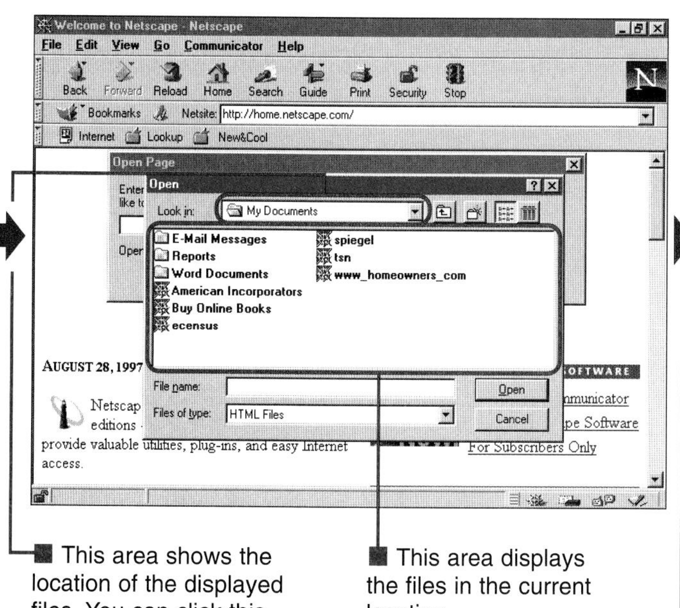

■ This area shows the location of the displayed files. You can click this area to change the location.

■ This area displays the files in the current location.

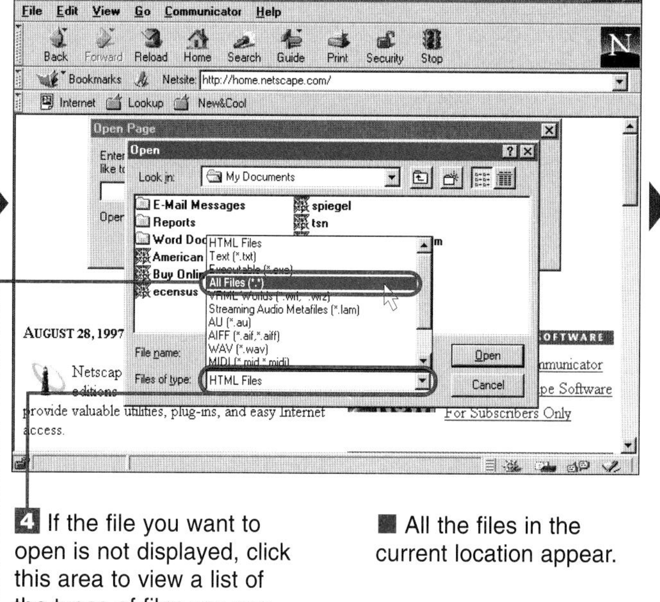

4 If the file you want to open is not displayed, click this area to view a list of the types of files you can display.

5 Click **All Files** to display all the files in the current location.

■ All the files in the current location appear.

CONTINUED

OPEN A SAVED WEB PAGE OR IMAGE

When you open a saved Web page, the images on the Web page do not appear. Navigator displays an icon for each image.

OPEN A SAVED WEB PAGE OR IMAGE (CONTINUED)

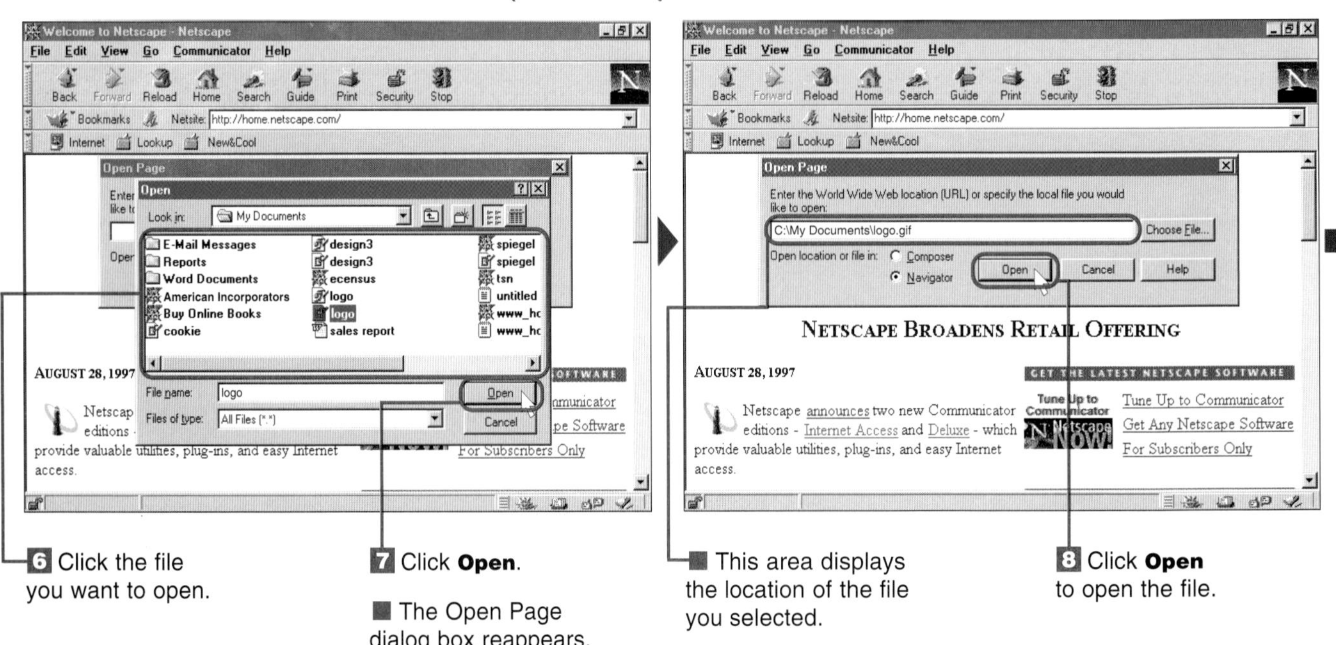

6 Click the file you want to open.

7 Click **Open**.

■ The Open Page dialog box reappears.

■ This area displays the location of the file you selected.

8 Click **Open** to open the file.

Is there a faster way to open Web pages or images I saved?

When you save a Web page or image, Navigator places the file in the location you specified on your computer. You can double-click the file to instantly open the file.

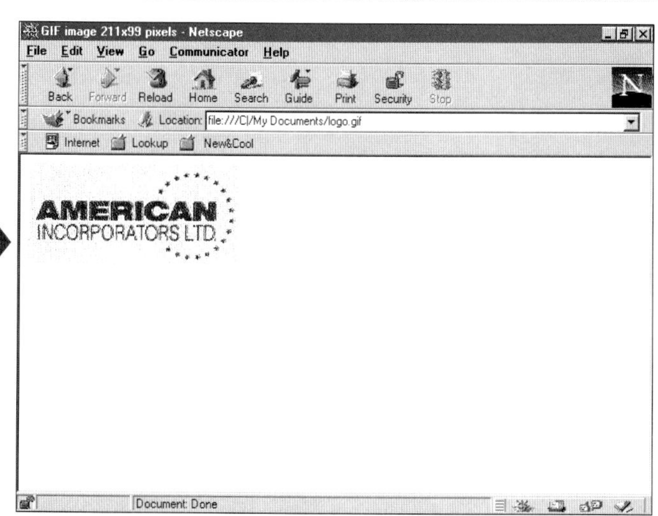

■ The image or Web page you selected appears on your screen.

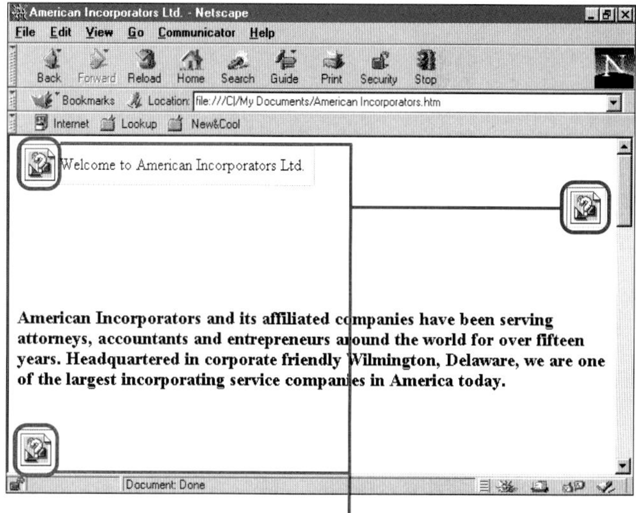

■ When you open a saved Web page, the images do not appear. Navigator stores only the text when you save a Web page.

■ Navigator displays a small icon ( ) where an image would usually appear on the Web page.

DS Memorial Quilt Website.
Memorial
The Lamborghini Diablo!
Lamborghini
Netscape
File Edit View Go Communicator Help
Adobe
Designing Business
Click through excerpts of a hot new Adobe Press book by designer Clement Mok.
The Design
Netscape
File Edit View Go Communicator Help
Mona Lisa
The Paint of this portrait has oxidized and is seen throu

CHAPTER 3

Do you want to learn more about Web browsing? This chapter teaches you how to play sounds and videos, view images and much more.

OPEN A NEW NAVIGATOR WINDOW

You can open a new window to display two Web pages at once.

When information is taking a long time to display, you can open a new window to view other Web pages while you wait. You can also open a new window to compare two Web pages.

OPEN A NEW NAVIGATOR WINDOW

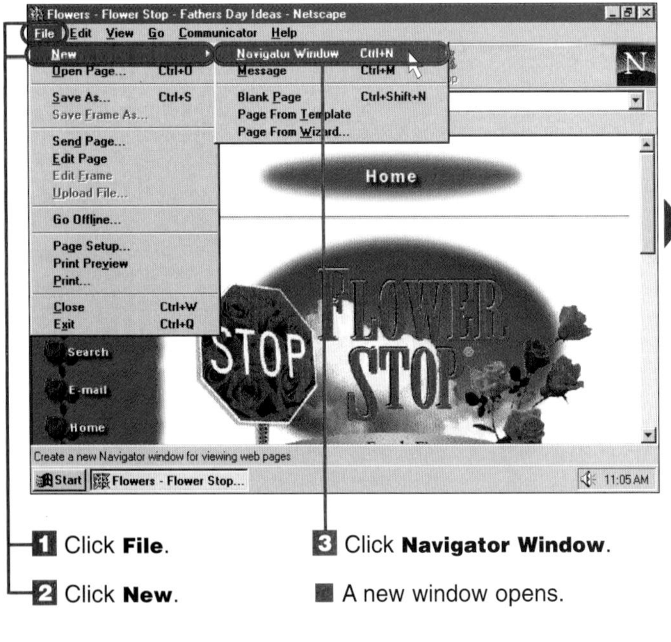

1 Click **File**.

2 Click **New**.

3 Click **Navigator Window**.

■ A new window opens.

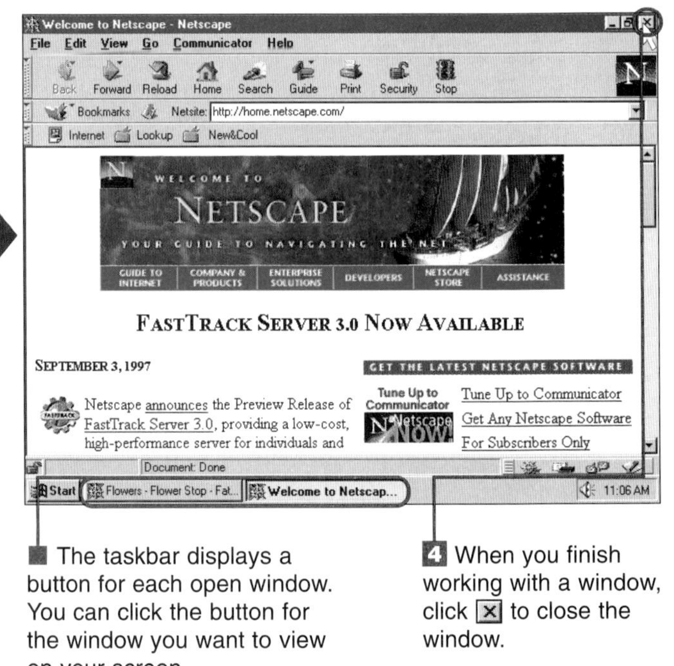

■ The taskbar displays a button for each open window. You can click the button for the window you want to view on your screen.

4 When you finish working with a window, click ☒ to close the window.

VIEW WEB PAGE SOURCE

You can view the HTML code used to create a Web page. This is useful if you want to see how an effect on a Web page was created.

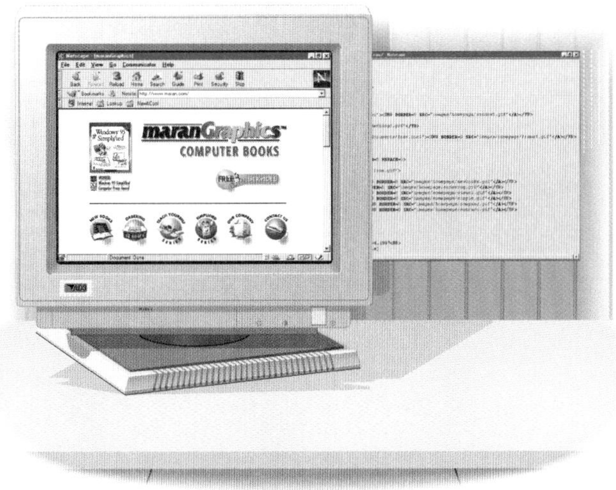

HyperText Markup Language (HTML) is a computer language used to create Web pages. Navigator interprets HTML code and displays the Web pages on your screen.

VIEW WEB PAGE SOURCE

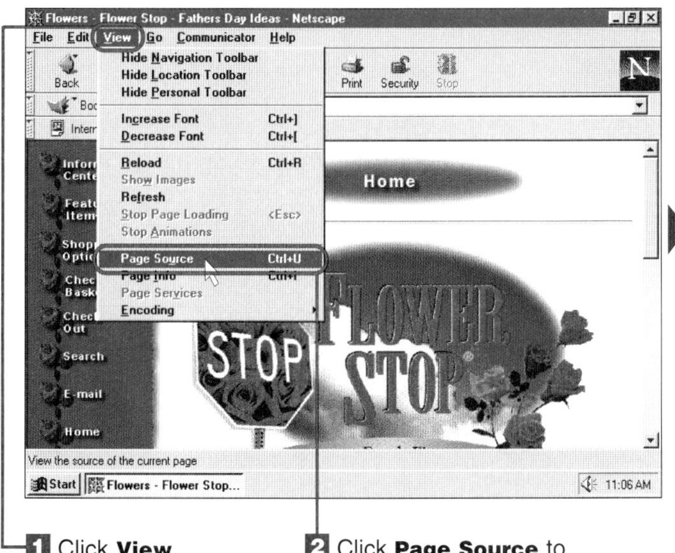

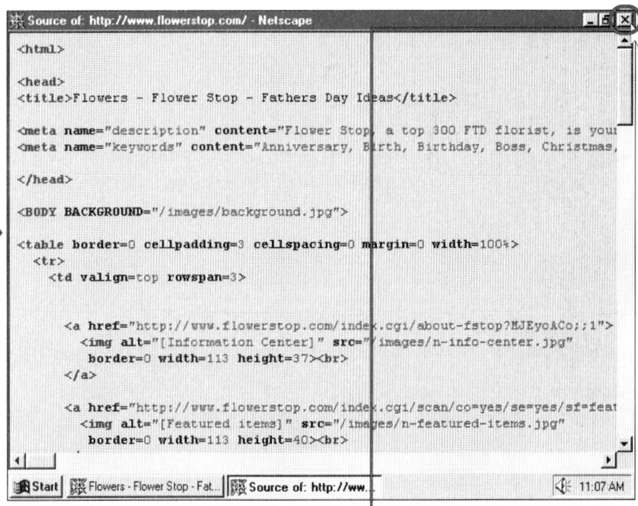

1 Click **View**.

2 Click **Page Source** to display the HTML code used to create the Web page displayed on your screen.

■ A window appears, displaying the HTML code for the Web page.

3 Click ☒ to close the window when you finish reviewing the HTML code.

You can choose which windows you want to open automatically each time you start Netscape Communicator.

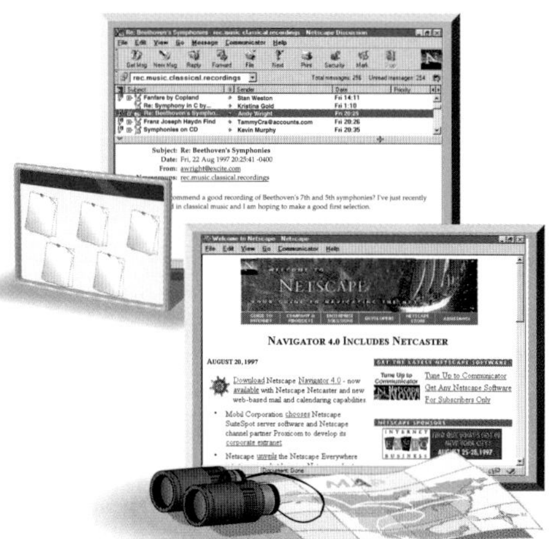

CHANGE STARTUP WINDOW

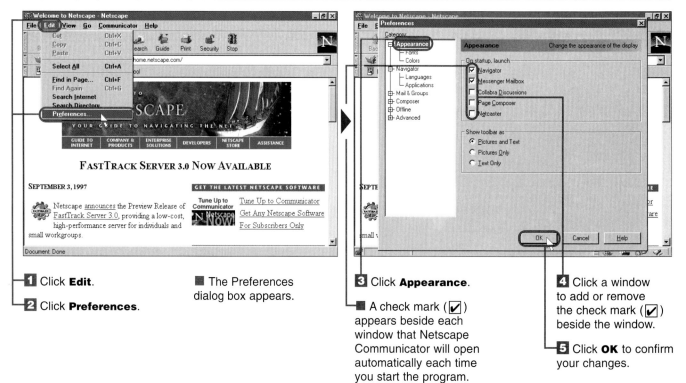

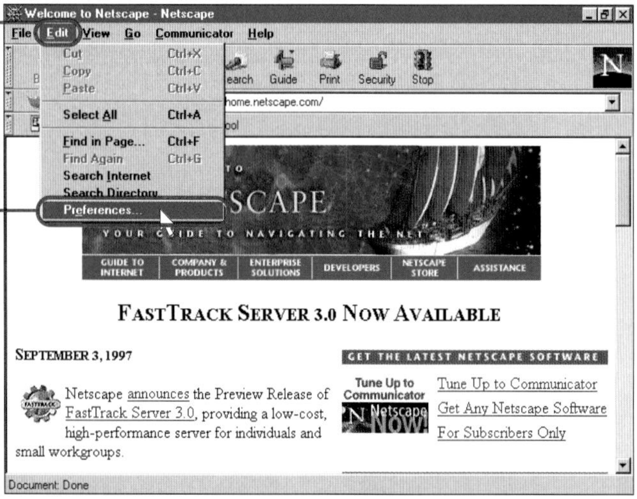

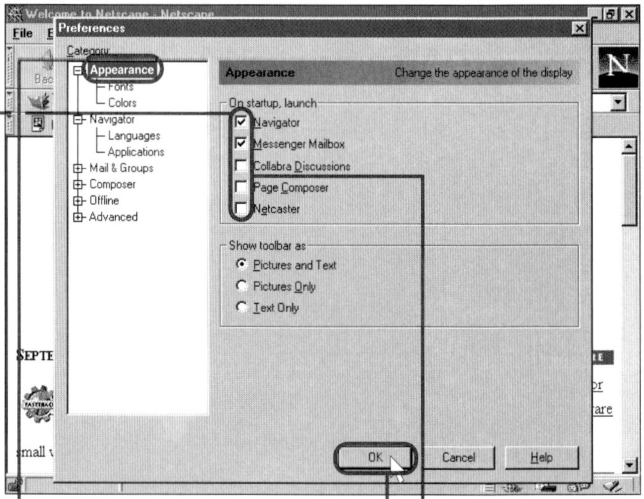

1 Click **Edit**.

2 Click **Preferences**.

■ The Preferences dialog box appears.

3 Click **Appearance**.

■ A check mark (☑) appears beside each window that Netscape Communicator will open automatically each time you start the program.

4 Click a window to add or remove the check mark (☑) beside the window.

5 Click **OK** to confirm your changes.

Some Web sites use frames to display several Web pages at the same time. Frames split a Web browser screen into different sections.

Frames are often used to display advertisements, logos or a table of contents. Information in one frame can stay on the screen while you browse through information in other frames.

WORK WITH FRAMES

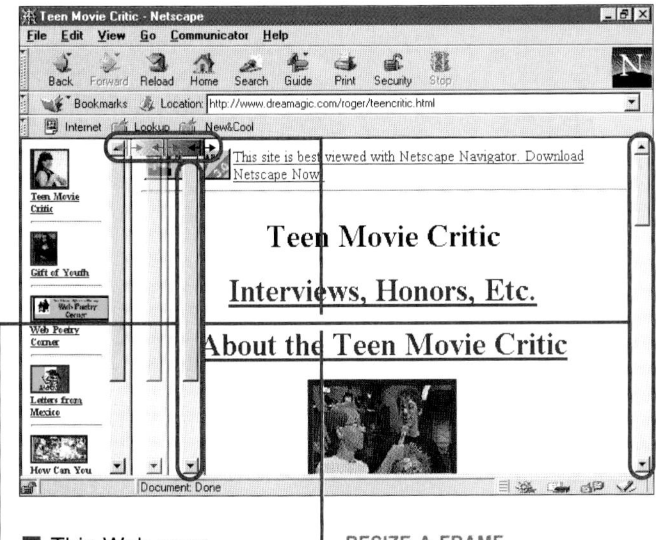

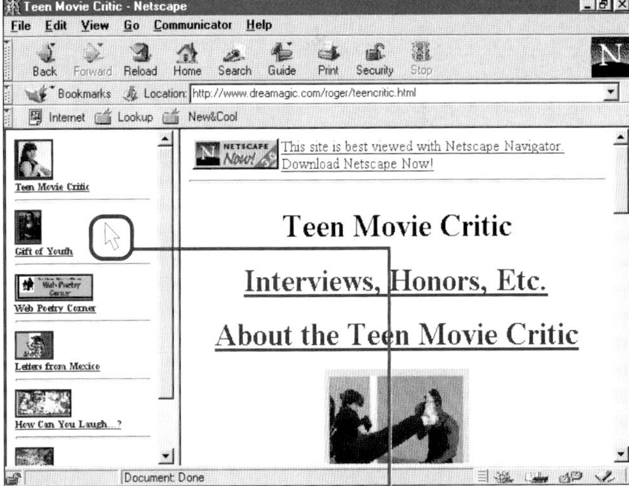

■ This Web page uses frames to display information.

■ You can use the scroll bars to scroll through the contents of a frame.

RESIZE A FRAME

1 Position the mouse over the edge of the frame (changes to ↔ or ↕) and then drag the frame to a new location.

Note: You cannot resize some frames.

SELECT A FRAME

■ Make sure you select the frame you want to work with when performing certain tasks such as printing a Web page.

1 To select the frame you want to work with, click a blank area in the frame.

You can change the text and background color of pages you view on the Web.

CHANGE WEB PAGE COLORS

1 Click **Edit**.

2 Click **Preferences**.

■ The Preferences dialog box appears.

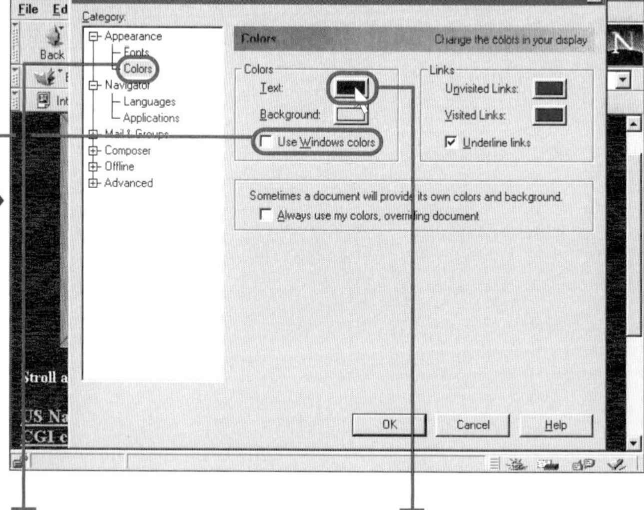

3 Click **Colors** to change the colors used to display Web pages.

4 Click this option if you want to choose your own colors rather than use Windows' colors (☑ changes to ☐).

5 Click this button to change the color of text used on Web pages.

■ The Color dialog box appears.

How do I change the color of links on Web pages?

You can change the color of links you have not selected (unvisited) and links you have selected (visited).

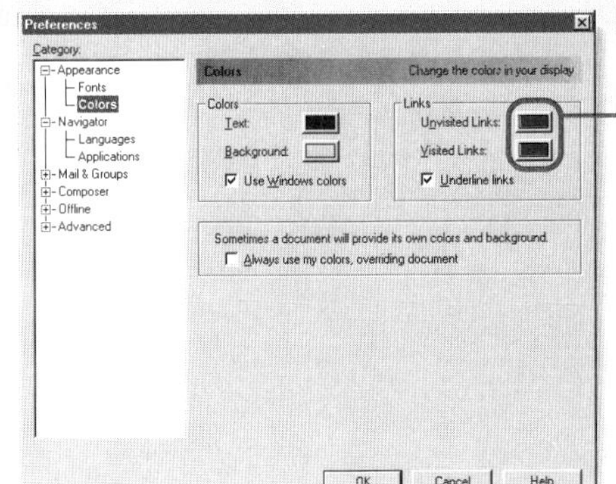

■ This area displays the colors used for links. You can click one of these buttons to change the color of links. Then perform steps **6** and **7** below to select a color.

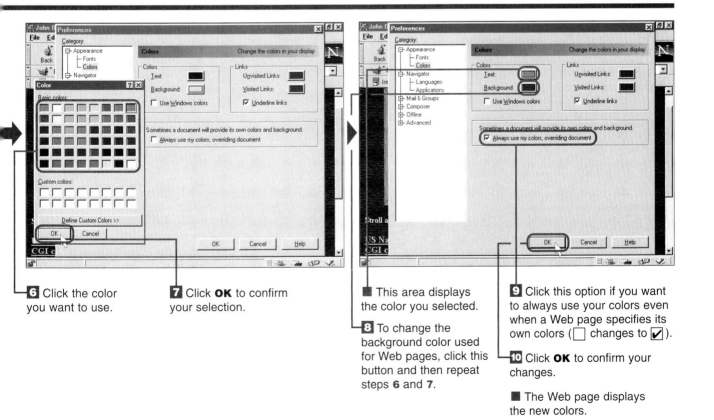

6 Click the color you want to use.

7 Click **OK** to confirm your selection.

■ This area displays the color you selected.

8 To change the background color used for Web pages, click this button and then repeat steps **6** and **7**.

9 Click this option if you want to always use your colors even when a Web page specifies its own colors (☐ changes to ☑).

10 Click **OK** to confirm your changes.

■ The Web page displays the new colors.

TURN OFF IMAGES

Images can take a while to transfer to your computer. Although images can make Web pages more attractive, you can save time by turning off the display of images.

TURN OFF IMAGES

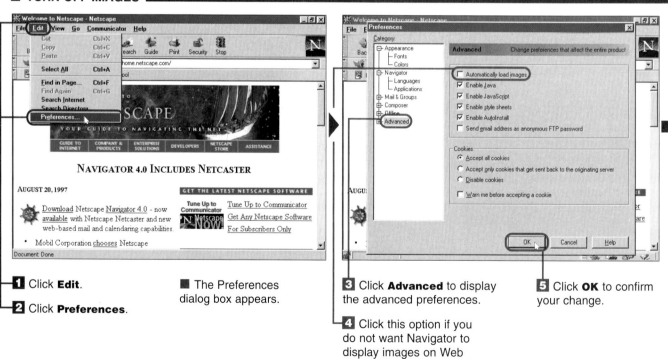

1. Click **Edit**.
2. Click **Preferences**.

■ The Preferences dialog box appears.

3. Click **Advanced** to display the advanced preferences.
4. Click this option if you do not want Navigator to display images on Web pages (☑ changes to ☐).
5. Click **OK** to confirm your change.

? **What types of image files will I find on the Web?**

The most common types of image files on the Web are GIF and JPEG.

GIF

Graphics Interchange Format (GIF) images are often used for logos, banners and computer-generated art.

JPEG

Joint Photographic Experts Group (JPEG) images are often used for photographs and very complex images.

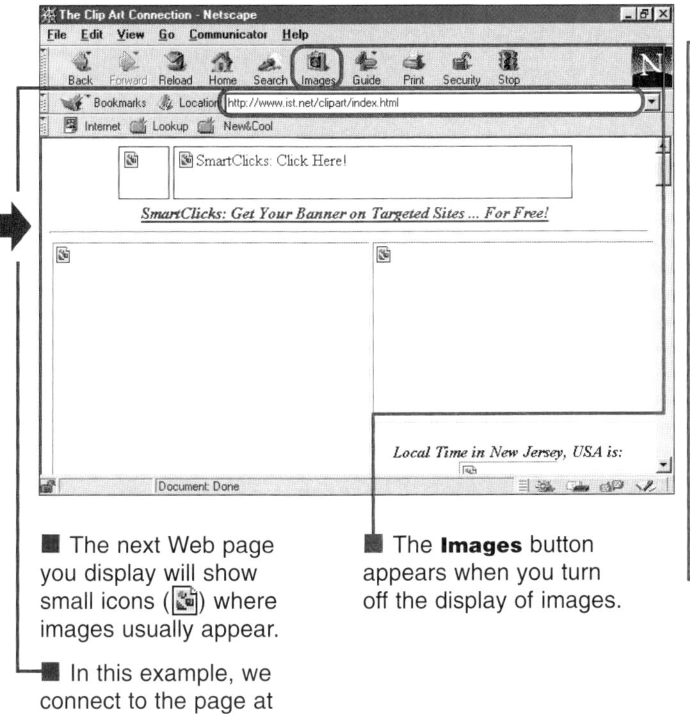

■ The next Web page you display will show small icons (▣) where images usually appear.

■ In this example, we connect to the page at this address.

■ The **Images** button appears when you turn off the display of images.

SHOW IMAGES

1 Click **Images** to show the images on the displayed page.

■ The images appear.

■ To once again show the images for every Web page you display, repeat steps **1** to **5** on page 62.

VIEW IMAGES

You can view images such as album covers, cartoons, celebrity pictures, famous paintings and weather maps on the Web.

GIF and JPEG images are the most common images on the Web. Communicator can display the following images:

Graphics Interchange Format (.gif)

Joint Photographic Experts Group (.jpeg, .jpg)

X Bitmap (.xbm)

VIEW IMAGES

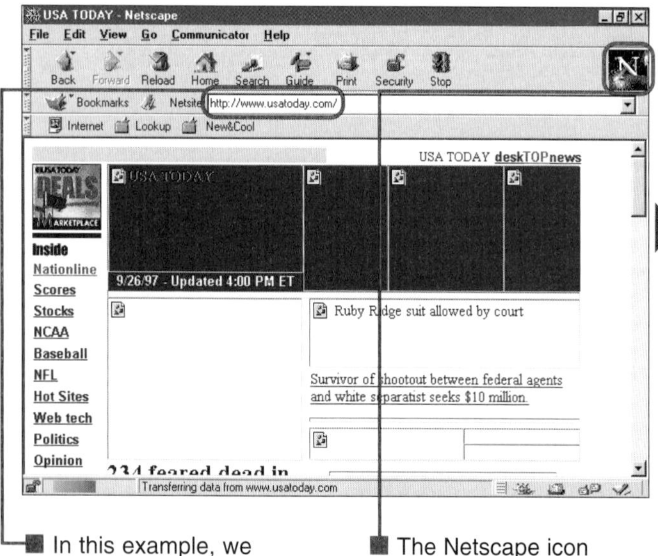

■ In this example, we connect to the Web page at this address.

■ Text transfers quickly to your computer so you can start reading the text right away. Images transfer more slowly.

■ The Netscape icon is animated as the page transfers to your computer. The animation stops when the page has finished transferring.

■ If the mouse ↖ changes to ☝ when over an image, the image is a link. You can click the image to take you to another Web page.

TYPES OF IMAGES

Background Images

A background image displays a solid color, texture or pattern behind the text and other images on a Web page. Background images are usually small images that repeat to fill the entire page.

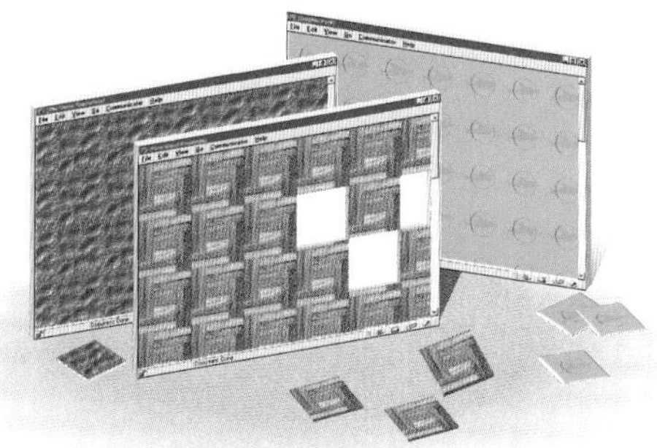

Imagemaps

An imagemap is an image divided into sections, called hotspots. Each hotspot contains a link to another page on the Web. Selecting a hotspot will take you to the linked page.

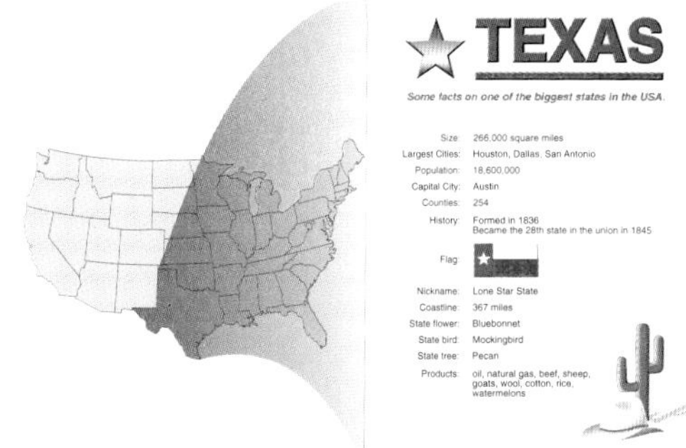

Inline Images

Most images on the Web are inline images. Inline images can include arrows, buttons, logos, photographs and pictures.

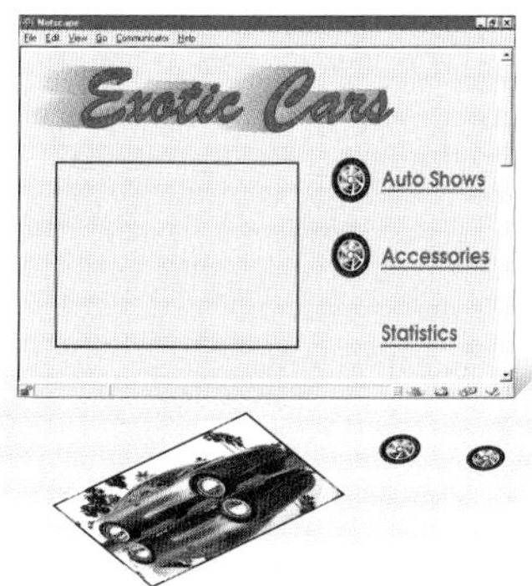

Thumbnail Images

A thumbnail image is a small version of a larger image that transfers quickly to your computer. If you want to see the larger image, select the thumbnail image.

PLAY SOUNDS

You can hear sounds such as historical speeches, movie soundtracks, newscasts, rock music, sound effects and TV theme songs on the Web.

You need a sound card and speakers to hear sounds on the Web.

Communicator can play the following types of sounds:

AIFF (.aif, .aiff)

Audio Player (.au)

MIDI (.mid, .midi)

Wave (.wav)

Note: To play some types of sounds, you may need a plug-in. Refer to page 72 for more information.

PLAY SOUNDS

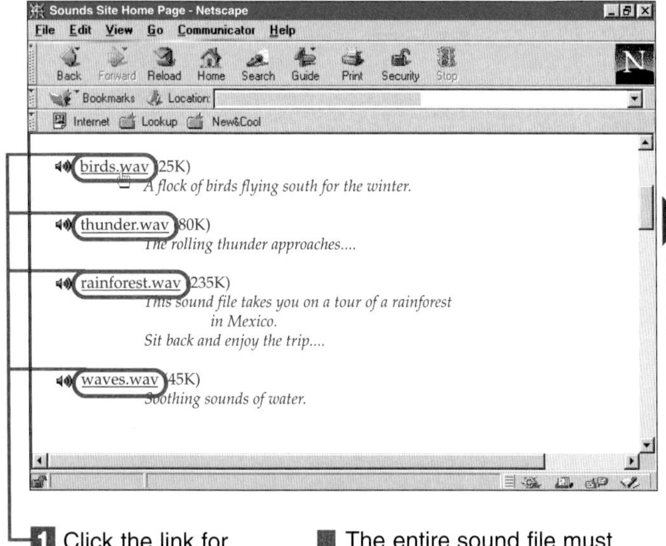

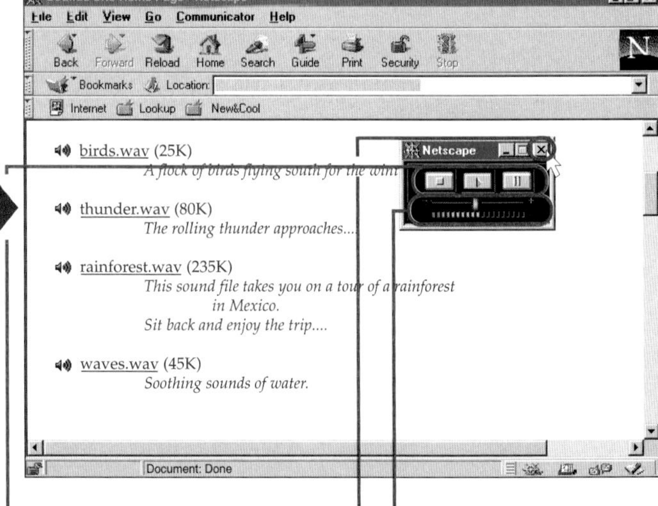

1 Click the link for the sound you want to play.

■ The entire sound file must transfer to your computer before you can listen to the sound. After a few moments, a window appears and the sound plays.

2 You can click one of these options to stop ( ), play ( ) or pause ( ) the sound.

Note: The sound controls do not appear until the entire sound file has transferred.

3 You can adjust the volume by dragging the slider ( ) to the left or right.

4 You can click ☒ to close the window when you finish listening to the sound.

How do I know if a link will play a sound?

Web pages usually use a phrase or image to indicate that a link will play a sound file. Web pages may also indicate the sound file type and size as well as the length of time the sound will play. This information allows you to decide if you want to play the sound file.

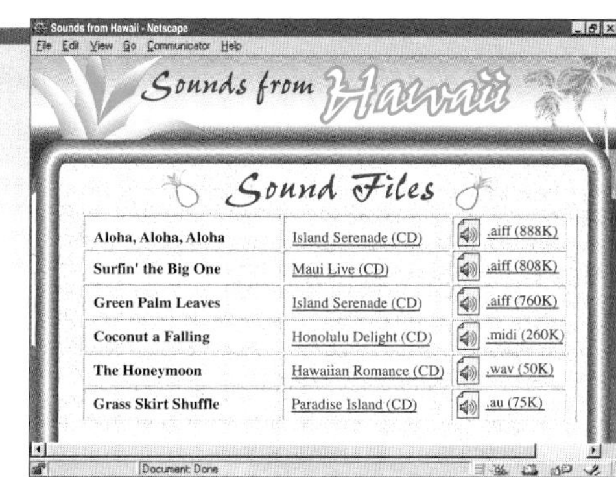

NETSCAPE'S STREAMING SOUND

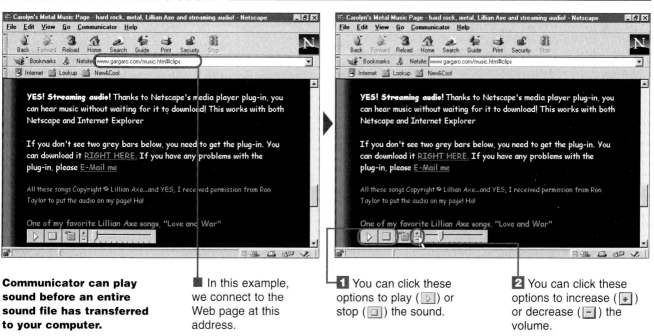

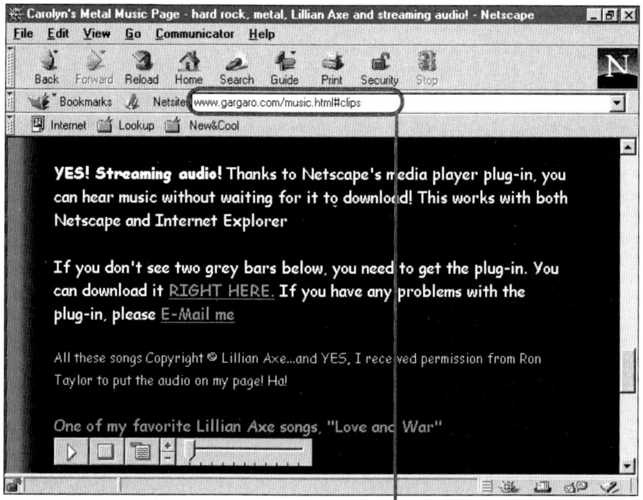

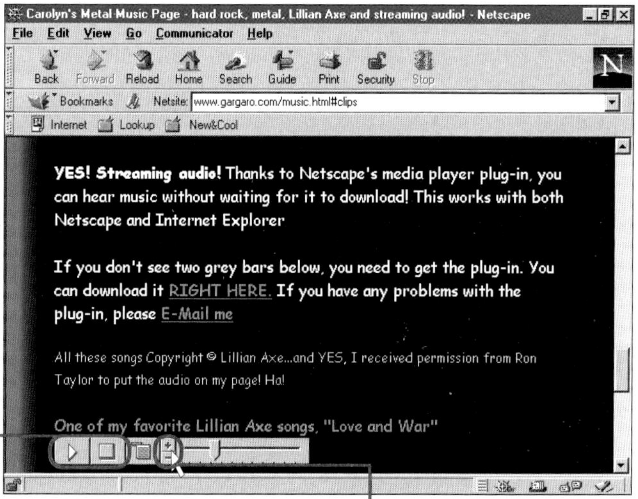

Communicator can play sound before an entire sound file has transferred to your computer.

■ In this example, we connect to the Web page at this address.

1 You can click these options to play (▷) or stop (□) the sound.

2 You can click these options to increase (+) or decrease (−) the volume.

PLAY VIDEOS

You can play videos such as advertisements, cartoons, celebrity interviews and movie clips on the Web.

Communicator can play Audio Video Interleaved (.avi) files. Other common types of video files on the Web include:

Motion Picture Experts Group (.mpeg, .mpg)

QuickTime (.mov)

Note: To play some types of videos, you may need a plug-in. Refer to page 72 for more information.

PLAY VIDEOS

Movie Clip Archive - Netscape

File Edit View Go Communicator Help

Back Forward Reload Home Search Guide Print Security Stop

Internet Lookup New&Cool

MOVIE CLIP ARCHIVE

Click a link from the list below and enjoy the show!

Name	Last Modified	Size
Journey through Africa	08 - Oct - 97 13:05	1 M
Summer Storm	08 - Oct - 97 13:12	87K
Invaders	08 - Oct - 97 13:06	676K
A Summer to Remember	08 - Oct - 97 13:06	656 K
Nick & Nancy	08 - Oct - 97 13:29	87K
Wedding Bells	08 - Oct - 97 13:39	117 K

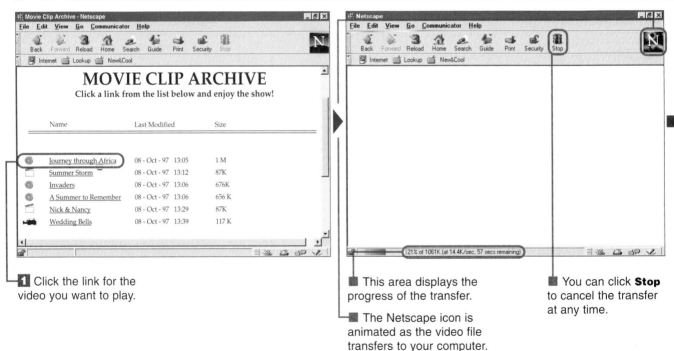

1 Click the link for the video you want to play.

Netscape

File Edit View Go Communicator Help

Back Forward Reload Home Search Guide Print Security Stop

Internet Lookup New&Cool

21% of 1061K (at 14.4K/sec, 57 secs remaining)

■ This area displays the progress of the transfer.

■ The Netscape icon is animated as the video file transfers to your computer.

■ You can click **Stop** to cancel the transfer at any time.

? How long will the video take to transfer?

A link to a video should display the file size and type. This will help you decide if you want to transfer the video to your computer.

File Size			Time
Bytes	Kilobytes (KB)	Megabytes (MB)	(estimated)
10,000,000	10,000	10	1 hour
5,000,000	5,000	5	30 minutes
2,500,000	2,500	2.5	15 minutes

You can use the chart above as a guide to determine how long the transfer will take. The chart is based on transferring files with a 28,800 bps modem.

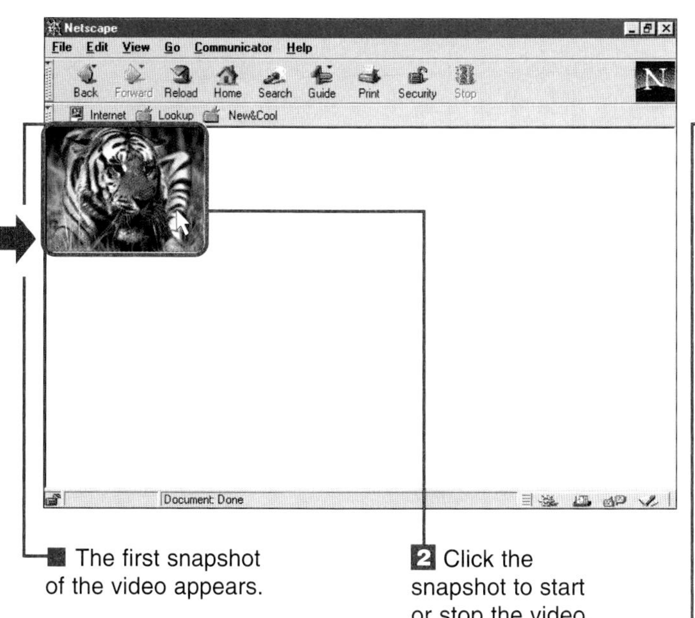

■ The first snapshot of the video appears.

2 Click the snapshot to start or stop the video.

LIVEVIDEO

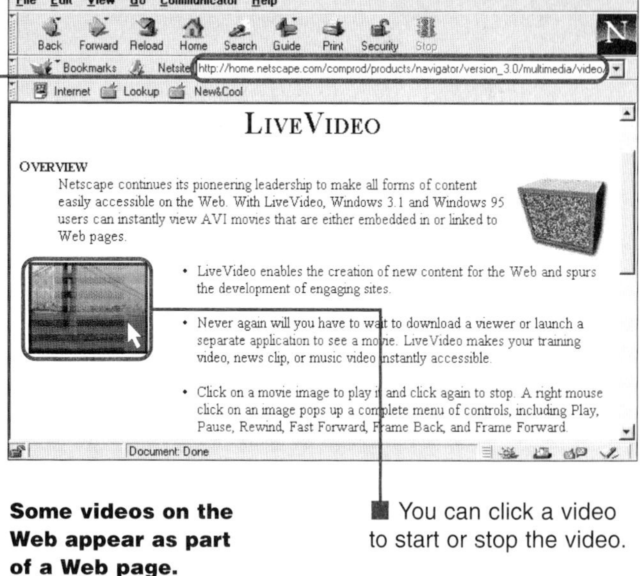

Some videos on the Web appear as part of a Web page.

■ In this example, we connect to the page at this address.

■ You can click a video to start or stop the video.

Java is a programming language that allows Web pages to display animation and moving text, play music and much more.

Programs written in Java are called Java applets.

You can find many examples of Java at www.gamelan.com

JAVA

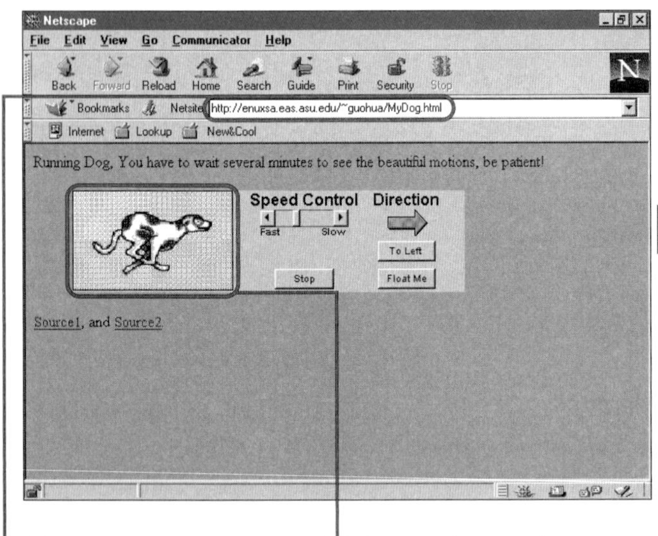

■ In this example, we connect to the page at this address.

■ People often use Java to enhance their Web pages. Java can display moving text or simple animation.

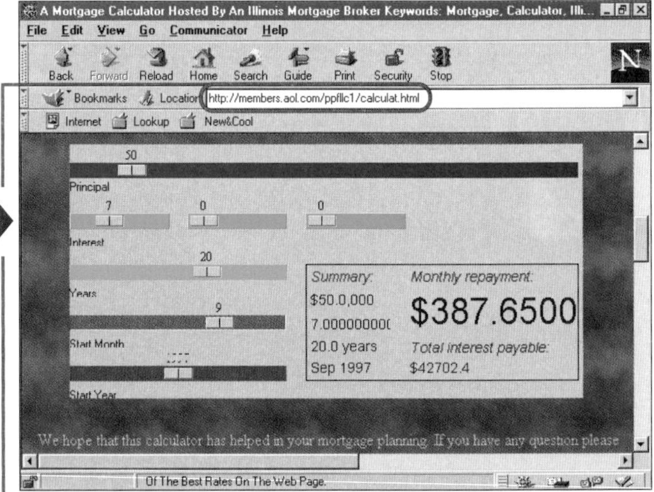

■ In this example, we connect to the page at this address.

■ Java allows you to interact with information on the screen. For example, you can perform calculations, play games or chat with other people.

You can move around and interact with three-dimensional worlds on the Web.

Virtual Reality Modeling Language (VRML) is the language used to create 3-D worlds on the Web.

You can find some interesting 3-D worlds at vrml.sgi.com

VRML

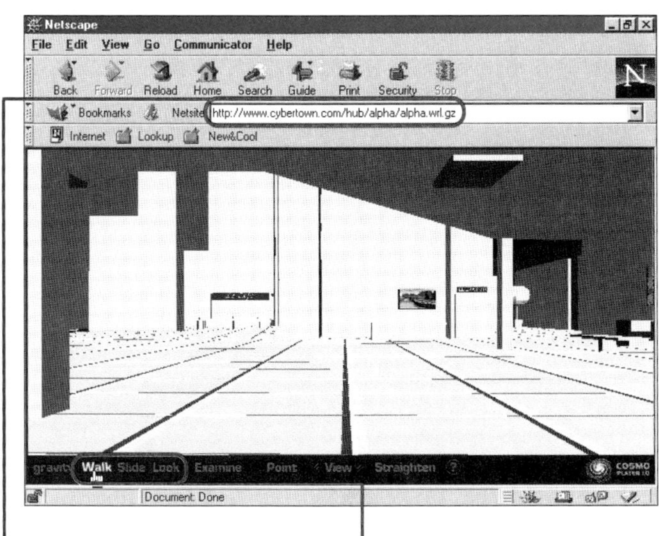

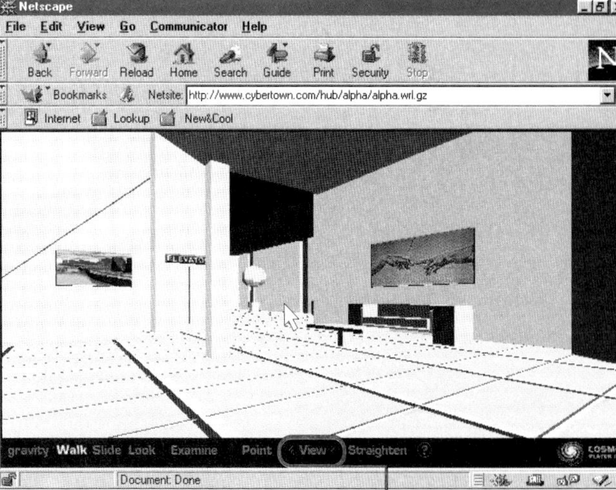

■ In this example, we connect to the page at this address.

1 You can click one of these options to determine how you want to move around the 3-D world.

2 You can use your mouse or keyboard to move around 3-D worlds and view objects from any angle.

■ You can click **View** at any time to return to the original appearance of the world.

Communicator needs special programs, called plug-ins, to display or play certain types of sound and video on the Web. Plug-ins add new capabilities that are not built into Communicator.

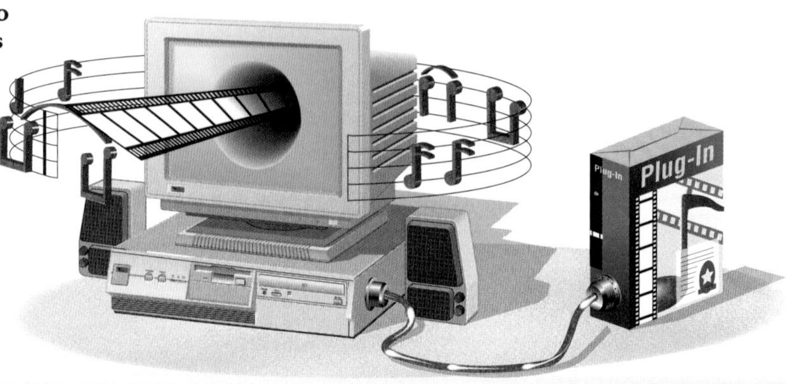

When Plug-ins Are Used

Communicator looks at the last few characters in a file name, called the extension, to determine how to display or play a file on a Web page. For example, **gif** in the file name porsche.**gif** tells Communicator the file is an image file.

When Communicator cannot display or play a file, Communicator will try to use a plug-in to display or play the file.

Where to Find Plug-ins

Some popular plug-ins are included with Communicator. You can obtain other plug-ins from the Web sites of the companies that offer the programs. After you download a plug-in, the program will work with Communicator to display or play files.

A list of plug-ins you can add to Communicator is available at the following Web site:

home.netscape.com/comprod/products/navigator/version_2.0/plugins/index.html

PLUG-IN MESSAGES

A message appears when Communicator cannot display or play a file you selected. You must get the appropriate plug-in before you can display or play the file.

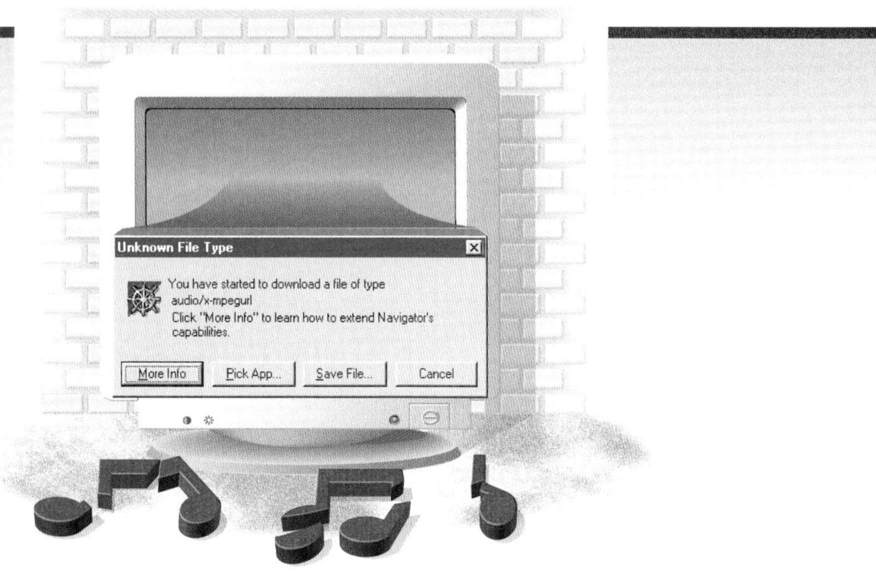

PLUG-IN NOT LOADED

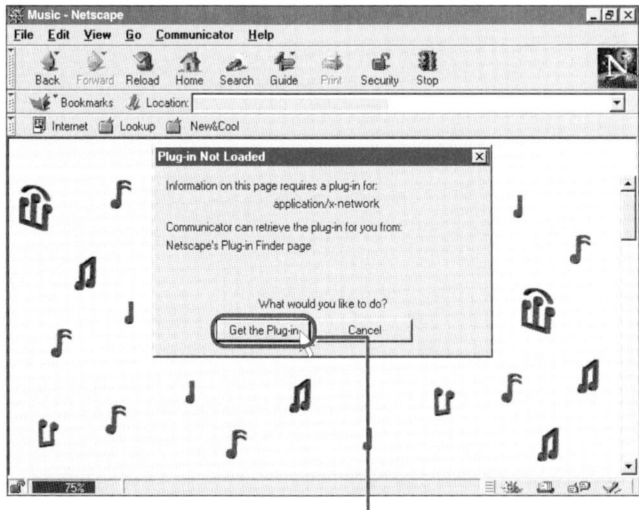

■ A dialog box appears when Communicator does not have a plug-in that can display or play the file.

1 Click **Get the Plug-in** to get a plug-in.

■ The Plug-in Finder page appears, listing the plug-ins that can display or play the file. You need to download and install a plug-in on your computer to display or play the file.

UNKNOWN FILE TYPE

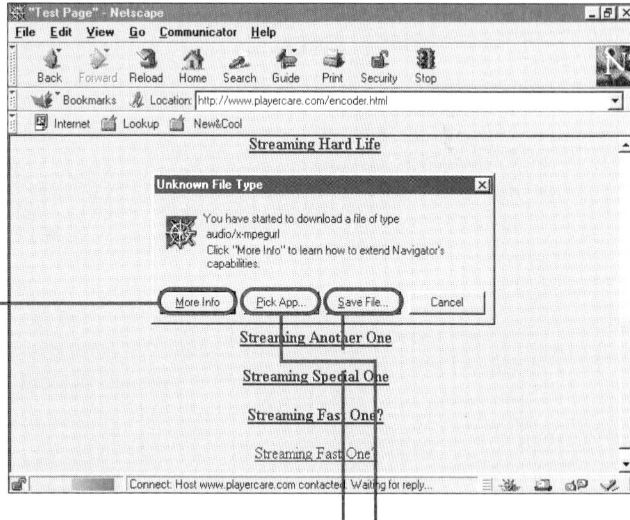

■ A dialog box appears when Communicator does not know how to handle the file.

■ Click **More Info** to get a plug-in on the Web that will display or play the file.

■ Click **Pick App** to find a program on your computer to display or play the file.

■ Click **Save File** to save the file on your computer.

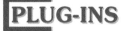

POPULAR PLUG-INS

Acrobat Reader

Acrobat Reader lets you view and print Portable Document Format (PDF) files. A PDF file is a high-quality file containing text, images and color. PDF files are well-organized and usually display an index and page numbers so you can easily find and print the information you want.

You can get a free copy of the Acrobat Reader plug-in at:

www.adobe.com

Crescendo

Crescendo is a plug-in that lets you listen to music as you browse through a Web site. You can get a free copy of the Crescendo plug-in at:

www.liveupdate.com

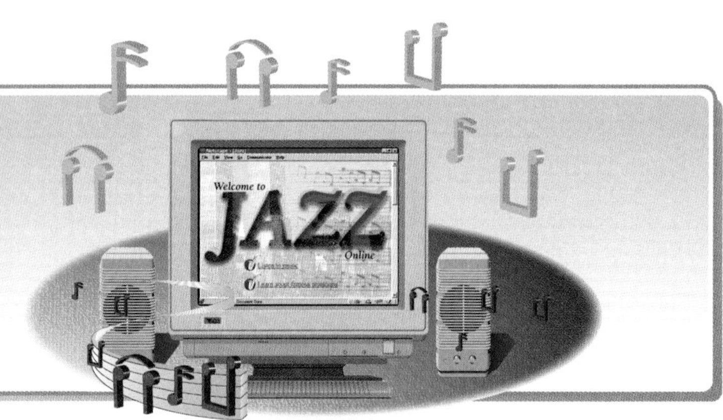

QuickTime

QuickTime lets you access a wide range of multimedia on the Web. QuickTime is used mostly for viewing video, but you can also use QuickTime to listen to music or explore virtual reality worlds. You can get the QuickTime plug-in free of charge at:

quicktime.apple.com

Shockwave

The Shockwave plug-in lets you interact with Web pages. You can use Shockwave to play games, view animation and listen to sounds and music on the Web. The Shockwave plug-in is available free of charge at:

www.macromedia.com

VDOLive Player

The VDOLive Player lets you view videos that are included in Web pages. Many Web sites use VDOLive to broadcast live events, such as interviews and announcements.

You can view a list of Web sites that use VDOLive and get a free version of the VDOLive plug-in at:

www.vdo.net

VXtreme

VXtreme's Web Theater Client lets you display videos available in Web pages. Many Web sites, such as CNN, use VXtreme to make television news clips available. The Web Theater software you need to view video clips is available for free at:

www.vxtreme.com

VIEW THE CACHE SETTINGS

The cache stores Web pages you recently viewed so you can quickly display these pages again.

Before transferring a Web page over the Internet to your computer, your computer checks to see if the page is stored in the cache. If the page is stored in the cache, your computer displays the page from the cache rather than wait for the page to transfer over the Internet.

VIEW THE CACHE SETTINGS

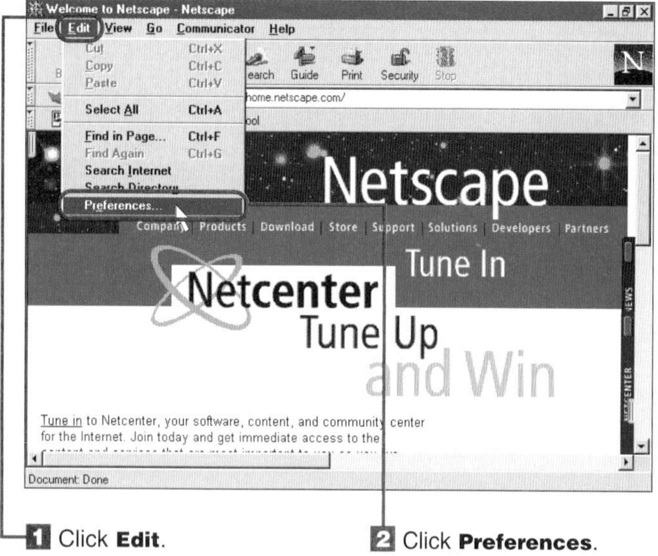

1 Click **Edit**.

2 Click **Preferences**.

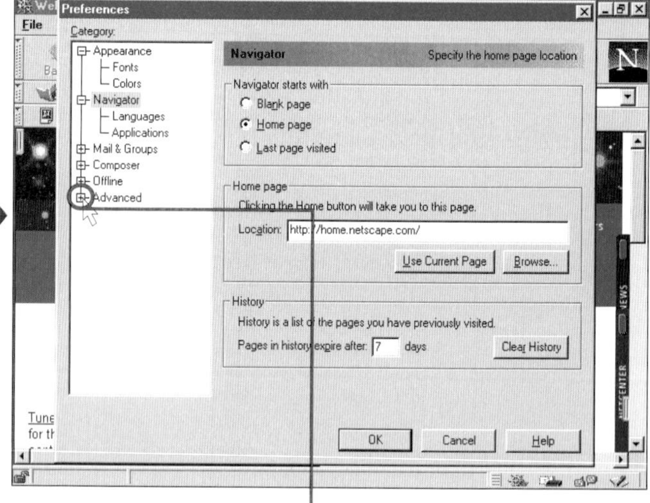

■ The Preferences dialog box appears.

3 Click the plus sign (⊞) beside **Advanced** (⊞ changes to ⊟).

What types of cache does Navigator use?

Memory cache is stored in the computer's memory and disappears when you turn off your computer. You may want to increase the memory cache if you have a lot of memory, such as 32 MB or more.

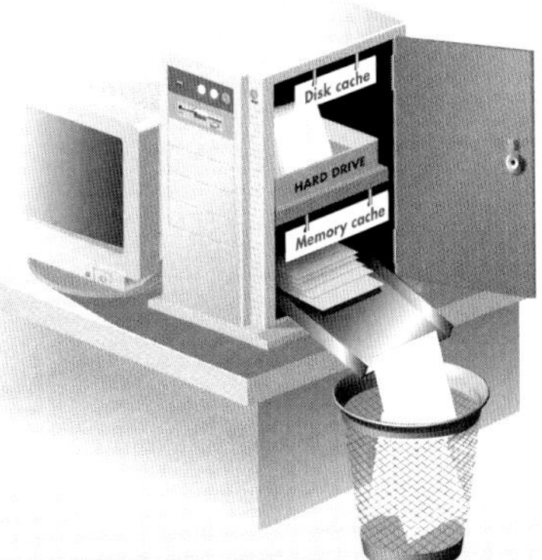

Disk cache is stored on your computer's hard drive and remains when you turn off your computer. You may want to reduce the disk cache if you are low on disk space.

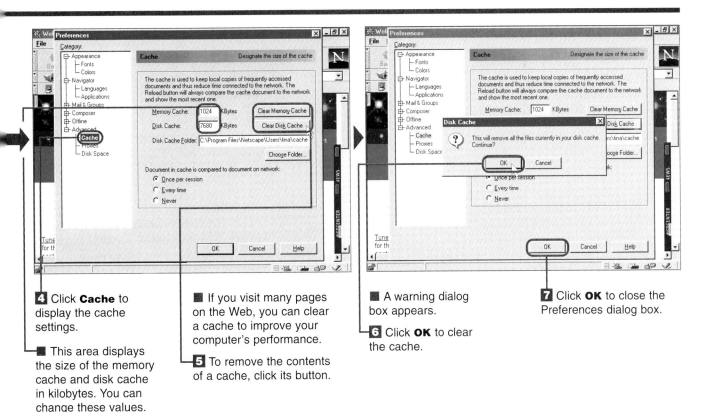

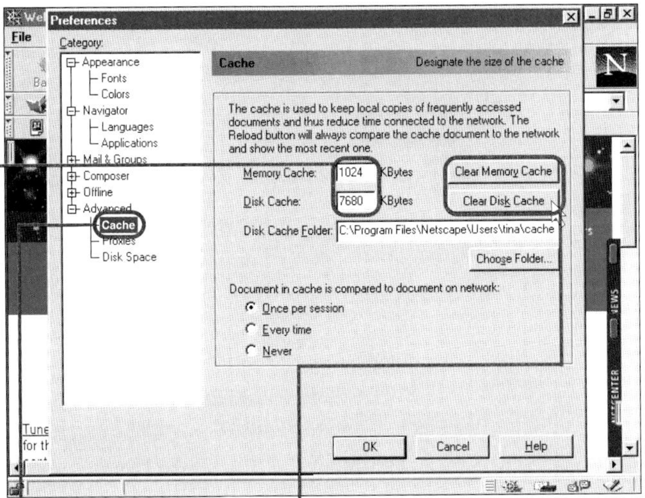

4 Click **Cache** to display the cache settings.

■ This area displays the size of the memory cache and disk cache in kilobytes. You can change these values.

■ If you visit many pages on the Web, you can clear a cache to improve your computer's performance.

5 To remove the contents of a cache, click its button.

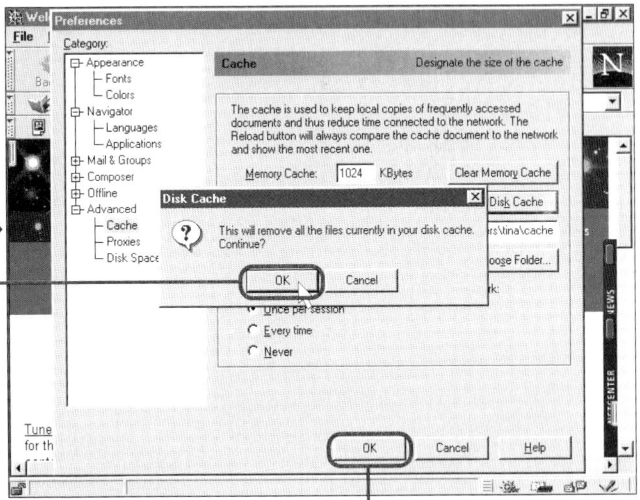

■ A warning dialog box appears.

6 Click **OK** to clear the cache.

7 Click **OK** to close the Preferences dialog box.

You can use Navigator to access FTP sites around the world. An FTP site is a computer on the Internet that stores a collection of files.

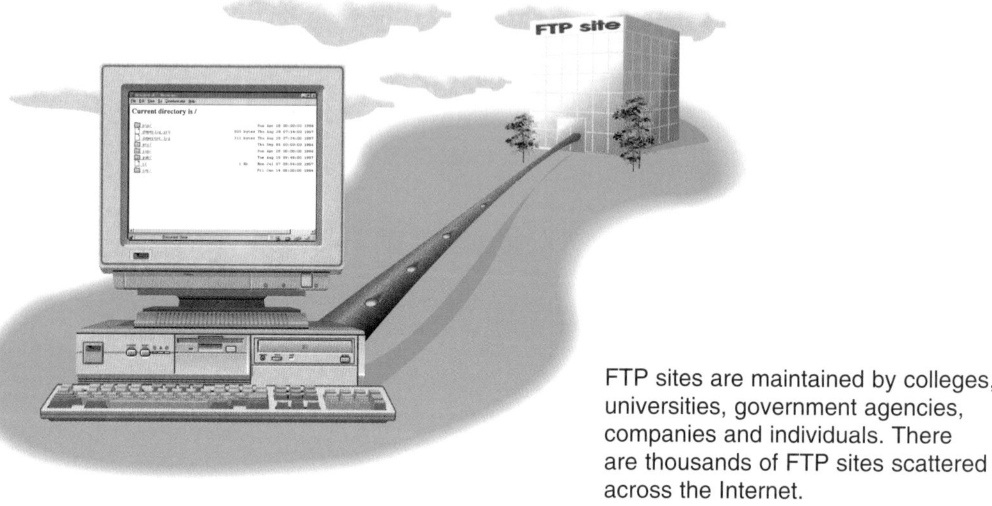

FTP sites are maintained by colleges, universities, government agencies, companies and individuals. There are thousands of FTP sites scattered across the Internet.

FTP stands for File Transfer Protocol.

FTP SITES

Private FTP Sites

Some FTP sites are private and require you to enter a password before you can access any files. Many corporations maintain private FTP sites to make files available to their employees and clients around the world.

Anonymous FTP Sites

Many FTP sites are anonymous. Anonymous FTP sites store collections of files that anyone can access free of charge.

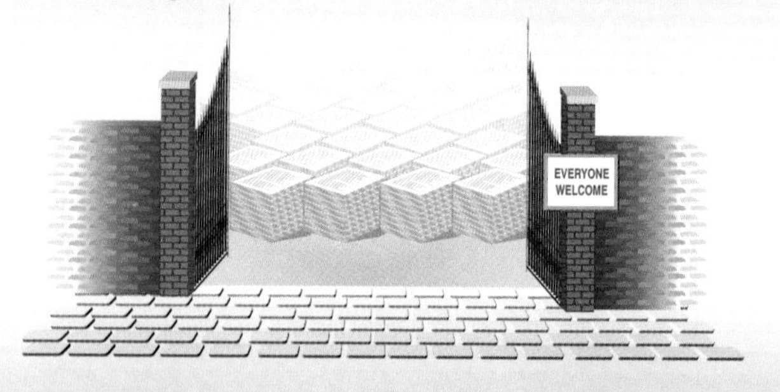

Popular FTP Sites

Library of Congress	ftp://ftp.loc.gov
Microsoft Corporation	ftp://ftp.microsoft.com
SunSITE USA	ftp://sunsite.unc.edu
Washington University	ftp://wuarchive.wustl.edu
Wiretap Library	ftp://wiretap.spies.com

The following Web site displays a list of popular FTP sites:

http://tile.net/ftp-list

Files at FTP sites are stored in different directories to help organize the information.

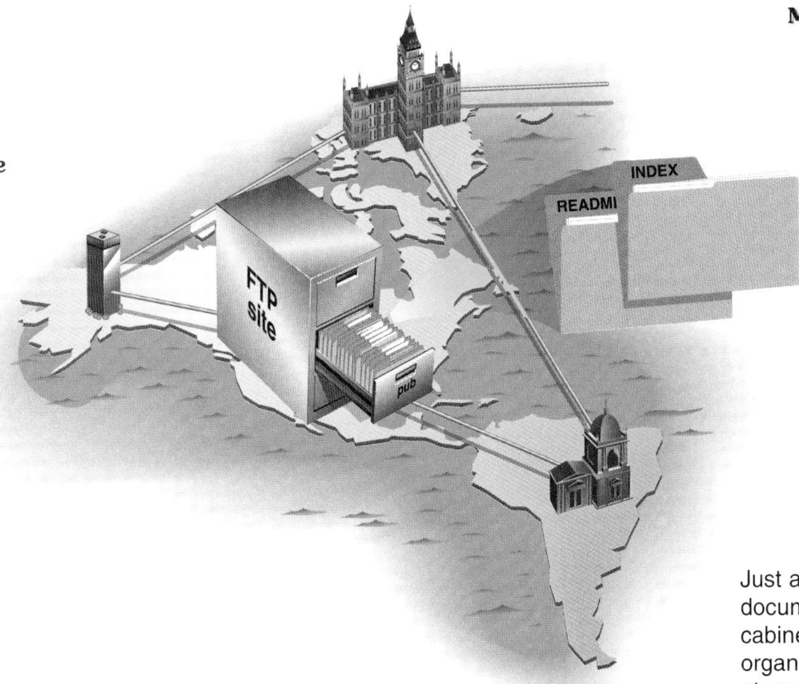

Just as folders organize documents in a filing cabinet, directories organize information at an FTP site.

DISPLAY AN FTP SITE

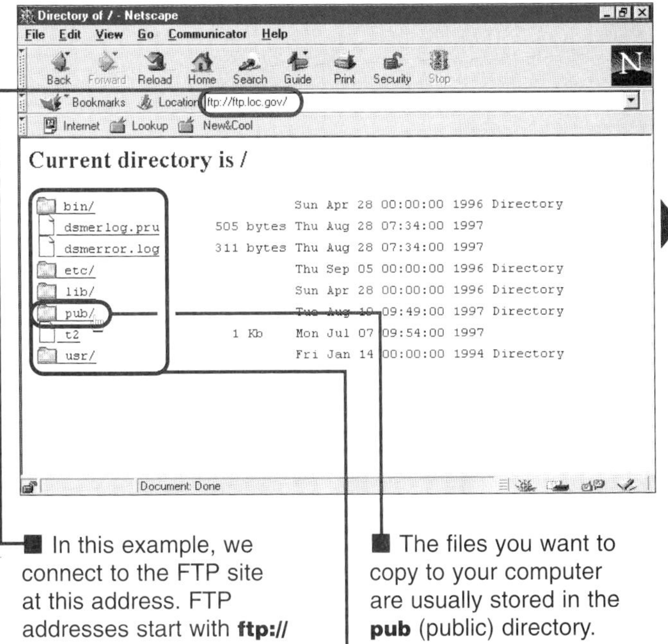

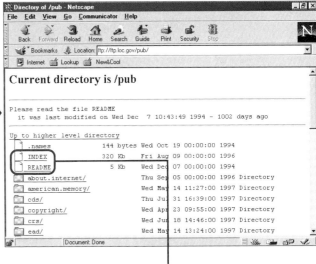

Directory of /pub - Netscape
File Edit View Go Communicator Help
Back Forward Reload Home Search Guide Print Security Stop
Bookmarks Location: ftp://ftp.loc.gov/pub/
Internet Lookup New&Cool

Current directory is /pub

Please read the file README
it was last modified on Wed Dec 7 10:43:49 1994 - 1002 days ago

Up to higher level directory
.names 144 bytes Wed Oct 19 00:00:00 1994
INDEX 320 Kb Fri Aug 09 00:00:00 1996
README 5 Kb Wed Dec 07 00:00:00 1994
about.internet/ Thu Sep 05 00:00:00 1996 Directory
american.memory/ Wed May 14 11:27:00 1997 Directory
cds/ Thu Jul 31 16:39:00 1997 Directory
copyright/ Wed Apr 23 09:55:00 1997 Directory
crs/ Wed Jun 18 14:46:00 1997 Directory
ead/ Wed May 14 13:24:00 1997 Directory
Document: Done

■ In this example, we connect to the FTP site at this address. FTP addresses start with **ftp://**

■ The files you want to copy to your computer are usually stored in the **pub** (public) directory.

1 Click the directory containing the files of interest.

■ The contents of the directory appear.

■ Most well-established FTP sites include files that describe the rest of the files offered at the site. Look for files named “index” or “readme”.

CONTINUED

Most files stored at an FTP site have a name and an extension, separated by a period (.).

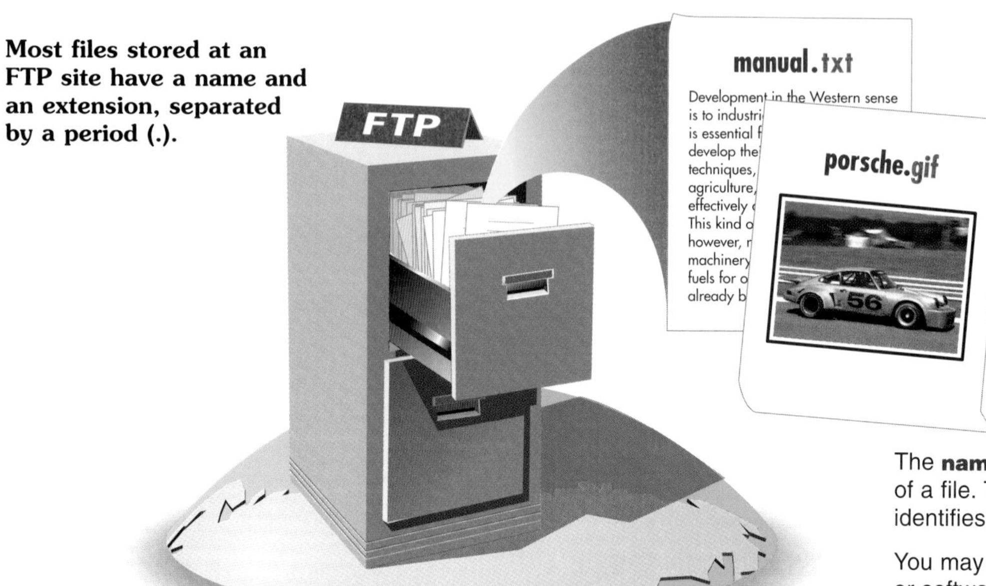

The **name** describes the contents of a file. The **extension** usually identifies the type of file.

You may need special hardware or software to view or play certain types of files on your computer. For example, you need a sound card and speakers to hear sound files.

Text

You can get interesting documents for research and for enjoyment. You can obtain books, journals, electronic magazines, computer manuals, government documents, news summaries and academic papers. Look for these extensions:

.asc .doc .msg .txt .wpd

Images

You can get images, such as computer-generated art, museum paintings and celebrity pictures. Look for these extensions:

.bmp .eps .gif .jpg .pct .png

Sound

You can get theme songs, sound effects, clips of famous speeches and lines from television shows and movies. Look for these extensions:

.au .ra .wav

Video

You can get movie clips, cartoons, educational videos and computer-generated animation. Look for these extensions:

.avi .mov .mpg

Programs

You can get programs to use on your computer, such as word processors, spreadsheets, databases, games and much more. Look for these extensions:

.bat .com .exe

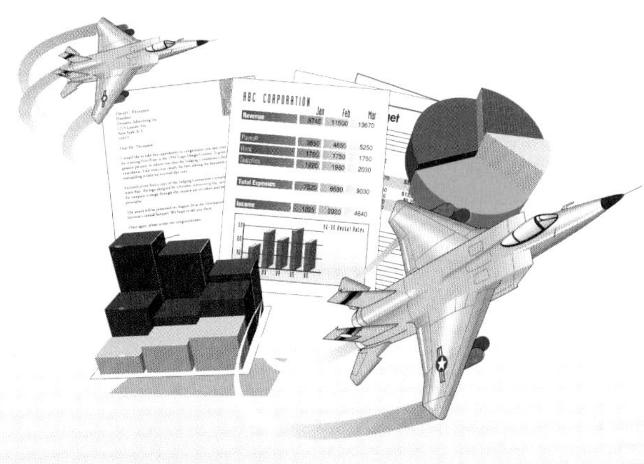

Compressed Files

Many large files stored at FTP sites are compressed, or squeezed, to make them smaller. Compressed files require less storage space and travel more quickly across the Internet. Before you can use a compressed file on your computer, you need to decompress the file. You can get the popular WinZip program to decompress files at www.winzip.com. Look for these extensions:

.arc .arj .gz .hqx .sit .tar .z .zip

PROGRAMS AVAILABLE AT FTP SITES

Public Domain

Public domain programs are free and have no copyright restrictions. You can change and distribute public domain programs as you wish.

Freeware

Freeware programs are free, but have copyright restrictions. The author may require you to follow certain rules if you want to change or distribute freeware programs.

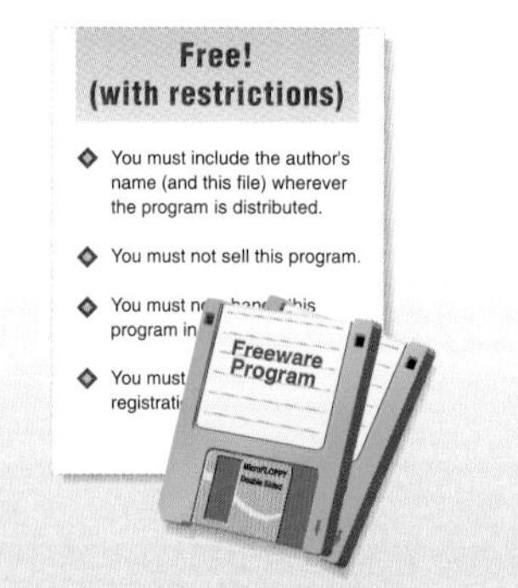

Shareware

You can try a shareware program free of charge for a limited time. If you like the program and want to continue using the program, you must pay the author of the program.

SEARCH FOR FTP FILES

Shareware.com lets you search for specific files or browse through files stored at FTP sites around the world. You can access shareware.com at:

www.shareware.com

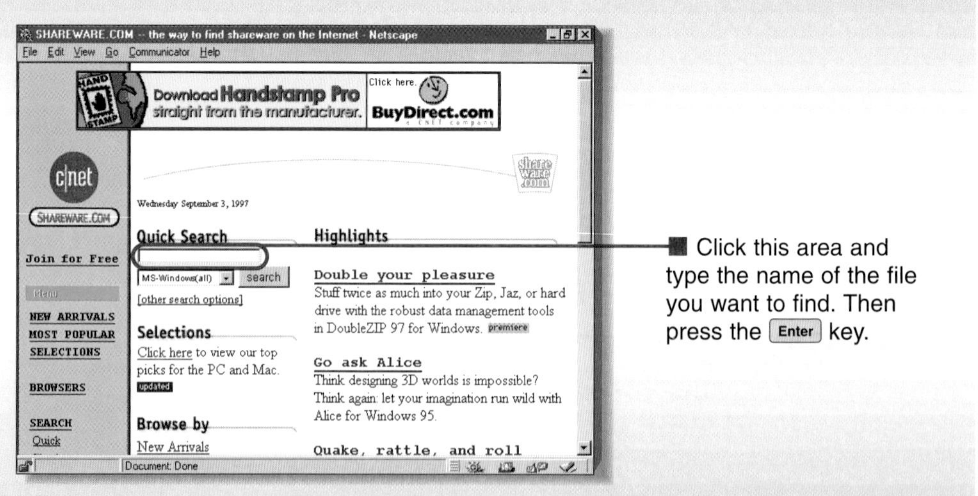

■ Click this area and type the name of the file you want to find. Then press the Enter key.

FTP TIPS

Avoid Traffic Jams

Each FTP site can only let a certain number of people use the site at once. If you get an error message when you try to connect, the site may already have as many people connected as it can handle. Try accessing FTP sites outside business hours, such as at night and on the weekend.

Use Mirror Sites

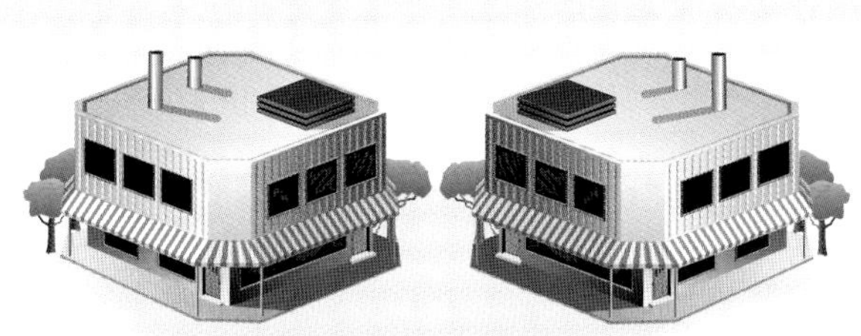

Some popular FTP sites have mirror sites. A mirror site stores exactly the same information as the original site, but is usually less busy. A mirror site may also be geographically closer to your computer, which can provide a faster connection.

Viruses

Files stored at FTP sites may contain viruses. A virus is a destructive program that can disrupt the normal operation of your computer. You should frequently make backup copies of the files on your computer and regularly check for viruses. There are anti-virus programs available at:

www.mcafee.com

CONNECT TO A SECURE WEB SITE

Navigator lets you know if a Web site is secure. You can safely transfer confidential information to a secure Web site.

Security is important when you want to send personal information such as credit card numbers or bank records over the Internet.

CONNECT TO A SECURE WEB SITE

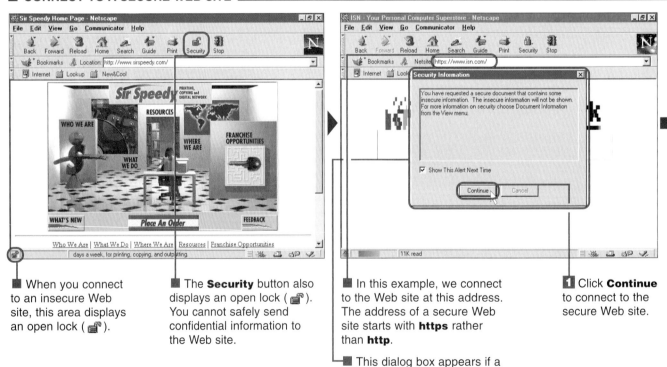

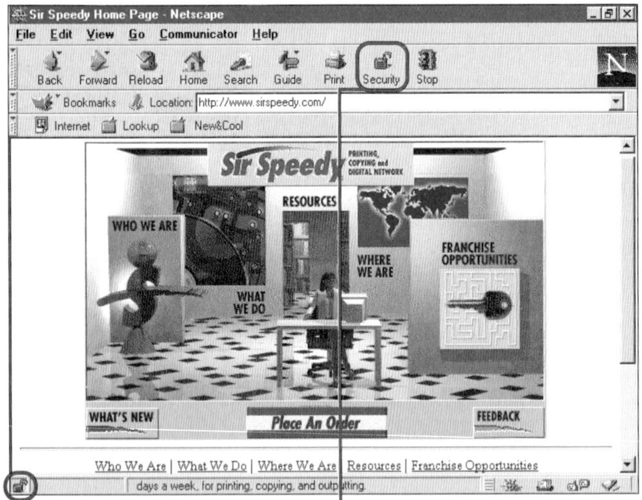

■ When you connect to an insecure Web site, this area displays an open lock (🔓).

■ The **Security** button also displays an open lock (🔓). You cannot safely send confidential information to the Web site.

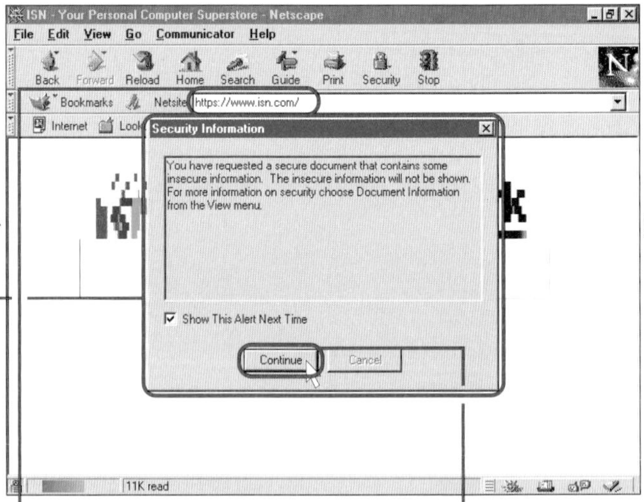

■ In this example, we connect to the Web site at this address. The address of a secure Web site starts with **https** rather than **http**.

■ This dialog box appears if a Web site you want to connect to is secure.

1 Click **Continue** to connect to the secure Web site.

How safe is a secure Web site?

Many people do not feel safe transmitting credit card numbers over the Internet. In fact, sending a credit card number to a secure Web site can be safer than giving the credit card number to an unknown person over the phone or by fax.

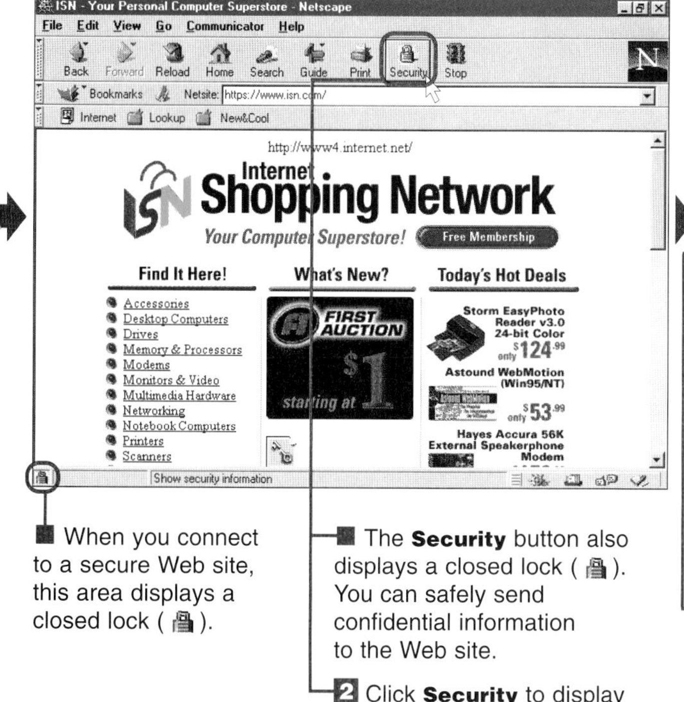

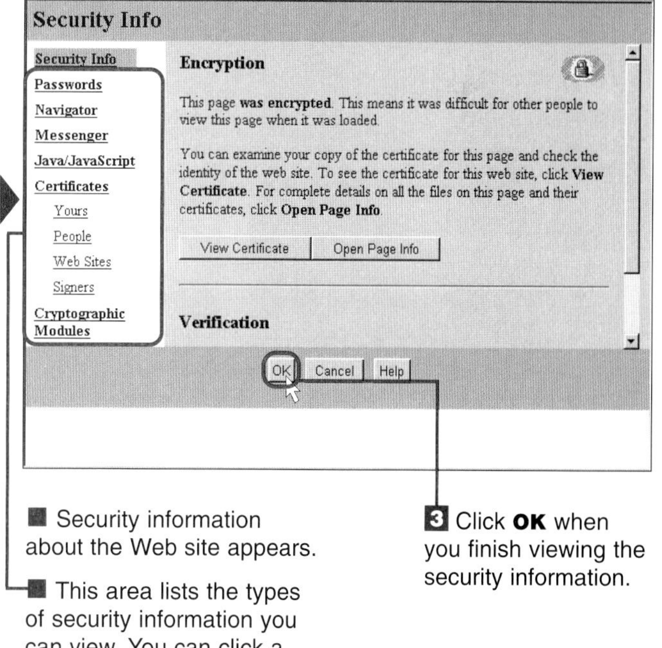

■ When you connect to a secure Web site, this area displays a closed lock (🔒).

■ The **Security** button also displays a closed lock (🔒). You can safely send confidential information to the Web site.

2 Click **Security** to display security information about the Web site.

■ Security information about the Web site appears.

■ This area lists the types of security information you can view. You can click a heading to view a different type of information.

3 Click **OK** when you finish viewing the security information.

SET UP COMMUNICATOR FOR SEVERAL PEOPLE

You can have several people share one copy of Netscape Communicator. Each person must set up their own profile. A profile contains the customized settings for one person.

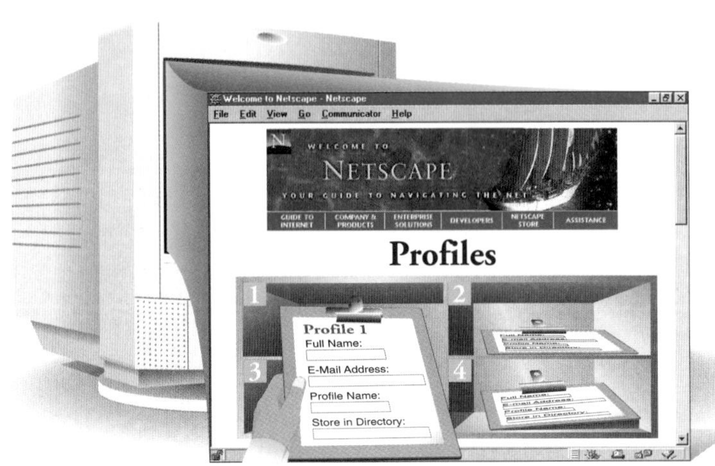

You set up a profile the first time you start Netscape Communicator. Setting up new profiles is useful when several family members or co-workers share the same computer.

SET UP COMMUNICATOR FOR SEVERAL PEOPLE

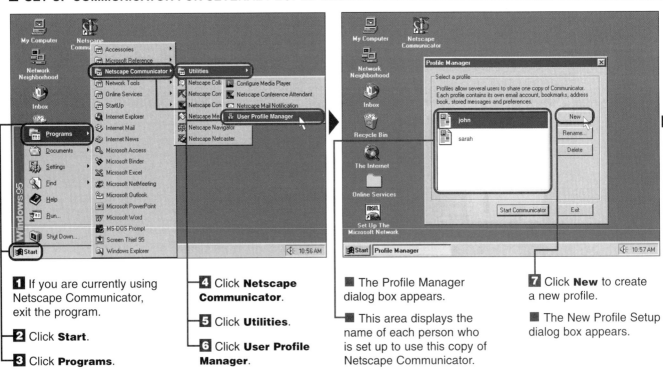

1 If you are currently using Netscape Communicator, exit the program.

2 Click **Start**.

3 Click **Programs**.

4 Click **Netscape Communicator**.

5 Click **Utilities**.

6 Click **User Profile Manager**.

■ The Profile Manager dialog box appears.

■ This area displays the name of each person who is set up to use this copy of Netscape Communicator.

7 Click **New** to create a new profile.

■ The New Profile Setup dialog box appears.

What information does a profile contain?

Each profile contains an e-mail account, bookmarks, address book, stored messages and preferences.

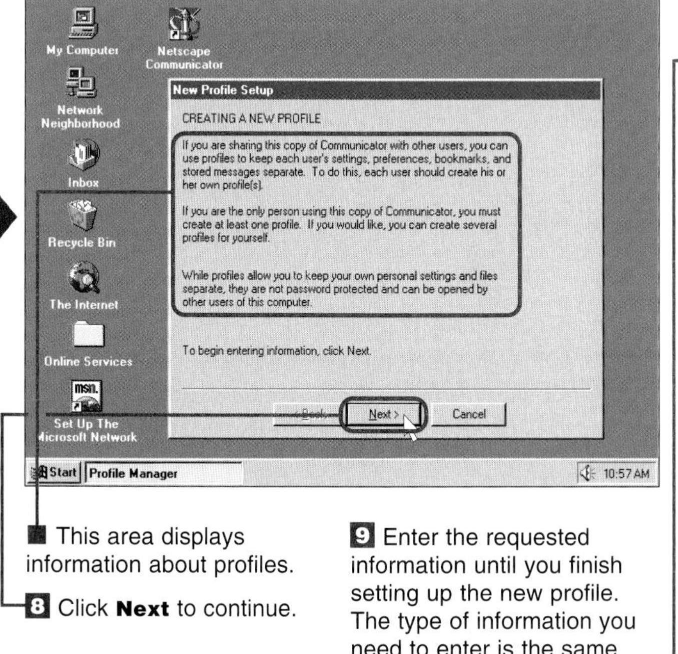

■ This area displays information about profiles.

8 Click **Next** to continue.

9 Enter the requested information until you finish setting up the new profile. The type of information you need to enter is the same as when you first set up Netscape Communicator. Refer to page 10.

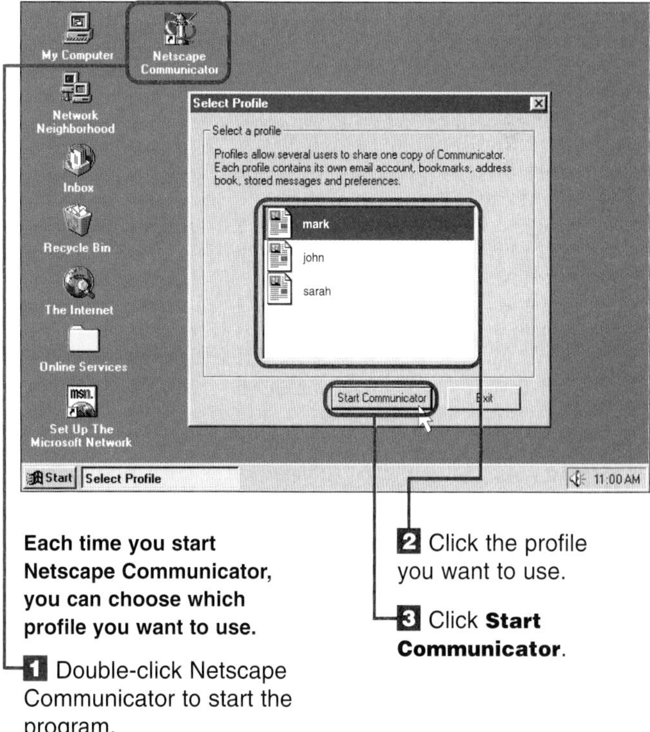

Each time you start Netscape Communicator, you can choose which profile you want to use.

1 Double-click Netscape Communicator to start the program.

2 Click the profile you want to use.

3 Click **Start Communicator**.

Infoseek
Lycos
Microsoft
USA Today
MINOLTA
http://www.sunkist.com
Welcome to the World of Sunkist - Netscape
File Edit View Go Communicator Help
Sunkist
Sunkist
of Quality
http://www
English - Netscape
Go Communicator Help
WELCOME TO TH
About

CHAPTER 4

Using Bookmarks

Do you want to store the addresses of Web pages you frequently visit? This chapter teaches you how to add, move and delete bookmarks for Web pages that interest you.

SELECT AND ADD BOOKMARKS

You can create bookmarks to store the addresses of your favorite Web pages. Bookmarks save you from having to remember and constantly retype your favorite Web page addresses.

Navigator provides bookmarks that are organized into various categories, such as Business Resources, Entertainment, Shopping and Sports.

SELECT A BOOKMARK

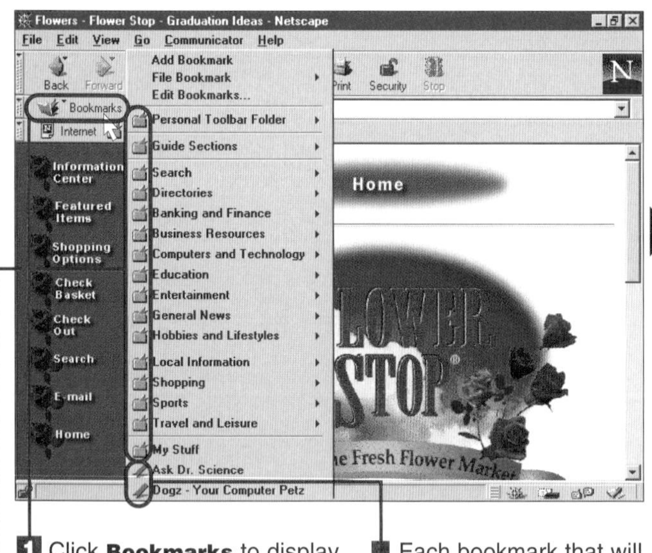

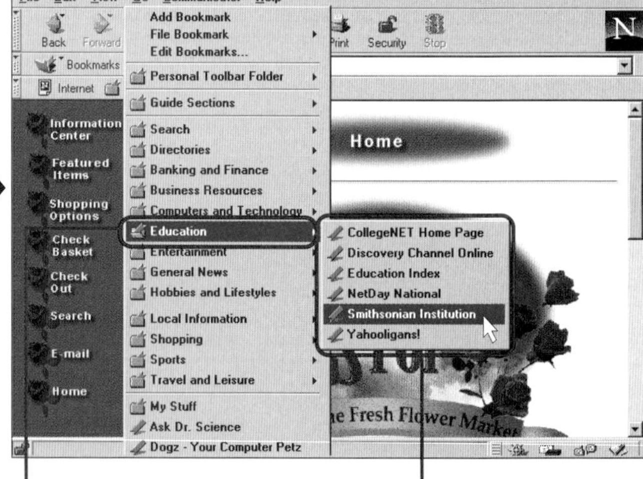

1 Click **Bookmarks** to display a list of your bookmarks.

■ Navigator uses folders to organize related bookmarks into categories. Each folder displays a folder symbol ( ).

■ Each bookmark that will take you to a specific Web page displays a bookmark symbol ( ).

2 To display the contents of a folder, position the mouse over the folder.

■ The bookmarks in the folder appear.

3 Click the name of the Web page you want to view.

■ The Web page you selected appears.

?

Is there another way to quickly access my favorite Web sites?

You can create a Web page that contains a list of your favorite Web sites. Each Web site can be a link that will instantly take you to each site. For information on creating Web pages, refer to pages 242 to 269.

ADD A BOOKMARK

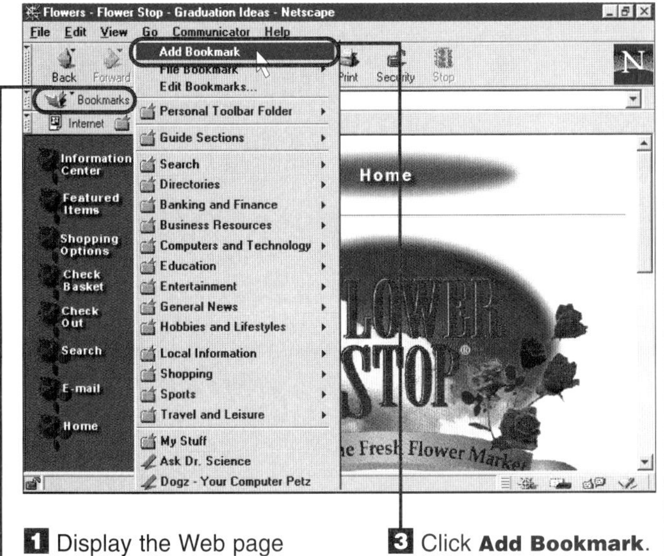

1 Display the Web page you want to add to your list of bookmarks.

2 Click **Bookmarks** and a menu appears.

3 Click **Add Bookmark**.

■ Navigator adds the bookmark to the bottom of the bookmark list.

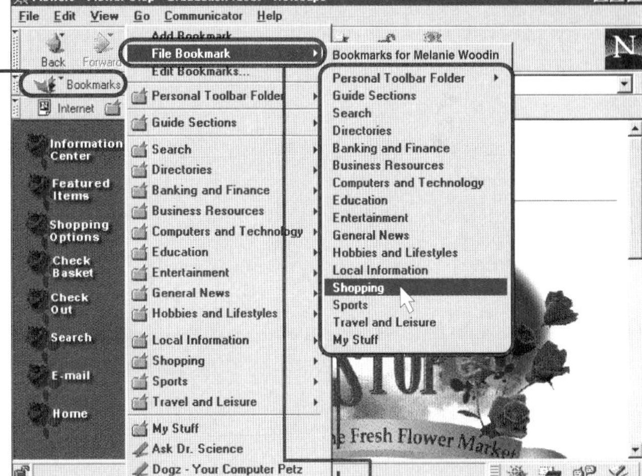

You can add a bookmark to a specific folder.

1 Click **Bookmarks** and a menu appears.

2 Click **File Bookmark**. A list of folders that store your bookmarks appears.

3 Click the folder you want to store the bookmark.

■ Navigator adds the bookmark to the folder.

DISPLAY THE BOOKMARKS WINDOW

You can display the Bookmarks window to view and make changes to your list of bookmarks.

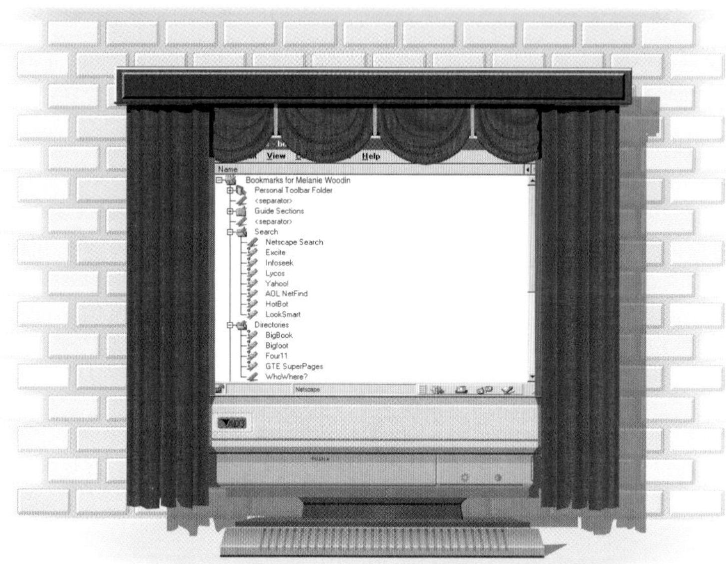

DISPLAY THE BOOKMARKS WINDOW

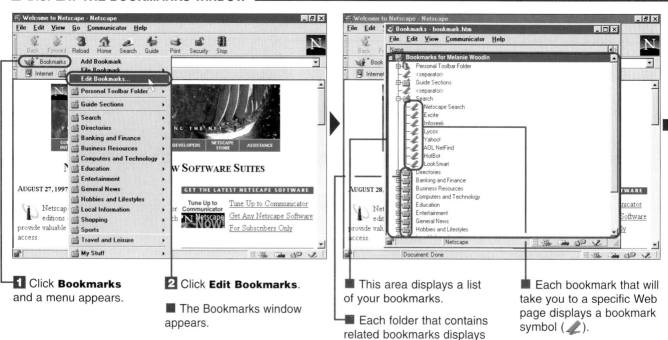

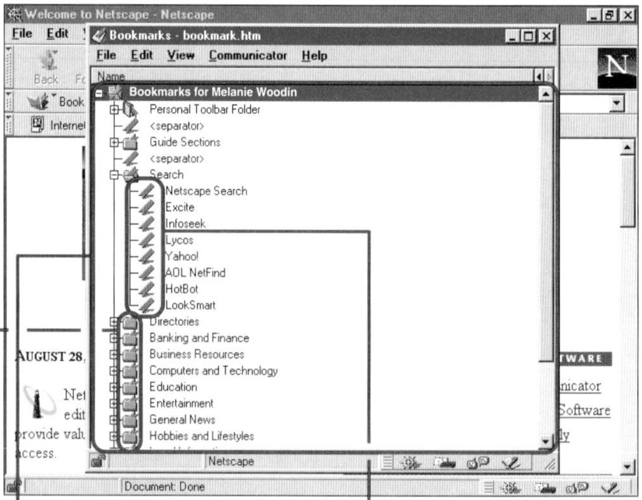

1 Click **Bookmarks** and a menu appears.

2 Click **Edit Bookmarks**.

■ The Bookmarks window appears.

■ This area displays a list of your bookmarks.

■ Each folder that contains related bookmarks displays a folder symbol ( ).

■ Each bookmark that will take you to a specific Web page displays a bookmark symbol ( ).

Are the items in the Bookmarks window and Bookmarks menu the same?

Yes. The items in the Bookmarks window are the same as the items in the Bookmarks menu. Changes you make in the Bookmarks window will appear in the Bookmarks menu.

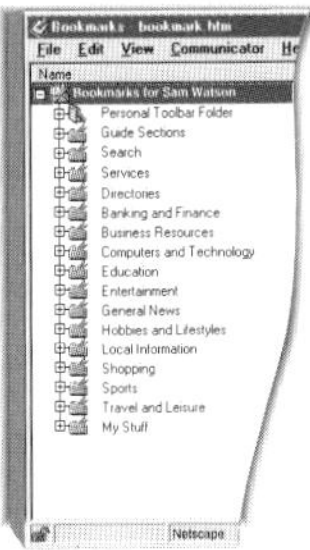

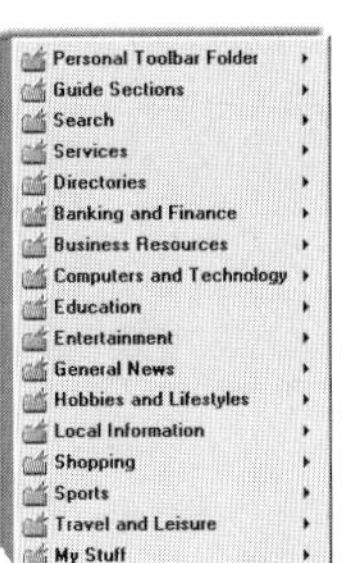

Bookmarks window **Bookmarks menu**

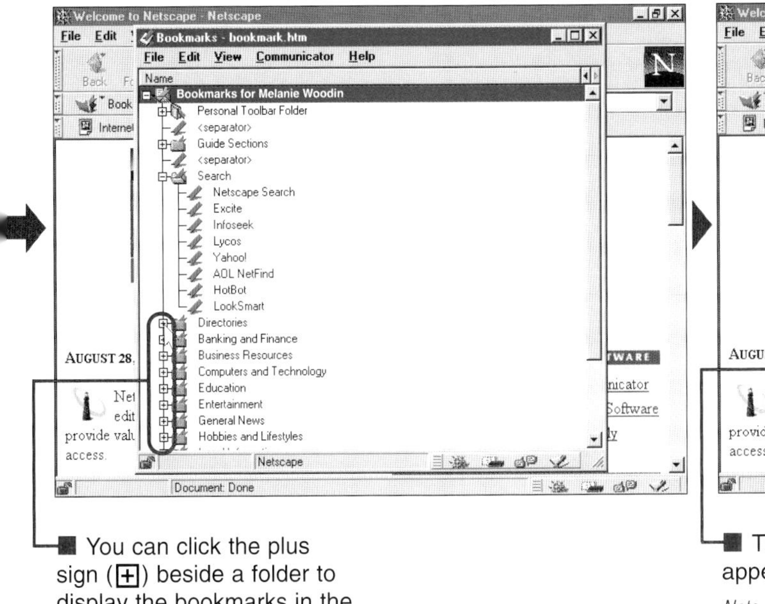

■ You can click the plus sign (⊞) beside a folder to display the bookmarks in the folder (⊞ changes to ⊟).

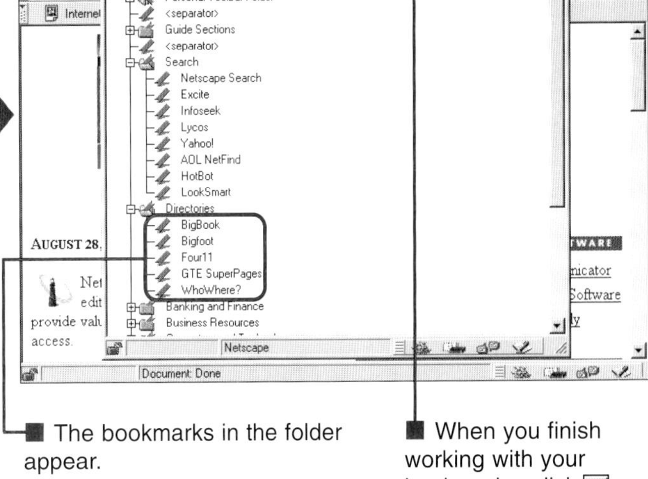

■ The bookmarks in the folder appear.

Note: You can click the minus sign (⊟) beside a folder to once again hide the contents of the folder.

■ When you finish working with your bookmarks, click ☒ to close the Bookmarks window.

RENAME A BOOKMARK

You can change the name of a bookmark to help you more easily identify where the bookmark will take you.

RENAME A BOOKMARK

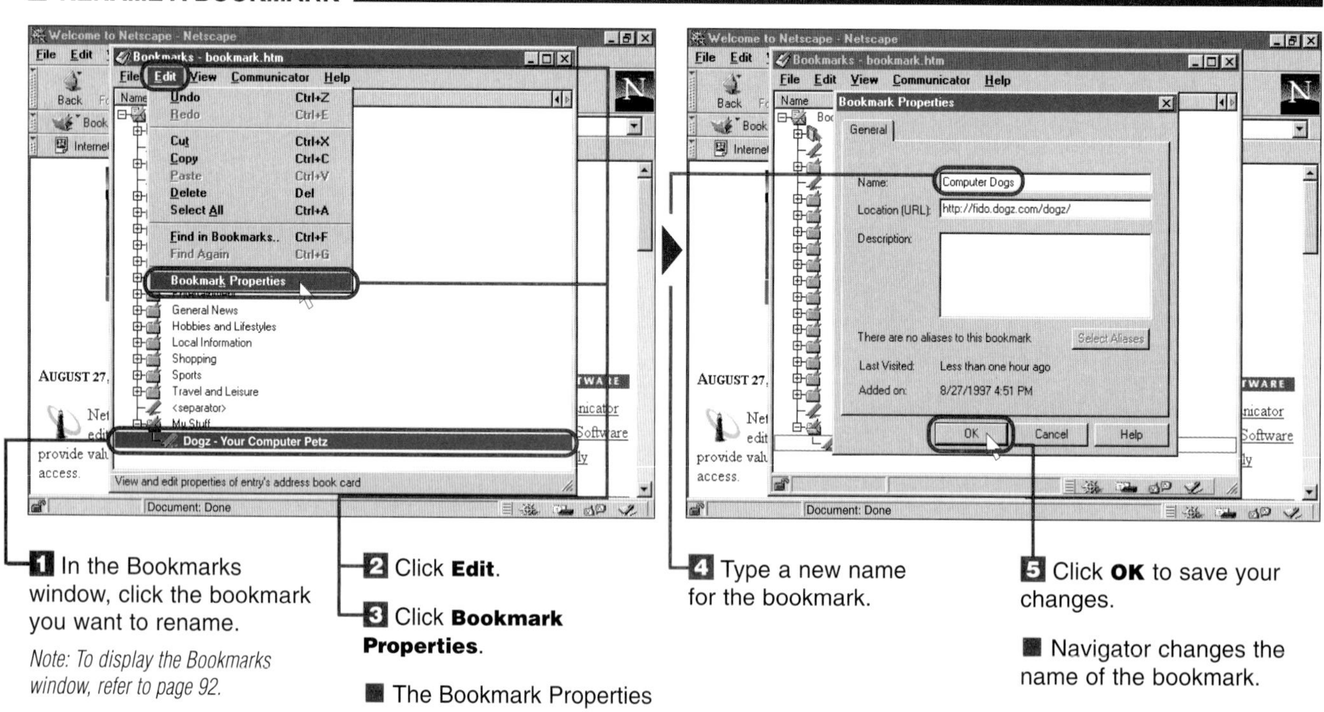

1 In the Bookmarks window, click the bookmark you want to rename.

Note: To display the Bookmarks window, refer to page 92.

2 Click **Edit**.

3 Click **Bookmark Properties**.

■ The Bookmark Properties dialog box appears.

4 Type a new name for the bookmark.

5 Click **OK** to save your changes.

■ Navigator changes the name of the bookmark.

DELETE A BOOKMARK

You should delete bookmarks you no longer need. Deleting bookmarks can help keep your bookmark list from becoming cluttered.

DELETE A BOOKMARK

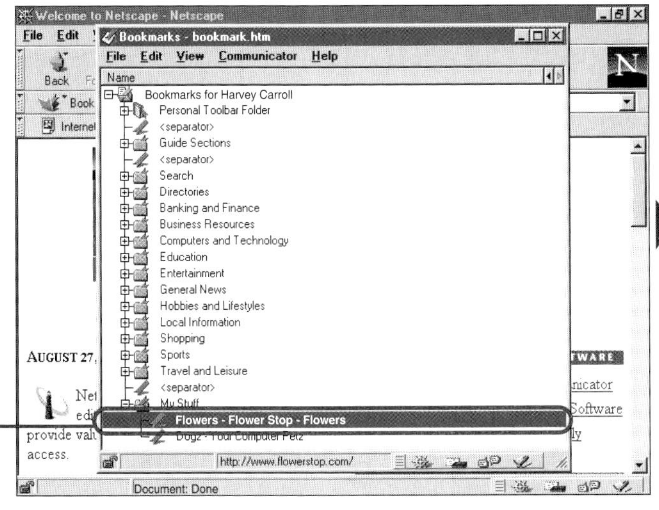

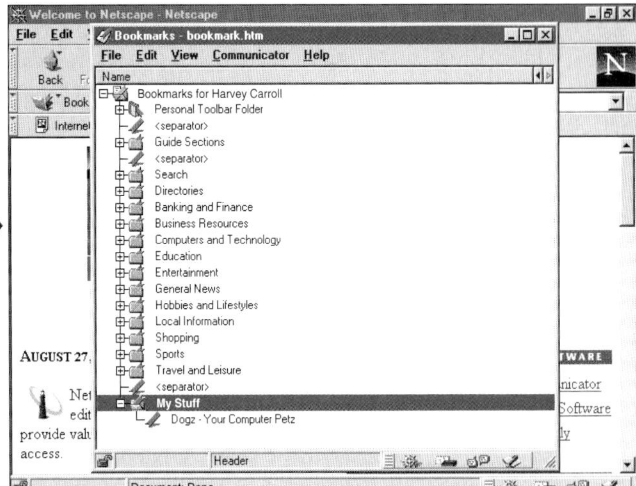

1 In the Bookmarks window, click the bookmark you want to delete.

Note: To display the Bookmarks window, refer to page 92.

2 Press the Delete key.

■ The bookmark disappears from the list.

MOVE A BOOKMARK

You can easily rearrange bookmarks in your list. You may want to move a bookmark to a specific folder or place a bookmark you frequently use at the top of your list.

MOVE A BOOKMARK

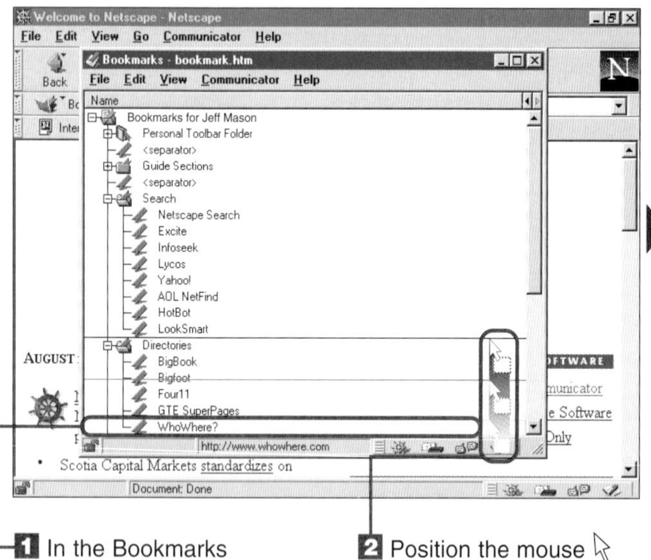

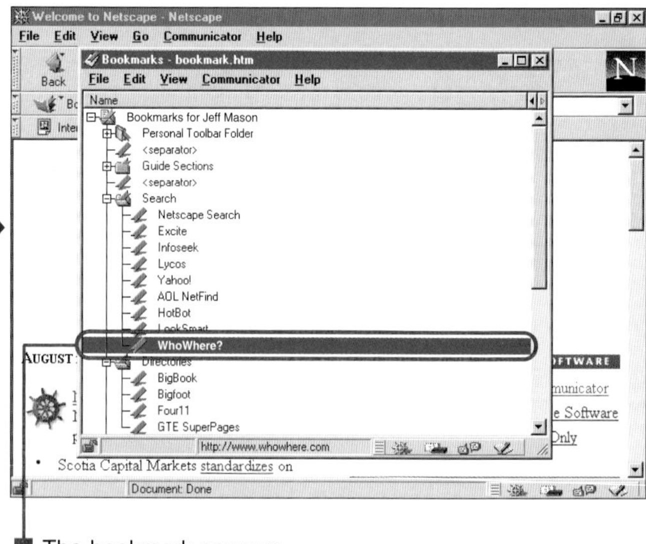

1 In the Bookmarks window, click the bookmark you want to move.

Note: To display the Bookmarks window, refer to page 92.

2 Position the mouse over the bookmark you want to move and then drag the bookmark to a new location.

Note: The bookmark will move to where the gray line appears on your screen or to the folder you highlight.

■ The bookmark appears in the new location.

ADD A SEPARATOR

You can add a separator to visually divide the bookmarks in your list.

ADD A SEPARATOR

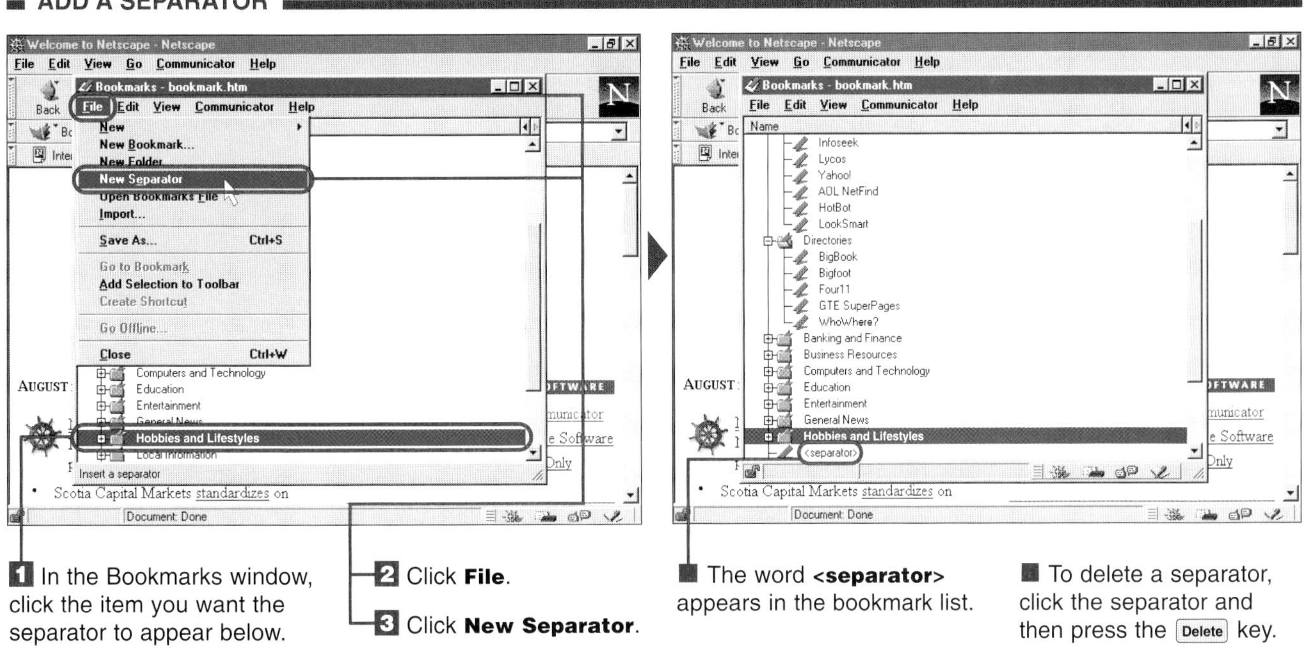

1 In the Bookmarks window, click the item you want the separator to appear below.

Note: To display the Bookmarks window, refer to page 92.

2 Click **File**.

3 Click **New Separator**.

■ The word **<separator>** appears in the bookmark list.

■ To delete a separator, click the separator and then press the Delete key.

CREATE A BOOKMARK FOLDER

You can create folders to help organize your list of bookmarks. This allows you to more easily find bookmarks of interest.

CREATE A BOOKMARK FOLDER

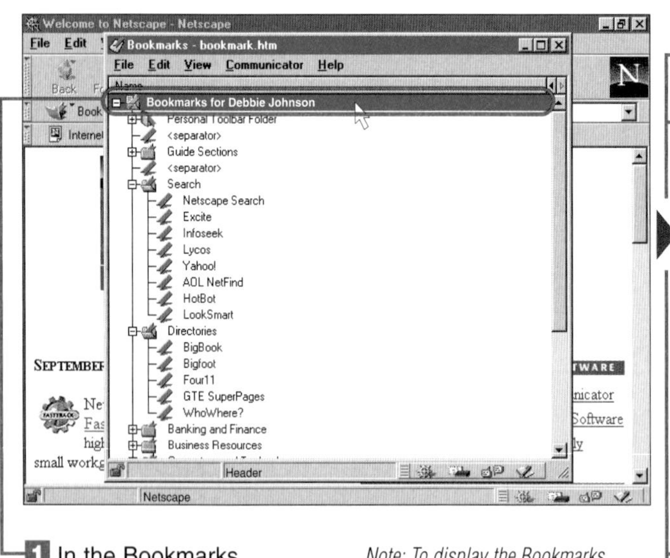

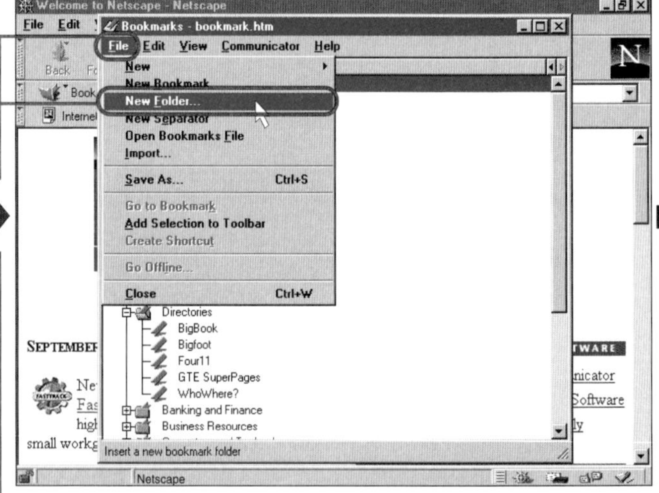

1 In the Bookmarks window, click the item you want the new folder to appear below.

Note: To display the Bookmarks window, refer to page 92.

2 Click **File**.

3 Click **New Folder**.

■ The Bookmark Properties dialog box appears.

?

How do I delete a folder I no longer want to appear in my bookmarks list?

When you delete a folder, Navigator also deletes the bookmarks in the folder. In the Bookmarks window, click the folder you want to remove and then press the Delete key.

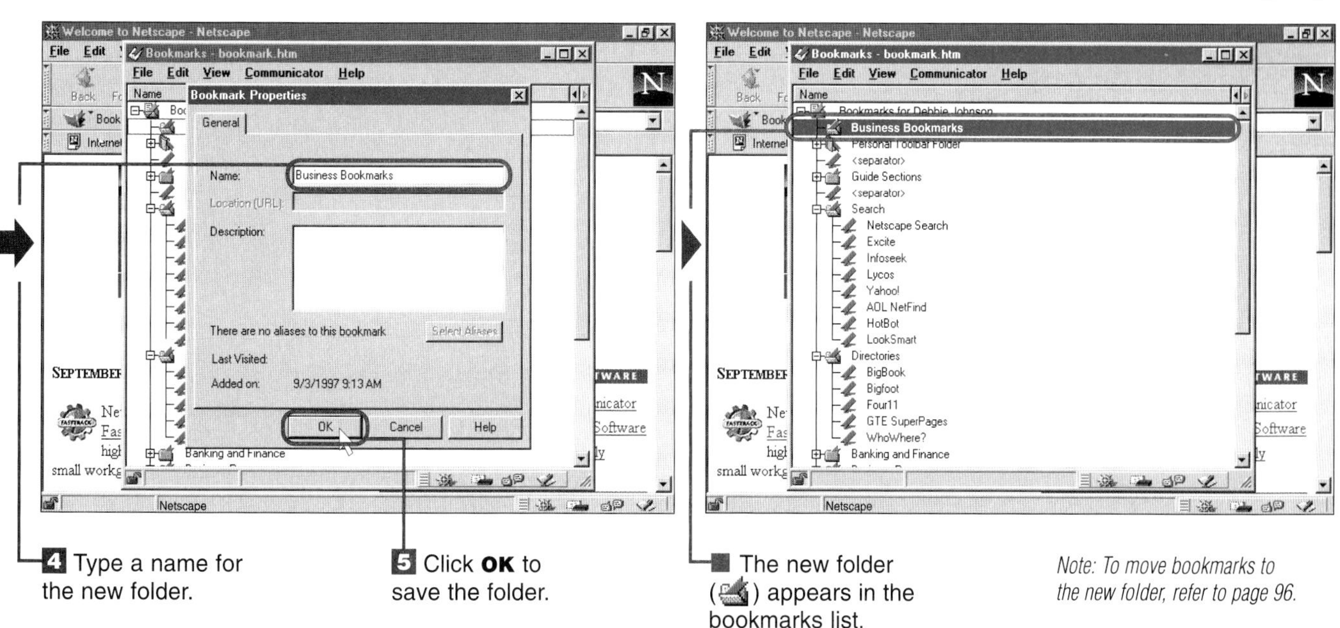

4 Type a name for the new folder.

5 Click **OK** to save the folder.

■ The new folder ( ) appears in the bookmarks list.

Note: To move bookmarks to the new folder, refer to page 96.

USING THE PERSONAL TOOLBAR

The Personal Toolbar can give you instant access to your favorite Web pages. You can place a bookmark on the Personal Toolbar for any page on the Web.

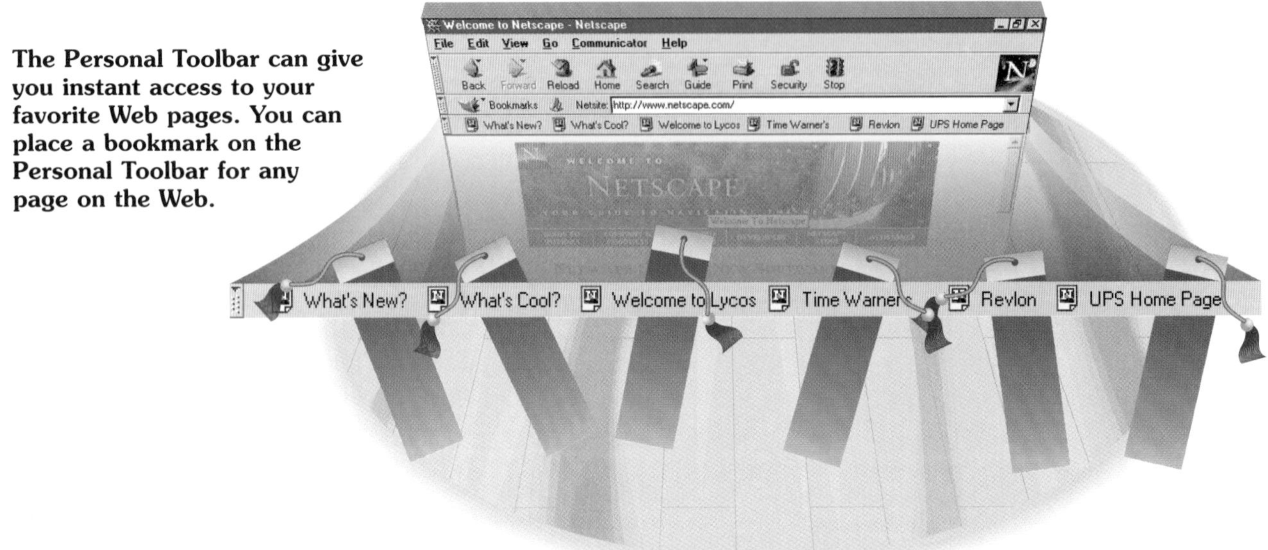

USING THE PERSONAL TOOLBAR

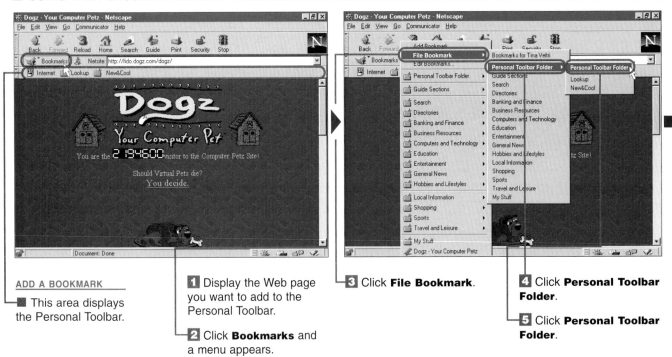

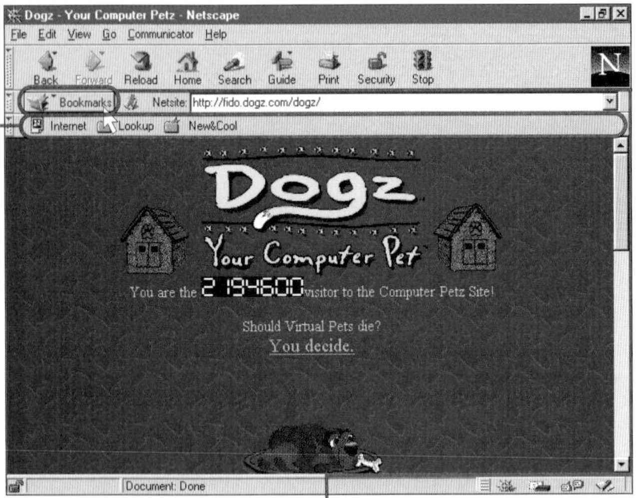

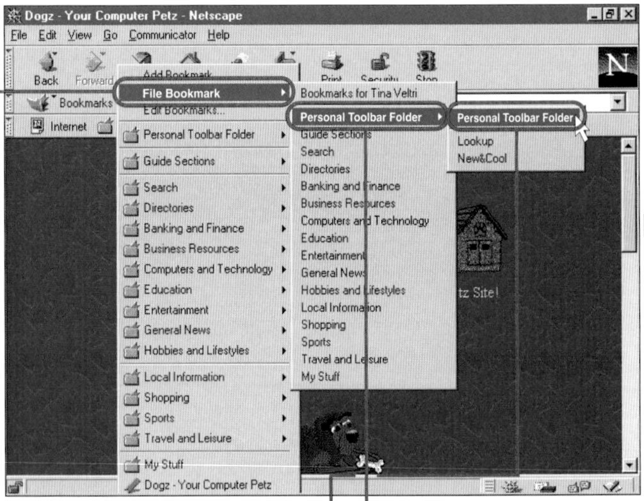

ADD A BOOKMARK

■ This area displays the Personal Toolbar.

1 Display the Web page you want to add to the Personal Toolbar.

2 Click **Bookmarks** and a menu appears.

3 Click **File Bookmark**.

4 Click **Personal Toolbar Folder**.

5 Click **Personal Toolbar Folder**.

?

How do I make changes to the items on the Personal Toolbar?

The items on the Personal Toolbar are displayed in the Personal Toolbar folder in the Bookmarks window. You can delete, move and rename the items in this folder as you would any items in the Bookmarks window. For more information, refer to pages 94 to 96.

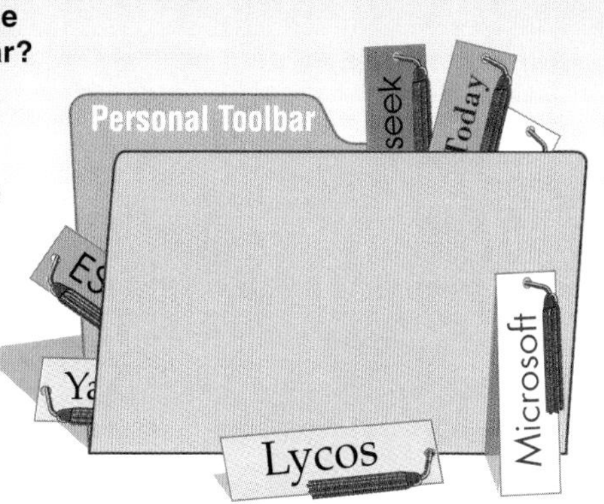

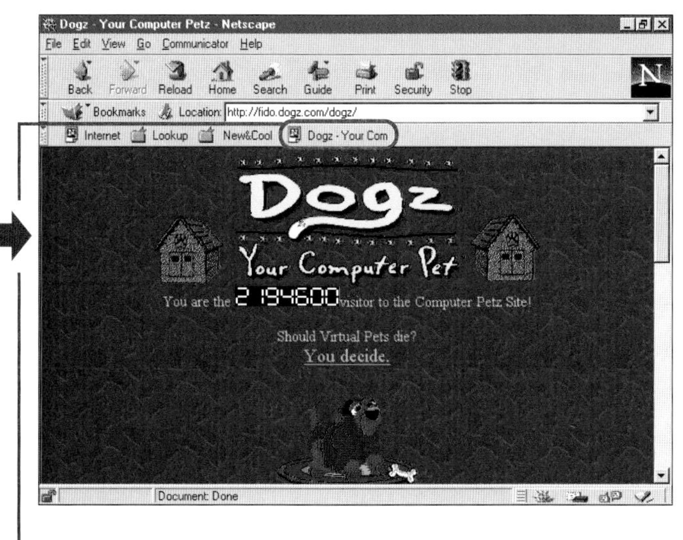

■ Navigator adds the bookmark to the Personal Toolbar.

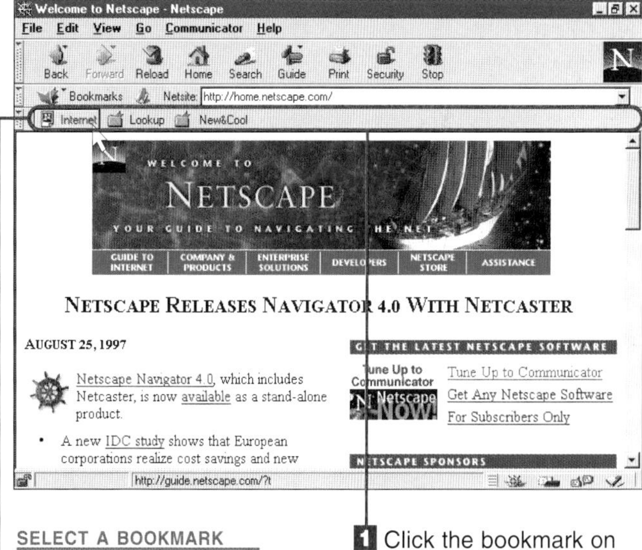

SELECT A BOOKMARK

■ Navigator provides a few bookmarks on the Personal Toolbar which take you to interesting places on the Web.

1 Click the bookmark on the toolbar for the Web page you want to view.

■ The Web page appears.

Jim,
I had a great time fishing this weekend. Thanks for inviting me. I've attached a picture of your catch. It's surely one for the record books!
Roger
Jim,
An emergency meeting of all stockholders has been called for 5PM today at The Plaza. Your attendance at this meeting is vital. If you cannot make it, notify me by fax, before noon.
Thanks,
Frank Peters
StockOptions Inc.
Jim,
In regards to the statement you wrote on the financial capabilities of this company, I must admit that I agree with many of your ideas. I, myself, feel that the company's growth potential is not being fully realized under the system that we have in place. I would be very interested in hearing any other ideas you may have on the subject.
Ross Jones
Vice-President

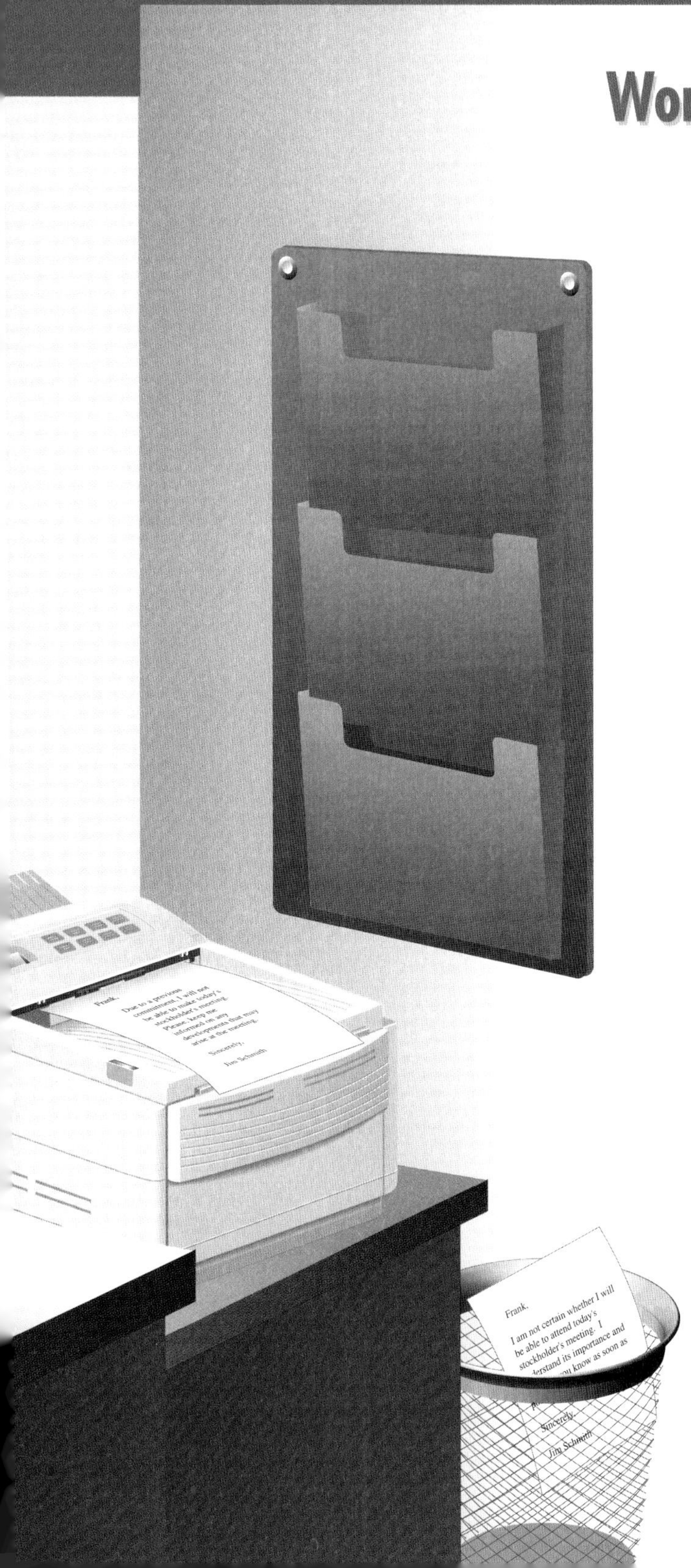

CHAPTER 5

Work with E-Mail Messages

Would you like to work with e-mail messages? In this chapter you will learn how to read and print messages, open attached files, use mail filters and much more.

INTRODUCTION TO E-MAIL

Netscape Messenger lets you exchange electronic mail (e-mail) with people around the world.

E-mail provides a fast, economical and convenient way to send messages to family, friends and colleagues.

Cost

Once you pay a service provider for a connection to the Internet, there is no charge for sending and receiving e-mail. You do not have to pay extra if you send a long message or the message travels around the world.

Exchanging e-mail can save you money on long distance calls. The next time you are about to pick up the telephone, consider sending an e-mail message instead.

Convenience

You can create and send e-mail messages at any time. Unlike telephone calls, the person receiving the message does not have to be at their computer when you send a message. E-mail makes communicating with people in different time zones very convenient.

E-MAIL ADDRESSES

You can send a message to anyone around the world if you know the person's e-mail address.

An e-mail address defines the location of an individual's mailbox on the Internet.

Parts of an E-mail Address

An e-mail address consists of two parts separated by the @ (at) symbol. An e-mail address cannot contain spaces.

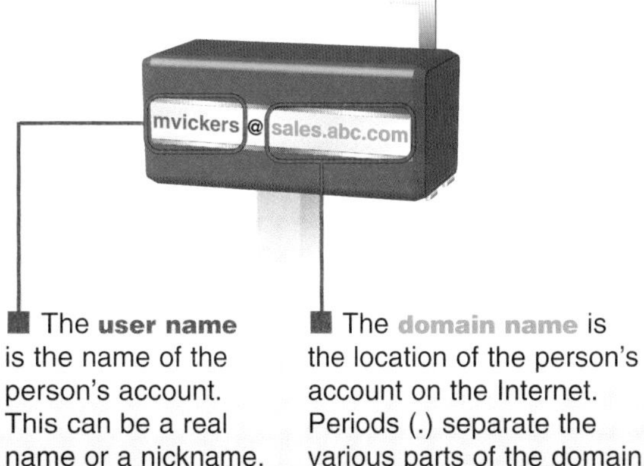

■ The **user name** is the name of the person's account. This can be a real name or a nickname.

■ The **domain name** is the location of the person's account on the Internet. Periods (.) separate the various parts of the domain name.

Organization or Country

The last few characters in an e-mail address usually indicate the type of organization or country to which the person belongs.

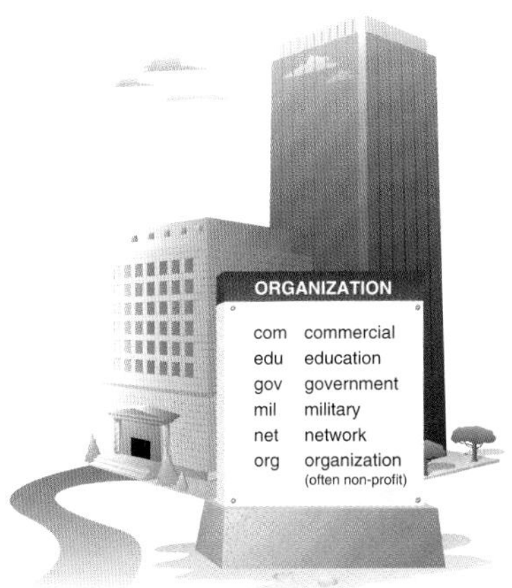

ORGANIZATION
com commercial
edu education
gov government
mil military
net network
org organization (often non-profit)

COUNTRY
au Australia
ca Canada
it Italy
jp Japan
uk United Kingdom
PASSPORT

Writing Style

Make sure every message you send is clear, concise and contains no spelling or grammar errors. Also make sure the message will not be misinterpreted. For example, the reader may not realize a statement is meant to be sarcastic.

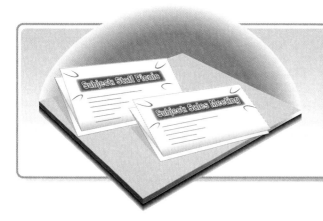

Subject

The subject of a message is usually the first item people read. Make sure the subject clearly identifies the contents of the message. For example, the subject "Read this now" or "For your information" is not very informative.

Abbreviations

Abbreviations are commonly used in messages to save time typing.

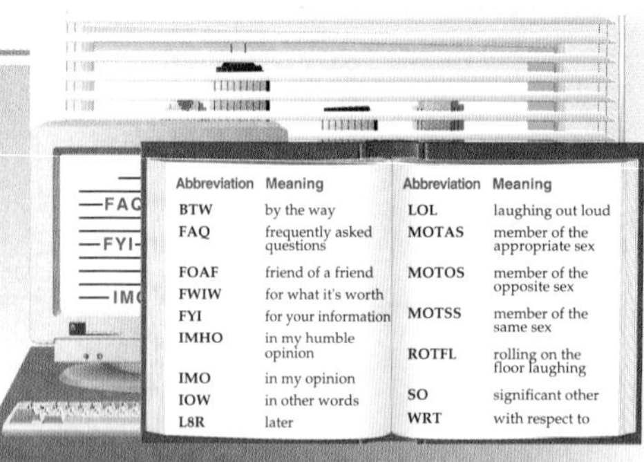

Abbreviation	Meaning	Abbreviation	Meaning
BTW	by the way	LOL	laughing out loud
FAQ	frequently asked questions	MOTAS	member of the appropriate sex
FOAF	friend of a friend	MOTOS	member of the opposite sex
FWIW	for what it's worth	MOTSS	member of the same sex
FYI	for your information	ROTFL	rolling on the floor laughing
IMHO	in my humble opinion	SO	significant other
IMO	in my opinion	WRT	with respect to
IOW	in other words		
L8R	later		

Smileys

You can use special characters, called smileys or emoticons, to express emotions in messages. These characters resemble human faces if you turn them sideways.

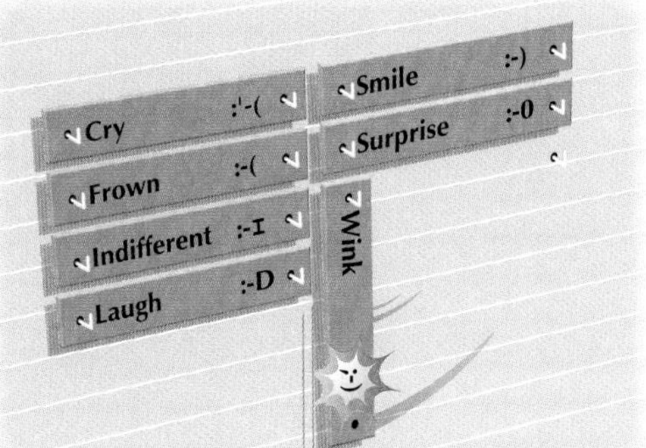

Shouting

A MESSAGE WRITTEN IN CAPITAL LETTERS IS ANNOYING AND HARD TO READ. THIS IS CALLED SHOUTING.

Always use upper and lower case letters when typing messages.

Bounced Messages

A bounced message is a message that returns to you because the message cannot reach its destination.

A message usually bounces because of typing mistakes in the e-mail address. Before sending a message, make sure you check the e-mail address for errors.

START NETSCAPE MESSENGER

You can start Netscape Messenger to send and receive e-mail messages with people around the world.

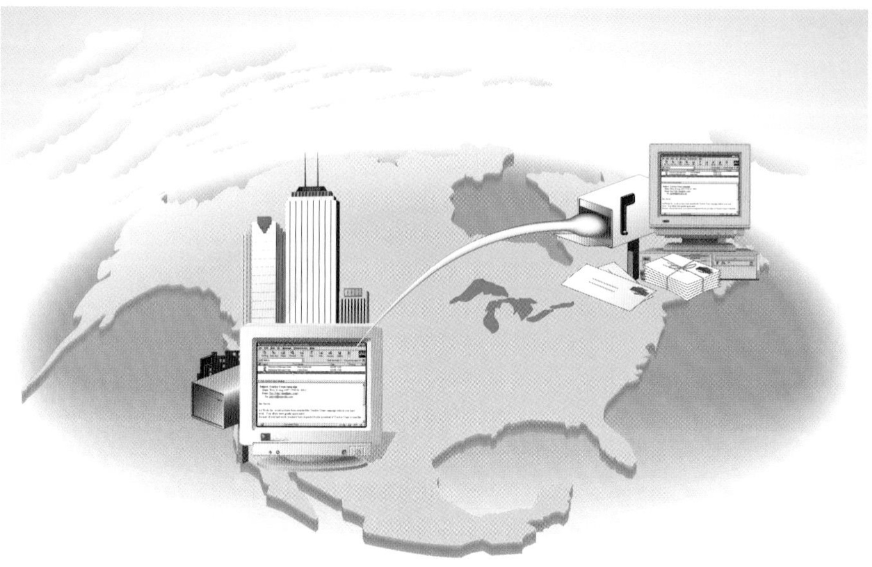

START NETSCAPE MESSENGER

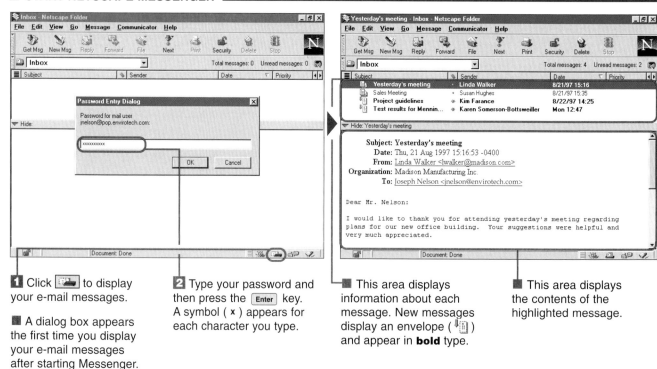

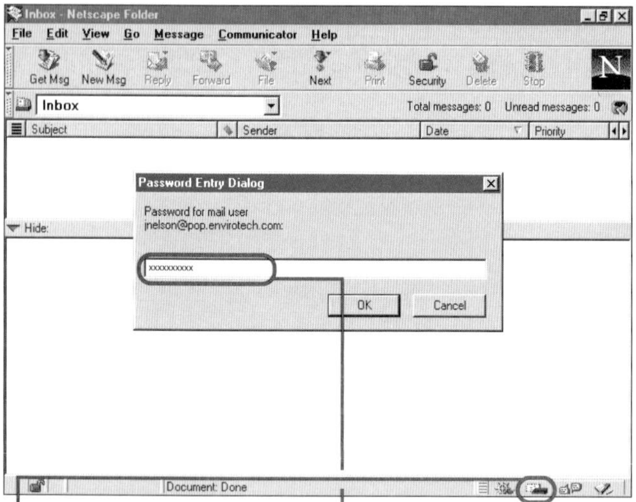

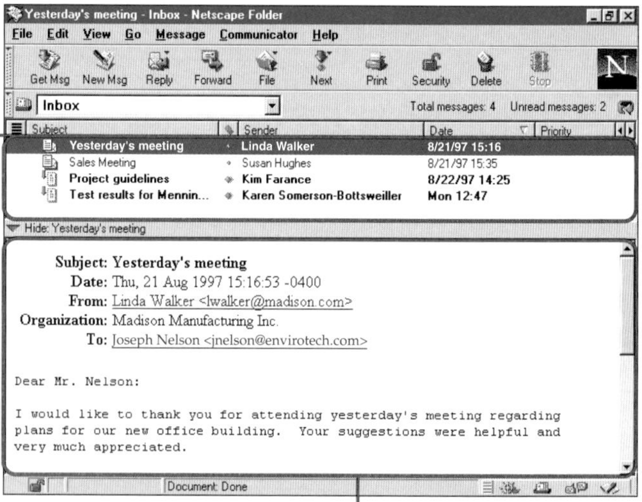

1 Click [Messenger icon] to display your e-mail messages.

■ A dialog box appears the first time you display your e-mail messages after starting Messenger.

2 Type your password and then press the Enter key. A symbol (x) appears for each character you type.

■ This area displays information about each message. New messages display an envelope ([envelope icon]) and appear in **bold** type.

■ This area displays the contents of the highlighted message.

THE NETSCAPE MESSENGER WINDOW

The Netscape Messenger window displays items to help you work with e-mail messages.

Toolbar

This area contains buttons to help you quickly perform common tasks.

Menus

This area offers menus that list related commands. Each command allows you to accomplish a specific task.

Folders

This area displays the name of the current folder, the total number of messages in the folder and the number of unread messages in the folder.

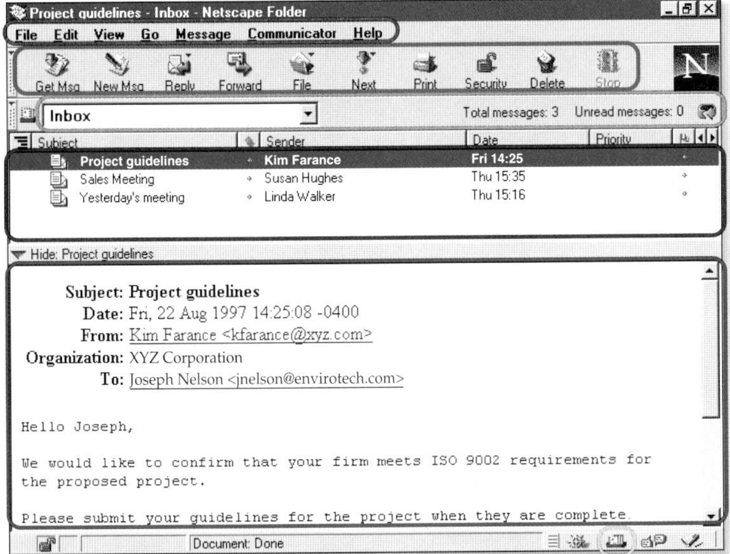

Messages

This area lists the messages in the current folder. Messenger displays the subject, sender, date and other information about each message.

Messages you have not read display a closed envelope ( ) and appear in **bold** type.

Messages you have read display an open envelope ( ) and appear in regular type.

Message Contents

This area displays the contents of the highlighted message.

Mailbox

This symbol indicates if you have ( ) or do not have ( ) any new messages.

Note: If you want Messenger to indicate when you have new messages, refer to page 116.

READ A MESSAGE

You can easily open a message to display its contents. A message can contain a few lines of text or several hundred.

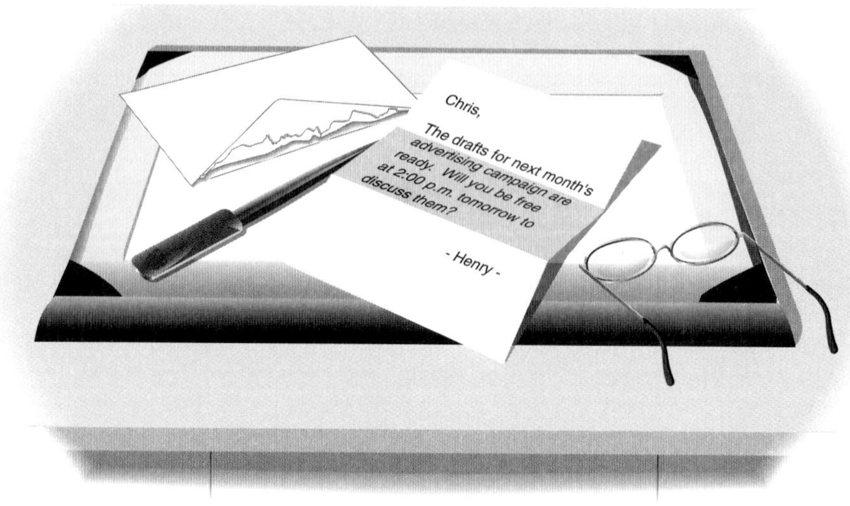

Chris,
The drafts for next month's advertising campaign are ready. Will you be free at 2:00 p.m. tomorrow to discuss them?
- Henry -

READ A MESSAGE

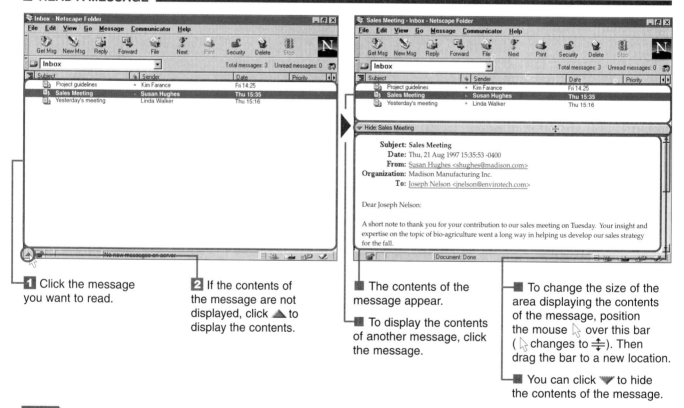

1 Click the message you want to read.

2 If the contents of the message are not displayed, click ▲ to display the contents.

■ The contents of the message appear.

■ To display the contents of another message, click the message.

■ To change the size of the area displaying the contents of the message, position the mouse ↖ over this bar (↖ changes to ≑). Then drag the bar to a new location.

■ You can click ▼ to hide the contents of the message.

? How can I quickly find new messages that I have not read?

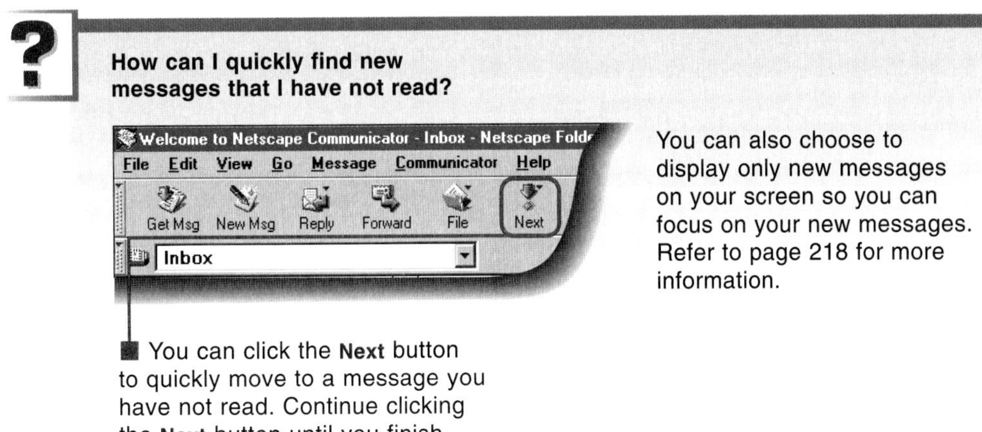

■ You can click the **Next** button to quickly move to a message you have not read. Continue clicking the **Next** button until you finish finding all of your new messages.

You can also choose to display only new messages on your screen so you can focus on your new messages. Refer to page 218 for more information.

READ A MESSAGE IN A SEPARATE WINDOW

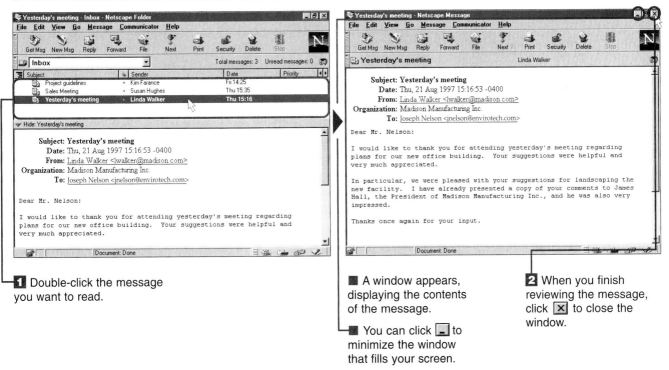

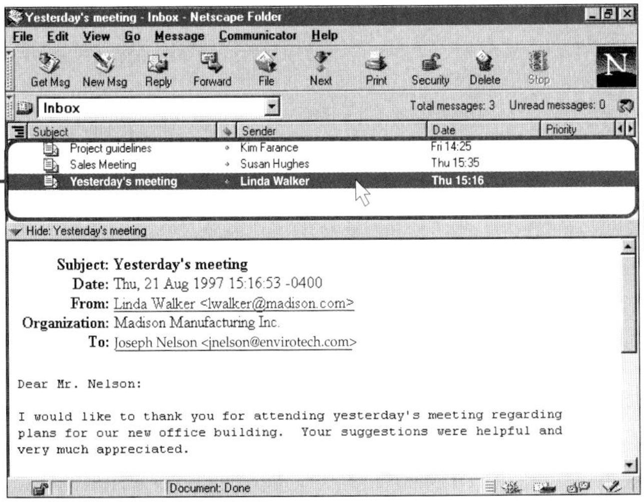

1 Double-click the message you want to read.

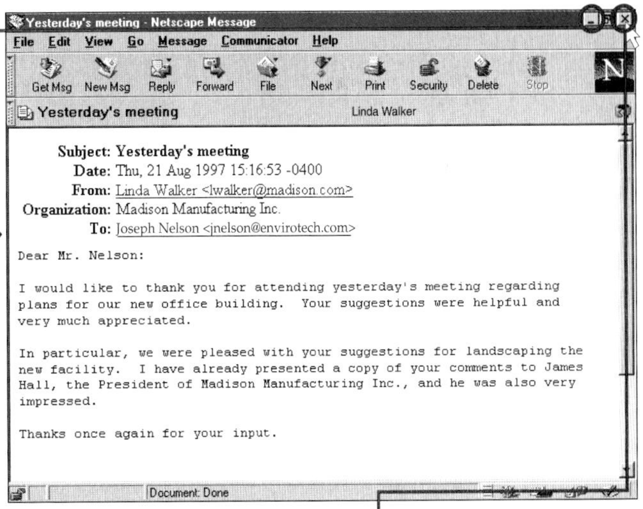

■ A window appears, displaying the contents of the message.

■ You can click [minimize] to minimize the window that fills your screen.

2 When you finish reviewing the message, click [X] to close the window.

WORK WITH COLUMNS

You can change the width and order of the columns that display information about your messages.

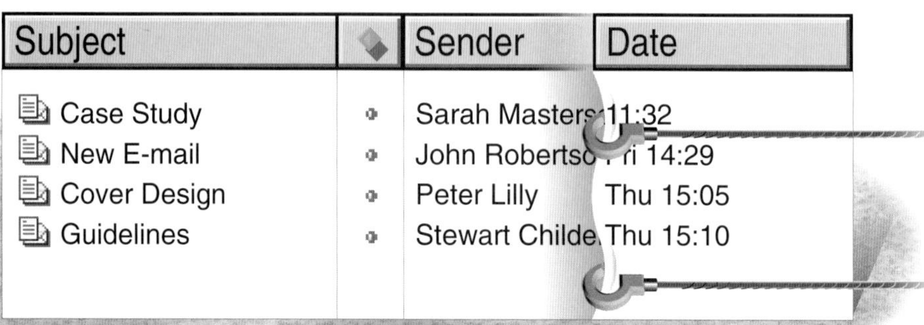

WORK WITH COLUMNS

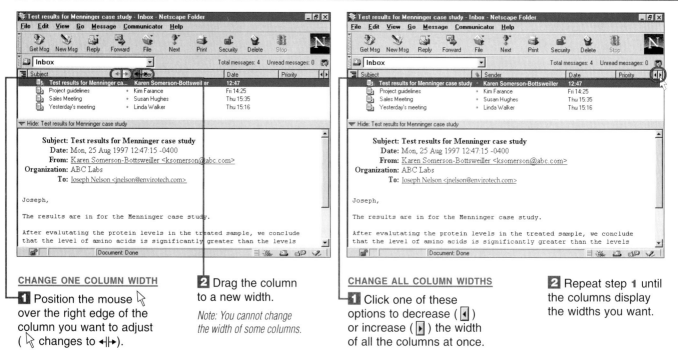

CHANGE ONE COLUMN WIDTH

1 Position the mouse over the right edge of the column you want to adjust (changes to ↔).

2 Drag the column to a new width.

Note: You cannot change the width of some columns.

CHANGE ALL COLUMN WIDTHS

1 Click one of these options to decrease (◂) or increase (▸) the width of all the columns at once.

2 Repeat step **1** until the columns display the widths you want.

What information is shown for each message?

Messenger initially shows several columns of information.

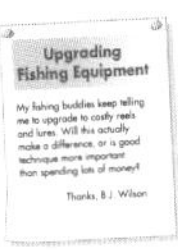

Subject

Read/Unread

Sender

Date

Priority

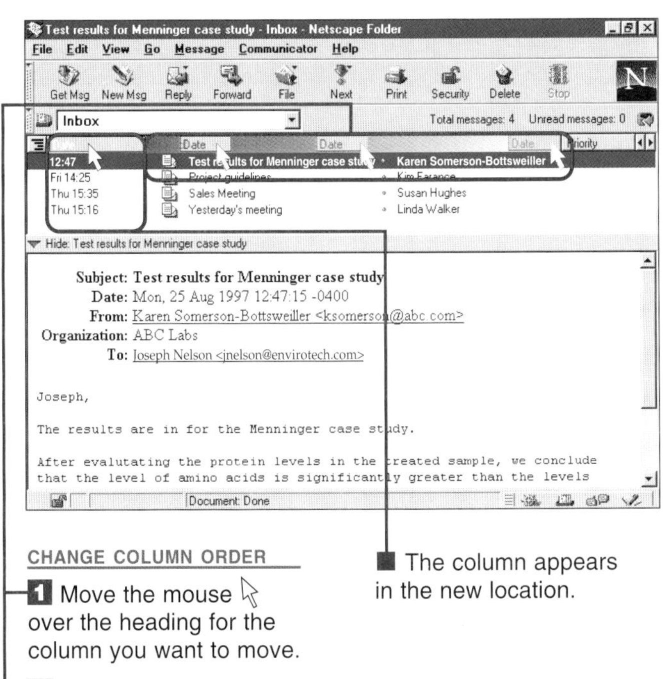

CHANGE COLUMN ORDER

1 Move the mouse over the heading for the column you want to move.

2 Hold down the left mouse button as you drag the column to a new location.

■ The column appears in the new location.

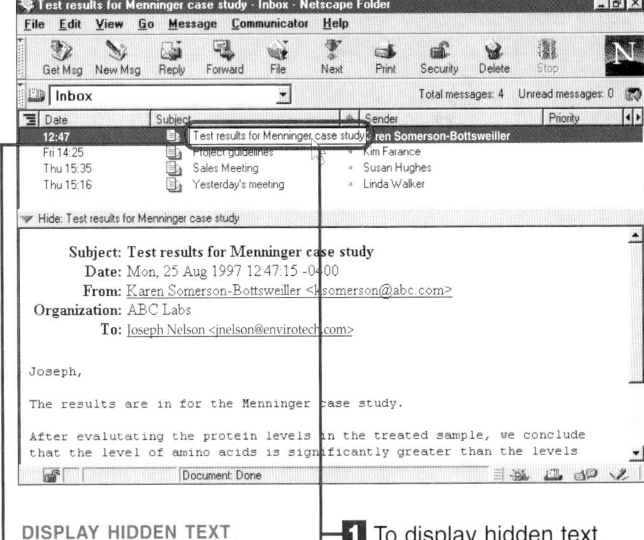

DISPLAY HIDDEN TEXT

■ A column may be too narrow to display all the information it contains.

1 To display hidden text without increasing the column width, position the mouse over an item displaying three dots (...).

■ All the text appears.

SORT MESSAGES

You can sort messages in a folder to help you easily find the messages you want to view.

You can sort messages in several ways, such as by subject, sender, date or priority.

SORT MESSAGES

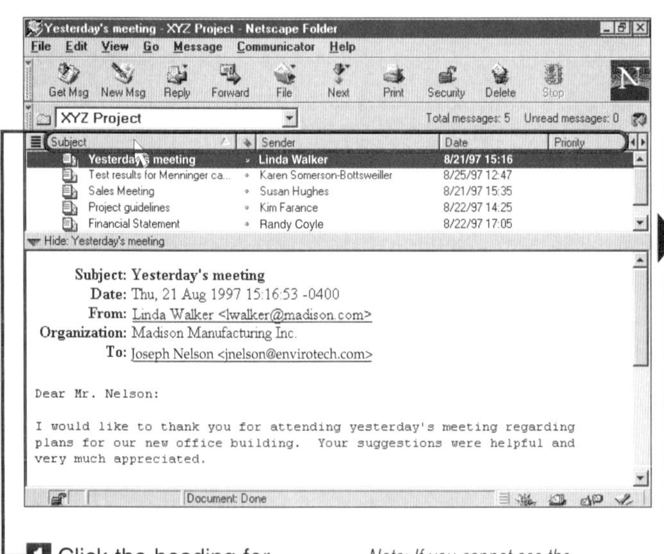

1 Click the heading for the column you want to use to sort the messages.

Note: If you cannot see the heading for the column you want to use, you can change the width of the columns to display the heading. To change the width of columns, refer to page 112.

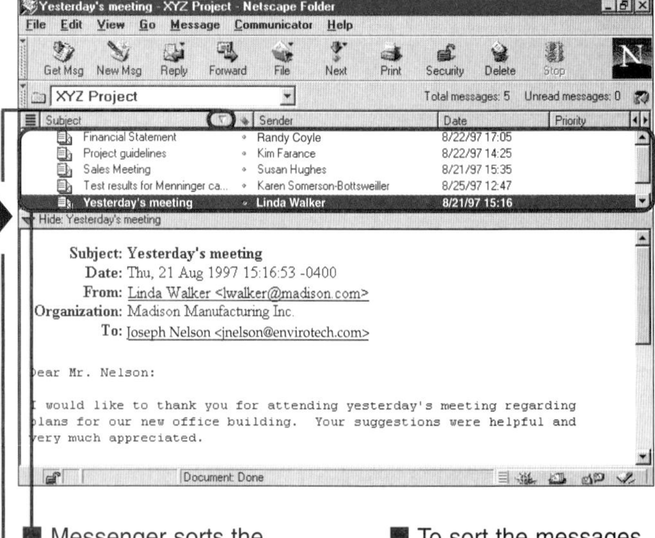

■ Messenger sorts the messages in the folder.

■ A small arrow (▽) appears in the heading of the column you used to sort the messages.

■ To sort the messages in the opposite order, repeat step **1**.

You can easily get new messages at any time.

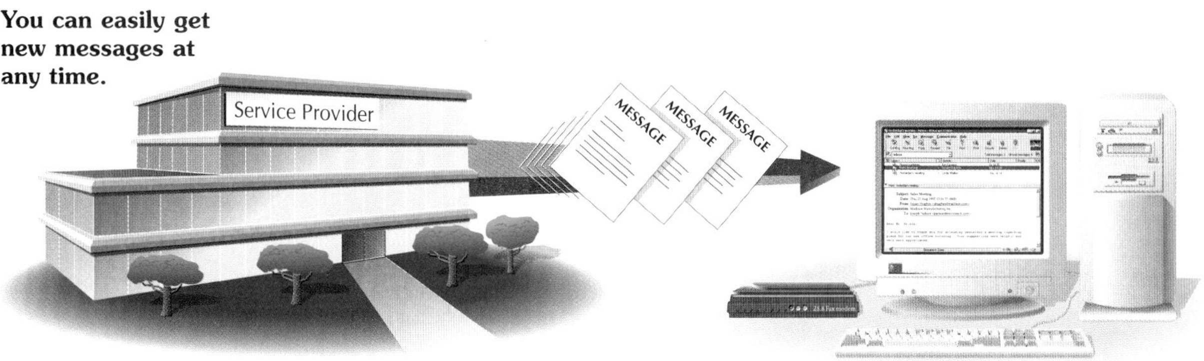

Your service provider stores your messages until you ask for them. When you get new messages, the messages are transferred to your computer and removed from the service provider's computer.

GET NEW MESSAGES

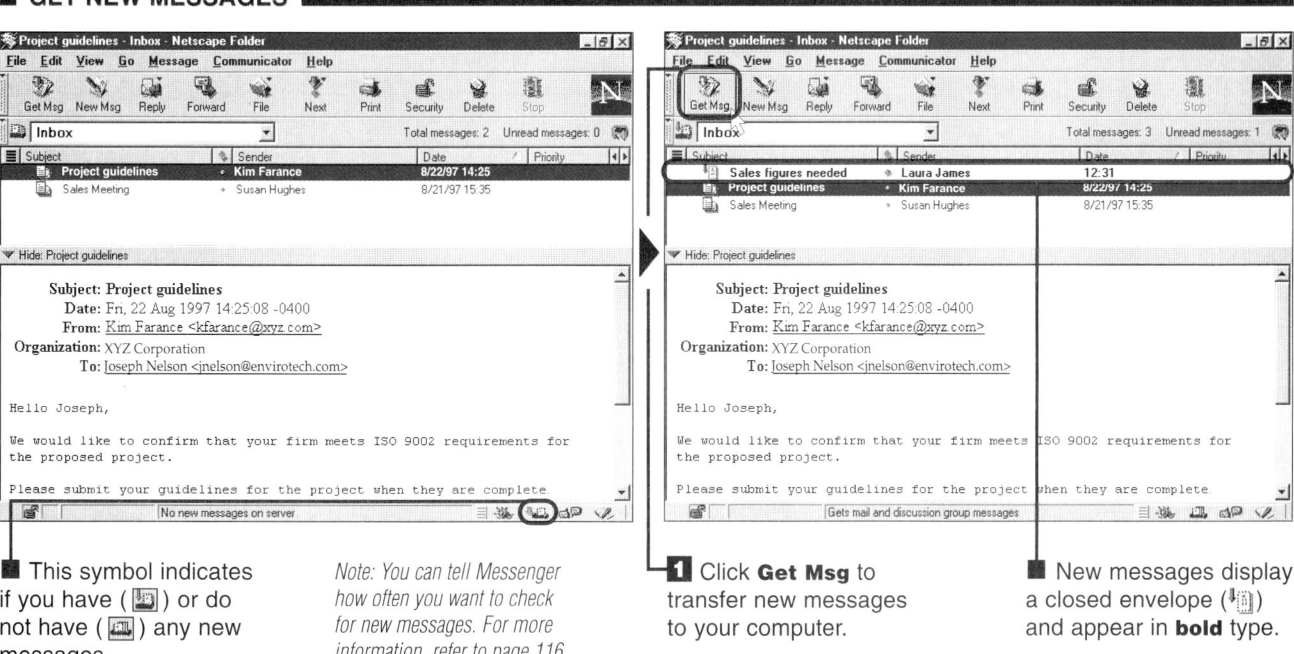

■ This symbol indicates if you have ( ) or do not have ( ) any new messages.

Note: You can tell Messenger how often you want to check for new messages. For more information, refer to page 116.

1 Click **Get Msg** to transfer new messages to your computer.

■ New messages display a closed envelope ( ) and appear in **bold** type.

CHANGE HOW OFTEN MESSENGER CHECKS MESSAGES

You can change how often Messenger will check for new messages.

Most people have Messenger check for new messages every ten minutes.

CHANGE HOW OFTEN MESSENGER CHECKS MESSAGES

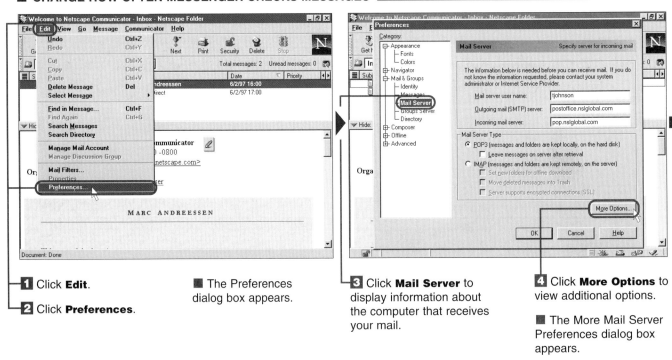

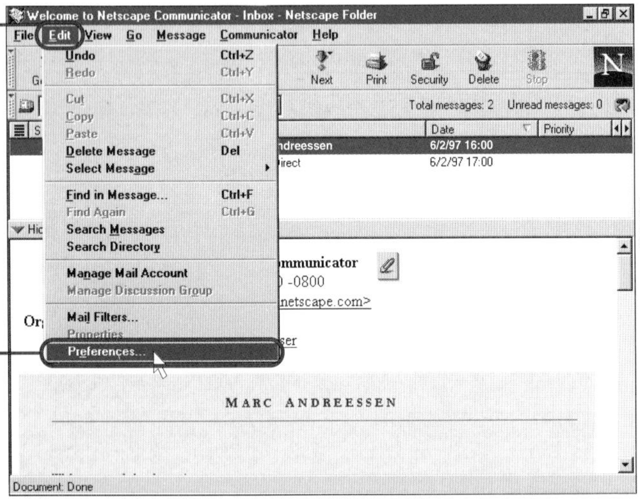

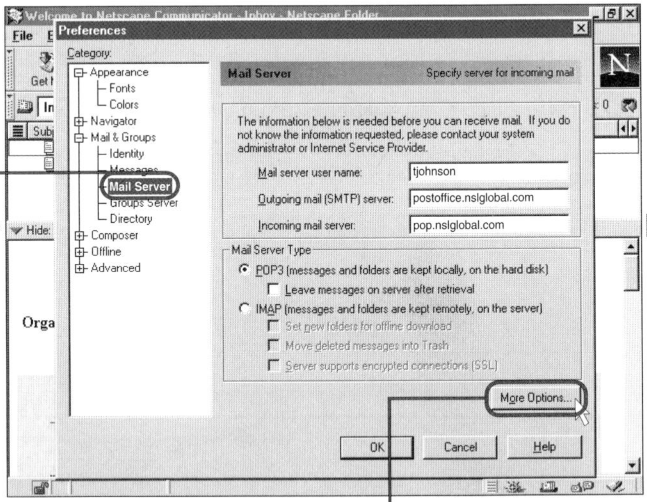

1 Click **Edit**.

2 Click **Preferences**.

■ The Preferences dialog box appears.

3 Click **Mail Server** to display information about the computer that receives your mail.

4 Click **More Options** to view additional options.

■ The More Mail Server Preferences dialog box appears.

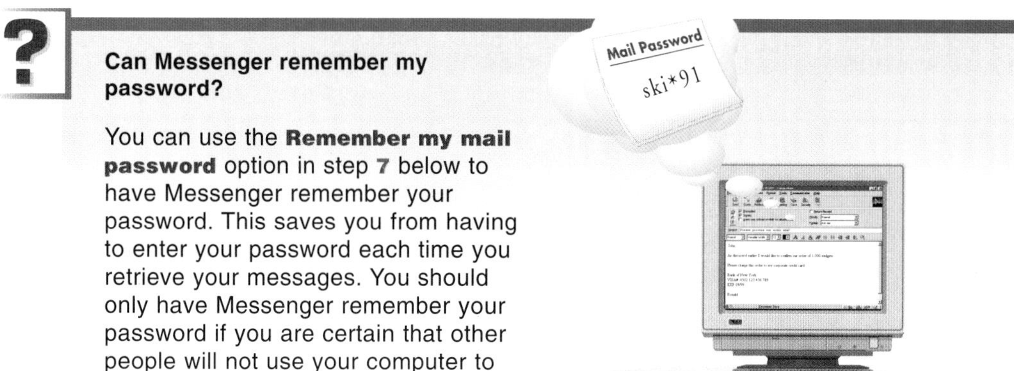

Can Messenger remember my password?

You can use the **Remember my mail password** option in step **7** below to have Messenger remember your password. This saves you from having to enter your password each time you retrieve your messages. You should only have Messenger remember your password if you are certain that other people will not use your computer to access your messages.

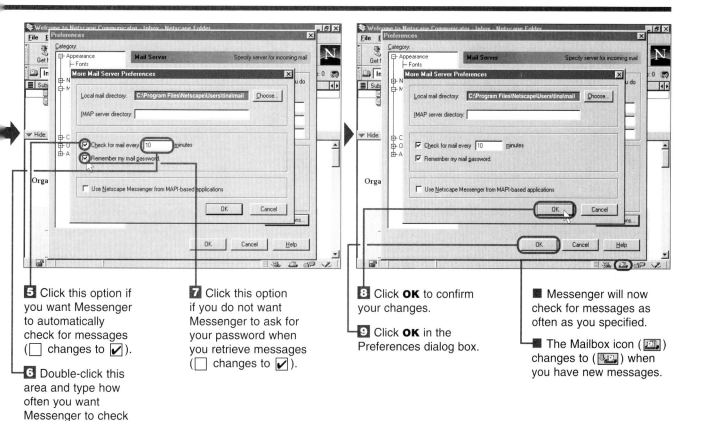

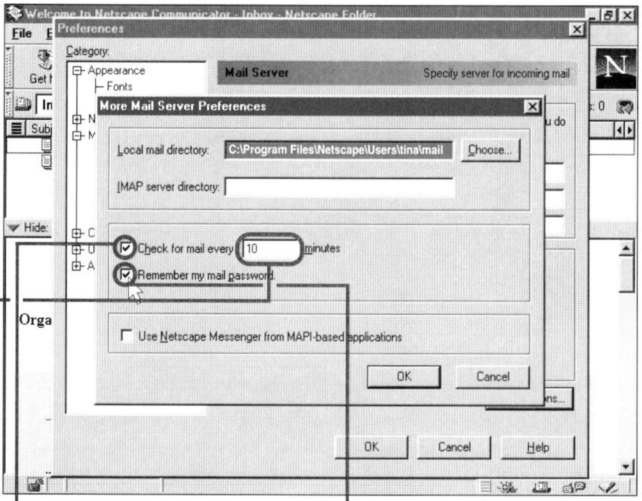

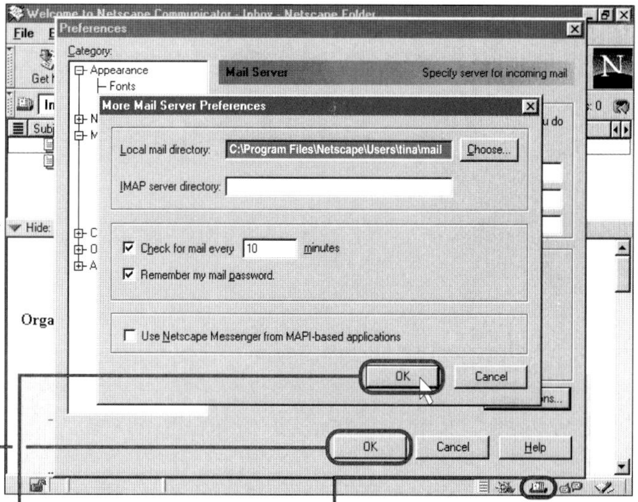

5 Click this option if you want Messenger to automatically check for messages (☐ changes to ☑).

6 Double-click this area and type how often you want Messenger to check for new messages.

7 Click this option if you do not want Messenger to ask for your password when you retrieve messages (☐ changes to ☑).

8 Click **OK** to confirm your changes.

9 Click **OK** in the Preferences dialog box.

■ Messenger will now check for messages as often as you specified.

■ The Mailbox icon ( ) changes to ( ) when you have new messages.

MARK A MESSAGE AS UNREAD

You can make a message appear as if you have not read the message. Marking a message as unread can help remind you to later review the message.

MARK A MESSAGE AS UNREAD

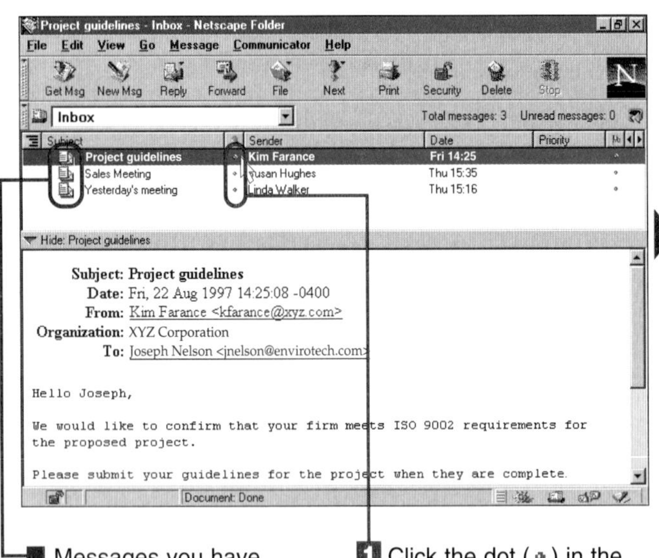

■ Messages you have read display an open envelope ( ) and appear in regular type.

1 Click the dot (◆) in the Read/Unread ( ) column beside the message you want to mark as unread.

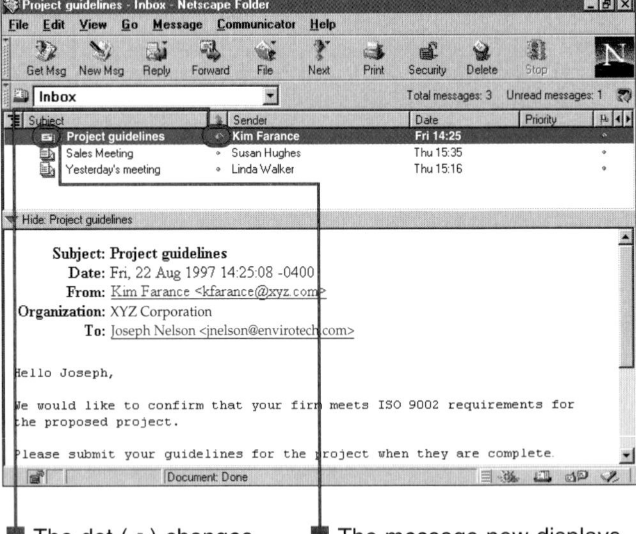

■ The dot (◆) changes to a diamond (◈).

■ The message now displays a closed envelope ( ) and appears in **bold** type.

*Note: You can once again mark the message as read by repeating step **1**.*

You can place a flag beside an important message. A flag will make the message stand out when you review your messages.

FLAG A MESSAGE

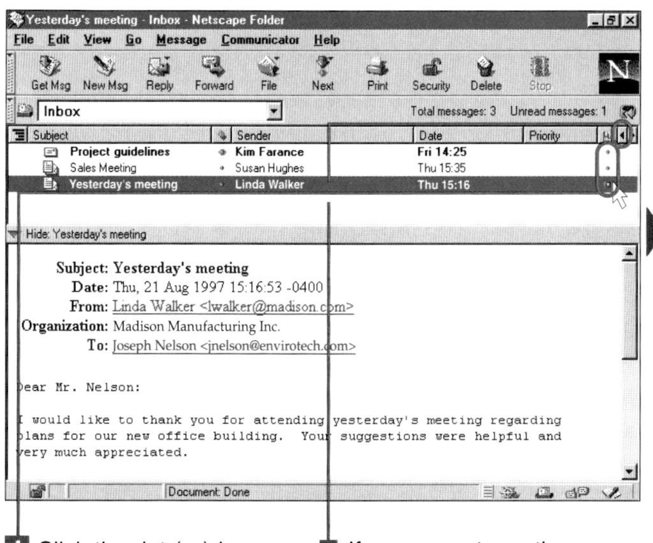

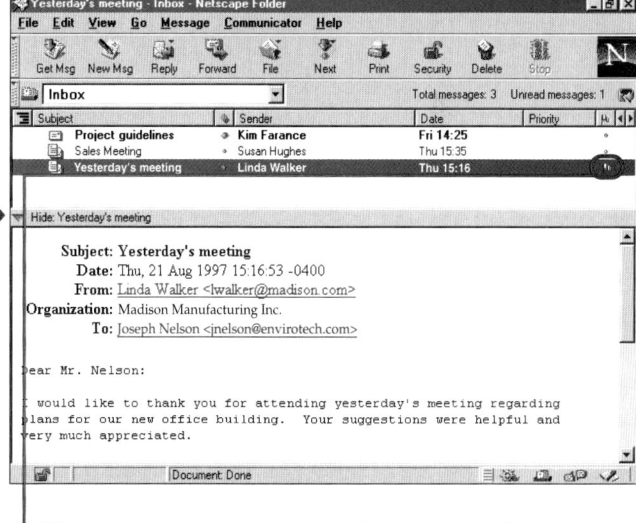

1 Click the dot (•) in the Flag ( ) column beside the message you want to flag.

■ If you cannot see the Flag column, click ◄ to display the Flag column.

■ The message displays a flag ( ).

Note: To remove a flag, repeat step ***1****.*

VIEW THREADS

You can group together related messages, called threads. A thread usually includes an original message and the replies to the message.

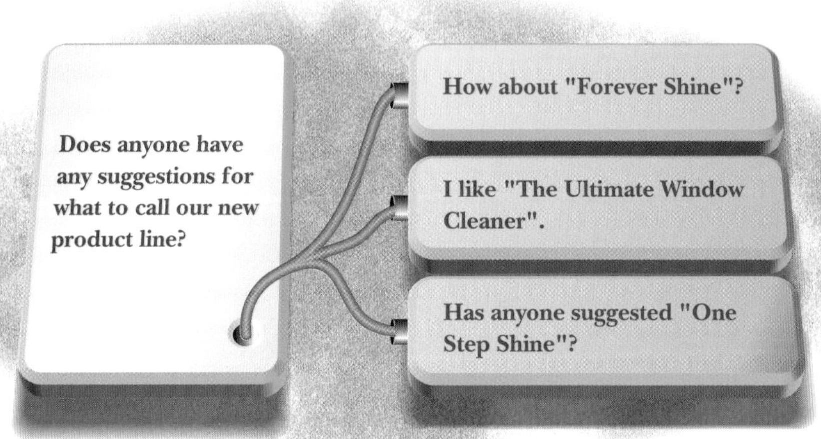

VIEW THREADS

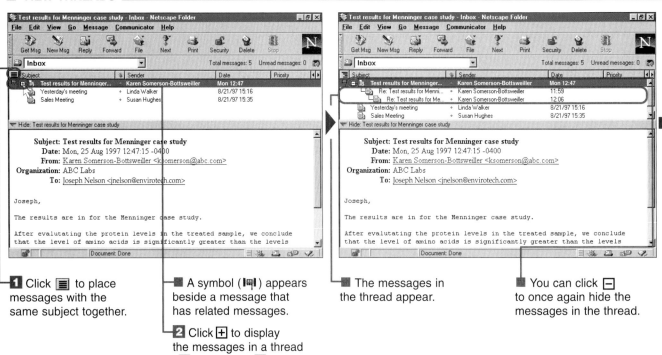

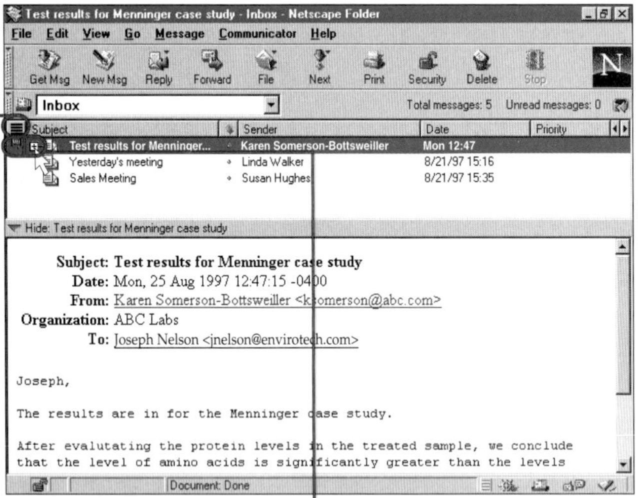

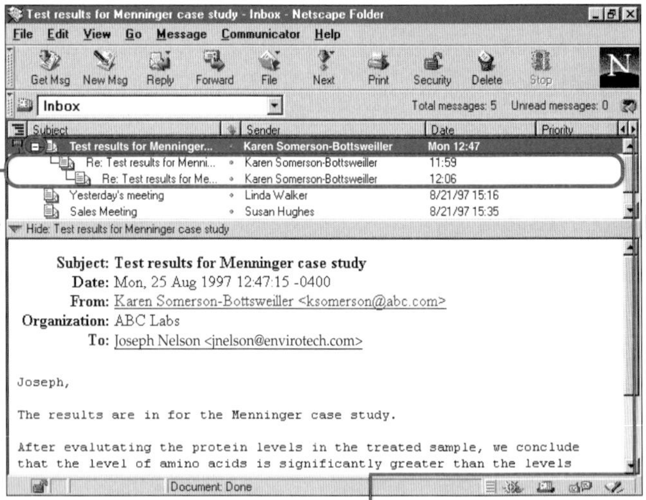

1 Click ▤ to place messages with the same subject together.

■ A symbol ([symbol]) appears beside a message that has related messages.

2 Click ⊞ to display the messages in a thread (⊞ changes to ⊟).

■ The messages in the thread appear.

■ You can click ⊟ to once again hide the messages in the thread.

How can I tell if a thread contains messages I have not read?

The symbol beside a thread displays a green arrow ( ) if the thread contains messages you have not read.

You can choose to display only threads with new messages. Displaying threads with new messages allows you to quickly find messages of interest. Refer to page 218 for more information.

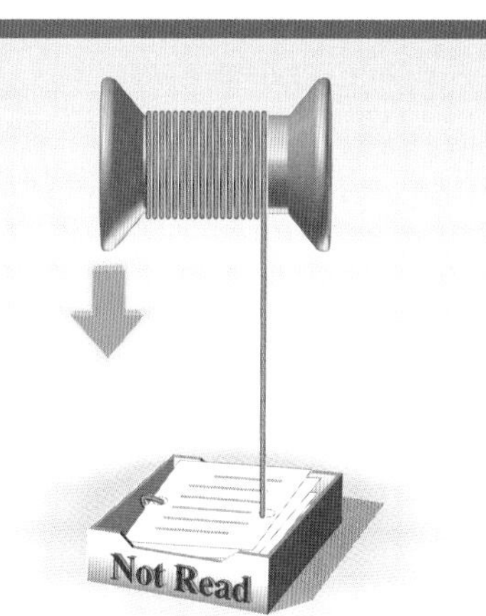

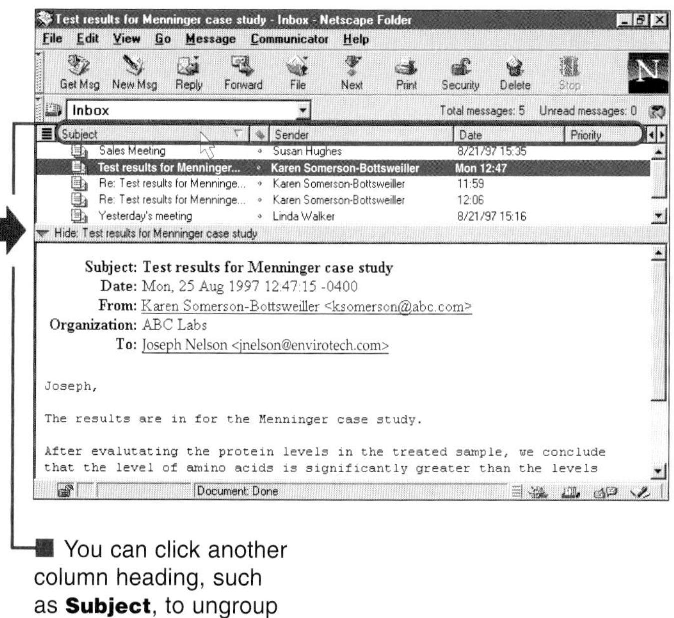

■ You can click another column heading, such as **Subject**, to ungroup related messages.

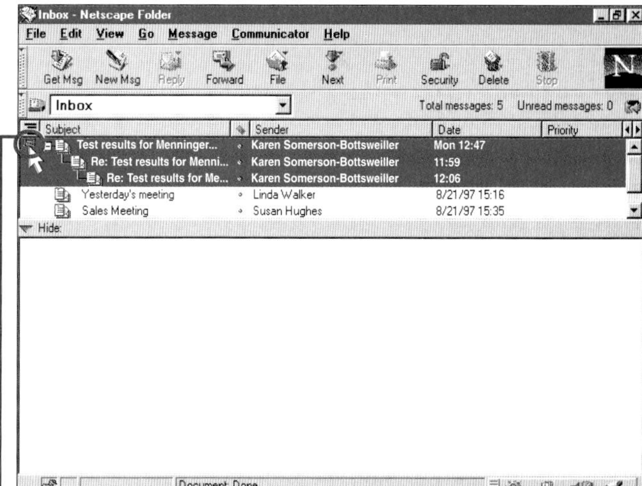

SELECT A THREAD

1 Click the symbol ( ) beside a thread to select all the messages in the thread.

■ Selecting all the messages in a thread allows you to delete all the messages or move all the messages to another folder at once.

DISPLAY MESSAGES IN OTHER FOLDERS

Messenger provides several folders to organize your messages. You can easily display the messages in any folder.

Inbox

Stores messages sent to you.

Unsent Messages

Stores messages that have not yet been sent.

Drafts

Stores messages you have not yet completed.

DISPLAY MESSAGES IN OTHER FOLDERS

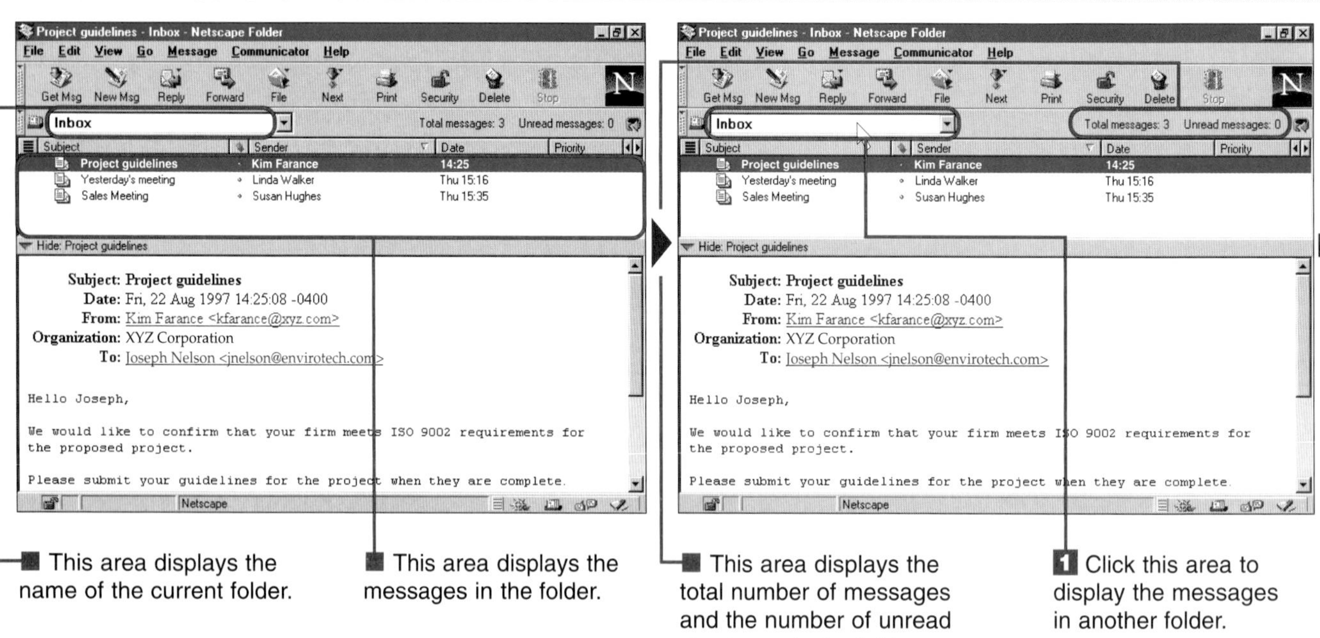

■ This area displays the name of the current folder.

■ This area displays the messages in the folder.

■ This area displays the total number of messages and the number of unread messages in the folder.

1 Click this area to display the messages in another folder.

Sent

Stores messages you have sent.

Trash

Stores messages you have deleted.

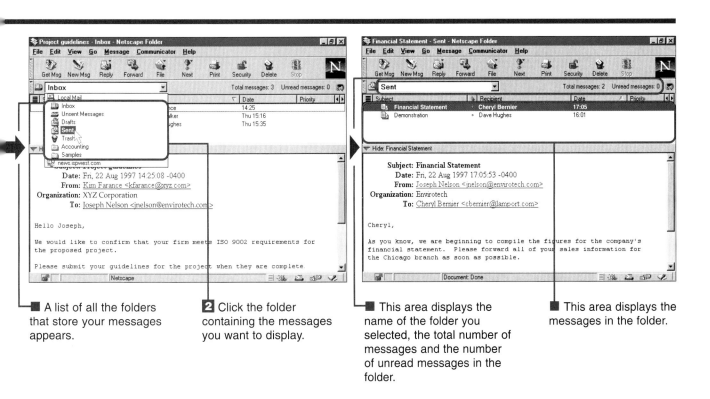

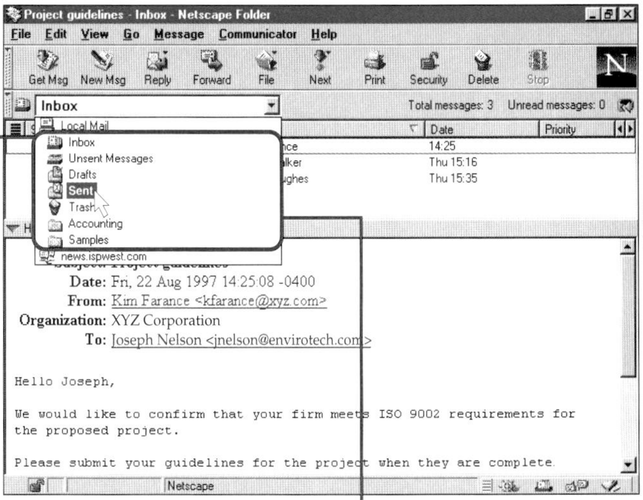

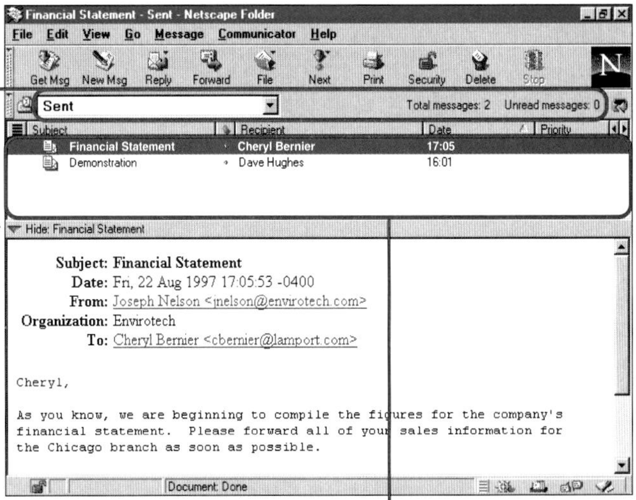

■ A list of all the folders that store your messages appears.

2 Click the folder containing the messages you want to display.

■ This area displays the name of the folder you selected, the total number of messages and the number of unread messages in the folder.

■ This area displays the messages in the folder.

CREATE A NEW FOLDER

You can create a new folder to help you organize your messages. A folder lets you keep related messages in one location.

CREATE A NEW FOLDER

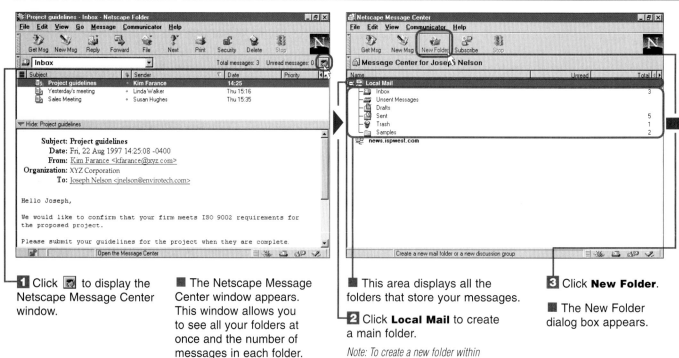

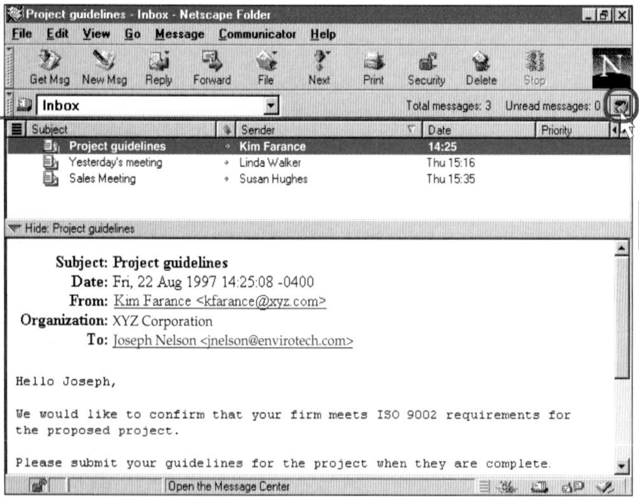

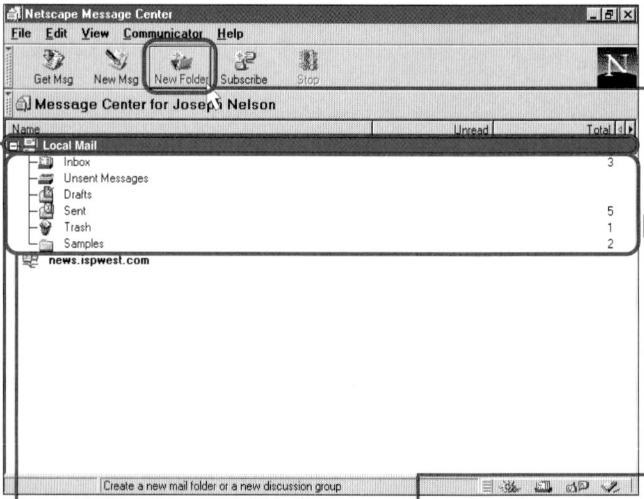

1 Click [icon] to display the Netscape Message Center window.

■ The Netscape Message Center window appears. This window allows you to see all your folders at once and the number of messages in each folder.

■ This area displays all the folders that store your messages.

2 Click **Local Mail** to create a main folder.

Note: To create a new folder within another folder, click the folder.

3 Click **New Folder**.

■ The New Folder dialog box appears.

?

How do I delete a folder I no longer need?

To delete a folder, click the folder you want to remove in the Netscape Message Center window and then press the Delete key. You should only delete folders that you have created.

When you delete a folder, Messenger places it in the Trash folder. To permanently remove the folder from your computer, empty the Trash folder. To empty the Trash folder, refer to page 129.

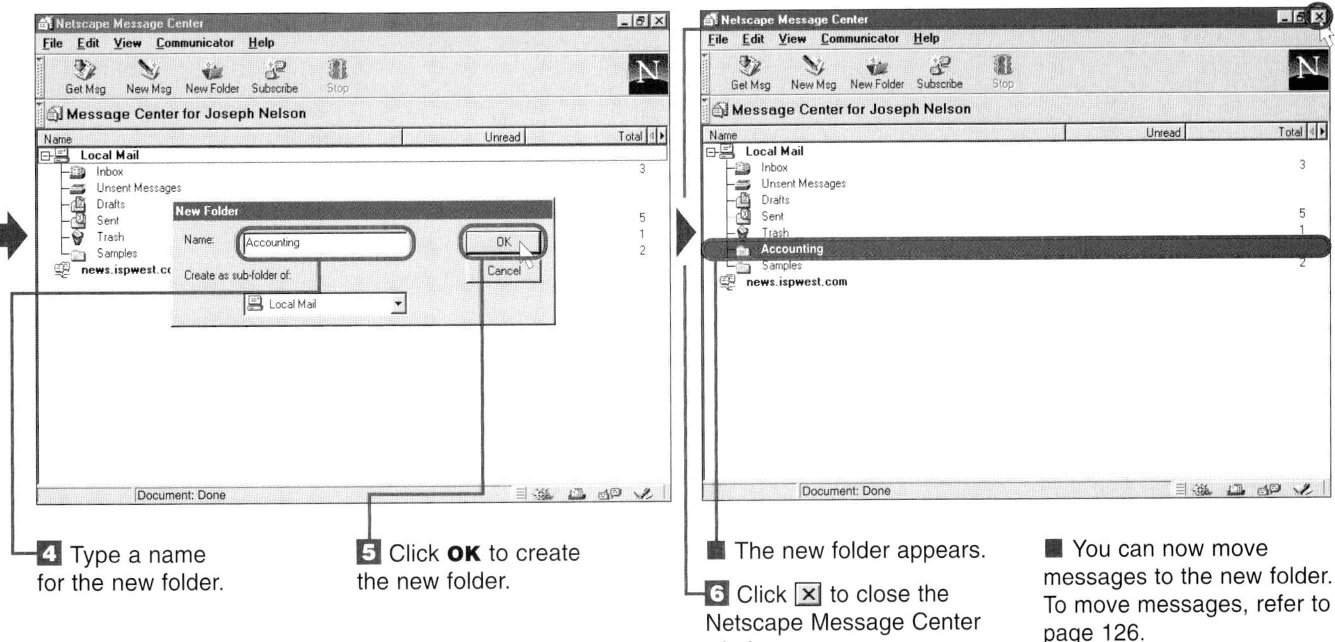

4 Type a name for the new folder.

5 Click **OK** to create the new folder.

■ The new folder appears.

6 Click ☒ to close the Netscape Message Center window.

■ You can now move messages to the new folder. To move messages, refer to page 126.

FILE A MESSAGE

You can place a message you want to later review in a folder you created. Keeping related messages in personalized folders helps you easily find messages.

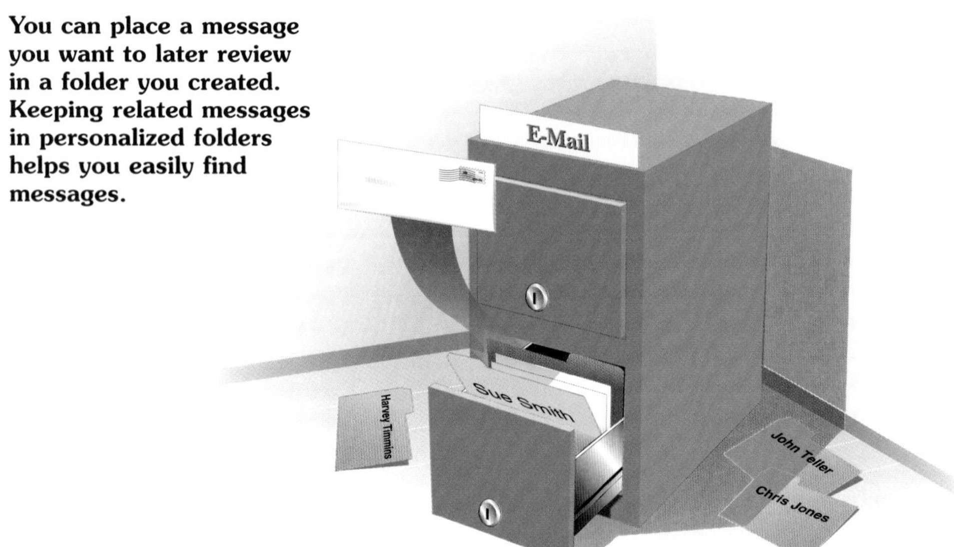

To create your own personalized folders, refer to page 124.

FILE A MESSAGE

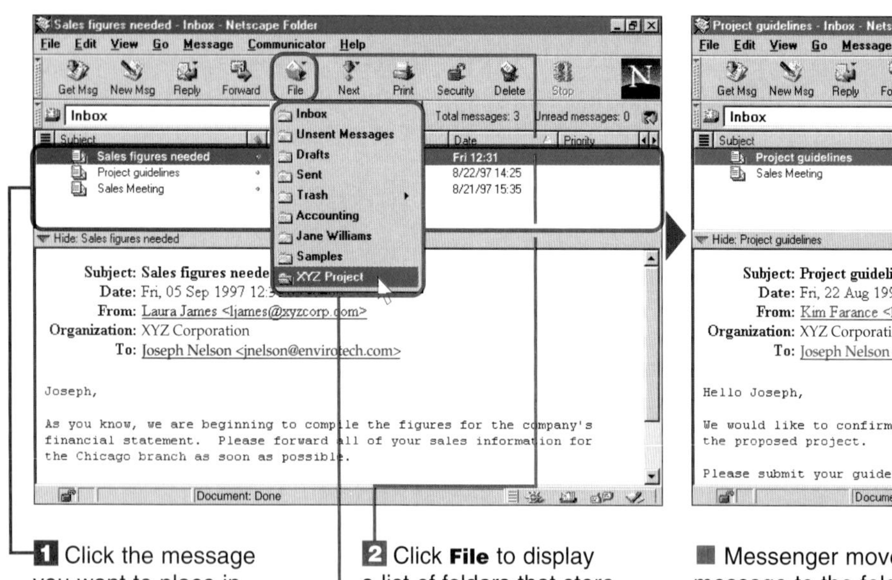

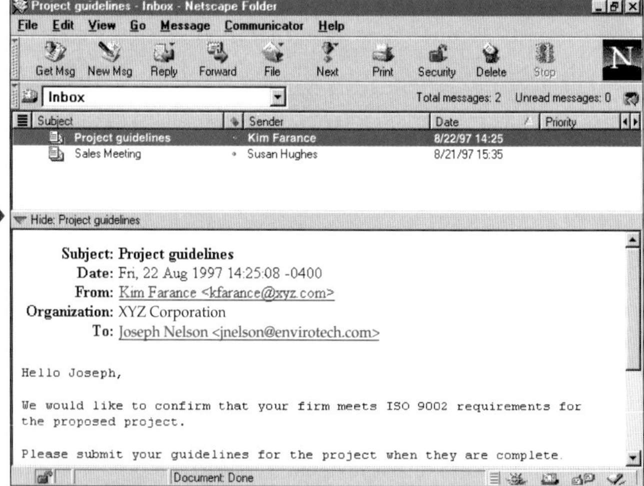

1 Click the message you want to place in another folder.

Note: To place several messages in another folder at once, hold down the Ctrl *key as you click each message.*

2 Click **File** to display a list of folders that store your messages.

3 Click the folder you want to store the message.

■ Messenger moves the message to the folder you selected.

You can produce a paper copy of a message displayed on your screen.

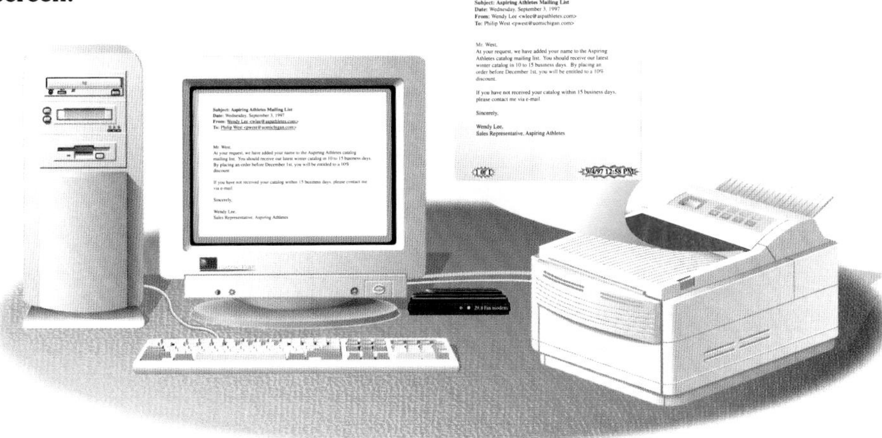

Messenger prints the subject of the message at the top of each page. The page number, total number of pages and current date and time print at the bottom of each page.

PRINT A MESSAGE

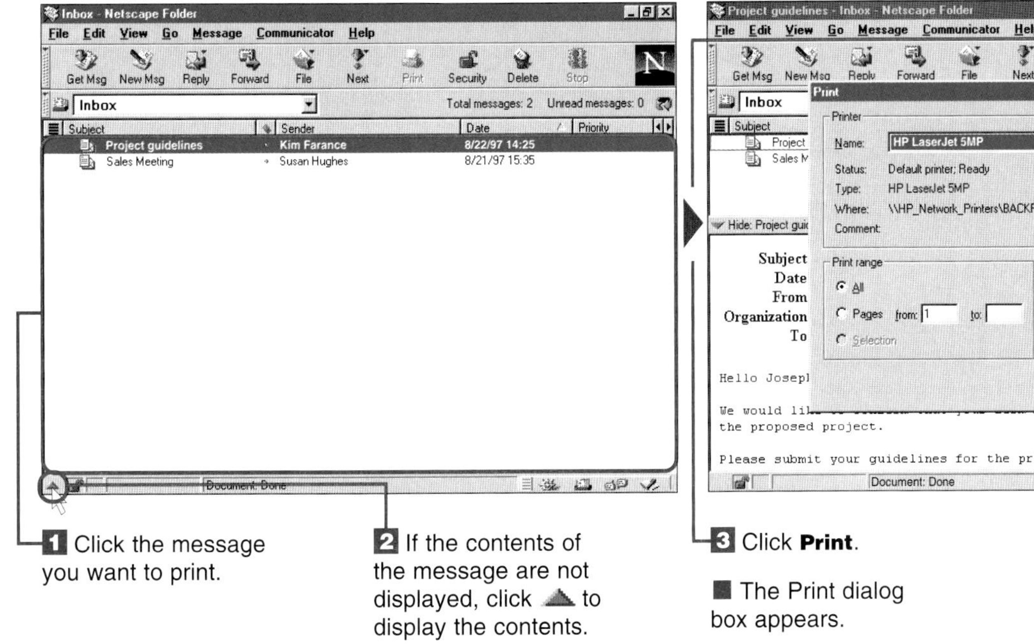

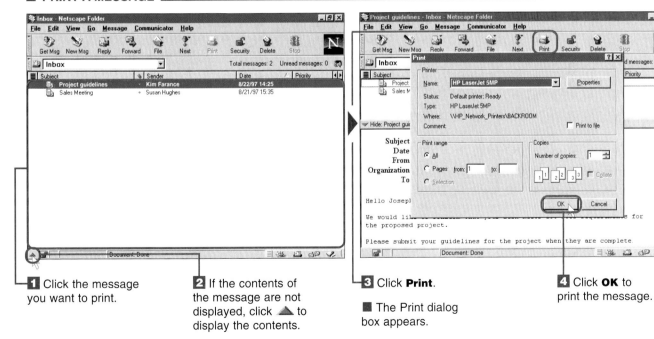

1 Click the message you want to print.

2 If the contents of the message are not displayed, click ▲ to display the contents.

■ The contents of the message appear.

3 Click **Print**.

■ The Print dialog box appears.

4 Click **OK** to print the message.

DELETE A MESSAGE

You can delete a message you no longer need. This prevents your folders from becoming cluttered with messages.

Make sure you regularly clean out your folders by deleting messages you no longer need.

DELETE A MESSAGE

Application for Product Tester - Inbox - Netscape Folder

File Edit View Go Message Communicator Help

Get Msg New Msg Reply Forward File Next Print Security Delete Stop

Inbox Total messages: 4 Unread messages: 0

Subject	Sender	Date	Priority
Application for Product Tester	Kevin Williams	Thu 15:41	
Project guidelines	Kim Farance	14:25	
Yesterday's meeting	Linda Walker	Thu 15:16	
Sales Meeting	Susan Hughes	Thu 15:35	

Hide: Application for Product Tester

Subject: Application for Product Tester
Date: Thu, 21 Aug 1997 15:41:59 -0400
From: Kevin Williams <kwilliams@xyzfreenet.org>
Organization: Madison Manufacturing Inc.
To: Joseph Nelson <jnelson@envirotech.com>

Dear Mr. Nelson,

I am highly interested in the Product Tester position recently advertised on the Internet. I am attaching my resume and hope to hear from you soon.

Delete the selected message

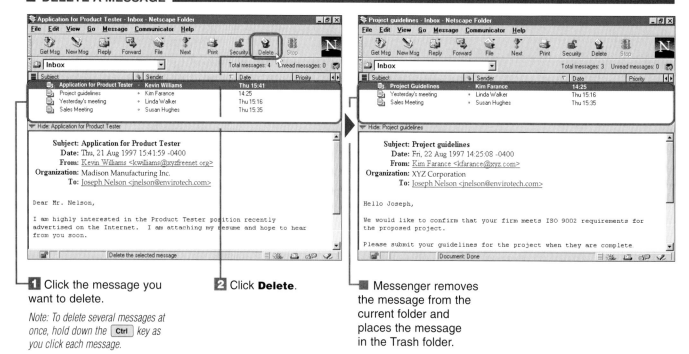

1 Click the message you want to delete.

Note: To delete several messages at once, hold down the Ctrl *key as you click each message.*

2 Click **Delete**.

Project guidelines - Inbox - Netscape Folder

File Edit View Go Message Communicator Help

Get Msg New Msg Reply Forward File Next Print Security Delete Stop

Inbox Total messages: 3 Unread messages: 0

Subject	Sender	Date	Priority
Project Guidelines	Kim Farance	14:25	
Yesterday's meeting	Linda Walker	Thu 15:16	
Sales Meeting	Susan Hughes	Thu 15:35	

Hide: Project guidelines

Subject: Project guidelines
Date: Fri, 22 Aug 1997 14:25:08 -0400
From: Kim Farance <kfarance@xyz.com>
Organization: XYZ Corporation
To: Joseph Nelson <jnelson@envirotech.com>

Hello Joseph,

We would like to confirm that your firm meets ISO 9002 requirements for the proposed project.

Please submit your guidelines for the project when they are complete.

Document: Done

■ Messenger removes the message from the current folder and places the message in the Trash folder.

EMPTY TRASH FOLDER

You can delete all the messages in the Trash folder to permanently remove the messages from your computer.

You should regularly empty the Trash folder to save space on your computer.

EMPTY TRASH FOLDER

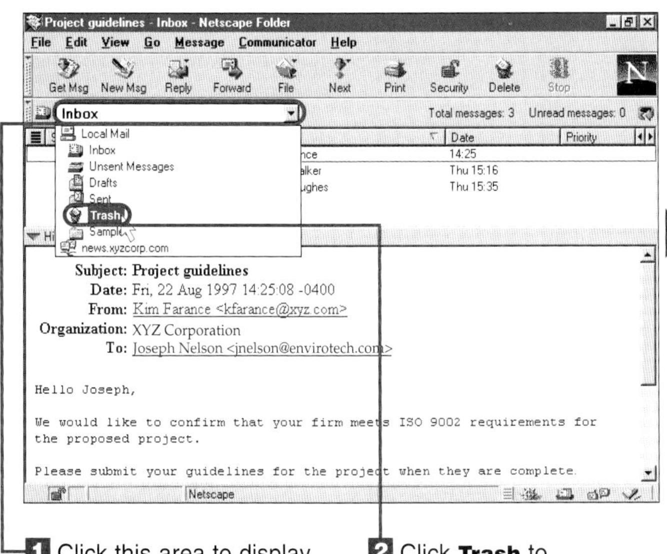

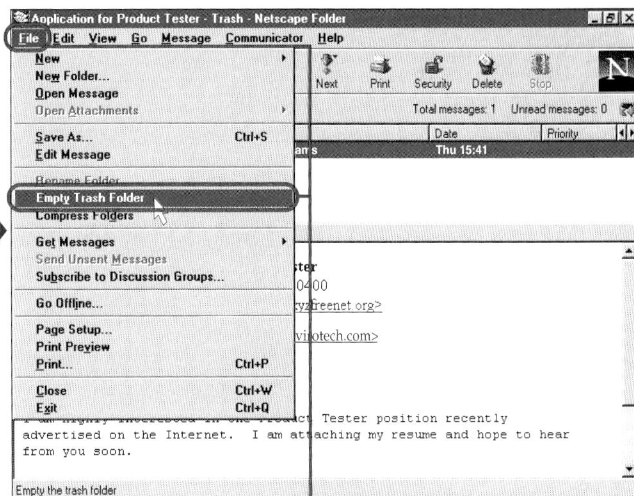

1 Click this area to display a list of the folders that store your messages.

2 Click **Trash** to display the messages in the Trash folder.

■ The messages in the Trash folder appear. Make sure the folder does not contain messages you want to keep.

3 Click **File**.

4 Click **Empty Trash Folder** to permanently delete all the messages in the Trash folder.

SAVE A MESSAGE

You can save a message so you can work with the message in another program, such as a word processor.

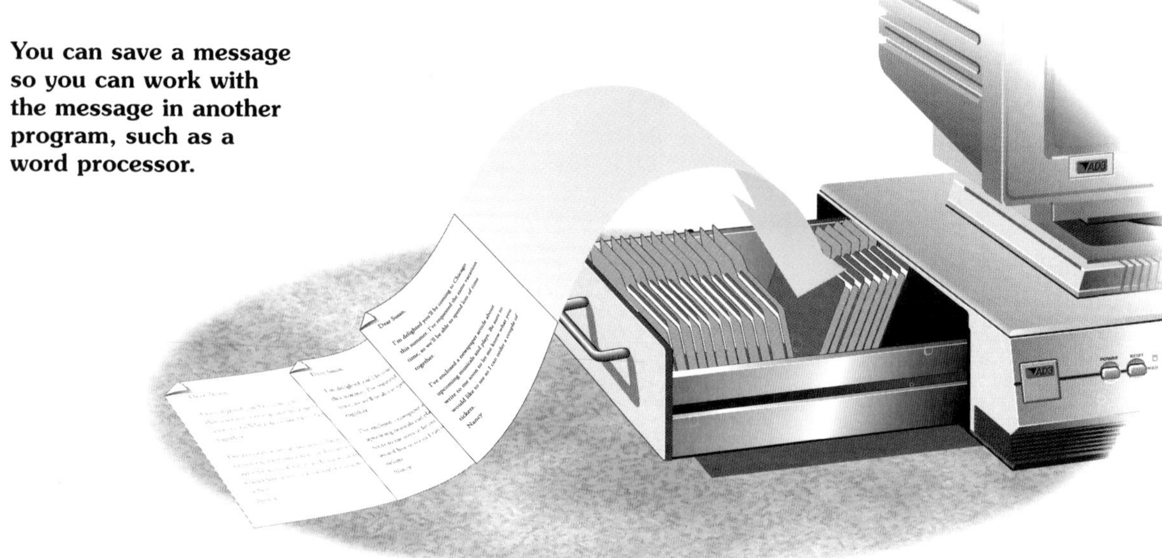

SAVE A MESSAGE

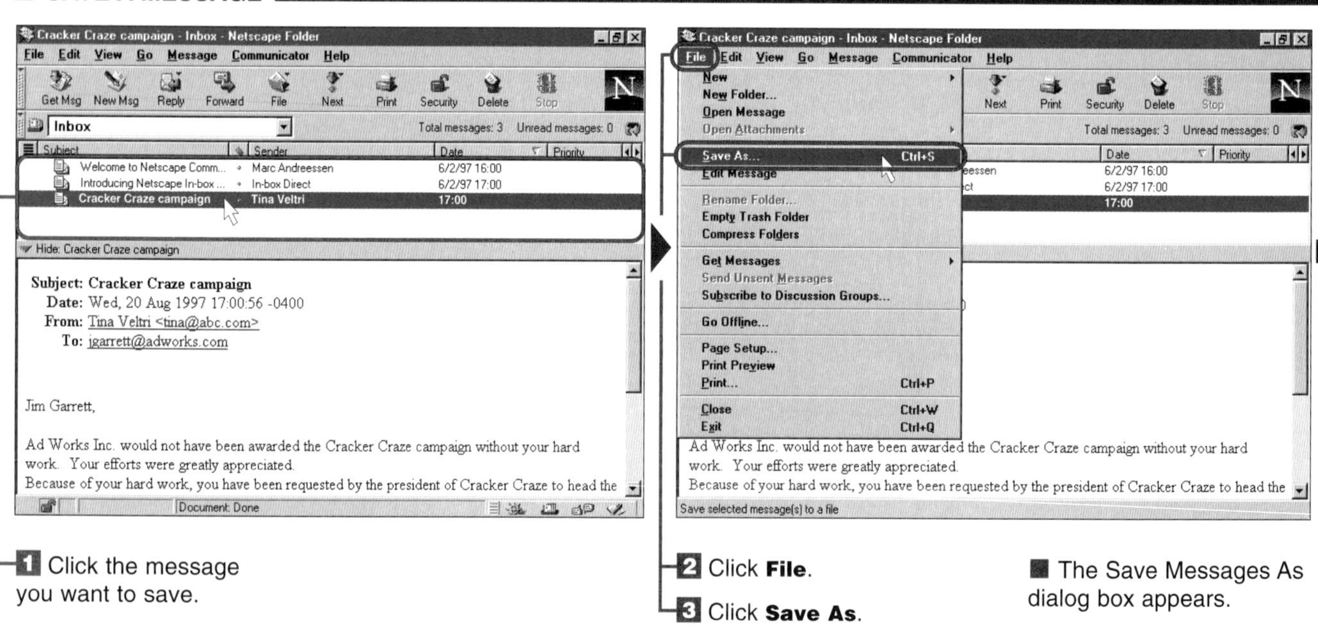

1 Click the message you want to save.

2 Click **File**.

3 Click **Save As**.

■ The Save Messages As dialog box appears.

? Why would I want to work with a message in a word processor?

You can use the powerful editing and formatting features offered by a word processor to enhance the readability and appearance of a saved message. You can then keep the message for personal reference or distribute the message to colleagues and friends.

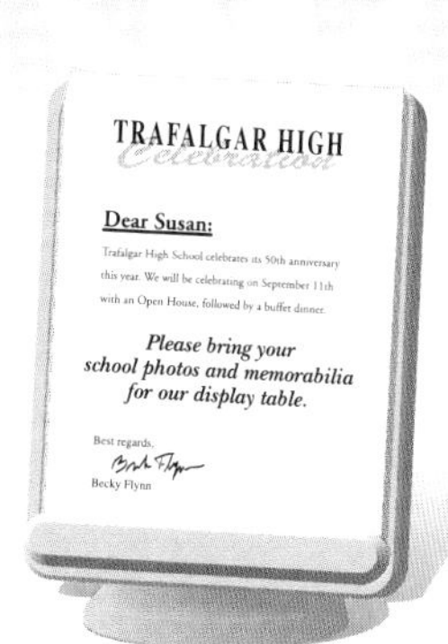

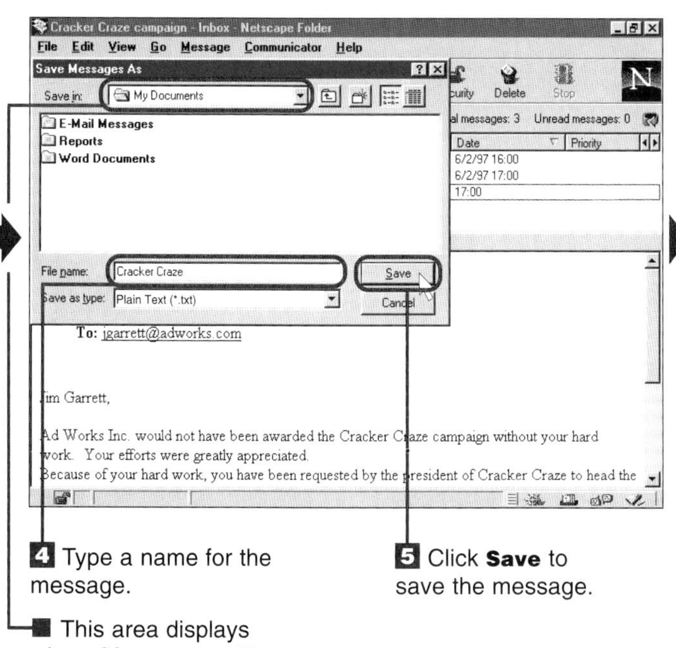

4 Type a name for the message.

■ This area displays where Messenger will save the message. You can click this area to change the location.

5 Click **Save** to save the message.

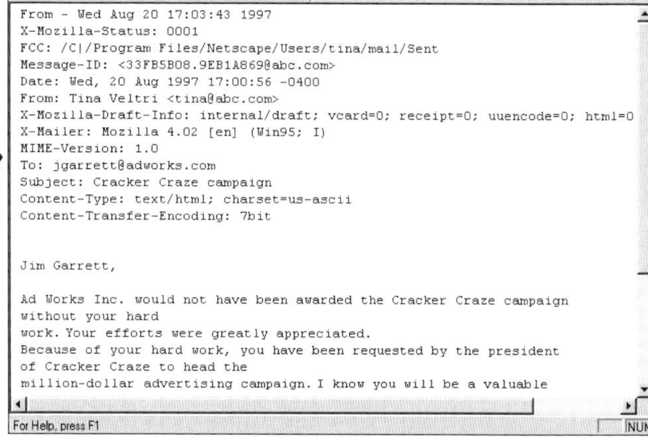

■ You can now open the saved message in another program.

■ In this example, we used a word processing program to display the message.

OPEN AN ATTACHED FILE

When you receive a message with an attached file, you can easily open the file.

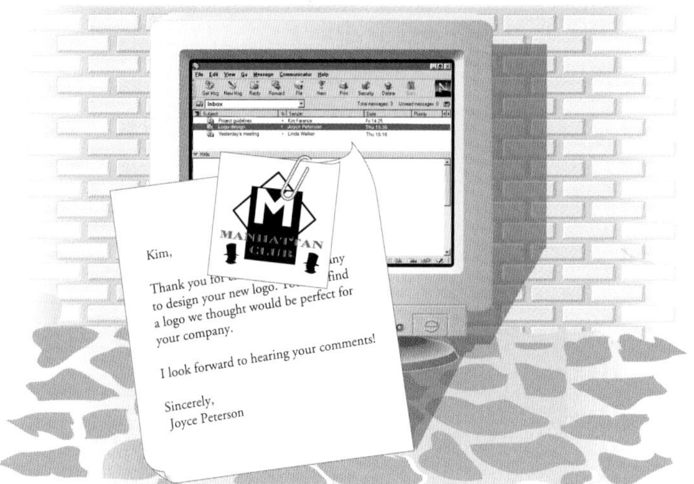

Attached files can contain text, images, sounds, videos or programs. Your computer must have the necessary software and hardware to display or play the files you receive.

OPEN AN ATTACHED FILE

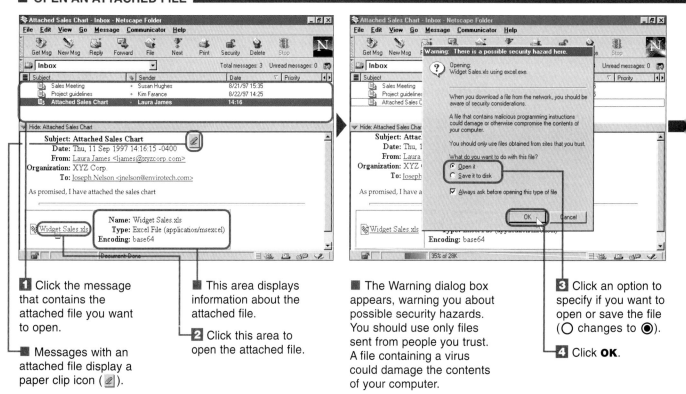

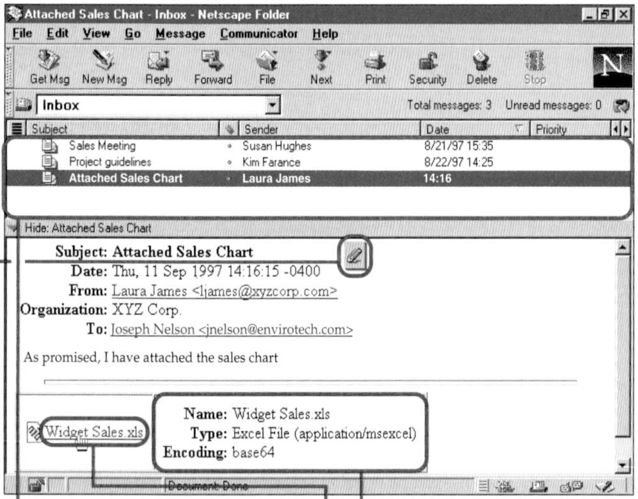

1 Click the message that contains the attached file you want to open.

■ Messages with an attached file display a paper clip icon ( ).

■ This area displays information about the attached file.

2 Click this area to open the attached file.

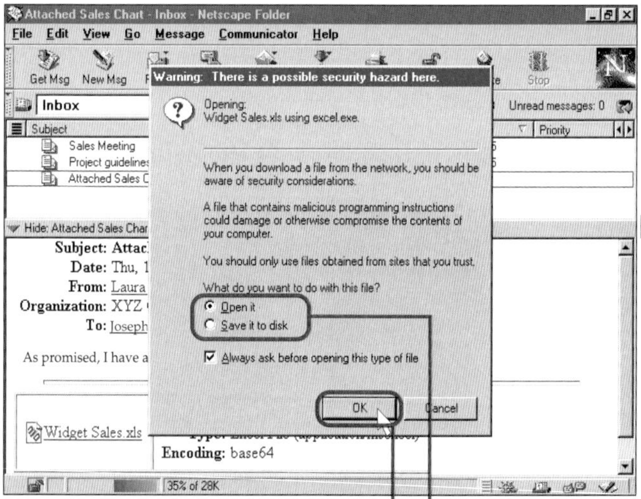

■ The Warning dialog box appears, warning you about possible security hazards. You should use only files sent from people you trust. A file containing a virus could damage the contents of your computer.

3 Click an option to specify if you want to open or save the file (○ changes to ◉).

4 Click **OK**.

Why did the Unknown File Type dialog box appear when I selected an attached file?

This dialog box appears when you select an attached file that Messenger does not know how to handle.

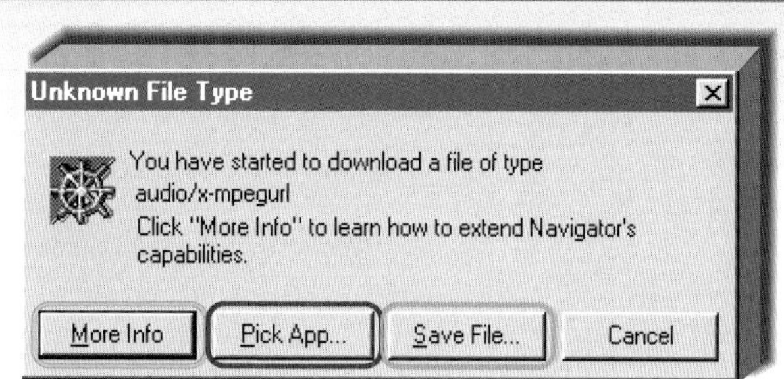

More Info

Get a program on the Web that will display or play the file.

Pick App

Find a program on your computer to display or play the file.

Save File

Saves the file on your computer.

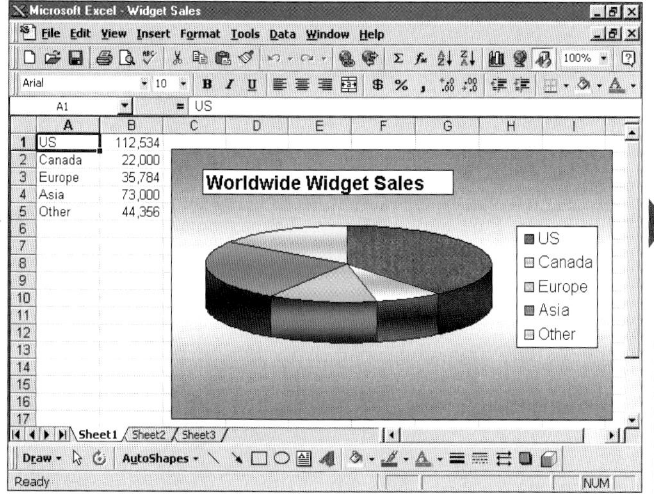

■ If you chose to open the file, the file opens in the appropriate program. You can review and work with the file on your computer.

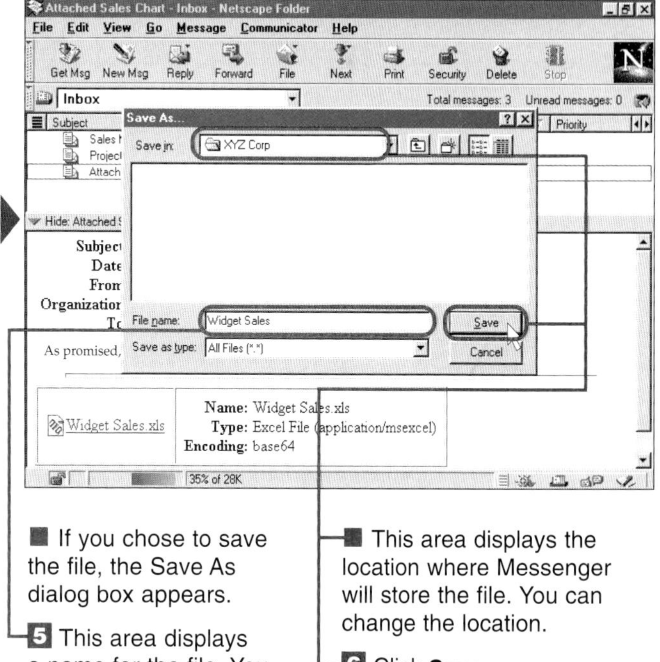

■ If you chose to save the file, the Save As dialog box appears.

5 This area displays a name for the file. You can type a new name.

■ This area displays the location where Messenger will store the file. You can change the location.

6 Click **Save**.

■ You can now open the file in the appropriate program.

FIND TEXT IN A MESSAGE

If you are reviewing a message that contains a lot of text, you can use the Find feature to quickly locate a word. This allows you to locate an area of interest in a long message.

FIND TEXT IN A MESSAGE

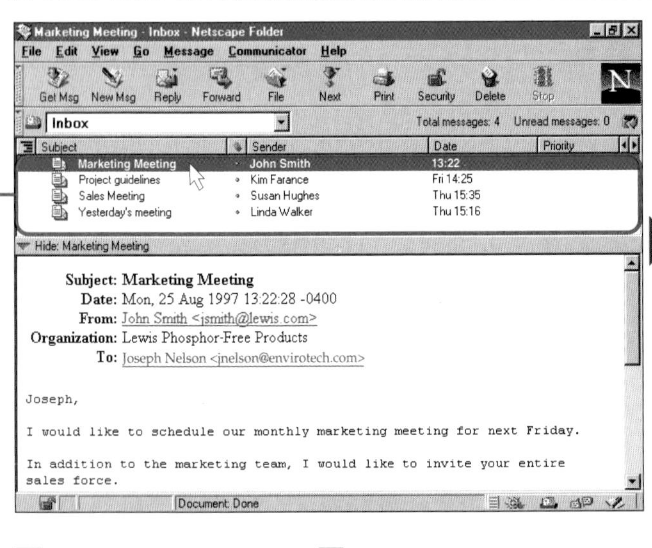

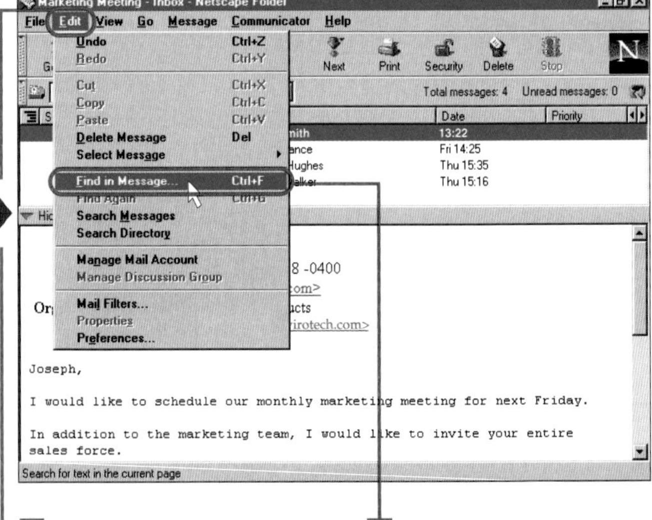

1 Click the message containing the text you want to find.

2 If the contents of the message are not displayed, refer to page 110.

3 Click **Edit**.

4 Click **Find in Message**.

■ The Find dialog box appears.

Will Messenger find words that are part of larger words?

When you search for a word in a message, Messenger will find the word even if it is part of a larger word. For example, if you search for **snow**, Messenger will also find **snow**ball, **snow**man and **snow**flake.

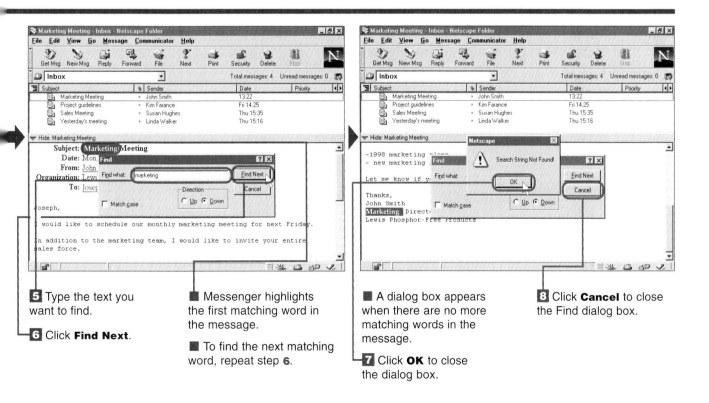

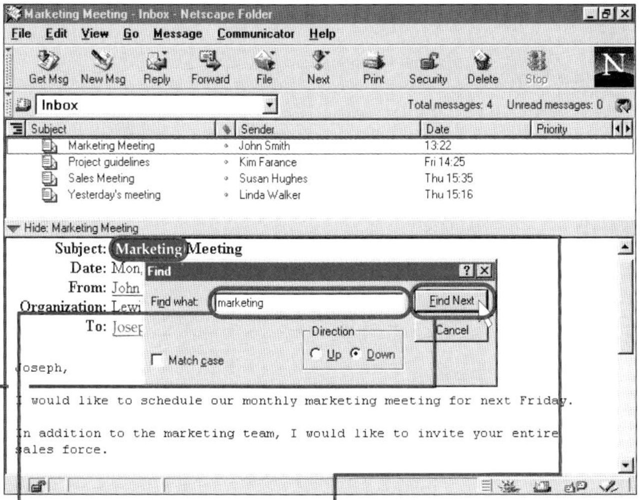

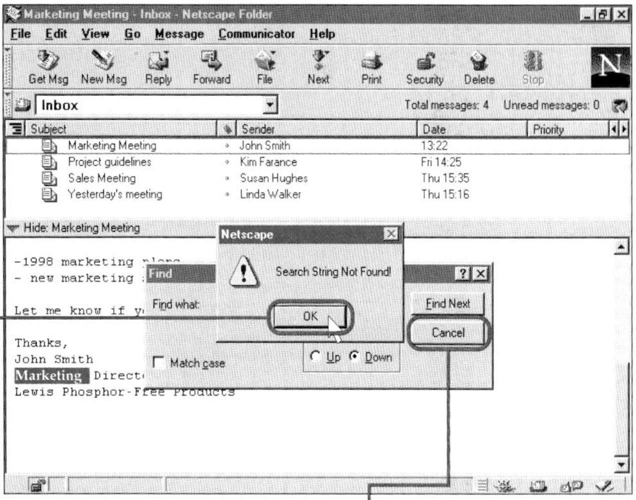

5 Type the text you want to find.

6 Click **Find Next**.

■ Messenger highlights the first matching word in the message.

■ To find the next matching word, repeat step **6**.

■ A dialog box appears when there are no more matching words in the message.

7 Click **OK** to close the dialog box.

8 Click **Cancel** to close the Find dialog box.

SEARCH FOR A MESSAGE

If you cannot find a message you want to review, you can have Messenger search for the message.

SEARCH FOR A MESSAGE

1 Click **Edit**.

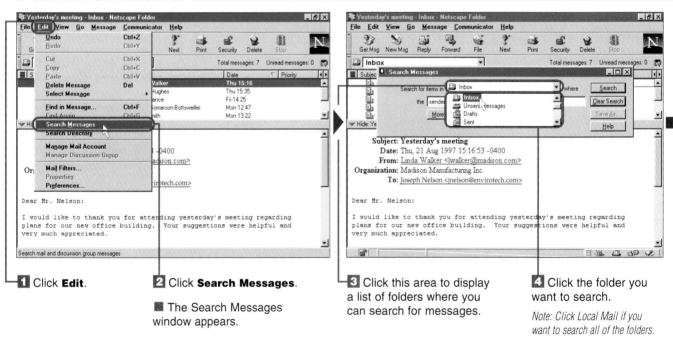

2 Click **Search Messages**.

■ The Search Messages window appears.

3 Click this area to display a list of folders where you can search for messages.

4 Click the folder you want to search.

Note: Click Local Mail if you want to search all of the folders.

? Which part of each message can I search?

There are several parts of each message you can search:

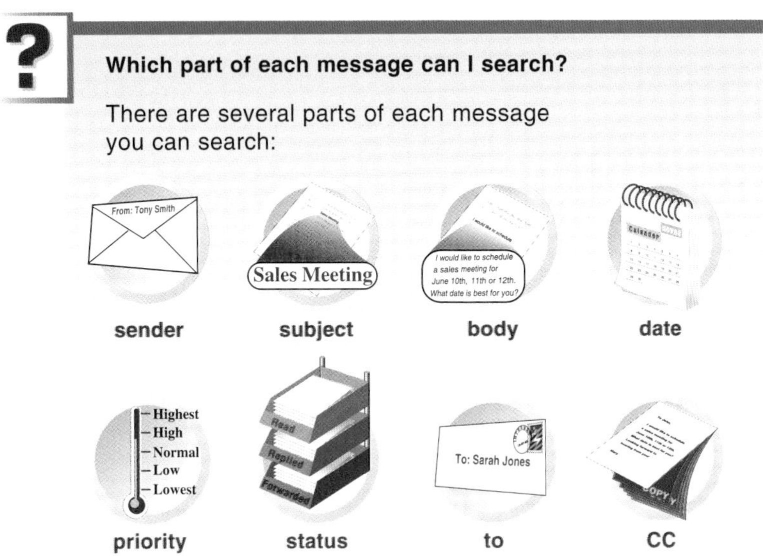

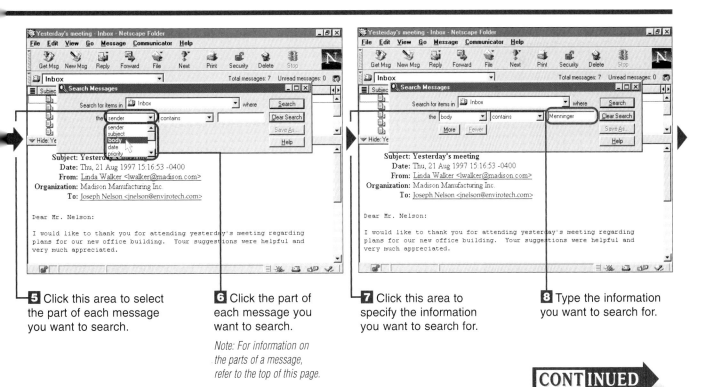

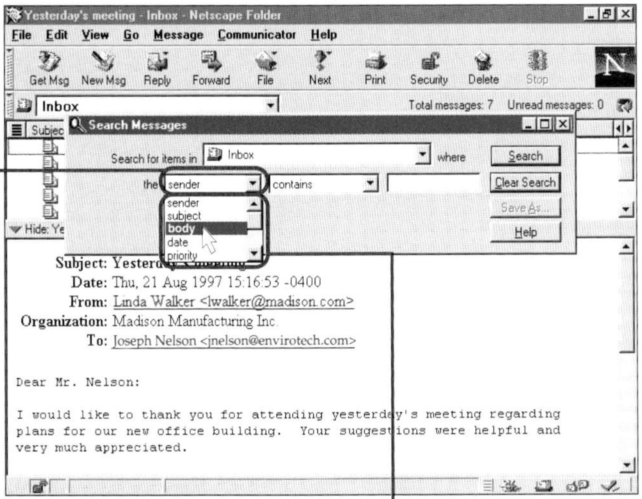

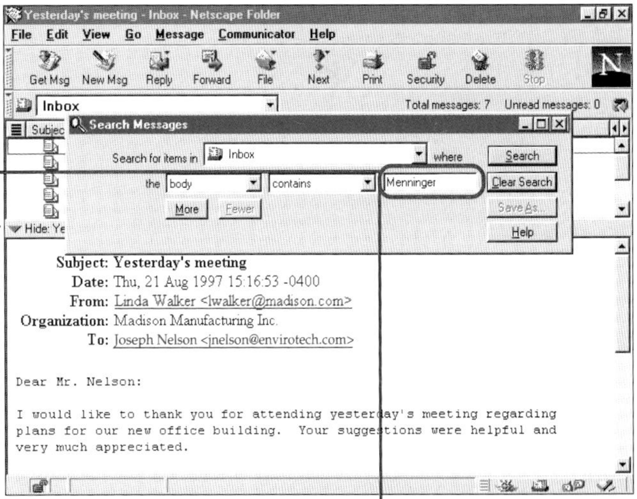

5 Click this area to select the part of each message you want to search.

6 Click the part of each message you want to search.

Note: For information on the parts of a message, refer to the top of this page.

7 Click this area to specify the information you want to search for.

8 Type the information you want to search for.

CONTINUED

SEARCH FOR A MESSAGE

When the search is complete, Messenger displays a list of the messages it found. You can display the contents of any of these messages.

SEARCH FOR A MESSAGE (CONTINUED)

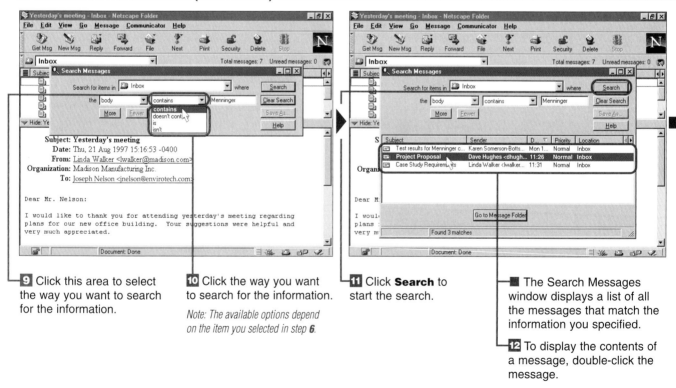

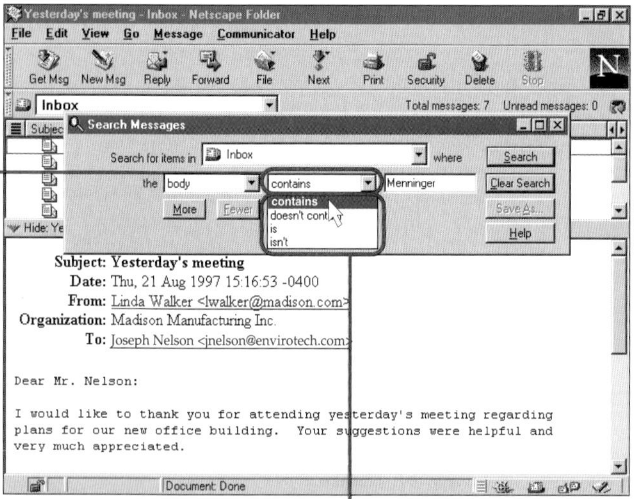

9 Click this area to select the way you want to search for the information.

10 Click the way you want to search for the information.

*Note: The available options depend on the item you selected in step **6**.*

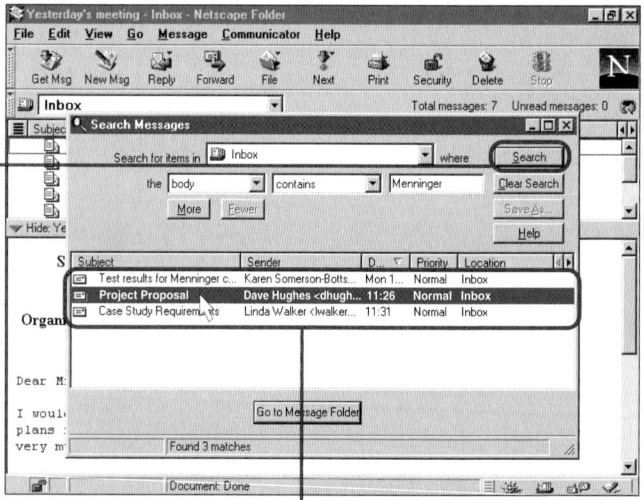

11 Click **Search** to start the search.

■ The Search Messages window displays a list of all the messages that match the information you specified.

12 To display the contents of a message, double-click the message.

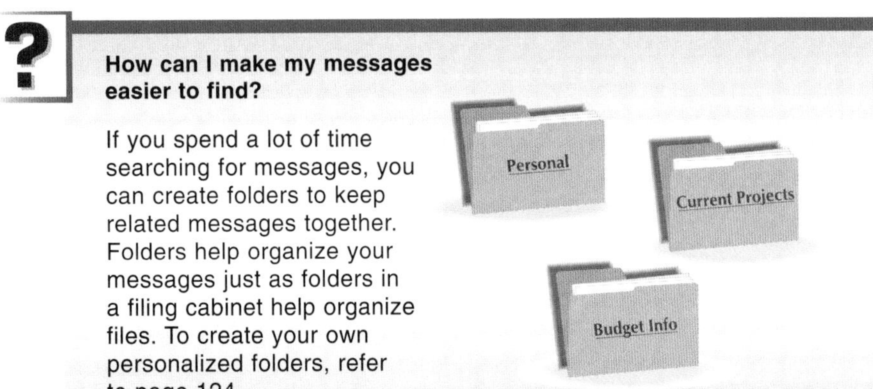

How can I make my messages easier to find?

If you spend a lot of time searching for messages, you can create folders to keep related messages together. Folders help organize your messages just as folders in a filing cabinet help organize files. To create your own personalized folders, refer to page 124.

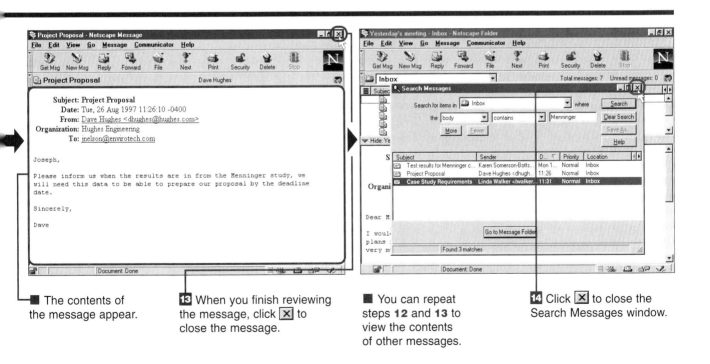

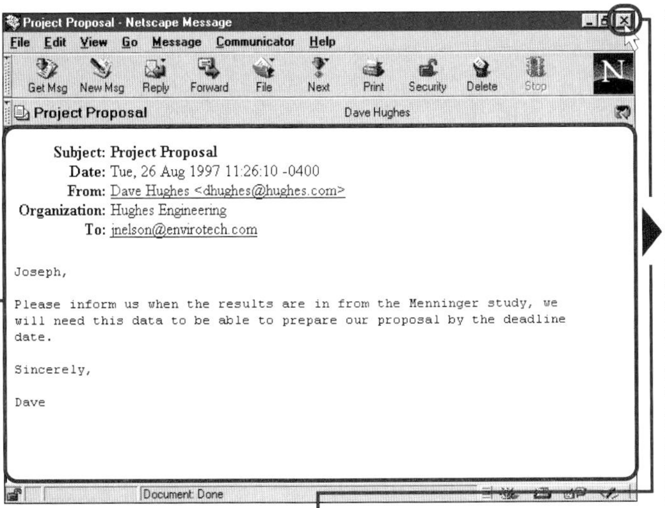

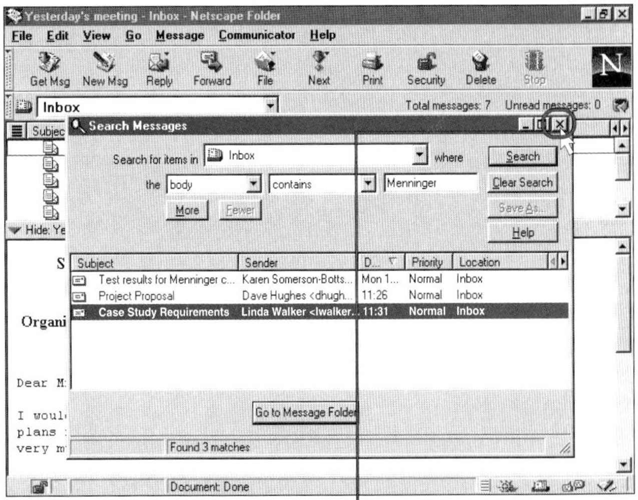

■ The contents of the message appear.

13 When you finish reviewing the message, click ☒ to close the message.

■ You can repeat steps **12** and **13** to view the contents of other messages.

14 Click ☒ to close the Search Messages window.

USE A MAIL FILTER

You can have Messenger act as your personal assistant by filtering messages you receive.

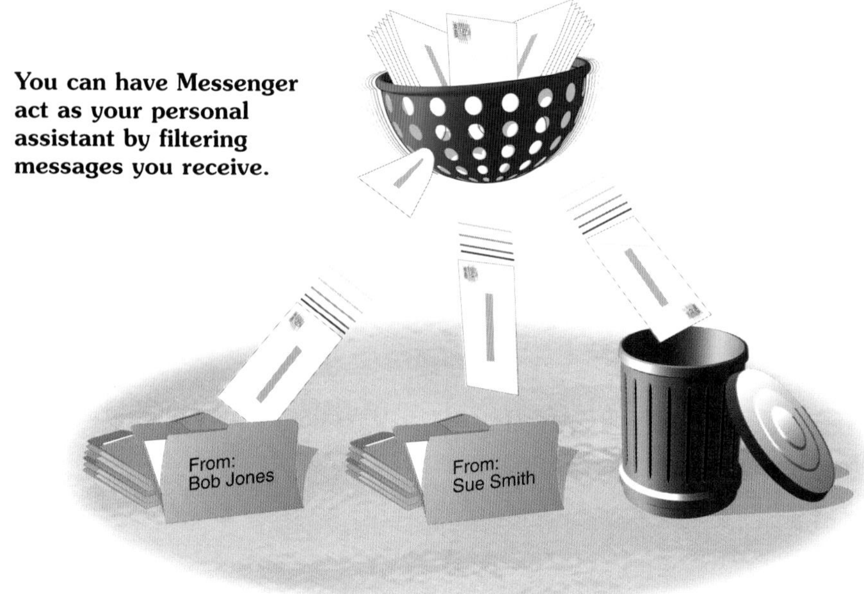

For example, you can use a filter to place specific messages you receive directly into personalized folders. You could also use a filter to immediately delete certain messages you receive.

USE A MAIL FILTER

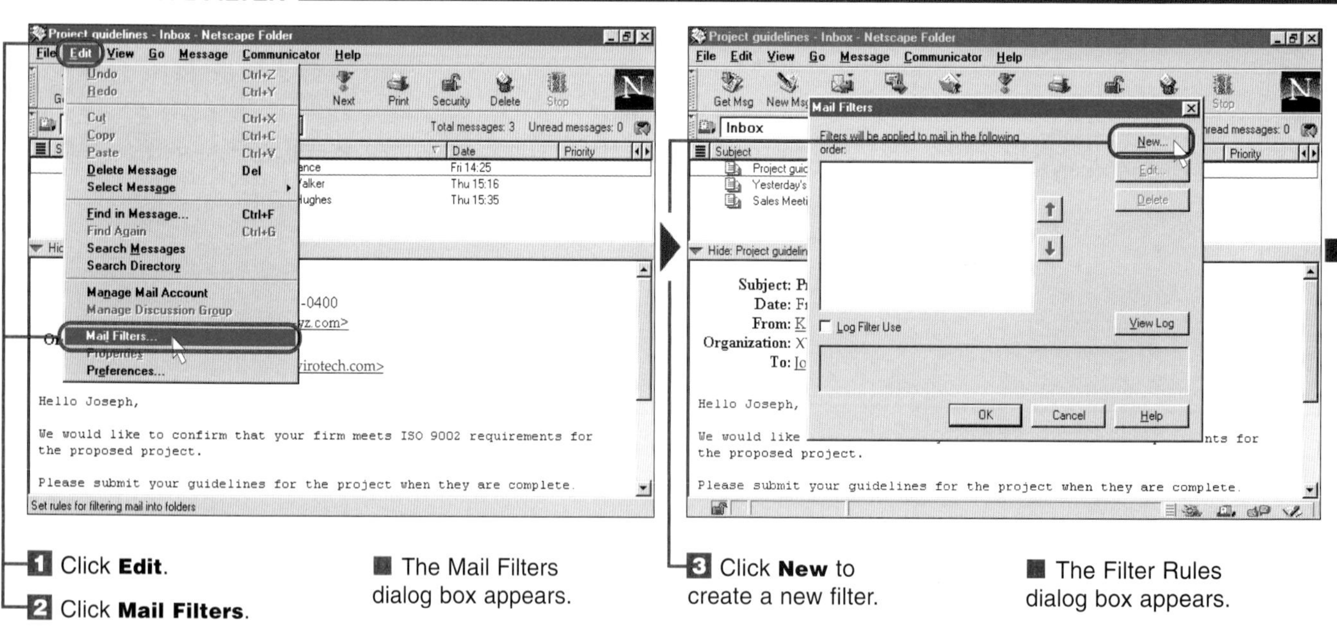

1 Click **Edit**.

2 Click **Mail Filters**.

■ The Mail Filters dialog box appears.

3 Click **New** to create a new filter.

■ The Filter Rules dialog box appears.

Which part of each message can Messenger search to filter my messages?

There are several parts of each message that you can have Messenger search.

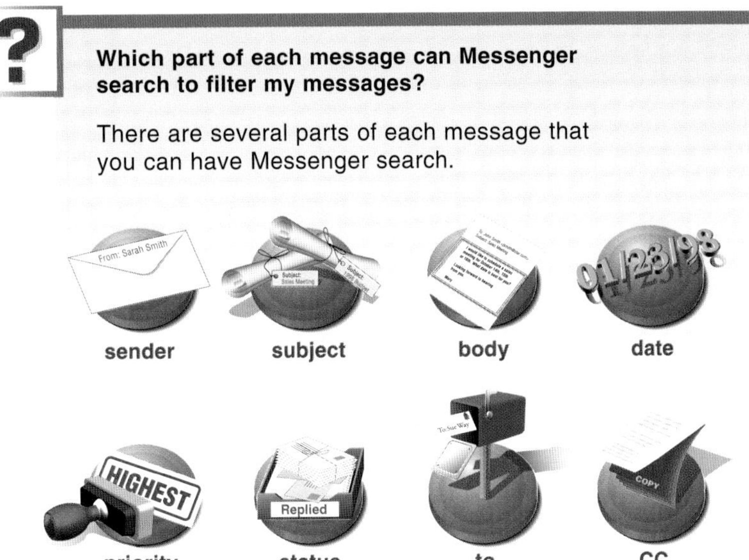

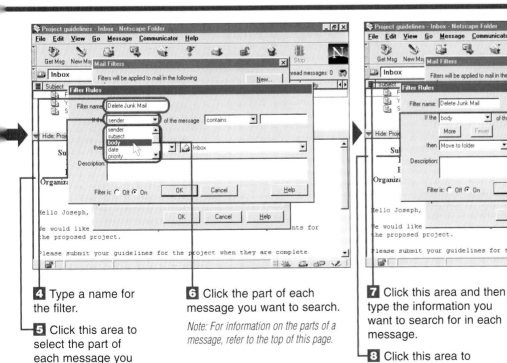

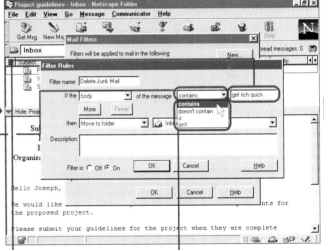

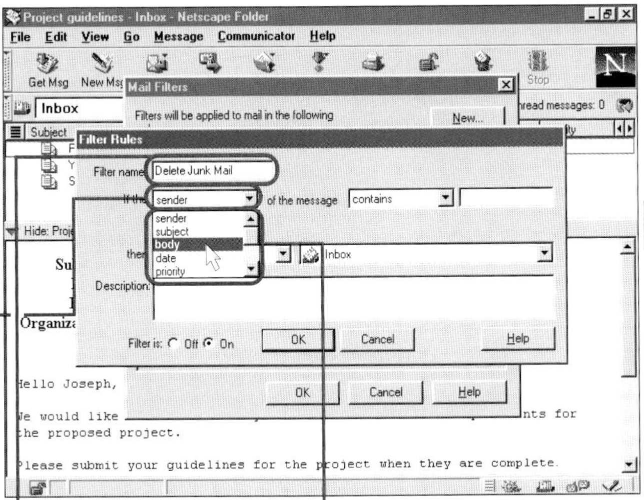

4 Type a name for the filter.

5 Click this area to select the part of each message you want to search to filter your messages.

6 Click the part of each message you want to search.

Note: For information on the parts of a message, refer to the top of this page.

7 Click this area and then type the information you want to search for in each message.

8 Click this area to select the way you want to search for the information.

9 Click the way you want to search for the information.

*Note: The available options depend on the item you selected in step **6**.*

CONTINUED

You can specify what you want Messenger to do with received messages that match the information you specified.

Move to folder

Place messages in a folder you specify.

Change priority

Change the priority of the messages.

Delete

Place messages in the Trash folder.

USE A MAIL FILTER (CONTINUED)

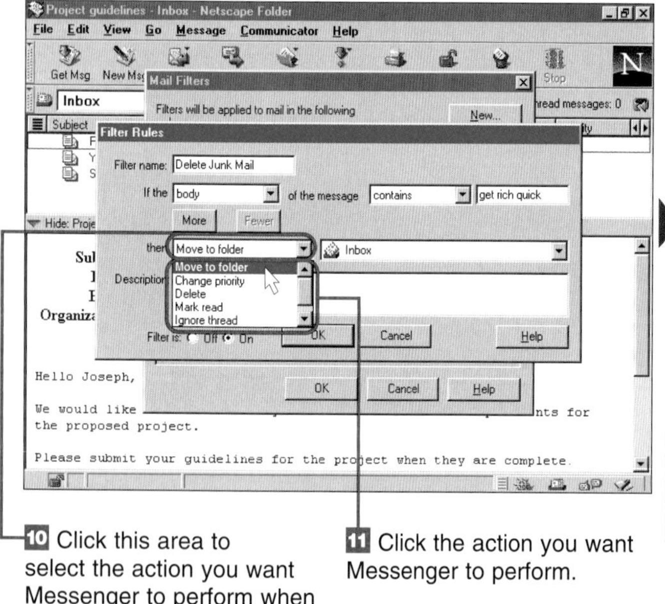

10 Click this area to select the action you want Messenger to perform when a message matches the information you specified.

11 Click the action you want Messenger to perform.

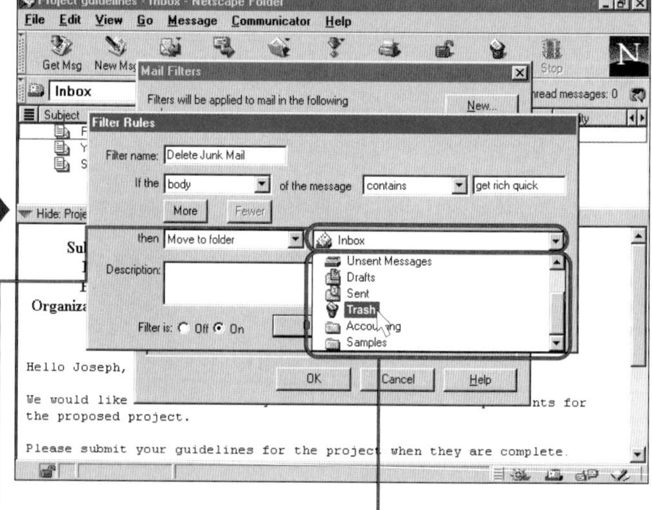

12 Click this area to display a list of folders where Messenger can place the messages.

*Note: This area may be blank or display different options, depending on the action you selected in step **11**.*

13 Click the folder where you want Messenger to place the messages.

Mark read

Mark the messages as read.

Ignore thread

Ignore messages in the thread.

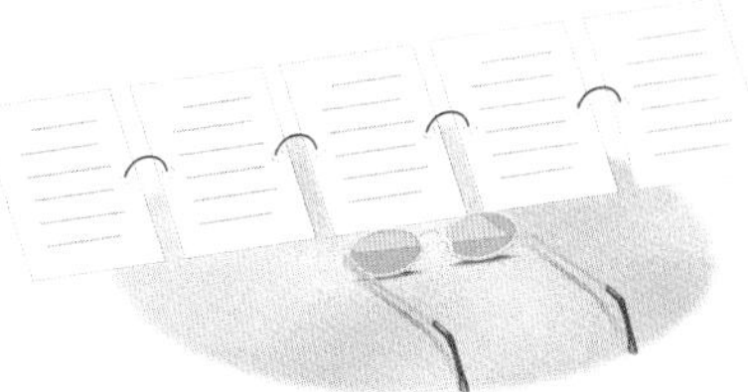

Watch thread

Watch messages in the thread.

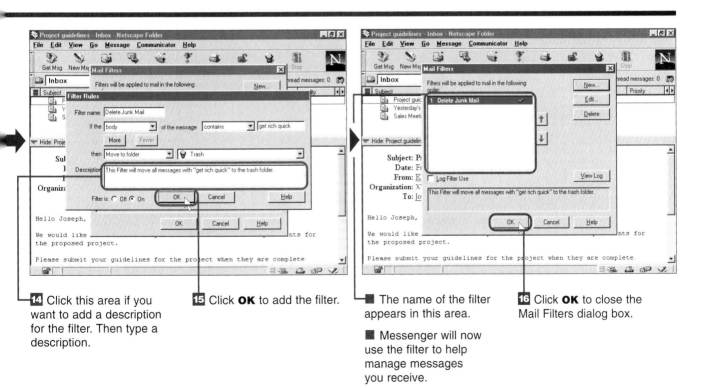

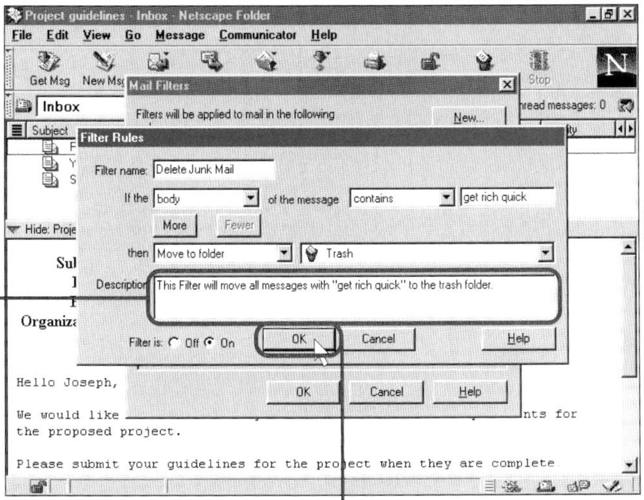

14 Click this area if you want to add a description for the filter. Then type a description.

15 Click **OK** to add the filter.

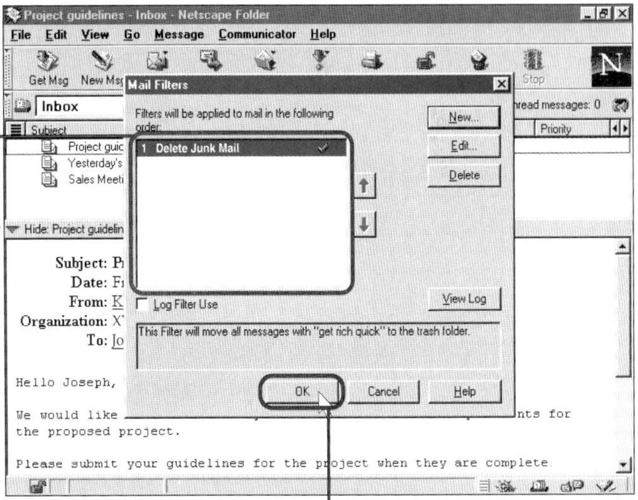

■ The name of the filter appears in this area.

■ Messenger will now use the filter to help manage messages you receive.

16 Click **OK** to close the Mail Filters dialog box.

WORK WITH FILTERS

You can easily work with filters you have created.

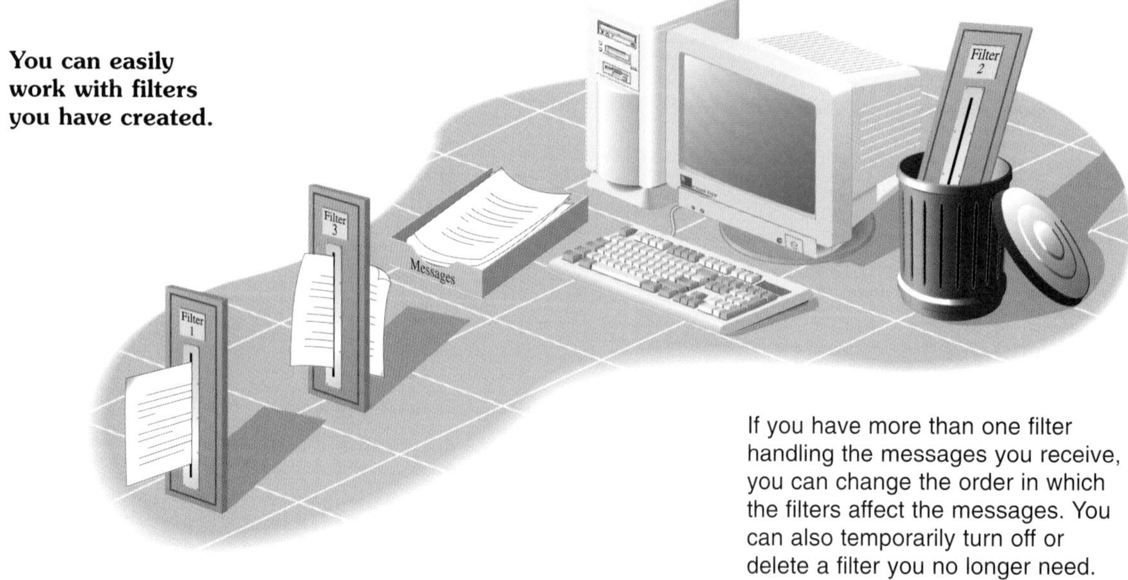

If you have more than one filter handling the messages you receive, you can change the order in which the filters affect the messages. You can also temporarily turn off or delete a filter you no longer need.

WORK WITH FILTERS

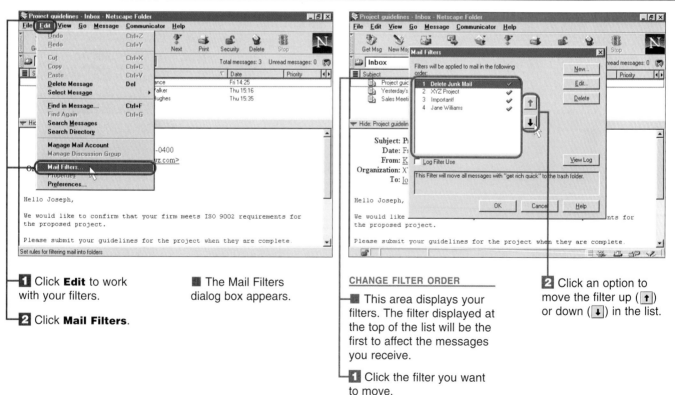

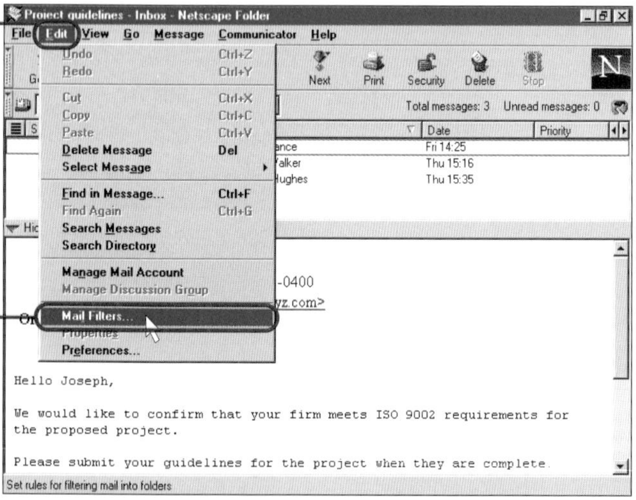

1 Click **Edit** to work with your filters.

2 Click **Mail Filters**.

■ The Mail Filters dialog box appears.

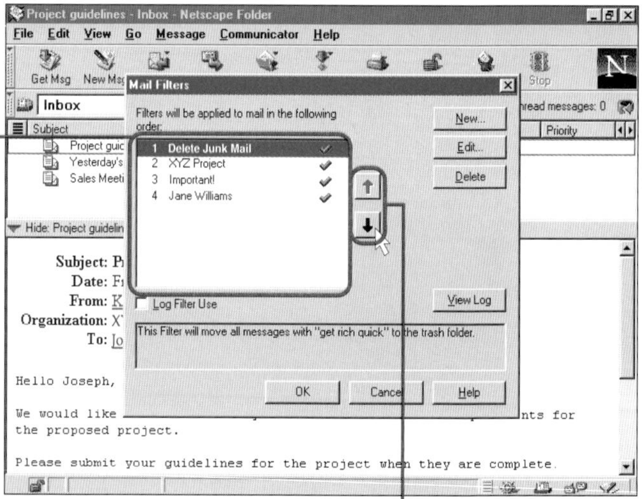

CHANGE FILTER ORDER

■ This area displays your filters. The filter displayed at the top of the list will be the first to affect the messages you receive.

1 Click the filter you want to move.

2 Click an option to move the filter up (↑) or down (↓) in the list.

? Why would I need to change the order of my filters?

You may need to change the order of your filters to make sure the filters affect messages in the proper order. For example, one filter could place messages from a colleague directly into a personalized folder. Another filter could delete any messages containing the phrase "make money fast." You should filter your colleague's messages first in case your colleague sends you a message containing the phrase "make money fast." This ensures that your colleague's messages will not be accidentally deleted.

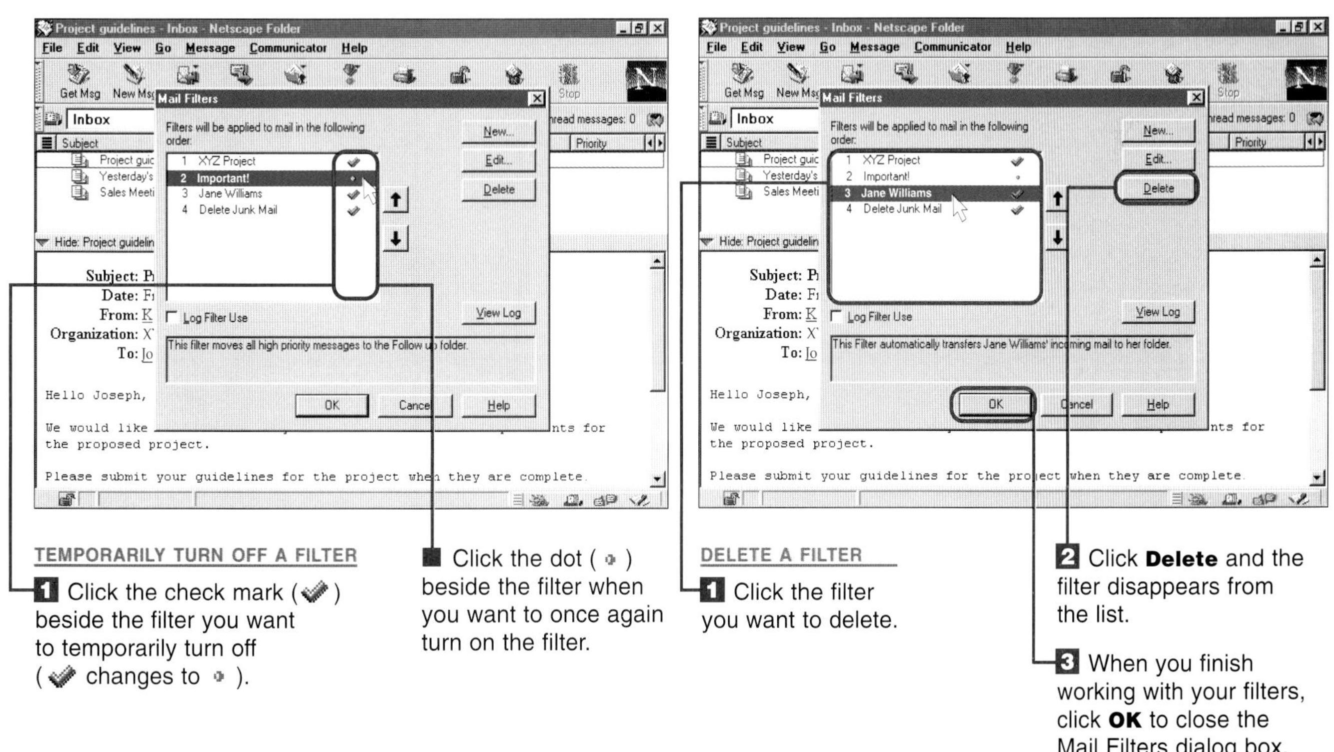

TEMPORARILY TURN OFF A FILTER

1 Click the check mark (✔) beside the filter you want to temporarily turn off (✔ changes to •).

■ Click the dot (•) beside the filter when you want to once again turn on the filter.

DELETE A FILTER

1 Click the filter you want to delete.

2 Click **Delete** and the filter disappears from the list.

3 When you finish working with your filters, click **OK** to close the Mail Filters dialog box.

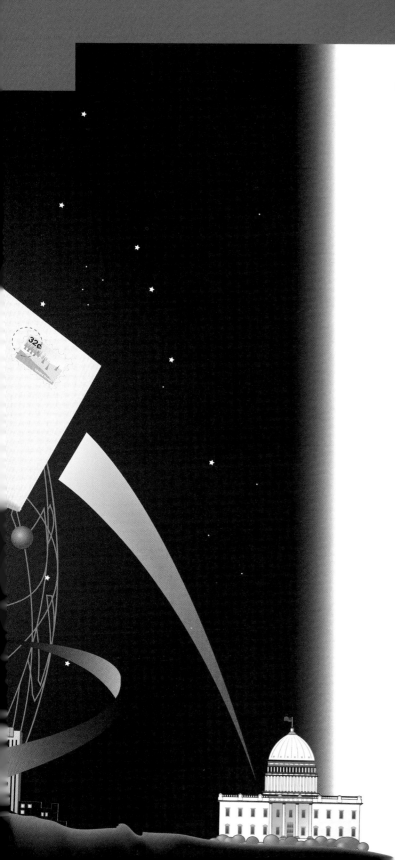

CHAPTER 6

Send E-Mail Messages

Are you ready to send e-mail messages to friends and colleagues around the world? This chapter shows you how to create new messages, attach files and Web pages to messages, find e-mail addresses and much more.

REPLY TO A MESSAGE

You can reply to a message to answer a question, express an opinion or supply additional information.

REPLY TO A MESSAGE

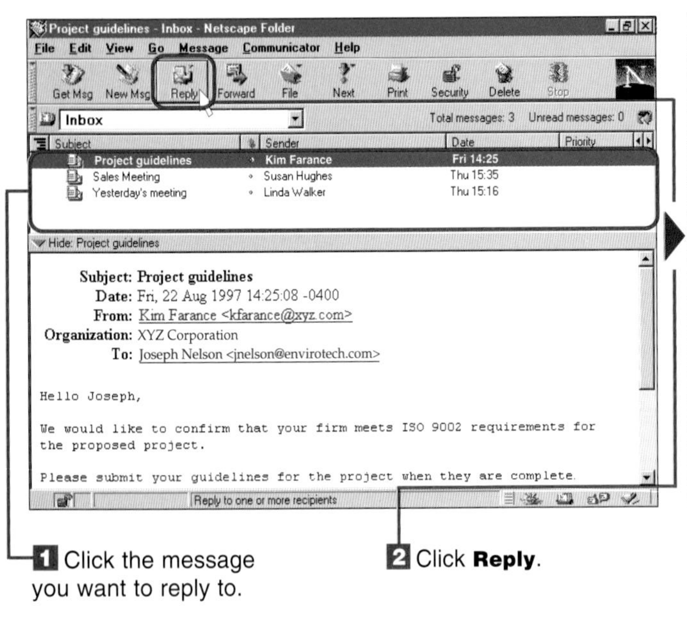

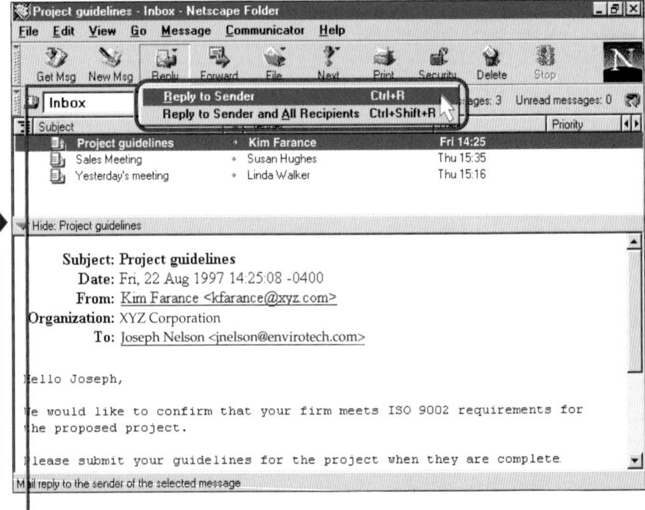

1 Click the message you want to reply to.

2 Click **Reply**.

3 Click an option to reply just to the sender or to the sender and everyone who received the original message.

? How can I emphasize information in my reply?

You can emphasize information in your reply in many ways, such as changing the design of text or using the bold or underline features. For more information, refer to pages 154 to 157.

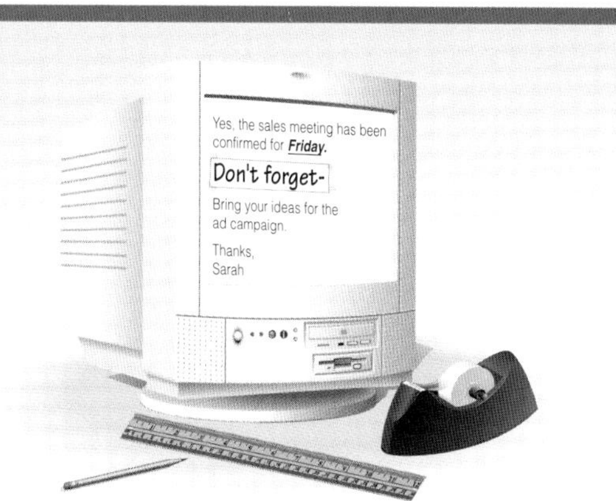

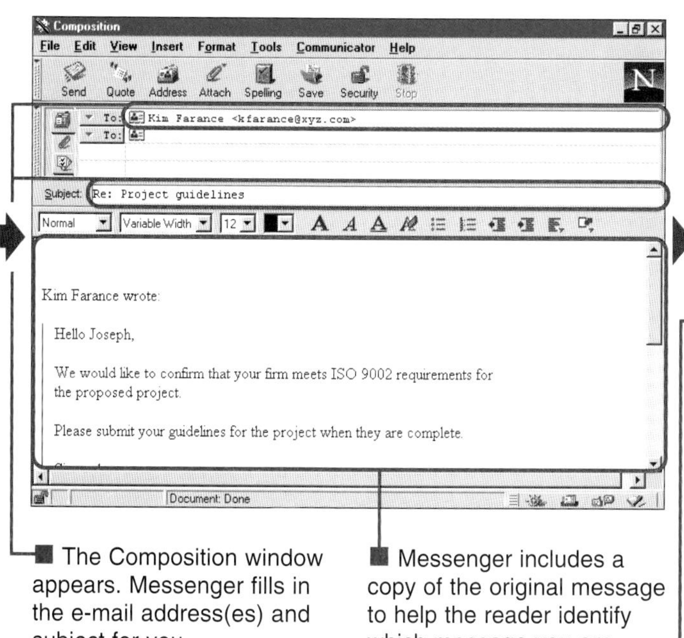

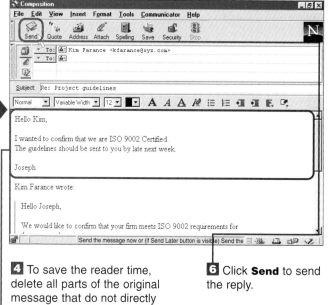

■ The Composition window appears. Messenger fills in the e-mail address(es) and subject for you.

■ Messenger includes a copy of the original message to help the reader identify which message you are replying to. This is called quoting. A blue line appears beside the quoted text.

4 To save the reader time, delete all parts of the original message that do not directly relate to your reply.

5 To add your comments to the message, click the area where you want the reply to appear and then type your reply.

6 Click **Send** to send the reply.

FORWARD A MESSAGE

After reading a message you received, you can add comments and then send the message to a friend or colleague.

FORWARD A MESSAGE

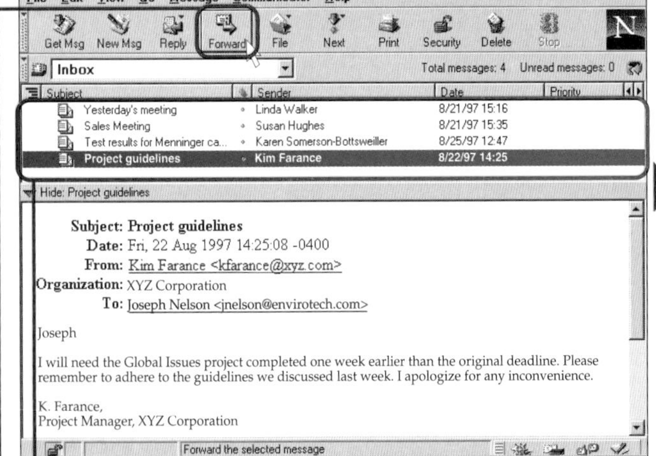

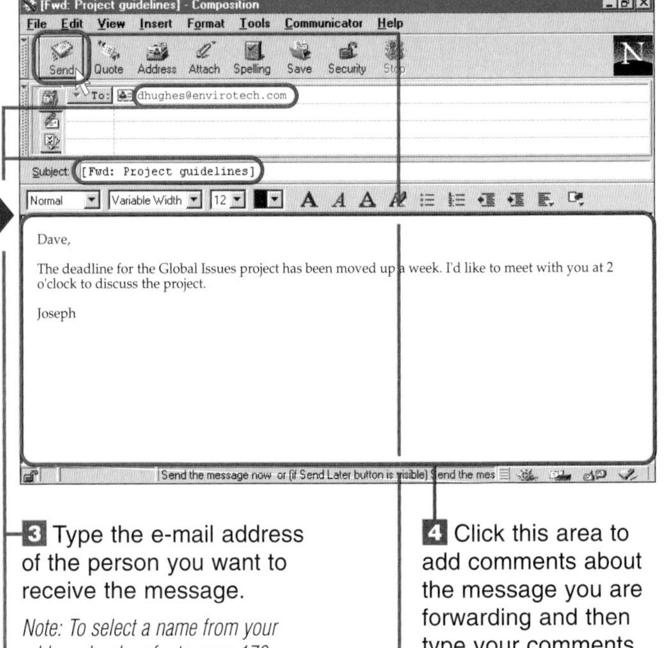

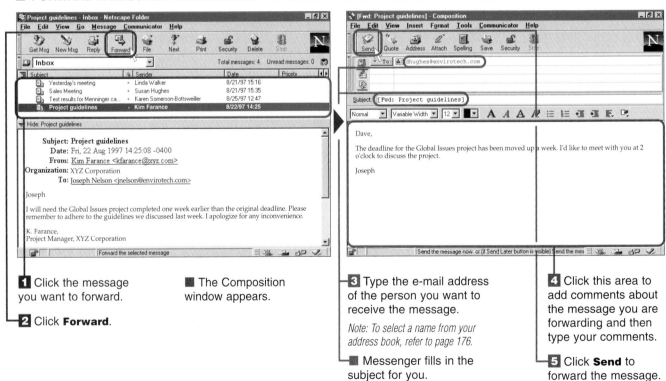

1 Click the message you want to forward.

2 Click **Forward**.

■ The Composition window appears.

3 Type the e-mail address of the person you want to receive the message.

Note: To select a name from your address book, refer to page 176.

■ Messenger fills in the subject for you.

4 Click this area to add comments about the message you are forwarding and then type your comments.

5 Click **Send** to forward the message.

?

Why would I forward a quoted message?

Forwarding a quoted message displays the message in the Composition window. This allows you to make changes to the text before forwarding the message.

Jim,
Would you be interested in going?
The sales conference will be held this Friday at 4 PM.

FORWARD A QUOTED MESSAGE

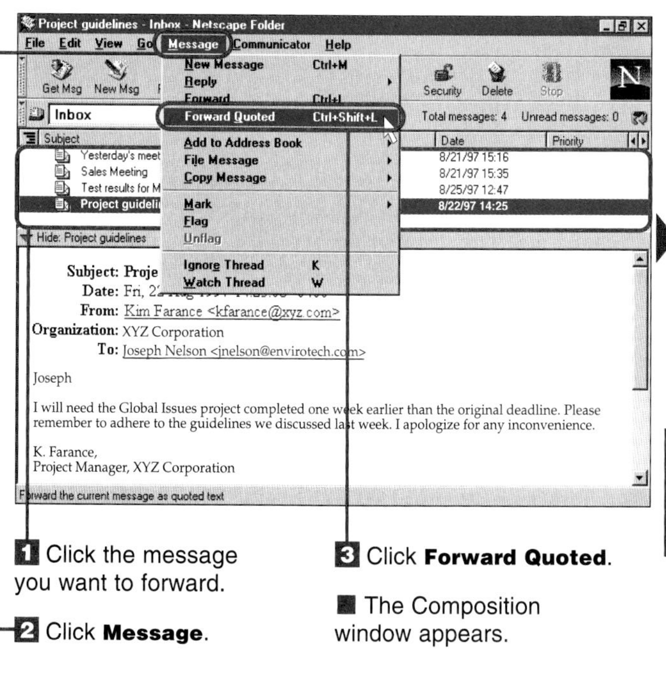

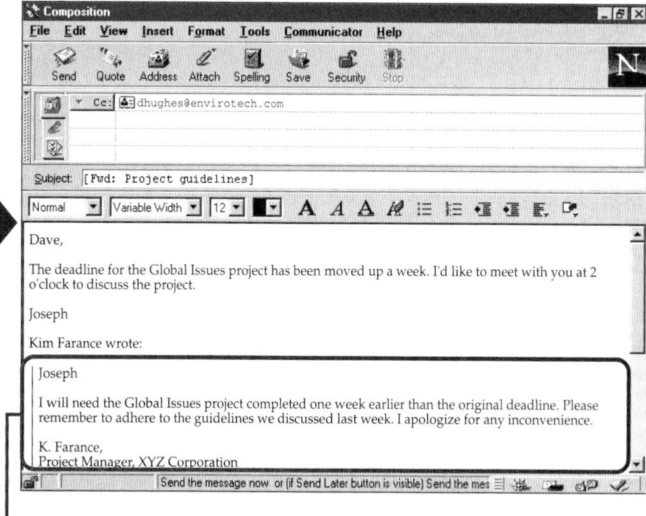

1 Click the message you want to forward.

2 Click **Message**.

3 Click **Forward Quoted**.

■ The Composition window appears.

■ The message you are forwarding appears in the window. A blue line appears beside the text.

4 To complete the message, perform steps **3** to **5** on page 150.

CREATE A NEW MESSAGE

You can send a message to exchange ideas or request information.

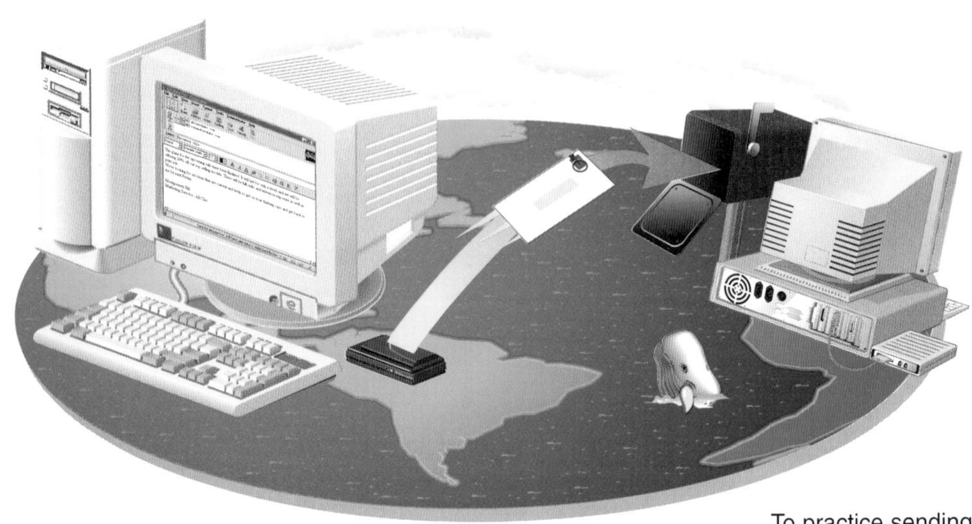

To practice sending a message, you can send a message to yourself.

CREATE A NEW MESSAGE

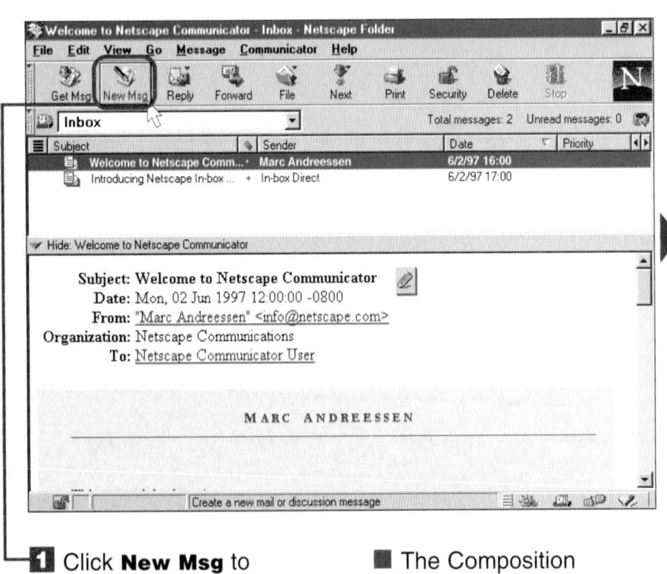

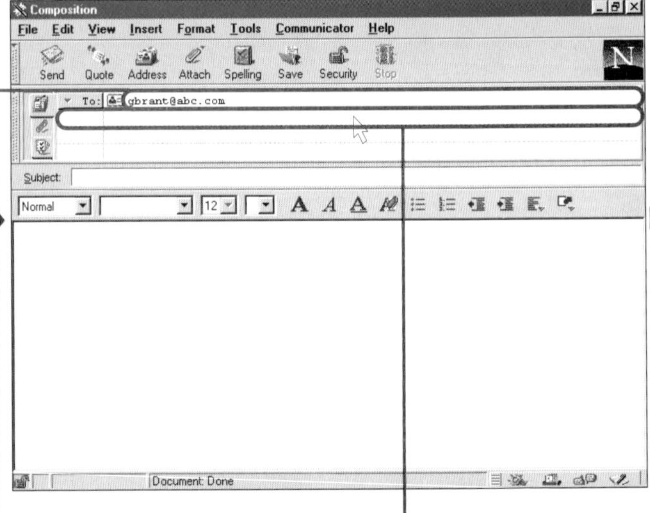

1 Click **New Msg** to create a new message.

■ The Composition window appears.

2 Type the e-mail address of the person you want to receive the message.

*Note: To select a name from your address book, refer to page 176. Then skip to step **8**.*

3 To send the message to another person, click the first blank space below the To button.

How can I address a message I want to send to more than one person?

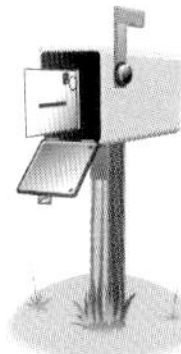

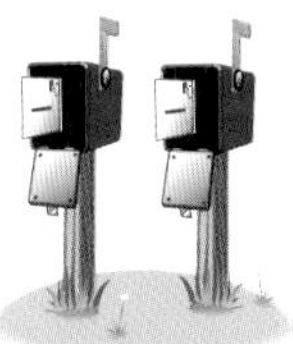

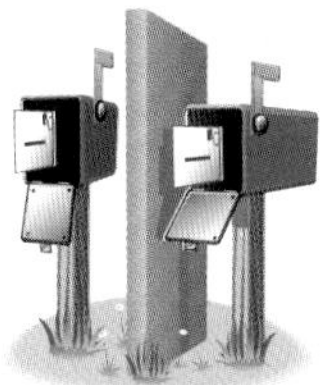

To

Sends the original message to the person you specify.

Carbon Copy (Cc)

Sends an exact copy of the message to a person who is not directly involved, but would be interested in the message.

Blind Carbon Copy (Bcc)

Sends an exact copy of the message to a person without anyone else knowing that the person received the message.

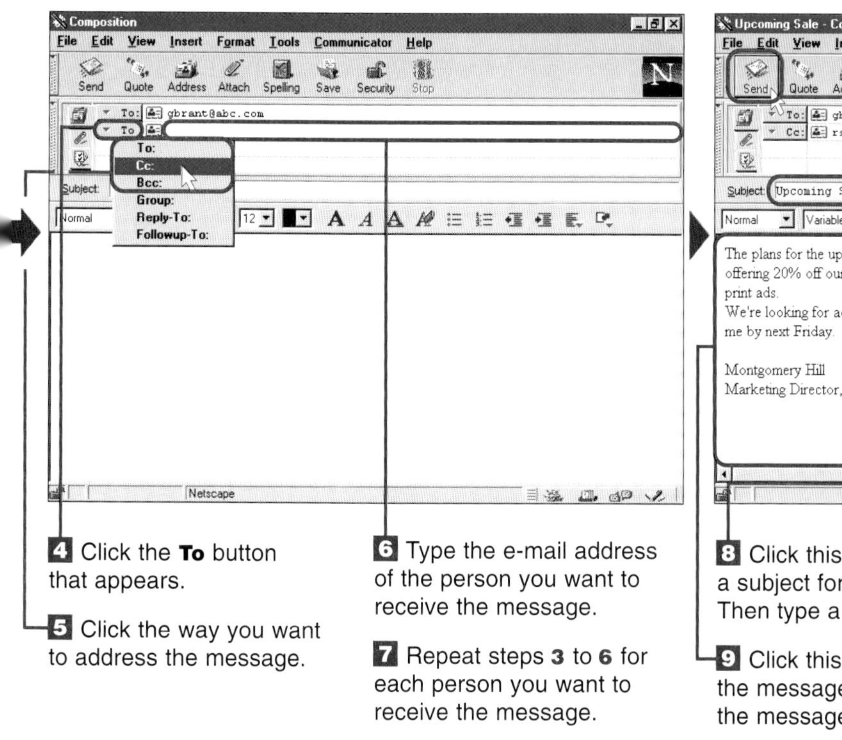

4 Click the **To** button that appears.

5 Click the way you want to address the message.

6 Type the e-mail address of the person you want to receive the message.

7 Repeat steps **3** to **6** for each person you want to receive the message.

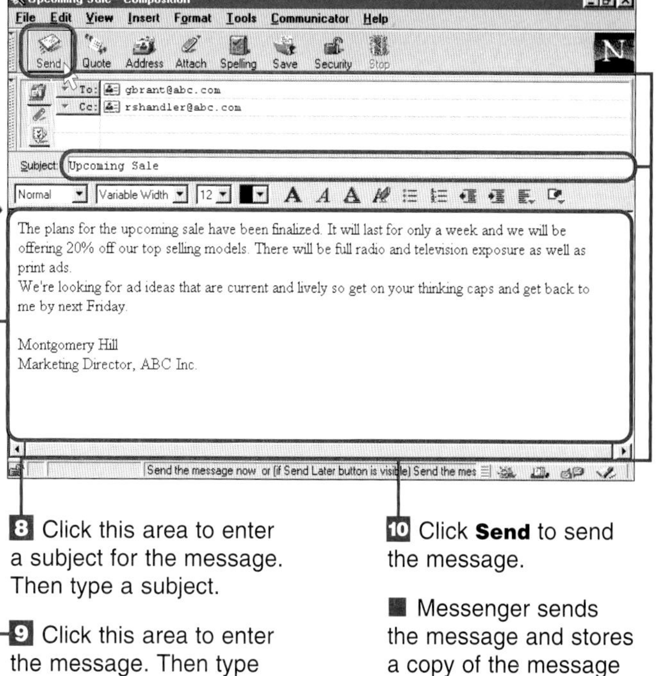

8 Click this area to enter a subject for the message. Then type a subject.

9 Click this area to enter the message. Then type the message.

10 Click **Send** to send the message.

■ Messenger sends the message and stores a copy of the message in the Sent folder.

CHANGE FONT AND FONT SIZE

You can change the design and size of text in a message.

Changing the design and size of text allows you to emphasize text and make your message more interesting and attractive.

CHANGE FONT

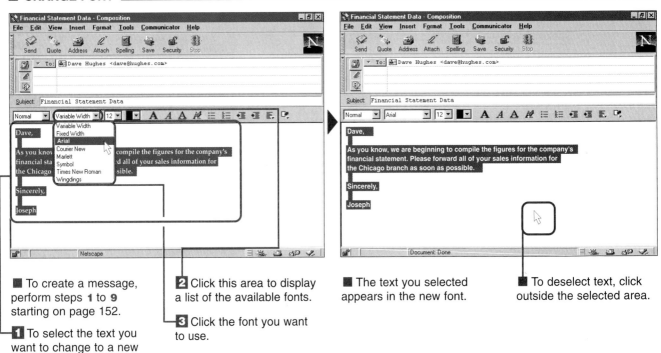

■ To create a message, perform steps 1 to 9 starting on page 152.

1 To select the text you want to change to a new font, drag the mouse over the text.

2 Click this area to display a list of the available fonts.

3 Click the font you want to use.

■ The text you selected appears in the new font.

■ To deselect text, click outside the selected area.

?

Why does a dialog box appear when I try to send a message?

Messenger may display a dialog box when you try to send a message that contains formatting. If the person you are sending the message to does not use Messenger or another e-mail program that can view formatting in messages, you should select the **Send in Plain Text Only** option.

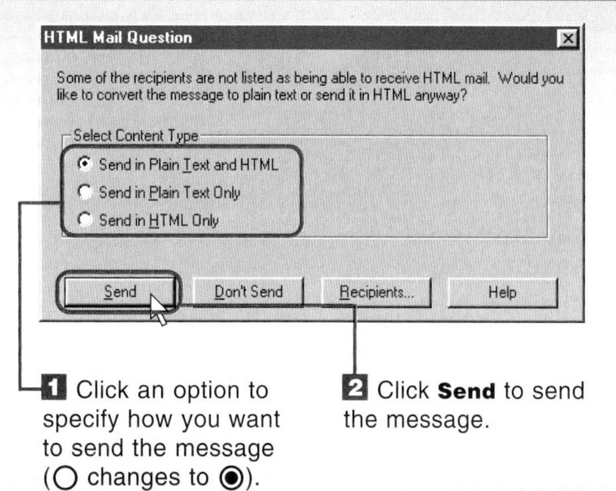

1 Click an option to specify how you want to send the message (○ changes to ◉).

2 Click **Send** to send the message.

CHANGE FONT SIZE

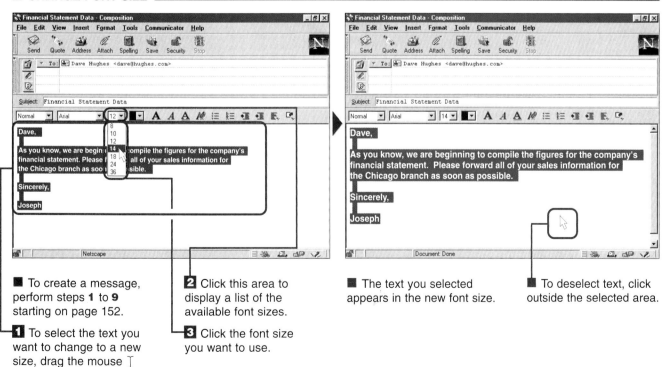

■ To create a message, perform steps **1** to **9** starting on page 152.

1 To select the text you want to change to a new size, drag the mouse I over the text.

2 Click this area to display a list of the available font sizes.

3 Click the font size you want to use.

■ The text you selected appears in the new font size.

■ To deselect text, click outside the selected area.

BOLD, ITALIC AND UNDERLINE

You can use the bold, italic and underline styles to emphasize information in a message.

BOLD, ITALIC AND UNDERLINE

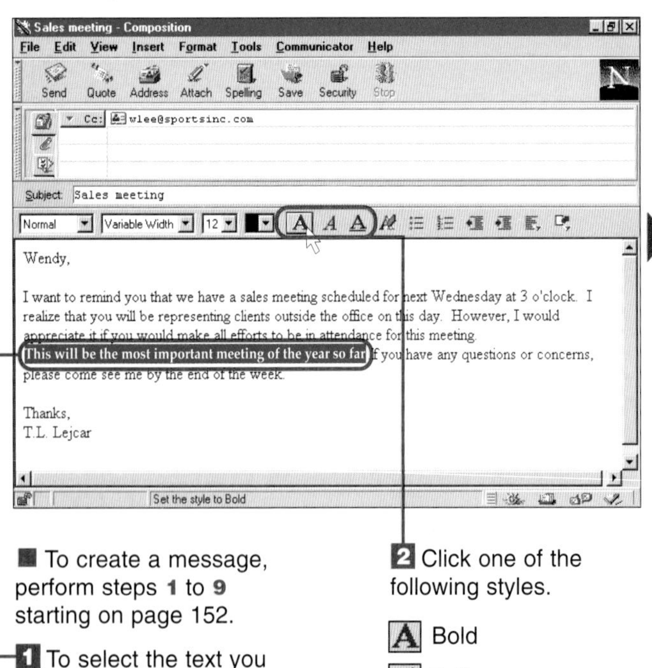

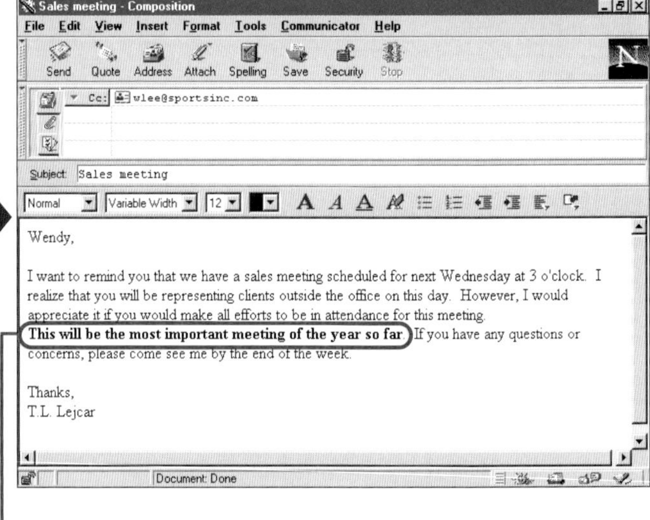

■ To create a message, perform steps **1** to **9** starting on page 152.

1 To select the text you want to change to a new style, drag the mouse over the text.

2 Click one of the following styles.

- Bold
- Italic
- Underline

■ The text you selected appears in the new style.

■ To deselect text, click outside the selected area.

■ To remove a bold, italic or underline style, repeat steps **1** and **2**.

Note: The HTML Mail Question dialog box may appear when you send the message. For information on this dialog box, refer to the top of page 155.

CHANGE TEXT COLOR

You can change the color of text in your message to draw attention to important information.

CHANGE TEXT COLOR

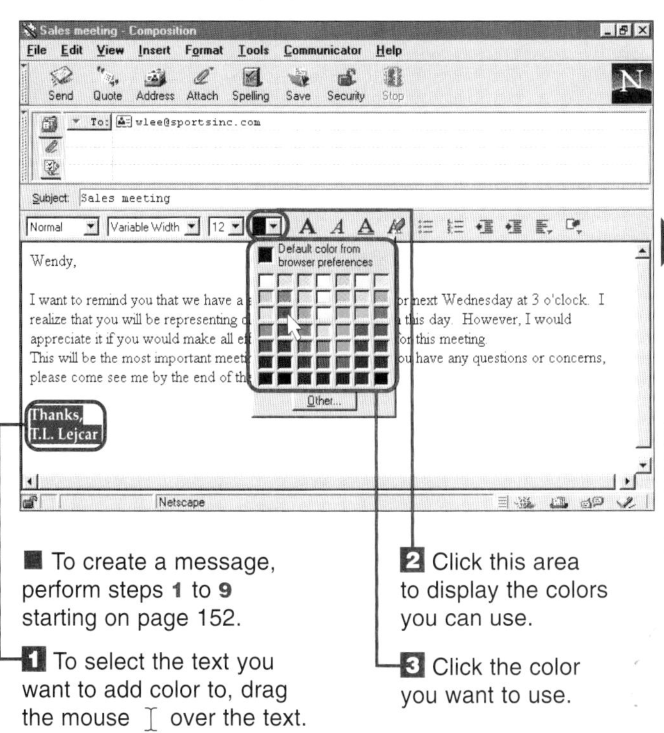

■ To create a message, perform steps **1** to **9** starting on page 152.

1 To select the text you want to add color to, drag the mouse I over the text.

2 Click this area to display the colors you can use.

3 Click the color you want to use.

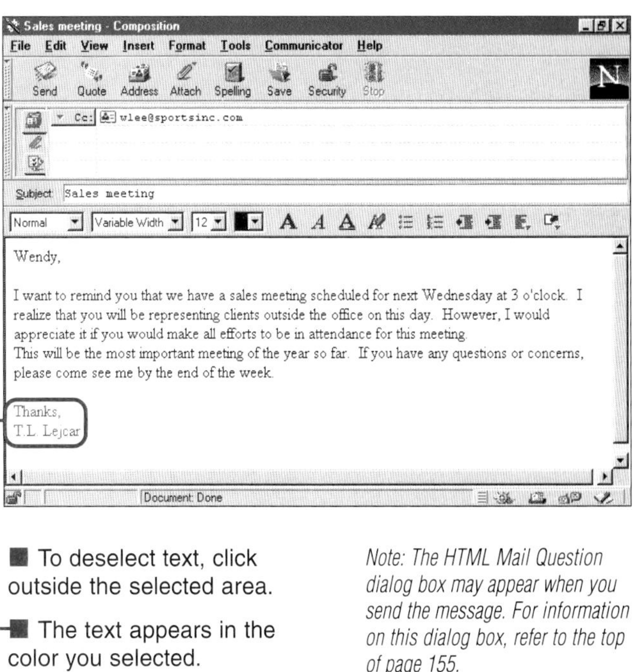

■ To deselect text, click outside the selected area.

■ The text appears in the color you selected.

Note: The HTML Mail Question dialog box may appear when you send the message. For information on this dialog box, refer to the top of page 155.

CHECK SPELLING

You can quickly find and correct all the spelling errors in a message you are about to send.

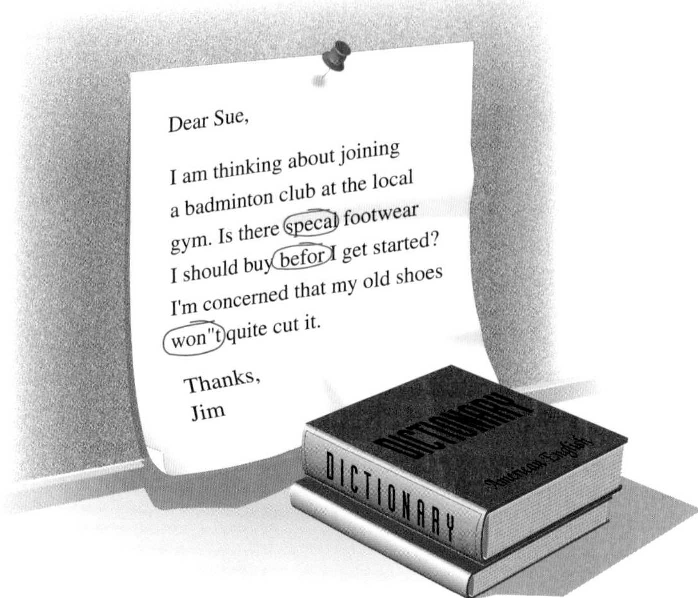

Dear Sue,
I am thinking about joining a badminton club at the local gym. Is there specal footwear I should buy befor I get started? I'm concerned that my old shoes won"t quite cut it.
Thanks,
Jim
DICTIONARY
American English

CHECK SPELLING

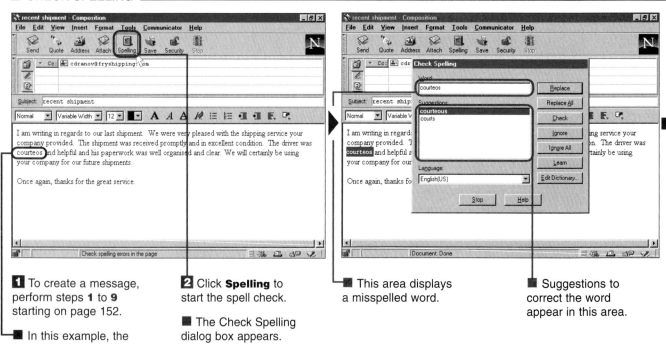

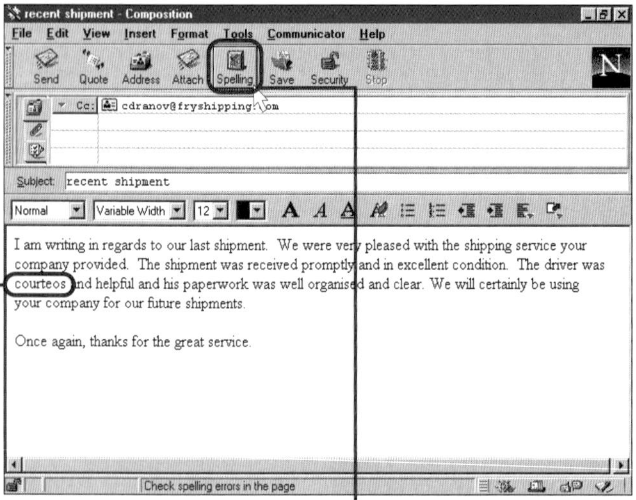

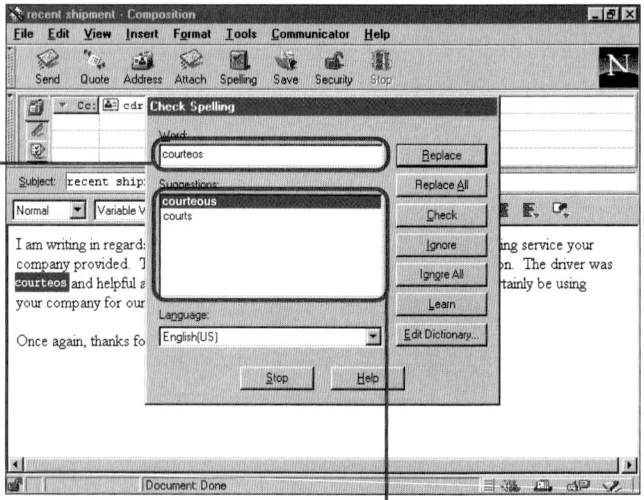

1 To create a message, perform steps **1** to **9** starting on page 152.

■ In this example, the spelling of **courteous** was changed to **courteos**.

2 Click **Spelling** to start the spell check.

■ The Check Spelling dialog box appears.

■ This area displays a misspelled word.

■ Suggestions to correct the word appear in this area.

? Will Messenger find all the spelling errors in my message?

Messenger compares every word in your message to words in its own dictionary. If a word does not exist in the dictionary, Messenger considers the word misspelled.

Messenger will not find a correctly spelled word used in the wrong context such as "The girl is **sit** years old". You should carefully reread your message to find this type of error.

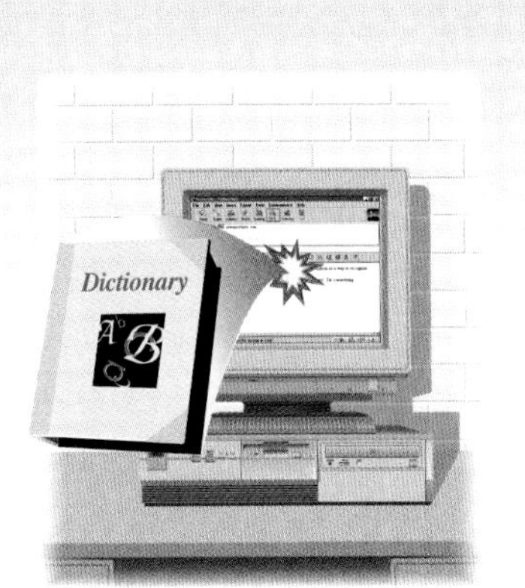

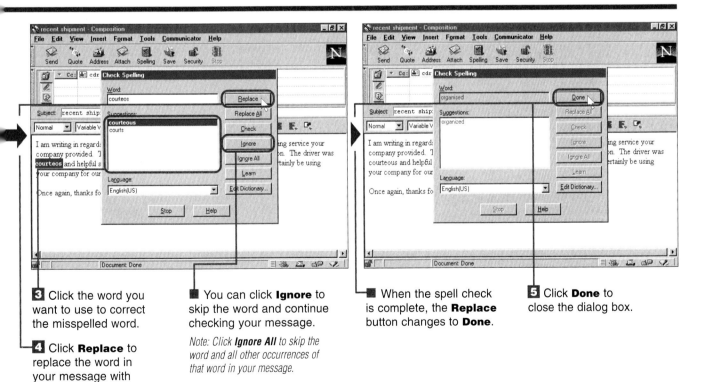

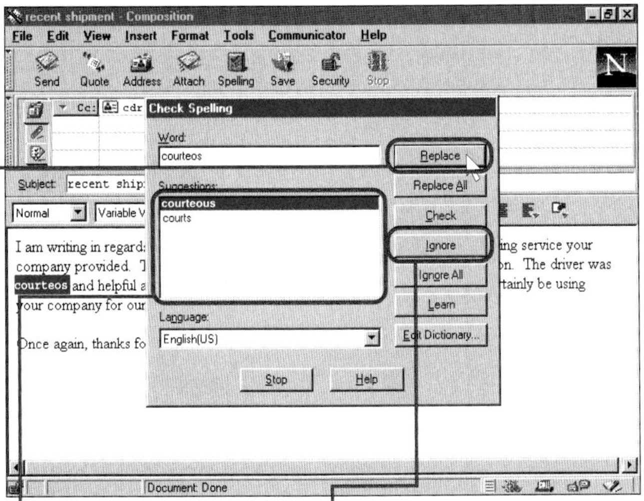

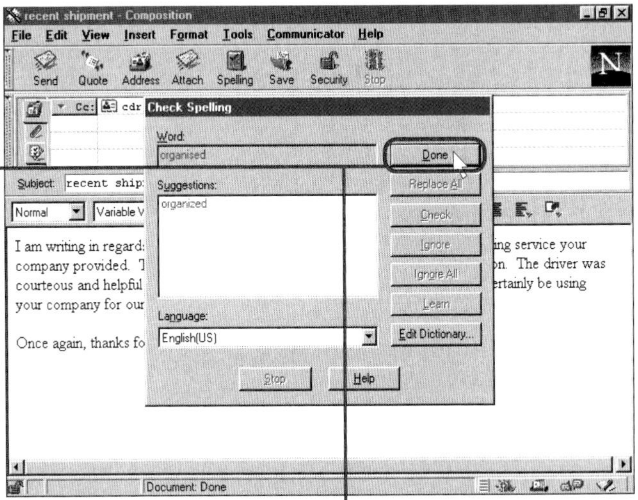

3 Click the word you want to use to correct the misspelled word.

4 Click **Replace** to replace the word in your message with the correct spelling.

■ You can click **Ignore** to skip the word and continue checking your message.

*Note: Click **Ignore All** to skip the word and all other occurrences of that word in your message.*

■ When the spell check is complete, the **Replace** button changes to **Done**.

5 Click **Done** to close the dialog box.

ATTACH A FILE TO A MESSAGE

You can attach a file to a message you are sending. Attaching a file is useful when you want to include additional information with a message.

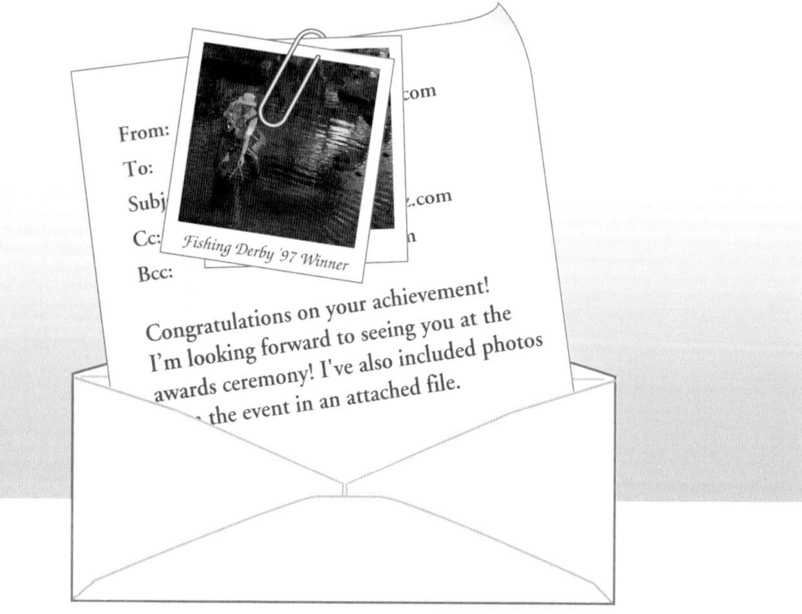

From:
To:
Cc:
Bcc:
Fishing Derby '97 Winner
Congratulations on your achievement!
I'm looking forward to seeing you at the
awards ceremony! I've also included photos
the event in an attached file.

ATTACH A FILE TO A MESSAGE

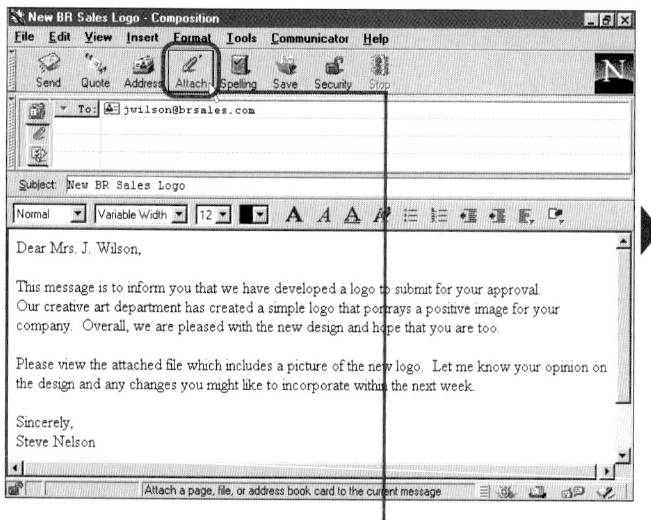

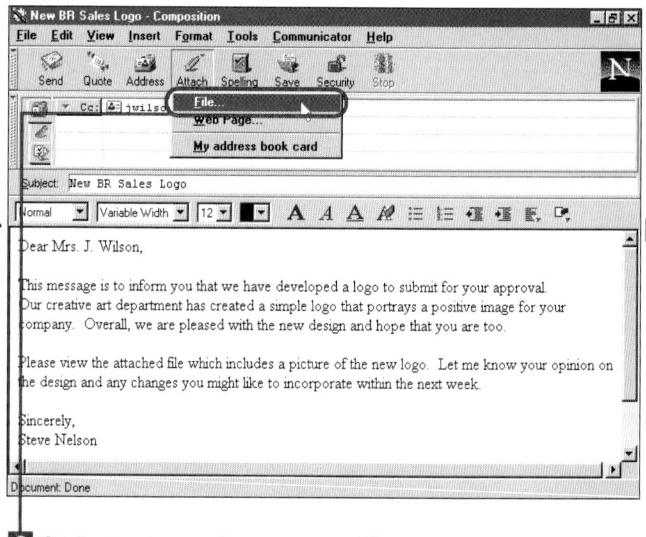

1 To create a message, perform steps **1** to **9** starting on page 152.

2 Click **Attach**.

3 Click **File** to attach a file to the message.

■ The Enter file to attach dialog box appears.

? What type of information can I attach to a message?

You can attach information such as documents, pictures, programs, sounds or videos to a message. The computer receiving the message must have the necessary software to display or play the file.

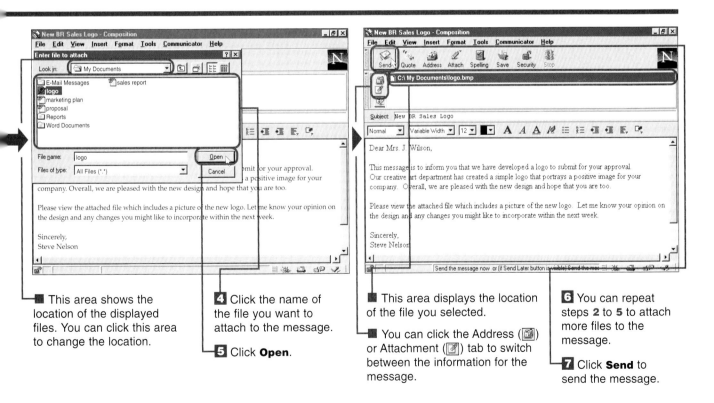

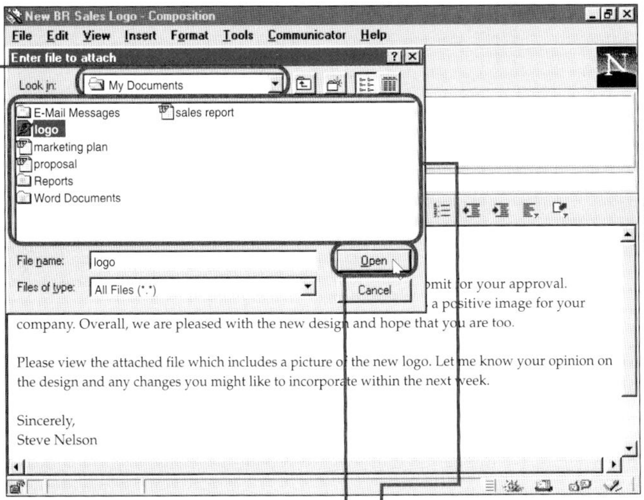

■ This area shows the location of the displayed files. You can click this area to change the location.

4 Click the name of the file you want to attach to the message.

5 Click **Open**.

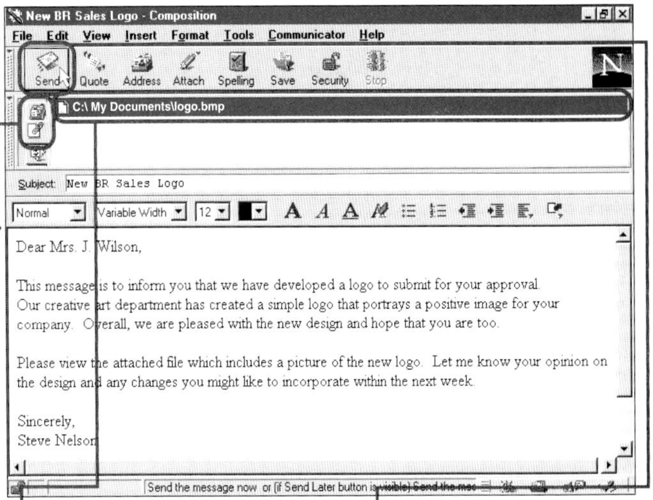

■ This area displays the location of the file you selected.

■ You can click the Address (📇) or Attachment (📎) tab to switch between the information for the message.

6 You can repeat steps **2** to **5** to attach more files to the message.

7 Click **Send** to send the message.

ATTACH A WEB PAGE TO A MESSAGE

When sending a message, you can attach a Web page that would be of interest to the person receiving the message.

ATTACH A WEB PAGE TO A MESSAGE

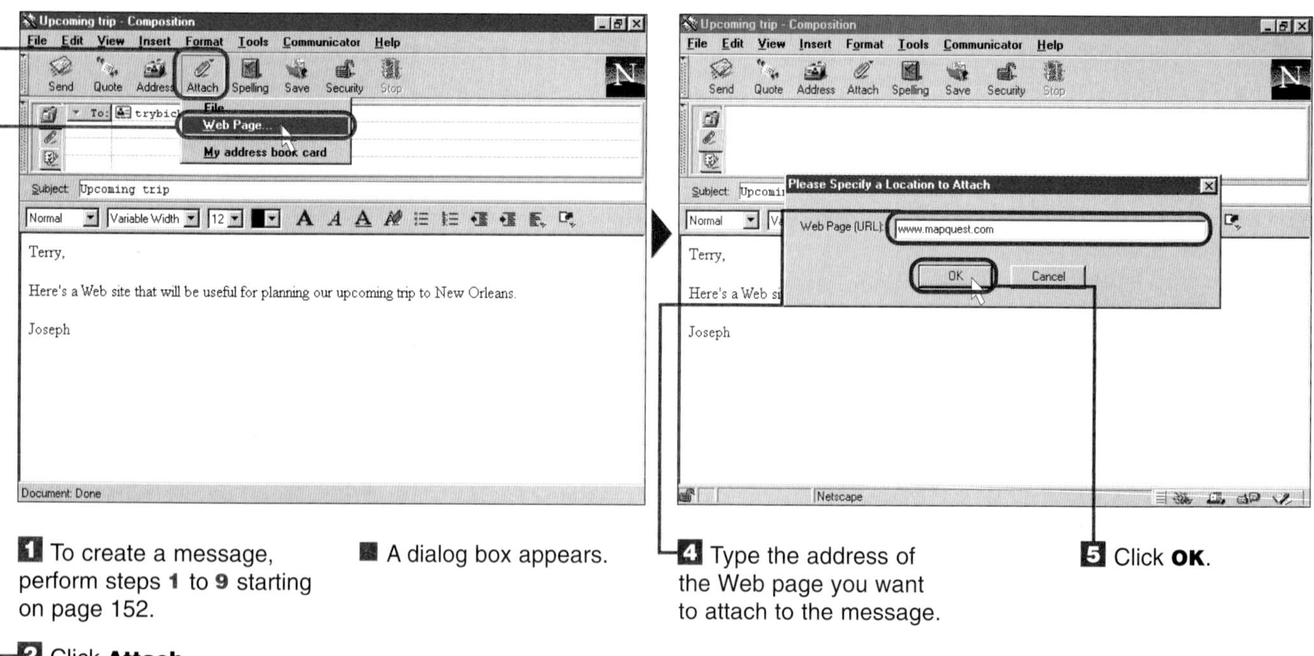

1 To create a message, perform steps **1** to **9** starting on page 152.

2 Click **Attach**.

3 Click **Web Page** to attach a Web page to the message.

■ A dialog box appears.

4 Type the address of the Web page you want to attach to the message.

5 Click **OK**.

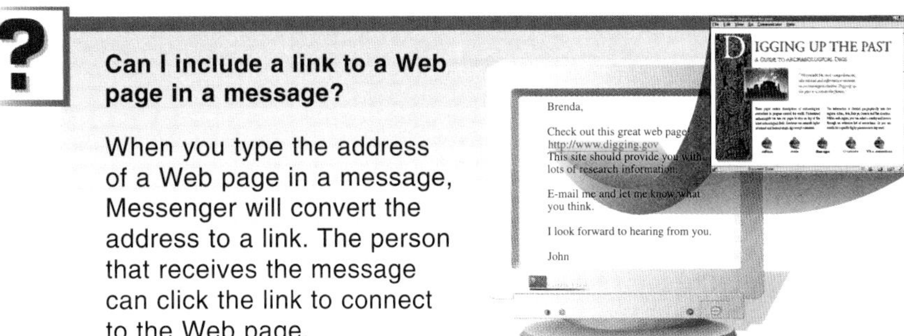

Can I include a link to a Web page in a message?

When you type the address of a Web page in a message, Messenger will convert the address to a link. The person that receives the message can click the link to connect to the Web page.

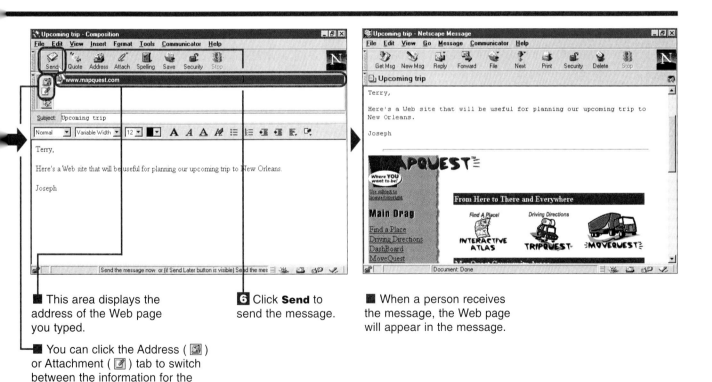

■ This area displays the address of the Web page you typed.

■ You can click the Address ( ) or Attachment ( ) tab to switch between the information for the message.

6 Click **Send** to send the message.

■ When a person receives the message, the Web page will appear in the message.

CHANGE MESSAGE PRIORITY

When sending a message, you can indicate the importance of the message by changing the priority.

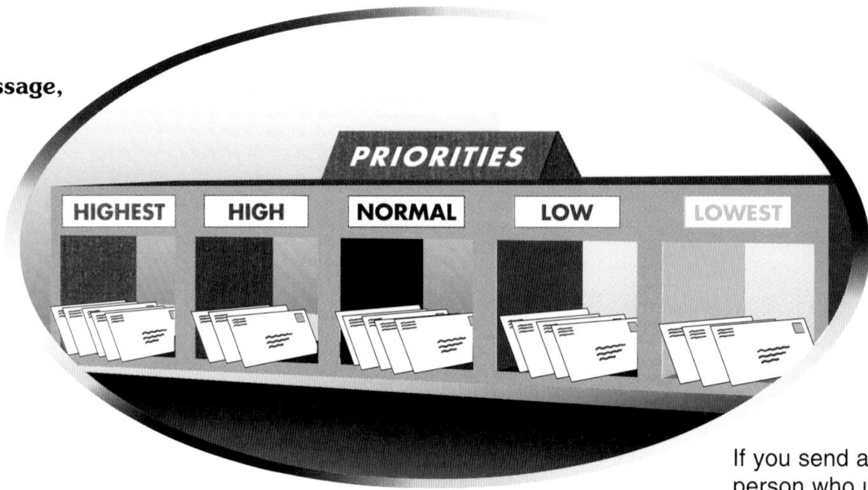

If you send a message to a person who uses another e-mail program, the priority of the message may be shown in a different way.

CHANGE MESSAGE PRIORITY

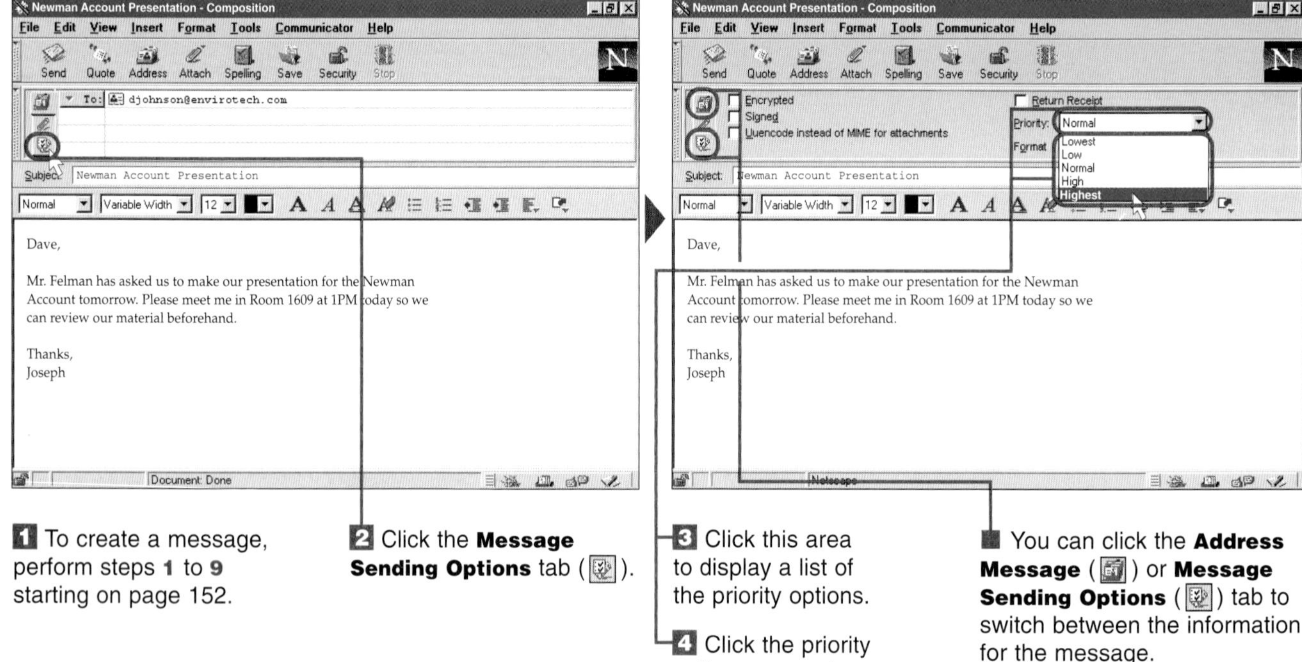

1 To create a message, perform steps **1** to **9** starting on page 152.

2 Click the **Message Sending Options** tab ( ).

3 Click this area to display a list of the priority options.

4 Click the priority option you want to use.

■ You can click the **Address Message** ( ) or **Message Sending Options** ( ) tab to switch between the information for the message.

Note: Messenger shows the priority of each message you receive in the Priority column. For more information on working with columns, refer to page 112.

REQUEST A RETURN RECEIPT

You can receive a confirmation message when your message arrives at its intended destination.

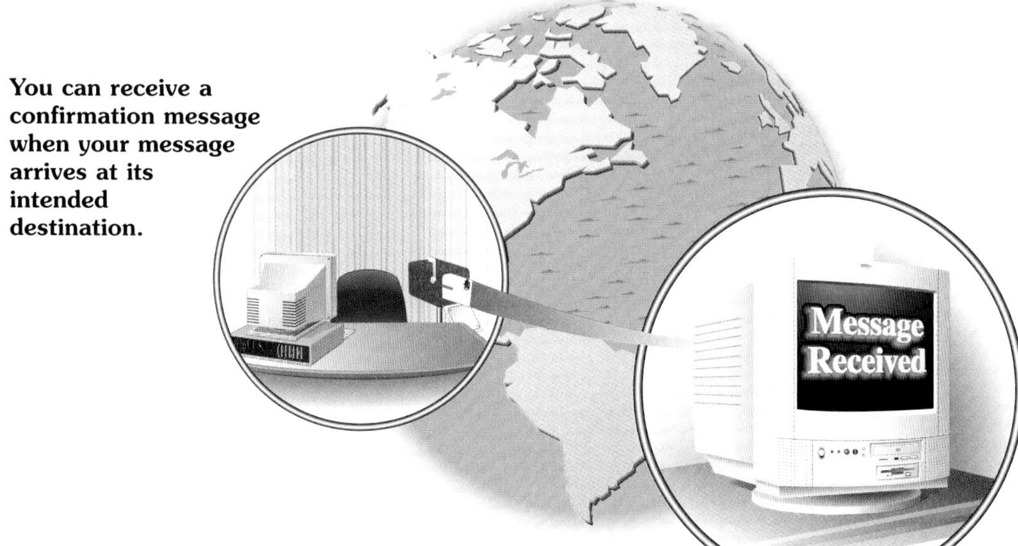

Most servers on the Internet do not support this feature. You will most likely use this feature on a corporate intranet.

REQUEST A RETURN RECEIPT

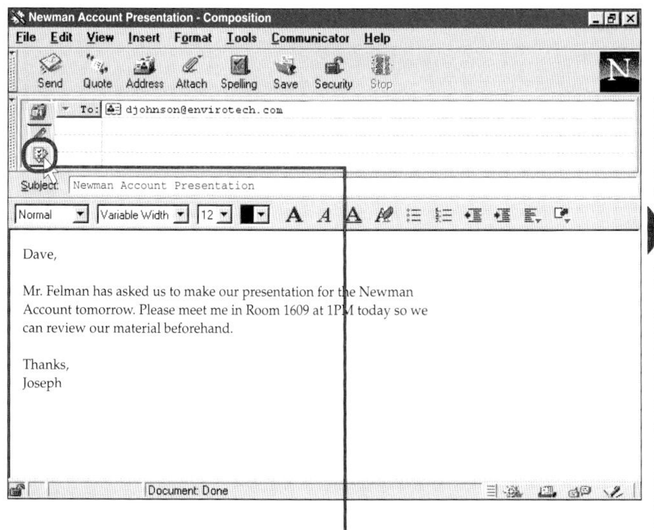

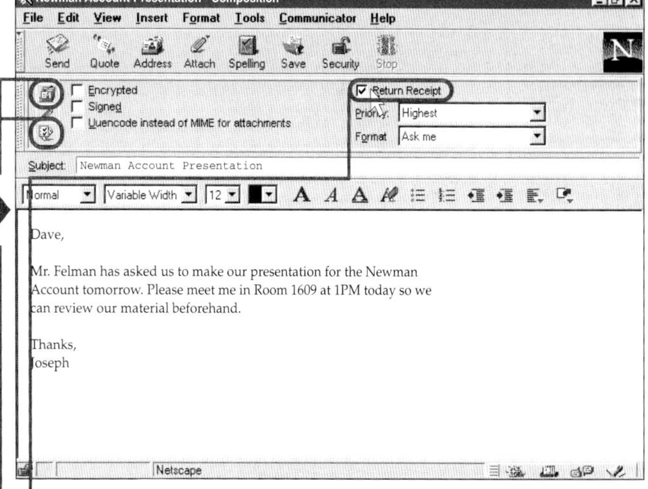

1 To create a message, perform steps **1** to **9** starting on page 152.

2 Click the **Message Sending Options** tab ( ).

3 Click **Return Receipt** (☐ changes to ☑).

■ You can click the **Address Message** ( ) or **Message Sending Options** ( ) tab to switch between the information for the message.

■ You will receive a confirmation message when the person receives the message.

CREATE A SIGNATURE FILE

You can have Messenger add information about yourself to the end of every message you send. A signature file saves you from having to type the same information every time you send a message.

CREATE A SIGNATURE FILE

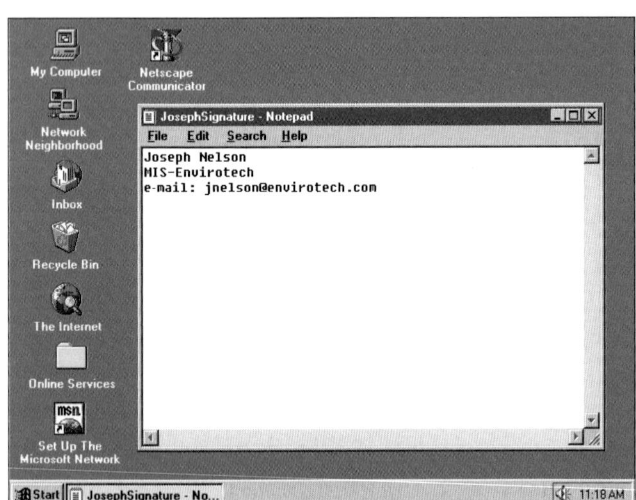

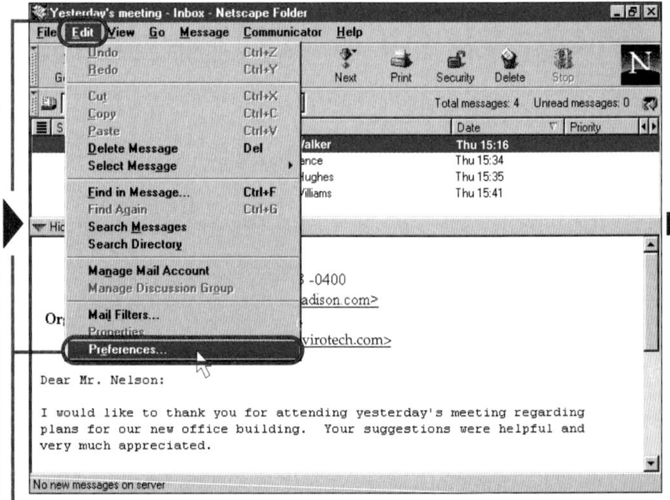

1 Create and save a document containing just text and no formatting.

■ You can use a text editor such as Microsoft Notepad or a word processor such as Microsoft Word to create the document. If you use a word processor, make sure you save the document as a text only document.

2 Display the Communicator Messenger window that shows your e-mail messages.

3 Click **Edit**.

4 Click **Preferences**.

■ The Preferences dialog box appears.

What can I include in a signature file?

A signature file can include information such as your name, e-mail address, occupation or favorite quotation. You can also use plain characters to display simple pictures. As a courtesy to others, do not create a signature file that is more than four lines long.

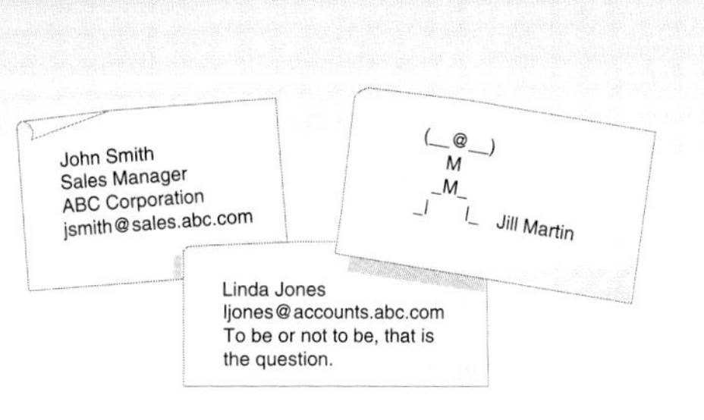

John Smith
Sales Manager
ABC Corporation
jsmith@sales.abc.com
Jill Martin
Linda Jones
ljones@accounts.abc.com
To be or not to be, that is
the question.

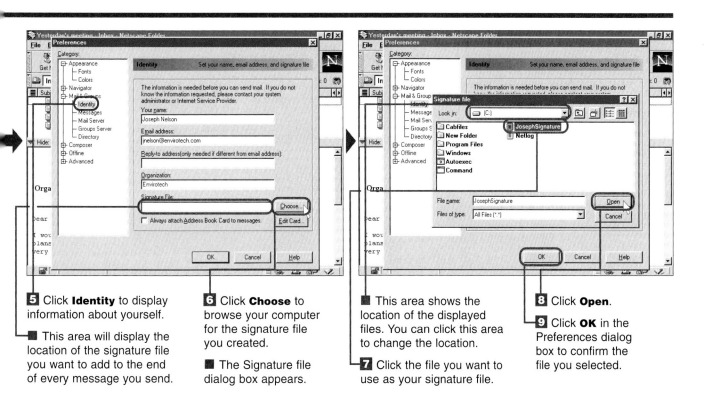

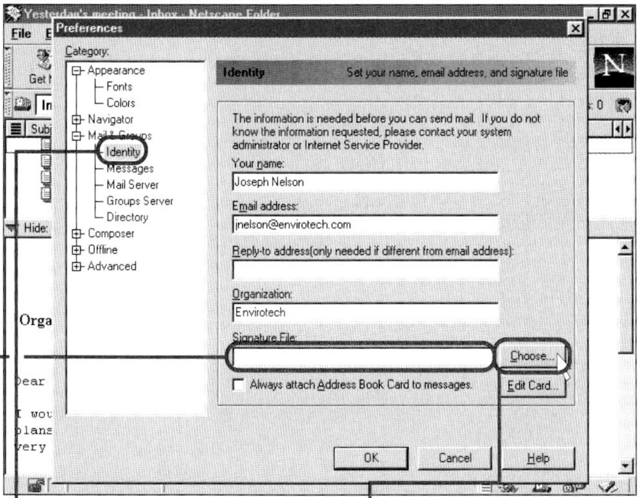

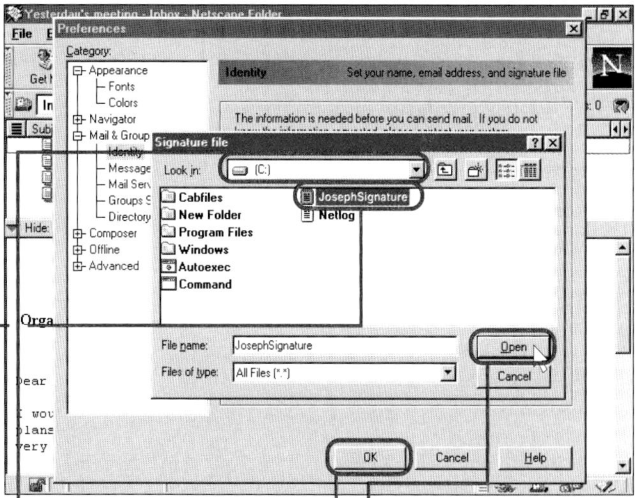

5 Click **Identity** to display information about yourself.

■ This area will display the location of the signature file you want to add to the end of every message you send.

6 Click **Choose** to browse your computer for the signature file you created.

■ The Signature file dialog box appears.

■ This area shows the location of the displayed files. You can click this area to change the location.

7 Click the file you want to use as your signature file.

8 Click **Open**.

9 Click **OK** in the Preferences dialog box to confirm the file you selected.

SAVE A DRAFT

If you are unable to finish creating a message, you can save a draft of the message. You can then finish the message at a later time.

SAVE A DRAFT

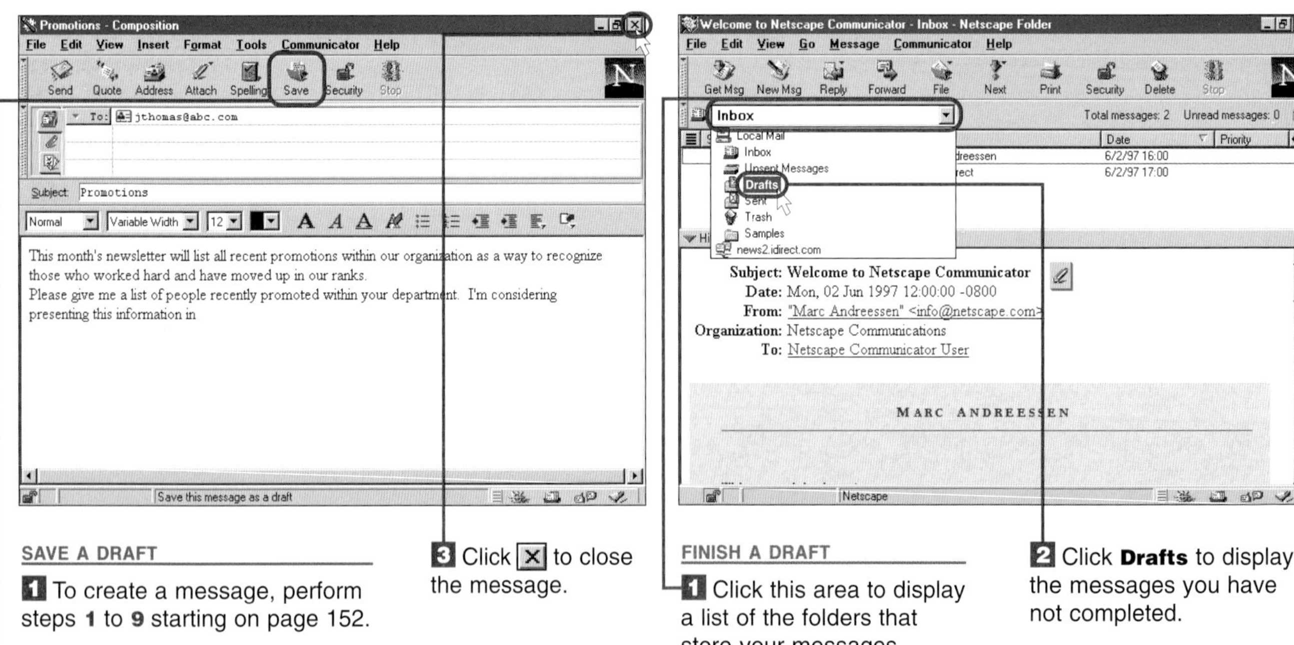

SAVE A DRAFT

1 To create a message, perform steps **1** to **9** starting on page 152.

2 Click **Save** to store the message in the Drafts folder until you are ready to complete and send the message.

3 Click ☒ to close the message.

FINISH A DRAFT

1 Click this area to display a list of the folders that store your messages.

2 Click **Drafts** to display the messages you have not completed.

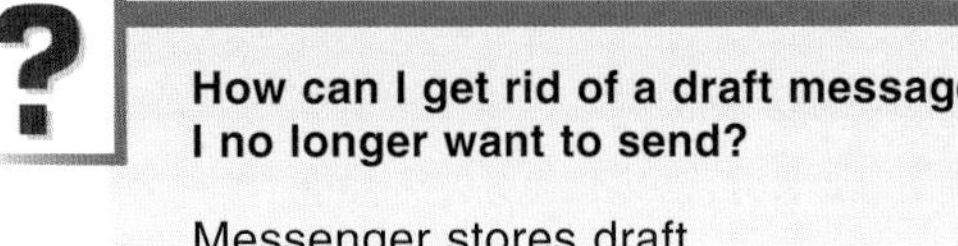

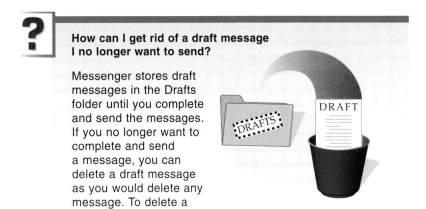

How can I get rid of a draft message I no longer want to send?

Messenger stores draft messages in the Drafts folder until you complete and send the messages. If you no longer want to complete and send a message, you can delete a draft message as you would delete any message. To delete a message, refer to page 128.

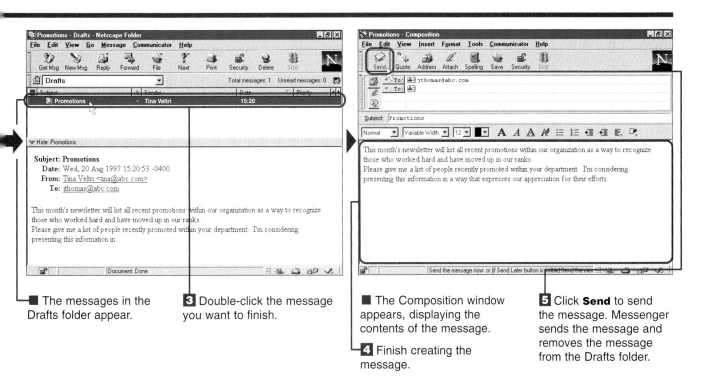

■ The messages in the Drafts folder appear.

3 Double-click the message you want to finish.

■ The Composition window appears, displaying the contents of the message.

4 Finish creating the message.

5 Click **Send** to send the message. Messenger sends the message and removes the message from the Drafts folder.

ADD NAME TO ADDRESS BOOK

Messenger provides an address book where you can store the e-mail addresses of people you frequently send messages to.

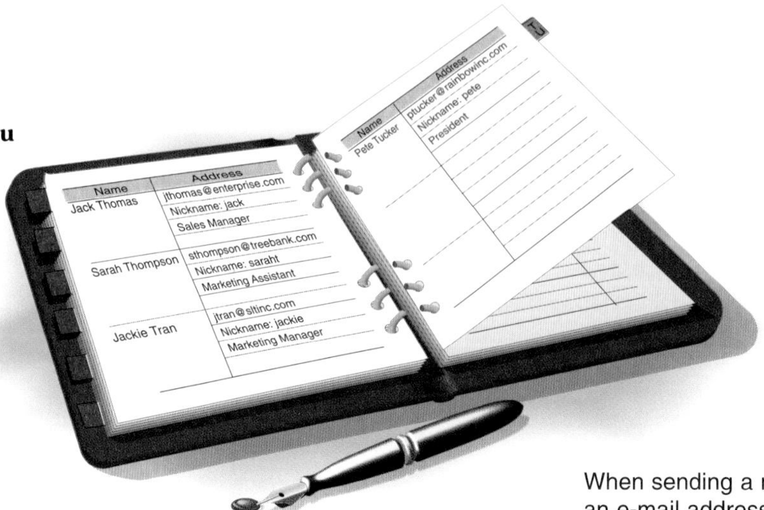

When sending a message, you can use an e-mail address stored in the address book. Selecting names from the address book saves you from having to type the same addresses over and over again.

ADD NAME TO ADDRESS BOOK

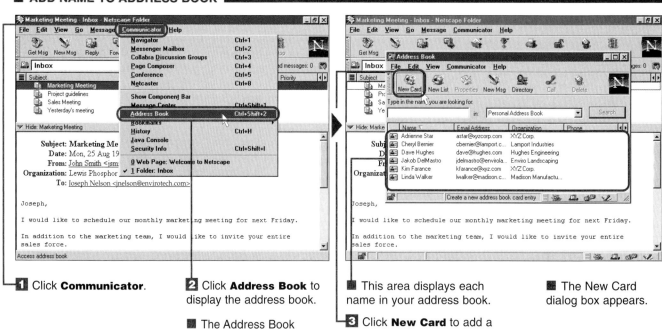

1 Click **Communicator**.

2 Click **Address Book** to display the address book.

■ The Address Book window appears.

■ This area displays each name in your address book.

3 Click **New Card** to add a name to the address book.

■ The New Card dialog box appears.

What is a nickname?

A nickname is a name or word that describes a person in your address book. Nicknames should be easy to remember.

When sending a message, you can address the message by typing the nickname of a person stored in your address book. Messenger will automatically fill in the e-mail address of the person for you.

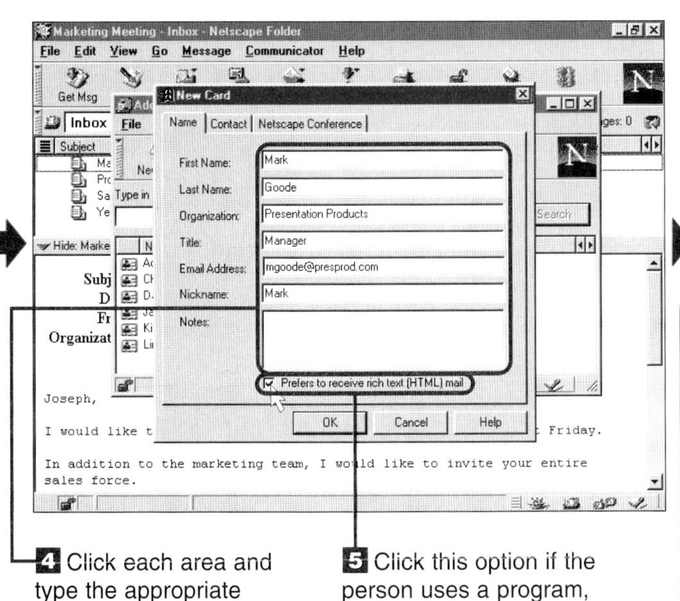

4 Click each area and type the appropriate information about the person.

5 Click this option if the person uses a program, such as Messenger, that can properly display messages that contain formatting (☐ changes to ☑). When you send messages that contain formatting, Messenger will not ask if you want to remove the formatting.

6 Click the **Contact** tab to enter additional information about the person. This information is optional.

7 Click each area and type the appropriate information about the person.

8 Click **OK** to add the name to your address book.

9 Click ☒ to close the Address Book window.

CONTINUED

ADD NAME TO ADDRESS BOOK

When you receive a message from a colleague or friend, you can quickly add the person's name to your address book.

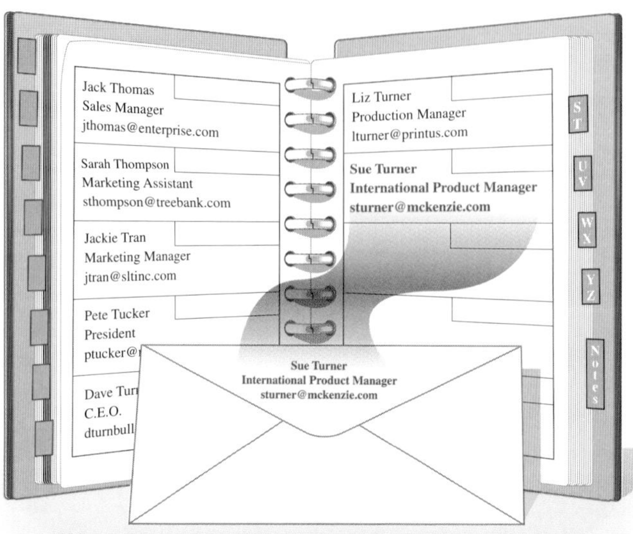

QUICKLY ADD NAME TO ADDRESS BOOK

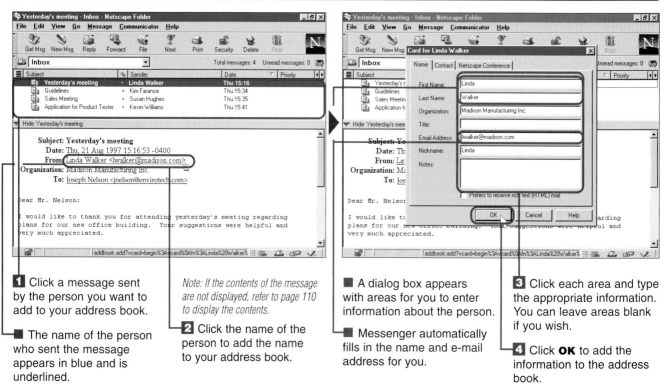

1 Click a message sent by the person you want to add to your address book.

■ The name of the person who sent the message appears in blue and is underlined.

Note: If the contents of the message are not displayed, refer to page 110 to display the contents.

2 Click the name of the person to add the name to your address book.

■ A dialog box appears with areas for you to enter information about the person.

■ Messenger automatically fills in the name and e-mail address for you.

3 Click each area and type the appropriate information. You can leave areas blank if you wish.

4 Click **OK** to add the information to the address book.

DELETE NAME FROM ADDRESS BOOK

When you no longer plan to send messages to a person in your address book, you can remove the person's name from the address book.

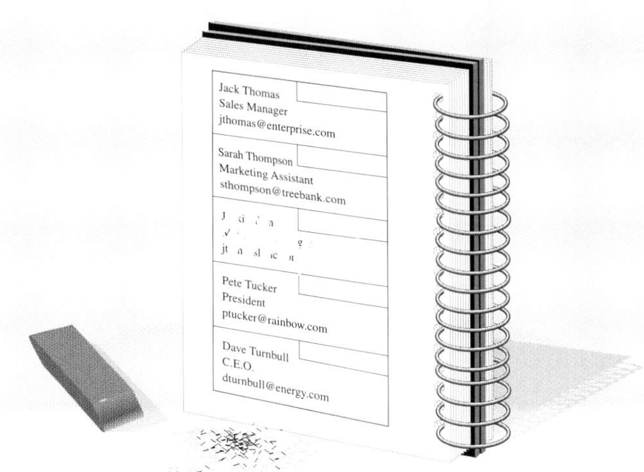

Removing addresses can make your address book less cluttered.

DELETE NAME FROM ADDRESS BOOK

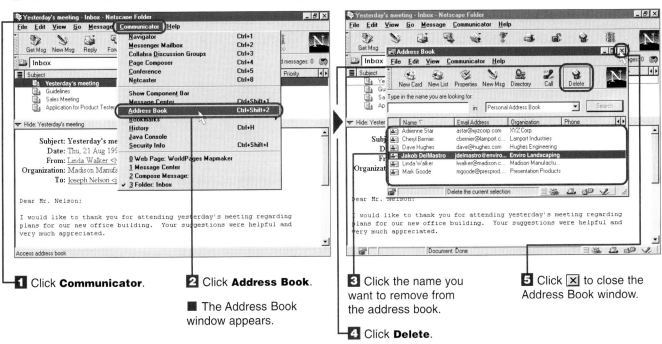

1 Click **Communicator**.

2 Click **Address Book**.

■ The Address Book window appears.

3 Click the name you want to remove from the address book.

4 Click **Delete**.

5 Click ☒ to close the Address Book window.

ADD LIST TO ADDRESS BOOK

You can send a message to many people at once by creating a list in your address book.

For example, you can create a list that contains the address of each person in a specific department. When you send a message to the list, every person on the list will receive the same message.

ADD LIST TO ADDRESS BOOK

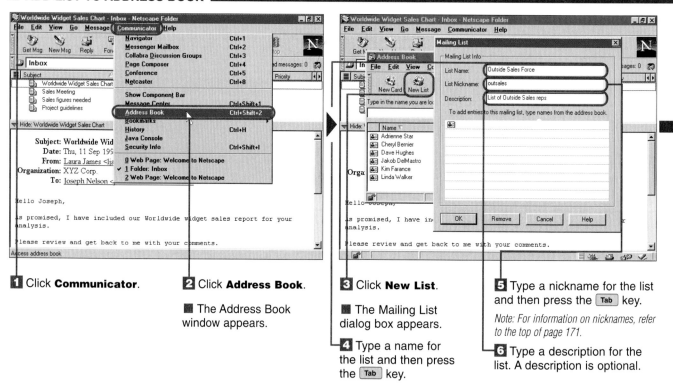

1 Click **Communicator**.

2 Click **Address Book**.

■ The Address Book window appears.

3 Click **New List**.

■ The Mailing List dialog box appears.

4 Type a name for the list and then press the Tab key.

5 Type a nickname for the list and then press the Tab key.

Note: For information on nicknames, refer to the top of page 171.

6 Type a description for the list. A description is optional.

Can my list contain names that are not in the address book?

No. If you want to add a name that is not in your address book, you must type the e-mail address for the person rather than their name. Messenger will ask you to add the name to the address book.

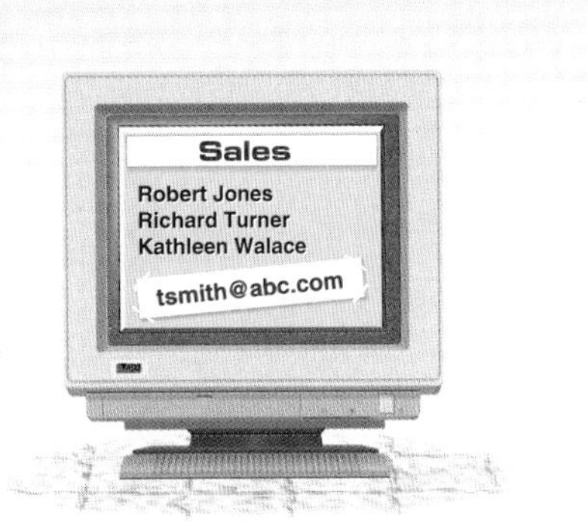

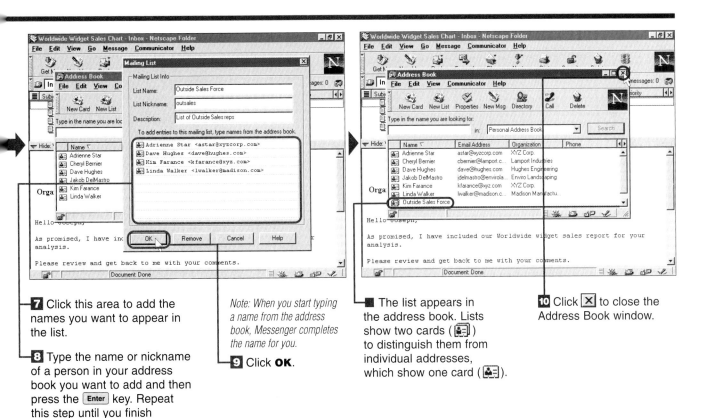

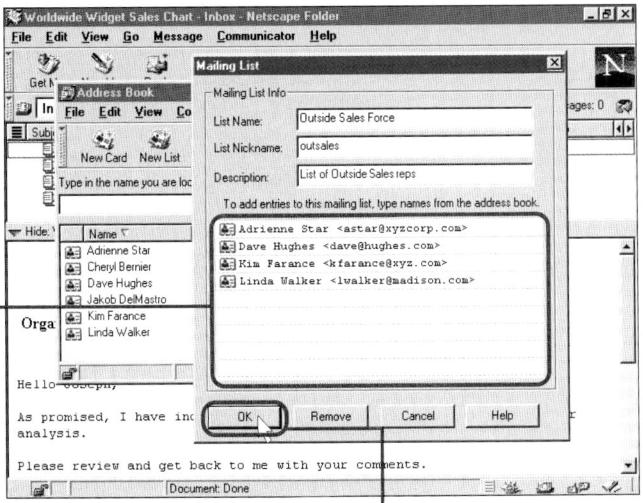

7 Click this area to add the names you want to appear in the list.

8 Type the name or nickname of a person in your address book you want to add and then press the Enter key. Repeat this step until you finish entering all of the names.

Note: When you start typing a name from the address book, Messenger completes the name for you.

9 Click **OK**.

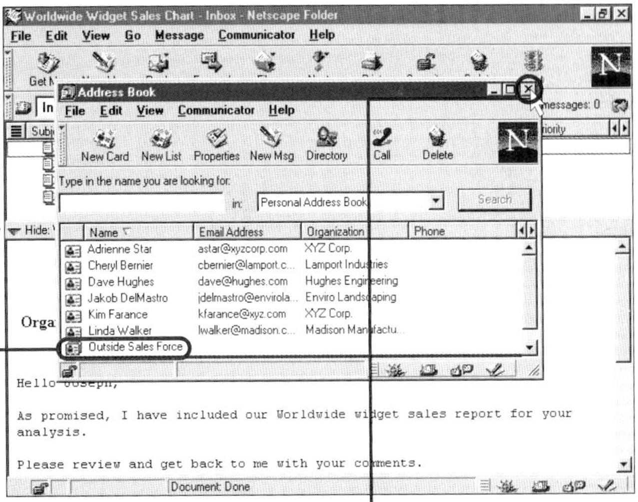

■ The list appears in the address book. Lists show two cards ( ) to distinguish them from individual addresses, which show one card ( ).

10 Click ☒ to close the Address Book window.

SELECT NAME FROM ADDRESS BOOK

When sending a message, you can select the name of the person you want to receive the message from your address book.

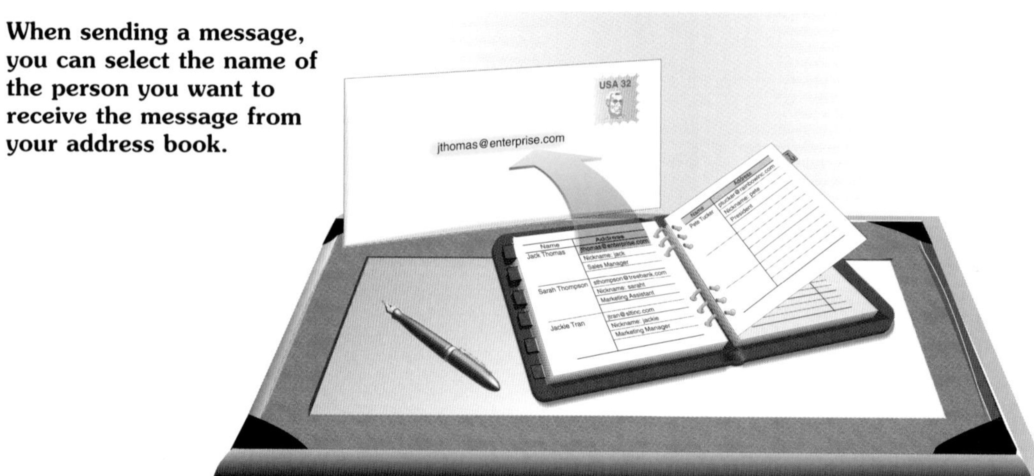

Selecting names from the address book saves you from having to remember e-mail addresses you often use.

SELECT NAME FROM ADDRESS BOOK

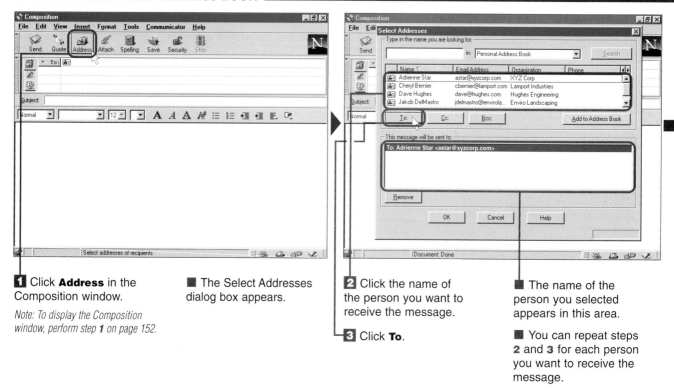

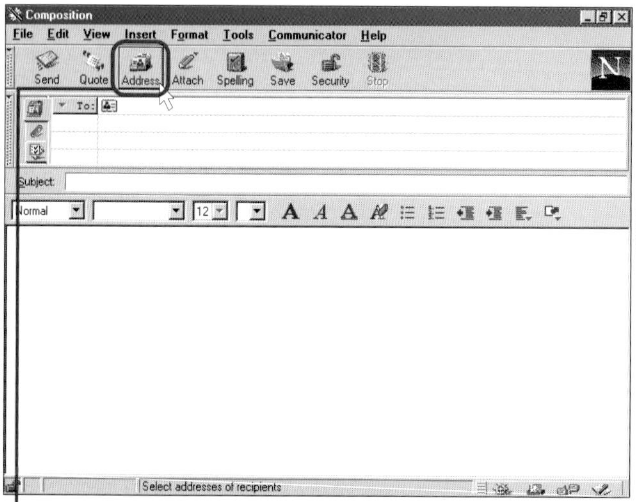

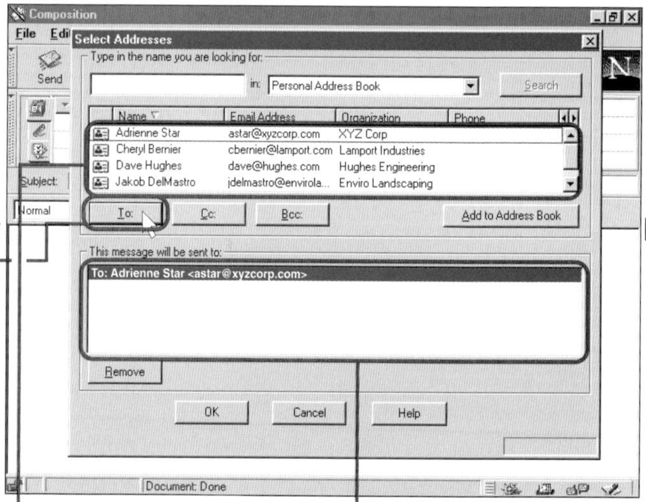

1 Click **Address** in the Composition window.

*Note: To display the Composition window, perform step **1** on page 152.*

■ The Select Addresses dialog box appears.

2 Click the name of the person you want to receive the message.

3 Click **To**.

■ The name of the person you selected appears in this area.

■ You can repeat steps **2** and **3** for each person you want to receive the message.

How can I address a message I want to send to more than one person?

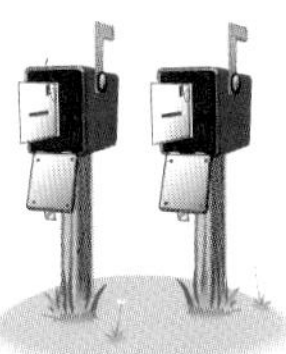

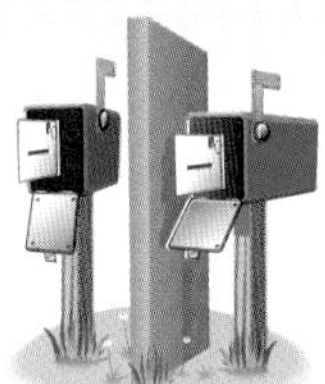

To

Sends the original message to a person you specify.

Carbon Copy (Cc)

Sends an exact copy of the message to a person who is not directly involved, but would be interested in the message.

Blind Carbon Copy (Bcc)

Sends an exact copy of the message to a person without anyone else knowing that the person received the message.

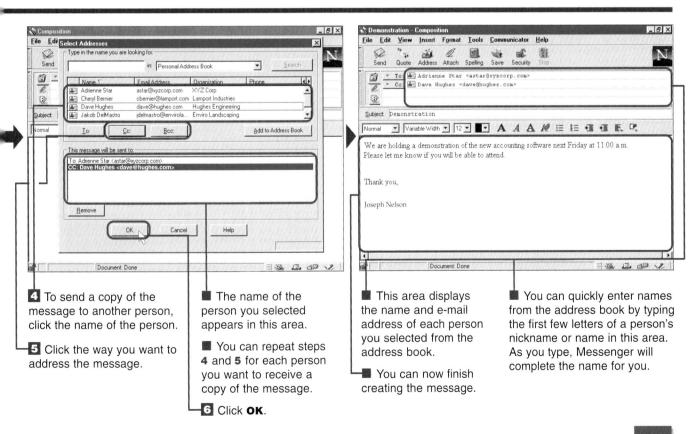

4 To send a copy of the message to another person, click the name of the person.

5 Click the way you want to address the message.

■ The name of the person you selected appears in this area.

■ You can repeat steps **4** and **5** for each person you want to receive a copy of the message.

6 Click **OK**.

■ This area displays the name and e-mail address of each person you selected from the address book.

■ You can now finish creating the message.

■ You can quickly enter names from the address book by typing the first few letters of a person's nickname or name in this area. As you type, Messenger will complete the name for you.

FIND AN E-MAIL ADDRESS

You can search for the e-mail address of a friend or colleague. This is helpful if you lost an address or you want to surprise someone with a message.

Communicator lets you search the Bigfoot, Four11, InfoSpace, Switchboard and WhoWhere directories. These directories contain millions of e-mail addresses.

FIND AN E-MAIL ADDRESS

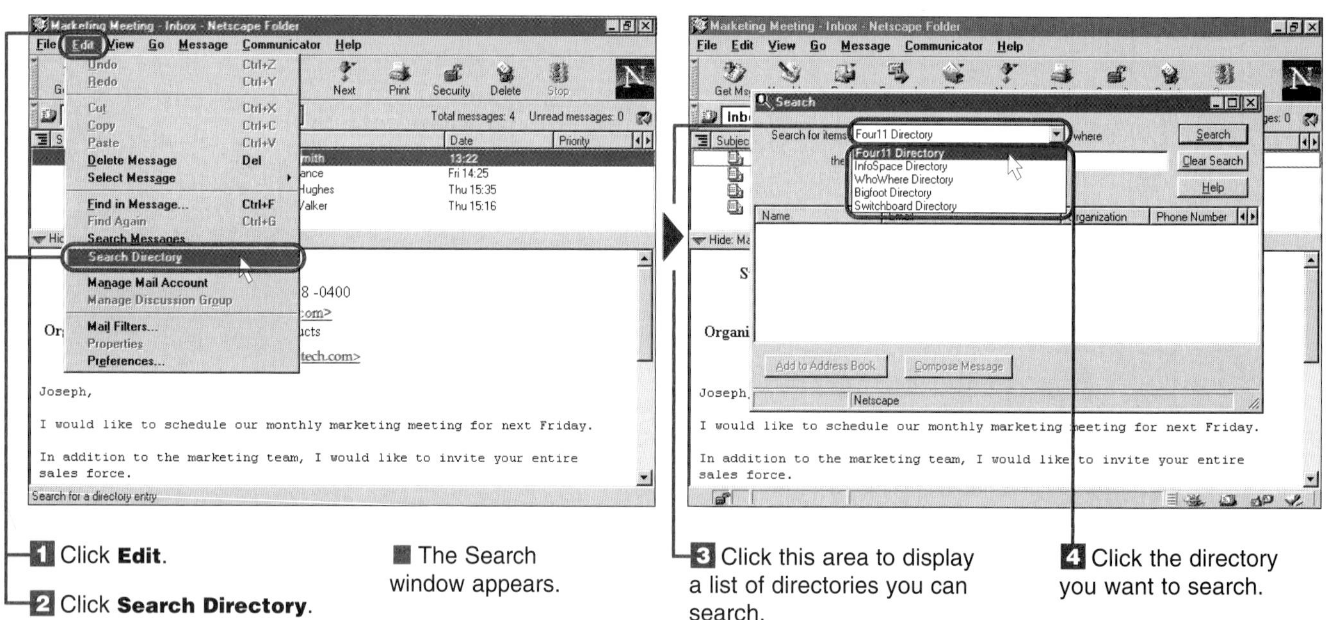

1 Click **Edit**.

2 Click **Search Directory**.

■ The Search window appears.

3 Click this area to display a list of directories you can search.

4 Click the directory you want to search.

?

Why can't I find an e-mail address?

There is no central listing of e-mail addresses. Directories such as Bigfoot and Four11 get addresses from newsgroups and from addresses people submit. Directories cannot possibly list every e-mail address on the Internet. The best way to find the e-mail address of a friend or colleague is to phone the person and ask.

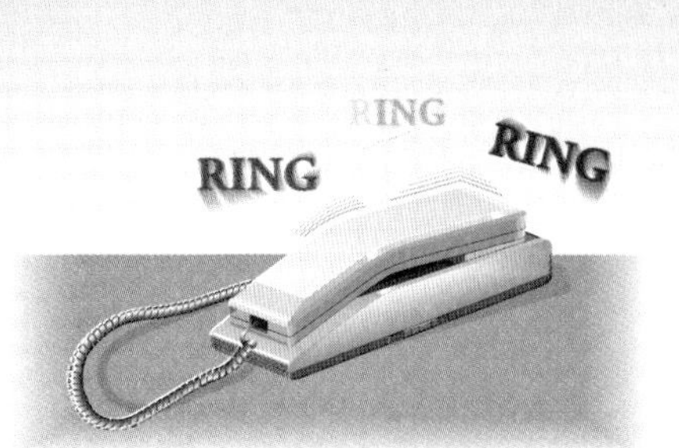

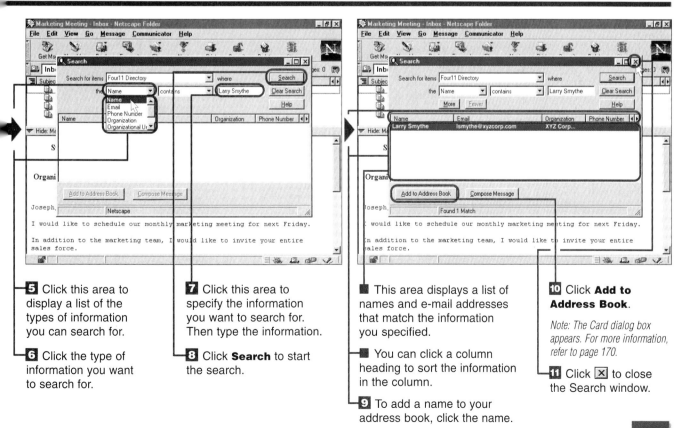

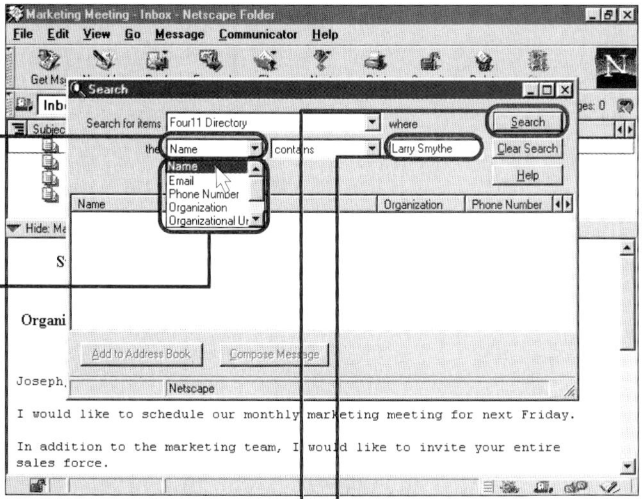

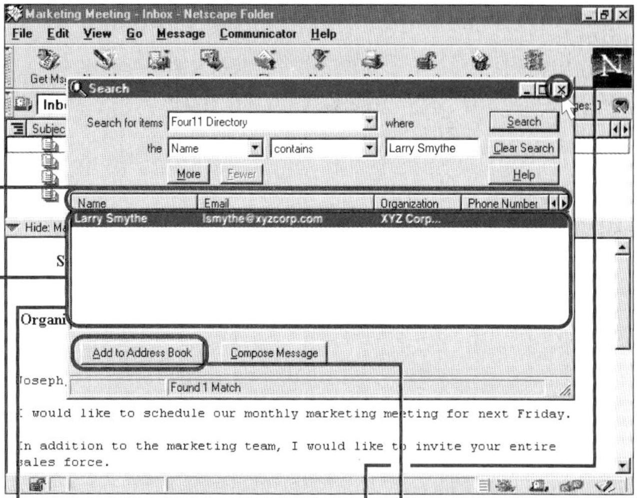

5 Click this area to display a list of the types of information you can search for.

6 Click the type of information you want to search for.

7 Click this area to specify the information you want to search for. Then type the information.

8 Click **Search** to start the search.

■ This area displays a list of names and e-mail addresses that match the information you specified.

■ You can click a column heading to sort the information in the column.

9 To add a name to your address book, click the name.

10 Click **Add to Address Book**.

Note: The Card dialog box appears. For more information, refer to page 170.

11 Click ☒ to close the Search window.

MAILING LISTS

You can use Messenger to send and receive messages in mailing lists that interest you. A mailing list is a discussion group on the Internet that uses e-mail to communicate.

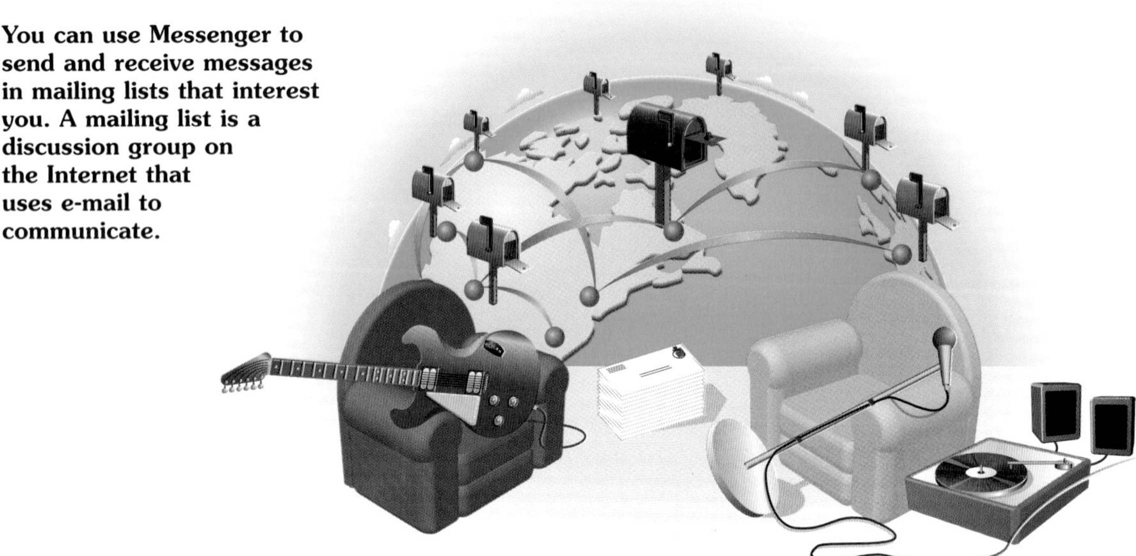

How Mailing Lists Work

When a mailing list receives a message, a copy of the message goes to everyone on the mailing list. Most mailing lists let you send and receive messages. Some mailing lists only let you receive messages.

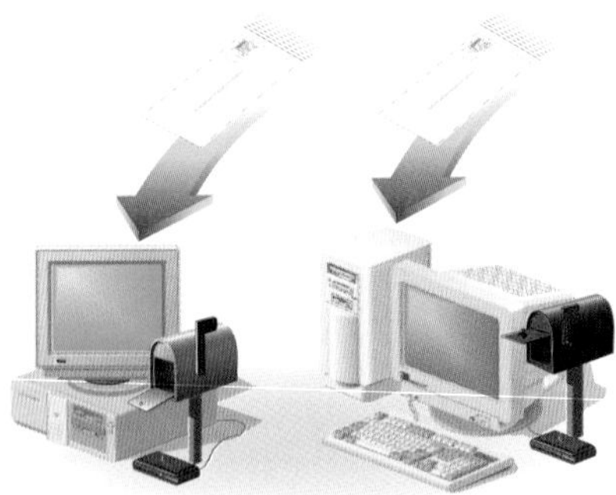

Make sure you read the messages in a mailing list for a week before sending a message. This allows you to see how people in the mailing list communicate and prevents you from sending inappropriate information to the mailing list.

Find Mailing Lists

There are thousands of mailing lists that cover a wide variety of topics such as actors, boating, food, golf, jokes, the paranormal, religion, stocks, weather and more. New mailing lists are created every week.

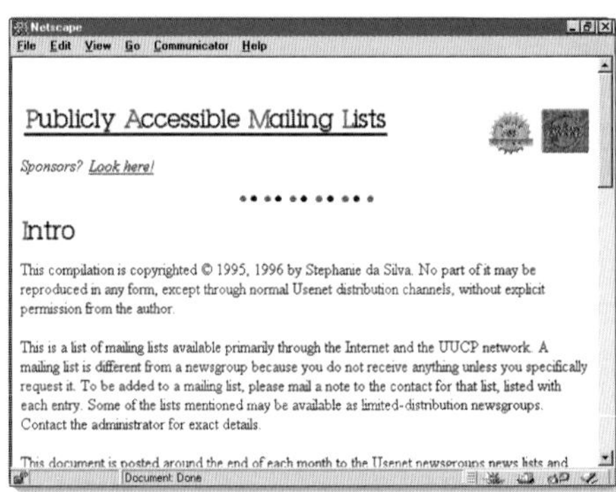

You can find mailing lists at:

www.neosoft.com/internet/paml

Subscribe to a Mailing List

Just as you would subscribe to a newspaper or magazine, you can subscribe to a mailing list that interests you. Subscribing adds your e-mail address to the mailing list.

After subscribing to a mailing list, make sure you frequently check for new messages. You can receive dozens of messages in a short period of time.

Unsubscribe From a Mailing List

If you no longer want to receive messages from a mailing list, you can unsubscribe from the mailing list at any time. Unsubscribing removes your e-mail address from the mailing list.

Mailing List Addresses

Each mailing list has two addresses. Make sure you send your messages to the appropriate address.

Mailing List Address

Use the mailing list address to send messages you want all the people on the list to receive. Do not send subscription or unsubscription requests to the mailing list address.

Administrative Address

Use the administrative address for administrative issues, such as subscribing to or unsubscribing from a mailing list.

E-MAIL SECURITY

You can send secure messages to other people on the Internet. Sending secure messages is useful when you need to send confidential information, such as sales figures, to a co-worker at another office.

You need a certificate to exchange secure messages. Netscape provides a Web page where you can find a list of companies that offer certificates at:

https://certs.netscape.com/client.html

SEND SECURE MESSAGES

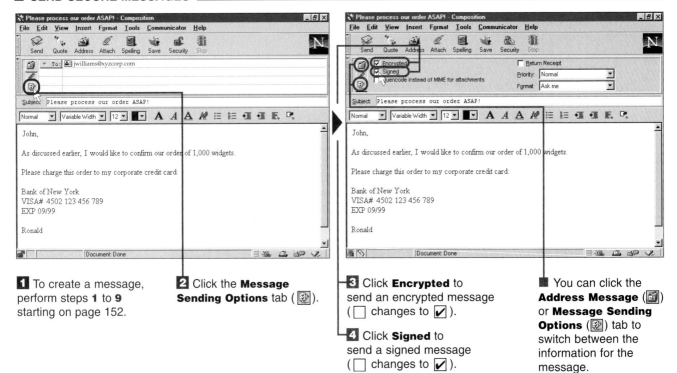

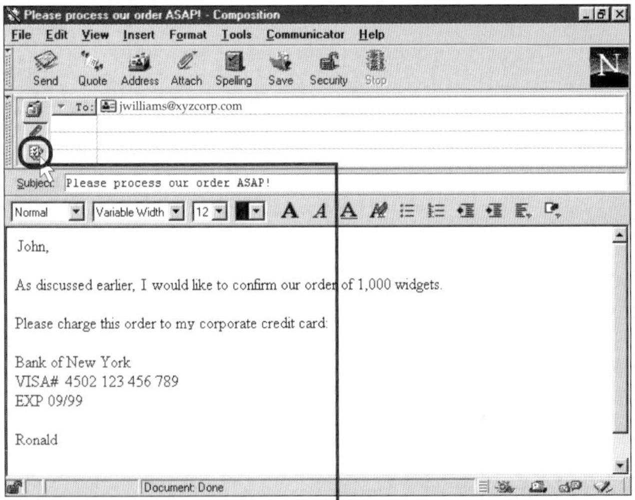

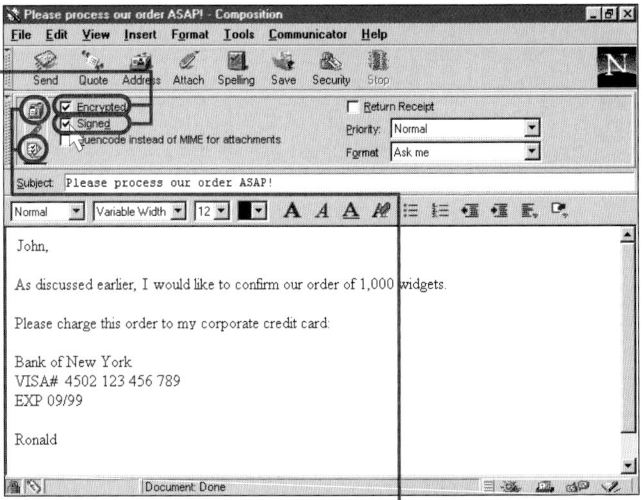

1 To create a message, perform steps **1** to **9** starting on page 152.

2 Click the **Message Sending Options** tab ( ).

3 Click **Encrypted** to send an encrypted message (☐ changes to ☑).

4 Click **Signed** to send a signed message (☐ changes to ☑).

■ You can click the **Address Message** ( ) or **Message Sending Options** ( ) tab to switch between the information for the message.

What is the difference between a signed and encrypted message?

Signed

Signed messages allow other people to confirm that a message actually came from you. The level of security of a signed message depends on the type of certificate you have.

Encrypted

Encrypted messages are scrambled so no one except the intended recipient can read the message. Before you can send someone an encrypted message, they must send you a signed message. The signed message will contain information needed for you to send the encrypted message.

RECEIVE SECURE MESSAGES

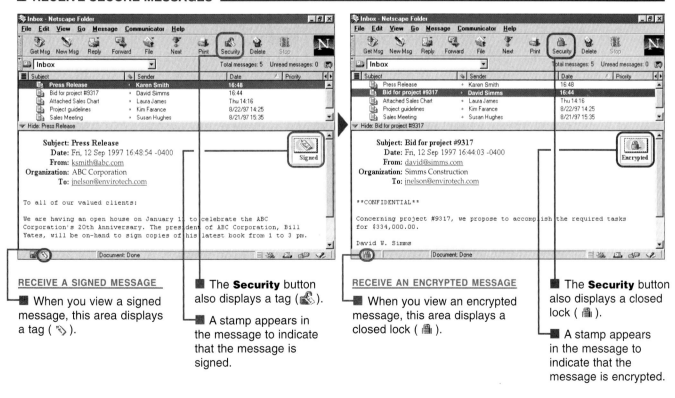

RECEIVE A SIGNED MESSAGE

- When you view a signed message, this area displays a tag ( ).

- The **Security** button also displays a tag ( ).

- A stamp appears in the message to indicate that the message is signed.

RECEIVE AN ENCRYPTED MESSAGE

- When you view an encrypted message, this area displays a closed lock ( ).

- The **Security** button also displays a closed lock ( ).

- A stamp appears in the message to indicate that the message is encrypted.

t.music
looking into
ying a new
yboard for my
udio. Does anyone
now what models
should be looking
at? Any advice would
be appreciated.
soc.politics
The Federal election is approaching and I'm not sure who to vote for. Where can I find information on my local candidates?
misc.fitness
Recently, I underwent surgery to remove my appendix. I was wondering how long after surgery I must wait before I can return to the gym?
sport.hockey
I have heard rumors
that Patrick Klimchuk
misc.financ
I would like to start saving for my retirement and I heard that investing in mutual funds is an excellent idea. Which books and magazines should I read?

CHAPTER 7

Work with Discussion Groups

Do you want to learn how to subscribe to a discussion group? This chapter will show you how to search for discussion groups, read messages and much more.

INTRODUCTION TO DISCUSSION GROUPS

Netscape Collabra lets you join discussion groups, which allow people with common interests to communicate with each other. Discussion groups are also called newsgroups.

There are thousands of discussion groups on every subject imaginable. Each discussion group discusses a particular topic, such as jobs offered, puzzles or medicine.

Usenet, short for Users' Network, refers to all the computers that distribute discussion group information.

DISCUSSION GROUP NAMES

The name of a discussion group describes the type of information discussed in the group. A discussion group name consists of two or more words, separated by periods (.).

The first word describes the main topic (example: **rec** for **rec**reation). Each of the following words narrows the topic.

MESSAGES

A discussion group can contain hundreds or thousands of messages.

Messages

A message is information that an individual sends (posts) to a discussion group. A message can be a few lines of text or the length of a book.

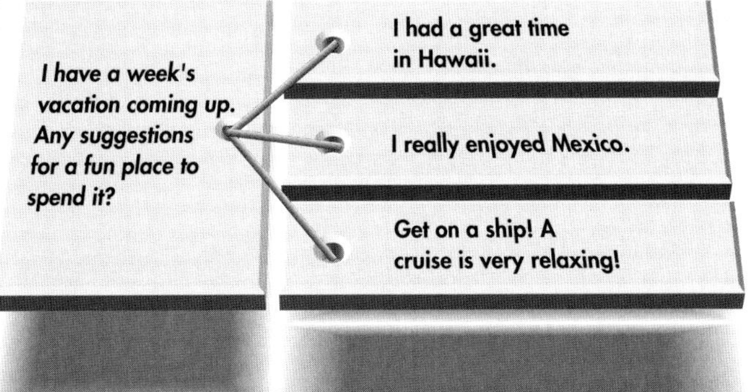

Threads

A thread is a message and all replies to the message. A thread may include an initial question and the responses from other readers.

MODERATED DISCUSSION GROUPS

Some discussion groups are moderated. In these discussion groups, a volunteer reads each message to decide if the message is appropriate for the group. If the message is appropriate, the volunteer posts the message for everyone to read.

Moderated discussion groups may have the word "moderated" at the end of the discussion group name (example: sci.military.moderated).

PRIVATE DISCUSSION GROUPS

Companies can set up private discussion groups on an intranet. An intranet is a small version of the Internet inside a company that only employees can access.

The groups can discuss information such as current projects, company news, job openings and management issues.

DISCUSSION GROUP ETIQUETTE

Writing Style

Make sure every message you send is clear, concise and contains no spelling or grammar errors. Also make sure the message will not be misinterpreted. For example, a reader may not realize a statement is meant to be sarcastic.

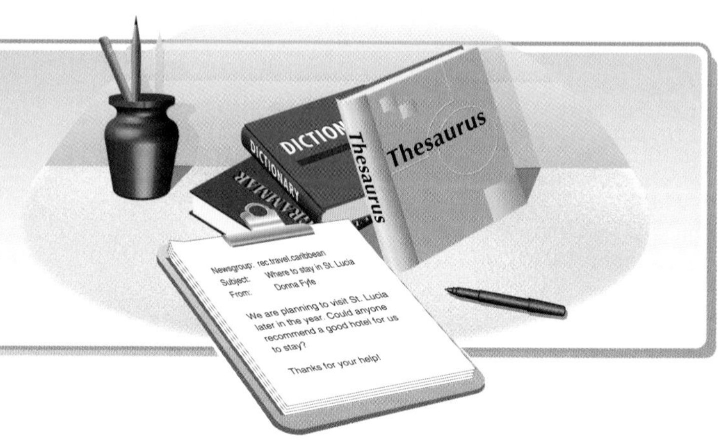

Subject

The subject of a message is the first item people read. Make sure the subject clearly identifies the contents of the message. For example, the subject "Read this now" or "For your information" is not very informative.

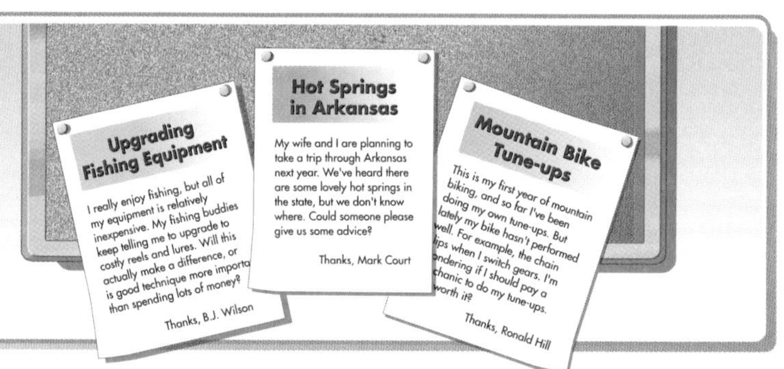

Read the FAQ

A FAQ (Frequently Asked Questions) is a message containing a list of questions and answers that regularly appear in a discussion group. The FAQ is designed to prevent new readers from asking questions that have already been answered.

If a discussion group has a FAQ, make sure you read it before sending any messages to the discussion group.

The **news.answers** discussion group provides FAQs for a wide variety of discussion groups.

NEWS SERVERS

A news server is a computer that stores discussion group messages.

News servers are maintained by service providers, which are companies that give you access to the Internet.

The discussion groups available to you depend on your service provider. Your service provider may limit the available discussion groups to save valuable storage space.

The amount of information sent to discussion groups each day is approximately equal to the amount of information in a set of encyclopedias.

When you send a message to a discussion group, the news server you are connected to keeps a copy of the message and then distributes the message to other news servers around the world.

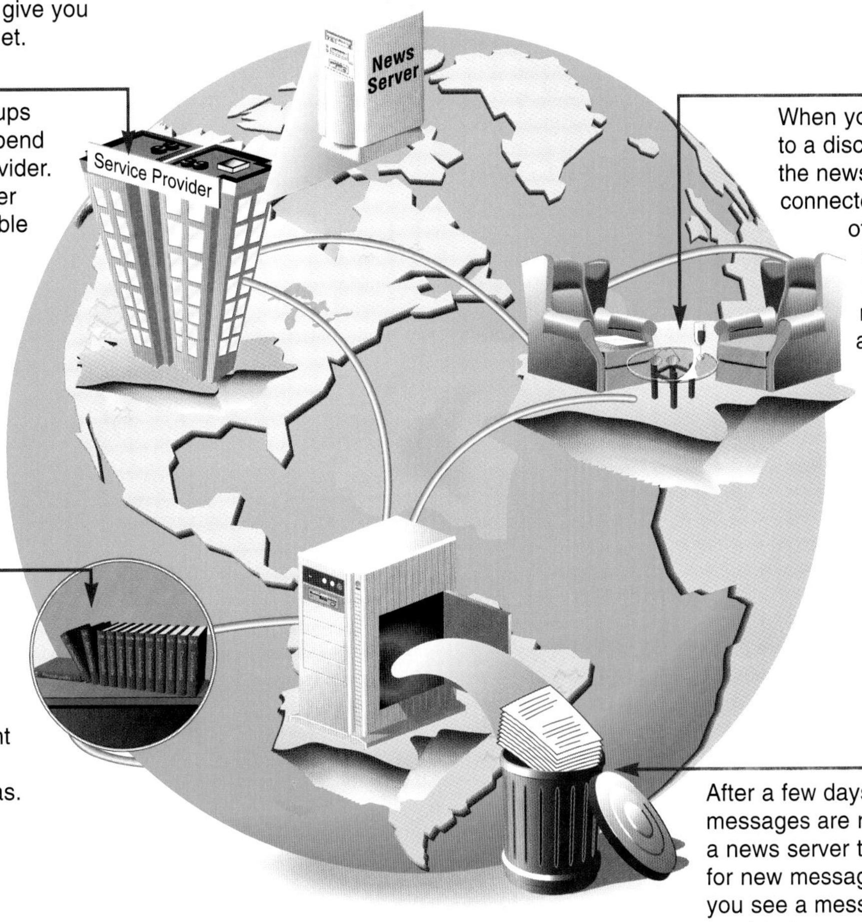

After a few days or weeks, messages are removed from a news server to make room for new messages. When you see a message you want to keep, make sure you file or print the message.

News Server

Service Provider

MAIN DISCUSSION GROUP CATEGORIES

alt (alternative)

General interest discussions that can include unusual or bizarre topics. Some of the material available in the **alt** discussion groups may be offensive to some people.

Examples

alt.binaries.sounds.movies

alt.fan.actors

alt.music.alternative

alt.ufo.reports

comp (computers)

Discussions of computer hardware, software and computer science. The **comp** discussion groups are a good source of technical support for computer-related problems.

Examples

comp.graphics

comp.security.misc

comp.software.testing

comp.sys.laptops

news

Discussions about Usenet discussion groups. Topics range from general information to specific advice on how to use discussion groups.

Examples

news.admin.misc

news.announce.newgroups

news.answers

news.newusers.questions

rec (recreation)

Discussions of recreational activities and hobbies. The messages in the **rec** discussion groups are often more entertaining than informative.

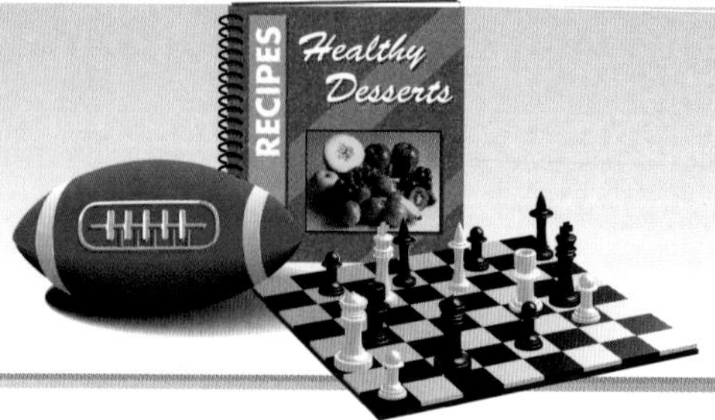

Examples

rec.autos

rec.food.recipes

rec.games.board

rec.sport.football.pro

sci (science)

Discussions about science, including research, applied science and the social sciences. Many of the discussions in the **sci** discussion groups are very technical.

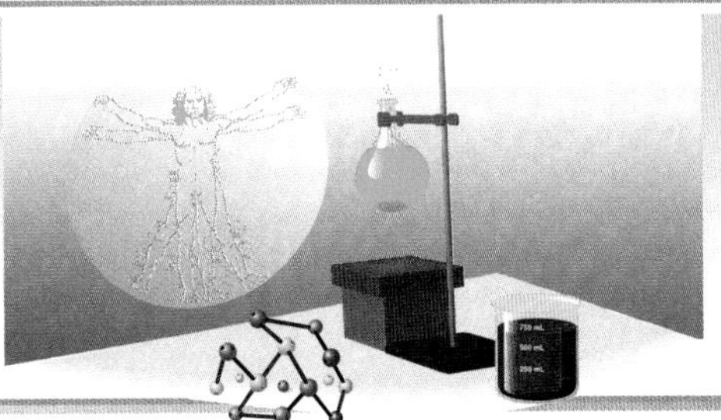

Examples

sci.agriculture

sci.energy

sci.med.dentistry

sci.physics

soc (social)

Discussions of social issues, including world cultures and political topics. The **soc** discussion groups also contain information about specific regions around the world.

Examples

soc.culture.caribbean

soc.history

soc.politics

soc.women

talk

Debates and long discussions, often about controversial subjects. Most of the messages in the **talk** discussion groups are quite long and very well-researched.

Examples

talk.environment

talk.philosophy.misc

talk.politics

talk.rumors

Regional Discussion Groups

Regional discussion groups focus on topics of interest to people living in specific geographic regions.

Examples

aus.environment.misc (Australia)

can.politics (Canada)

uk.legal (United Kingdom)

us.jobs.offered (United States)

START NETSCAPE COLLABRA

When you start Collabra, a window appears, displaying a list of the discussion groups you belong to.

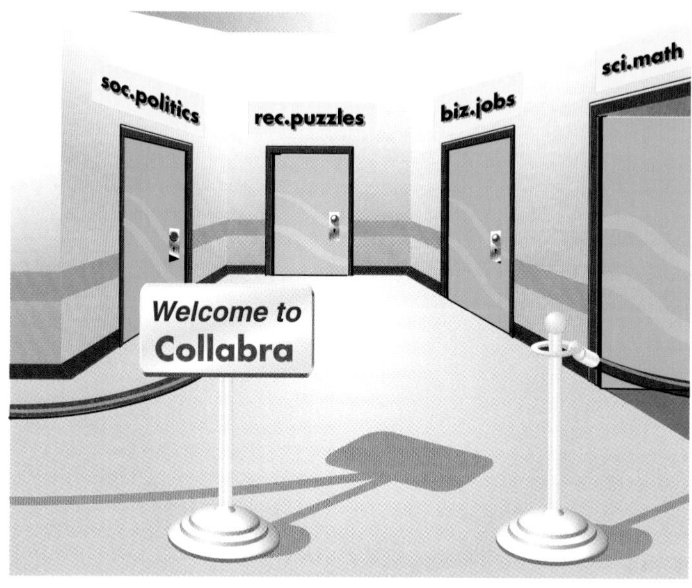

You need to subscribe to discussion groups before they will appear in the list. To find discussion groups of interest to you, refer to pages 194 to 199.

START NETSCAPE COLLABRA

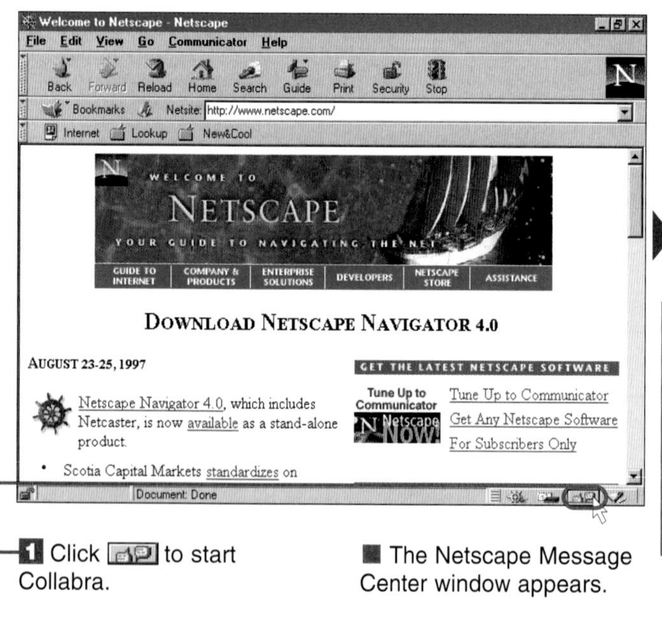

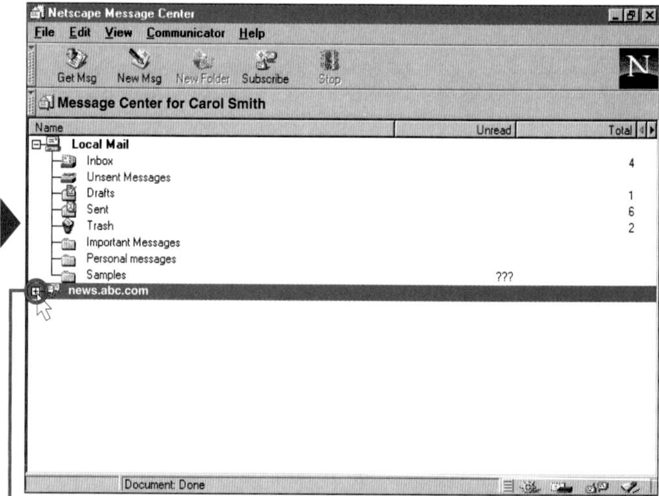

1 Click [icon] to start Collabra.

■ The Netscape Message Center window appears.

2 Click the plus sign (⊞) beside your discussion group server to display the discussion groups you are subscribed to (⊞ changes to ⊟). The name of a discussion group server usually begins with "news".

Note: If no symbol (⊞ or ⊟) appears beside the discussion group server, you are not subscribed to any discussion groups.

Are there any discussion groups that can help me get started?

There are several discussion groups that are useful for beginners. These discussion groups provide useful information and let you ask questions about discussion groups:

news.announce.newusers

news.answers

news.newusers.questions

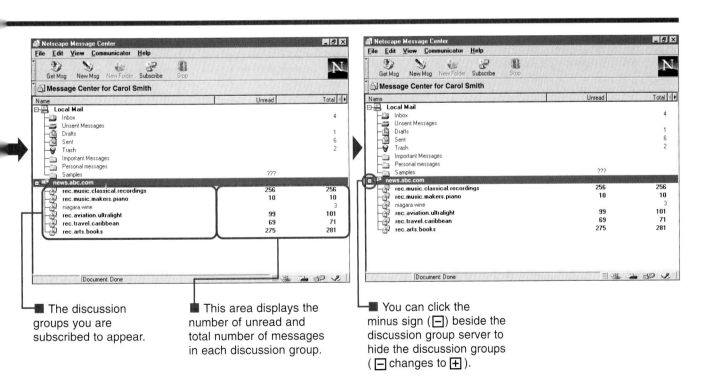

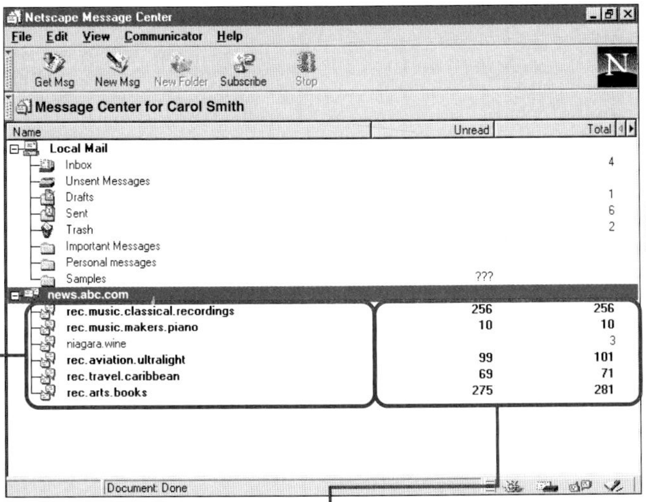

■ The discussion groups you are subscribed to appear.

■ This area displays the number of unread and total number of messages in each discussion group.

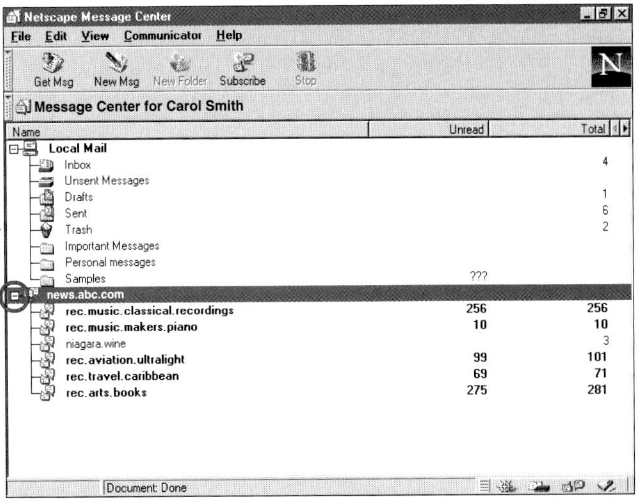

■ You can click the minus sign (⊟) beside the discussion group server to hide the discussion groups (⊟ changes to ⊞).

SUBSCRIBE TO DISCUSSION GROUPS

You can display a list of all the available discussion groups. When you find discussion groups of interest, you need to subscribe to the groups so you can read their messages.

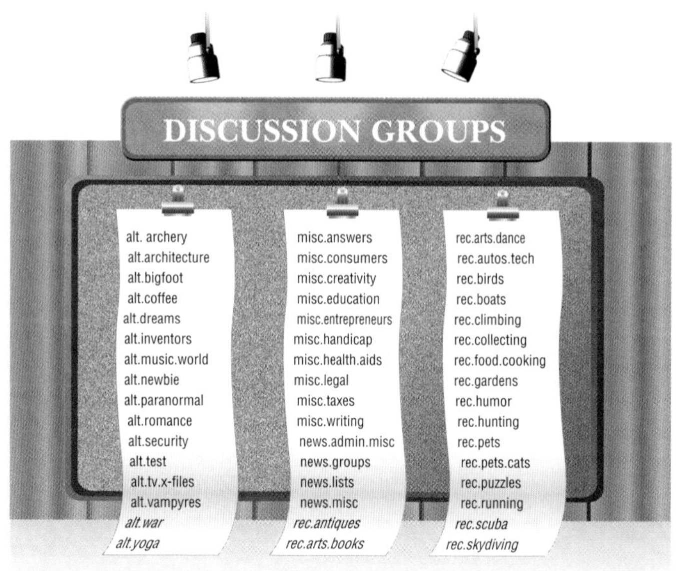

SUBSCRIBE TO DISCUSSION GROUPS

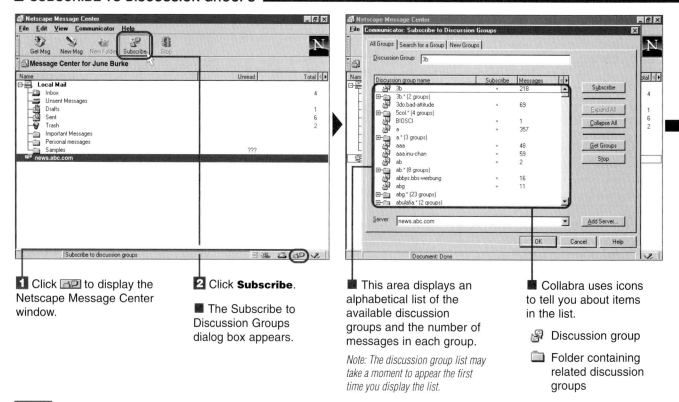

1 Click to display the Netscape Message Center window.

2 Click **Subscribe**.

■ The Subscribe to Discussion Groups dialog box appears.

■ This area displays an alphabetical list of the available discussion groups and the number of messages in each group.

Note: The discussion group list may take a moment to appear the first time you display the list.

■ Collabra uses icons to tell you about items in the list.

- Discussion group
- Folder containing related discussion groups

?

Why is my discussion group list different from the list shown in this book?

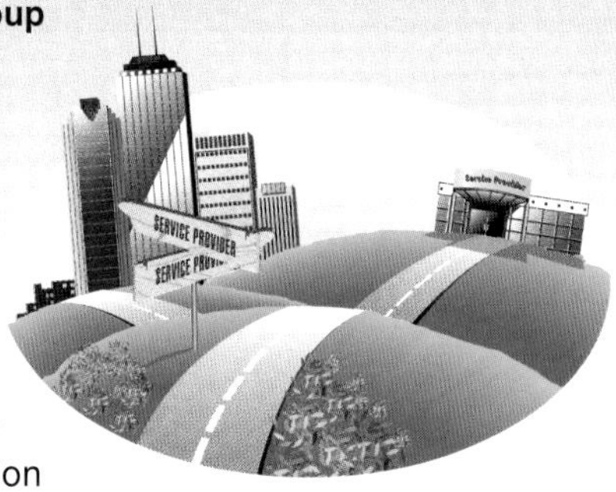

The discussion groups available to you depend on your service provider, which is the company that gives you access to the Internet. Your service provider may limit the available discussion groups to save valuable storage space.

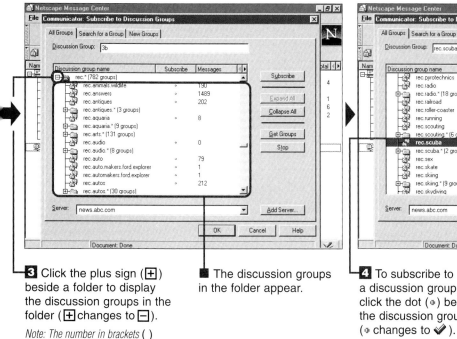

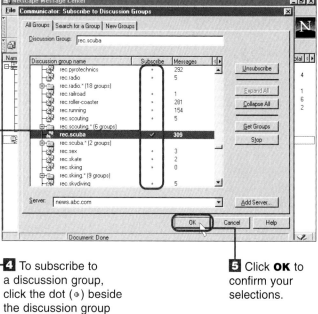

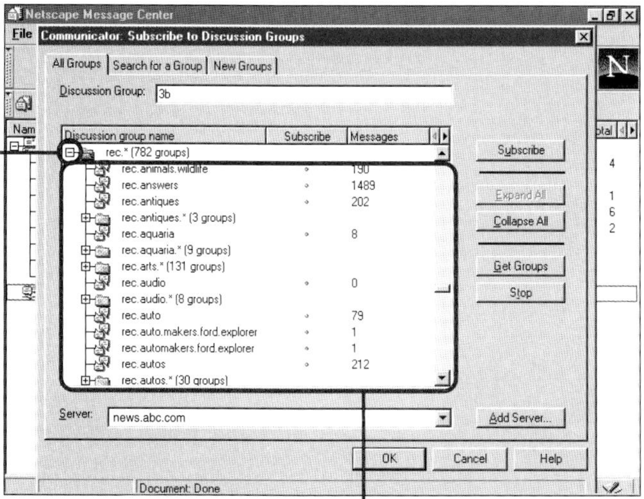

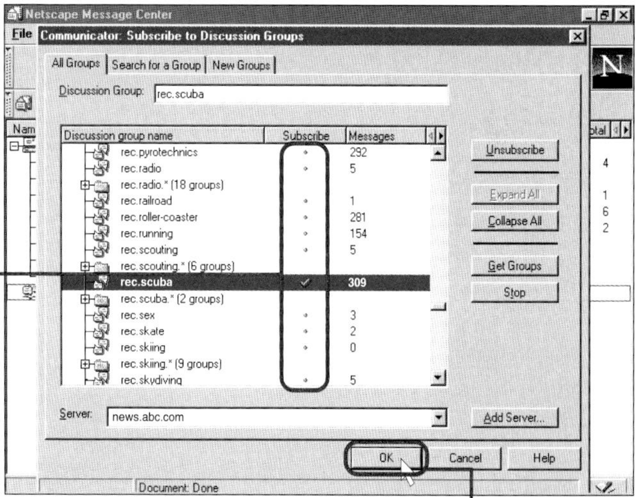

3 Click the plus sign (⊞) beside a folder to display the discussion groups in the folder (⊞ changes to ⊟).

Note: The number in brackets ( ) beside a folder tells you how many discussion groups are in the folder.

■ The discussion groups in the folder appear.

4 To subscribe to a discussion group, click the dot (•) beside the discussion group (• changes to ✔).

Note: To unsubscribe from a discussion group, refer to page 196.

5 Click **OK** to confirm your selections.

UNSUBSCRIBE FROM A DISCUSSION GROUP

You can unsubscribe from a discussion group at any time if the subject material no longer interests you.

UNSUBSCRIBE FROM A DISCUSSION GROUP

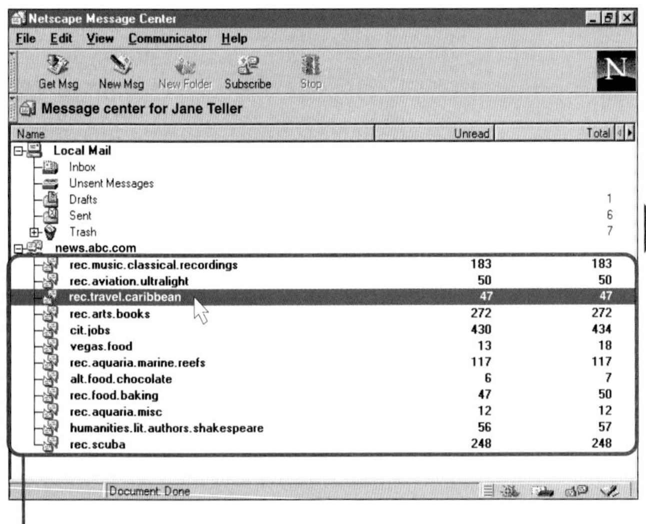

1 Click the discussion group you want to unsubscribe from.

2 Press the Delete key.

■ A confirmation dialog box appears.

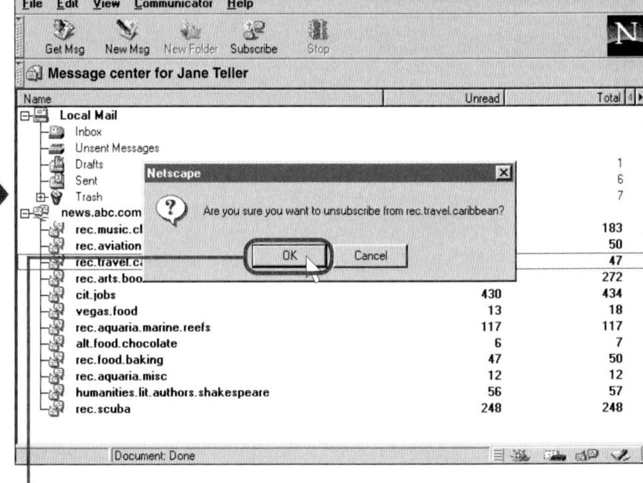

3 Click **OK** to unsubscribe from the discussion group.

■ The discussion group disappears from the list.

DISPLAY NEW DISCUSSION GROUPS

You can display a list of the new discussion groups that are available.

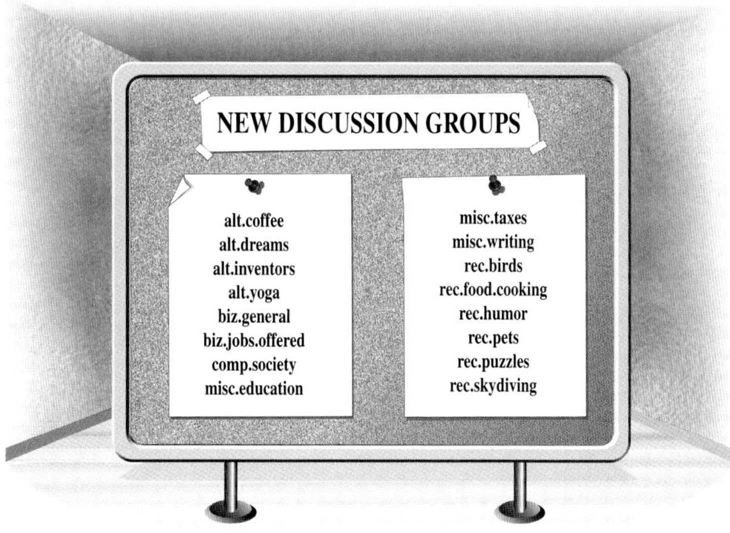

New discussion groups are created every week.

DISPLAY NEW DISCUSSION GROUPS

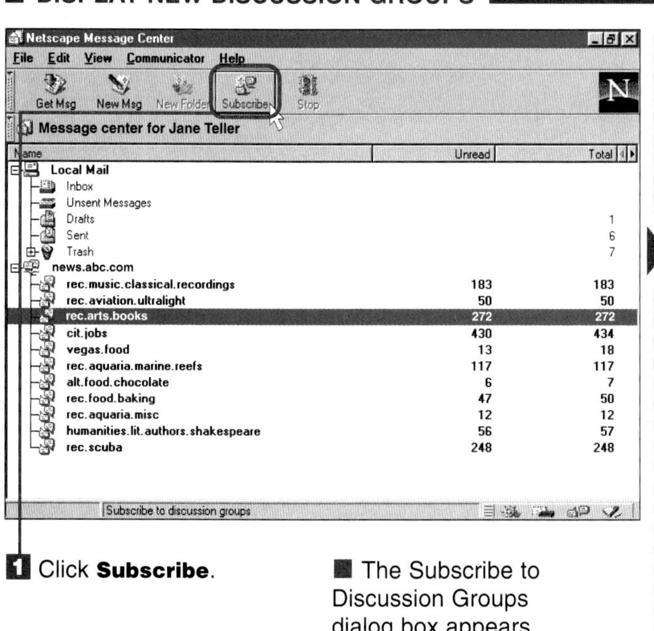

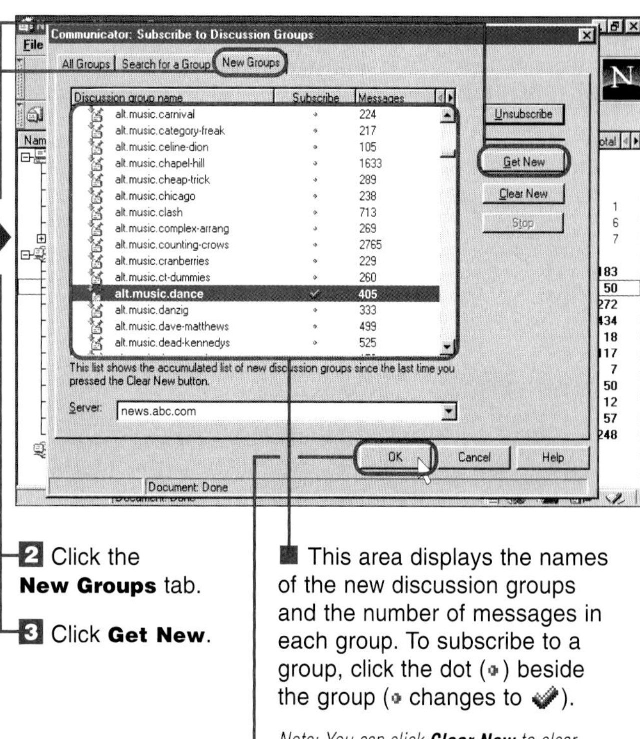

1 Click **Subscribe**.

■ The Subscribe to Discussion Groups dialog box appears.

2 Click the **New Groups** tab.

3 Click **Get New**.

■ This area displays the names of the new discussion groups and the number of messages in each group. To subscribe to a group, click the dot (•) beside the group (• changes to ✔).

*Note: You can click **Clear New** to clear the list of new discussion groups.*

4 Click **OK**.

SEARCH FOR DISCUSSION GROUPS

You can search for discussion groups that deal with topics of interest to you.

SEARCH FOR DISCUSSION GROUPS

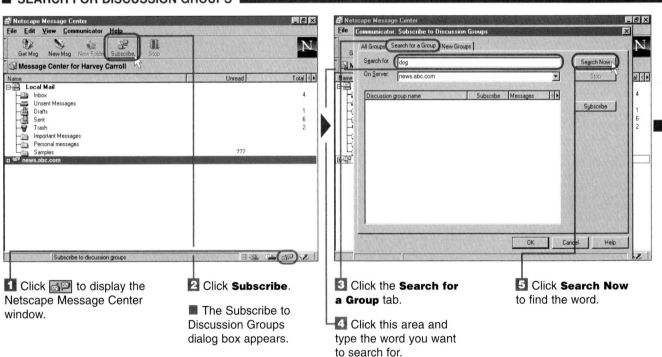

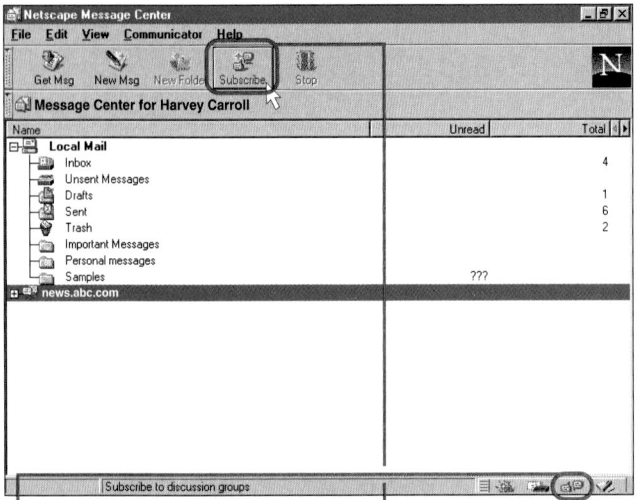

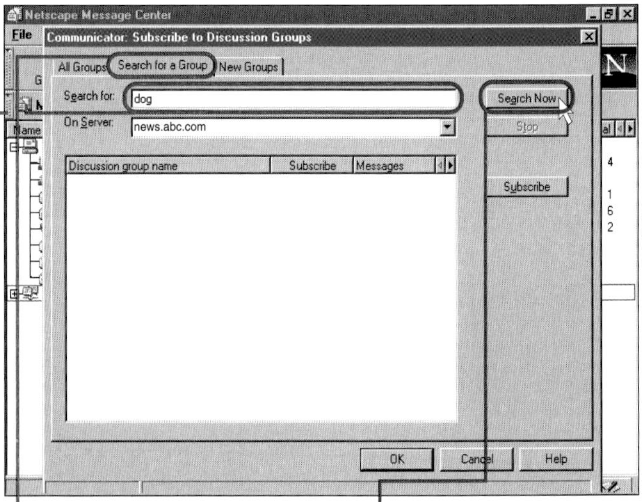

1 Click [icon] to display the Netscape Message Center window.

2 Click **Subscribe**.

■ The Subscribe to Discussion Groups dialog box appears.

3 Click the **Search for a Group** tab.

4 Click this area and type the word you want to search for.

5 Click **Search Now** to find the word.

Why can't I find a discussion group of interest?

You may need to perform several searches before you find a discussion group of interest. For example, if you want to find a discussion group on cars, you can first try searching for **car** and then try searching for **auto** or **vehicle**.

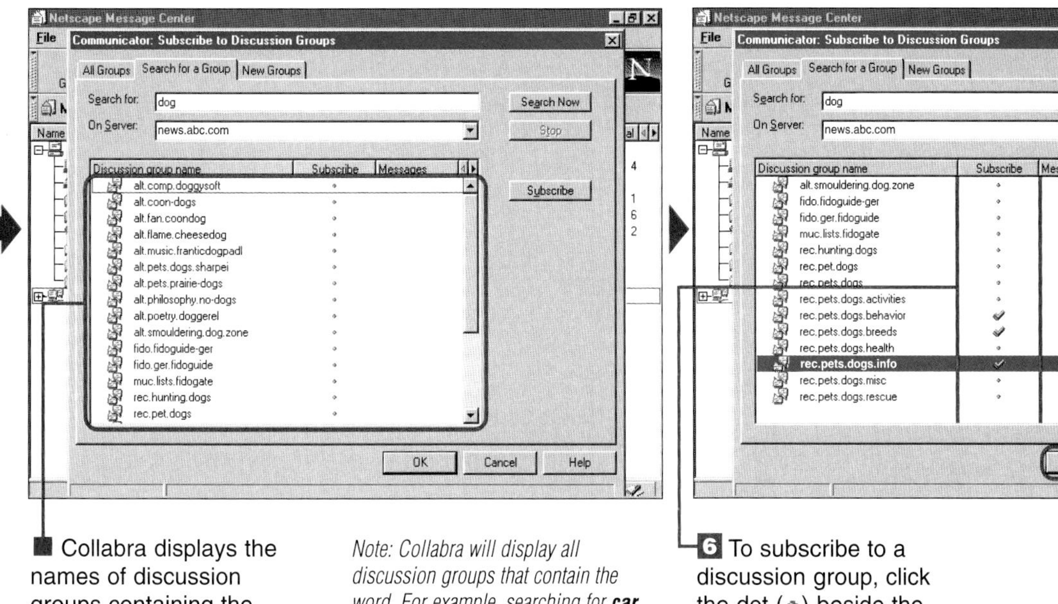

■ Collabra displays the names of discussion groups containing the word you typed.

*Note: Collabra will display all discussion groups that contain the word. For example, searching for **car** will also find **car**toons and child**car**e.*

6 To subscribe to a discussion group, click the dot (◦) beside the discussion group (◦ changes to ✔).

Note: To unsubscribe from a discussion group, refer to page 196.

7 Click **OK** to confirm your selections.

DISPLAY MESSAGES IN OTHER DISCUSSION GROUPS

You can quickly display the messages in another discussion group. This allows you to view the messages for another topic.

DISPLAY MESSAGES IN OTHER DISCUSSION GROUPS

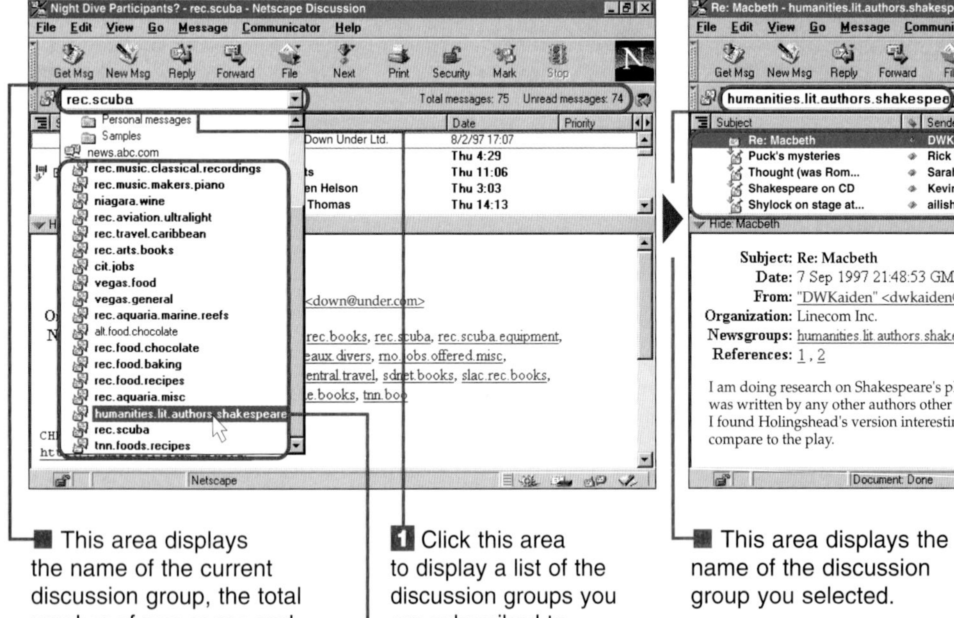

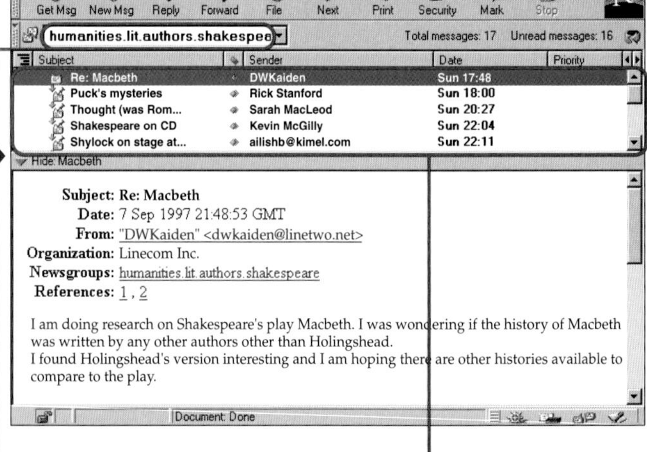

■ This area displays the name of the current discussion group, the total number of messages and the number of unread messages in the group.

1 Click this area to display a list of the discussion groups you are subscribed to.

2 Click the discussion group containing the messages you want to view.

■ This area displays the name of the discussion group you selected.

Note: If the discussion group you selected contains a lot of messages, a dialog box may appear. For information on the dialog box, refer to the top of page 203.

■ This area displays the messages in the discussion group.

CHANGE HEADER DISPLAY

You can change the amount of header information each message displays. The header displays information such as the subject and date of a message.

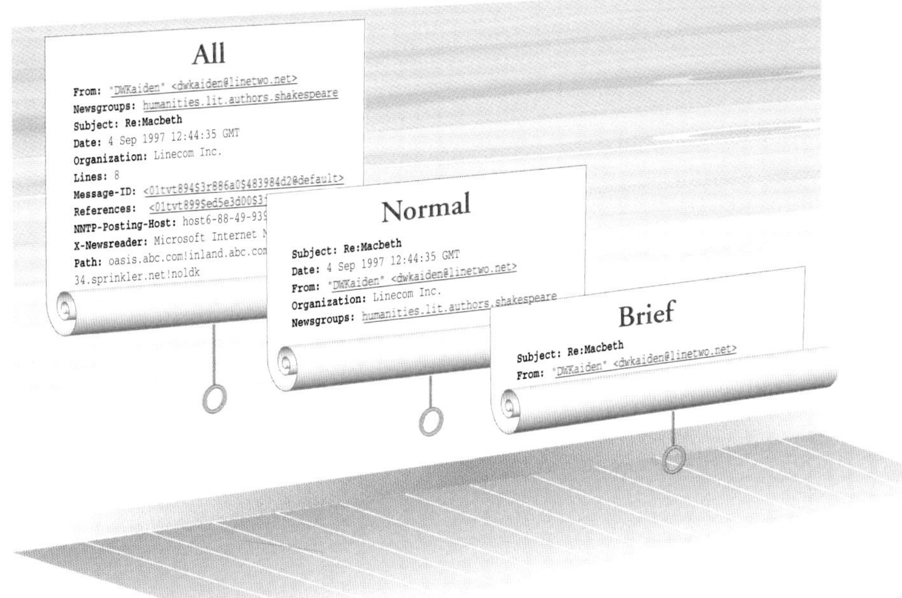

CHANGE HEADER DISPLAY

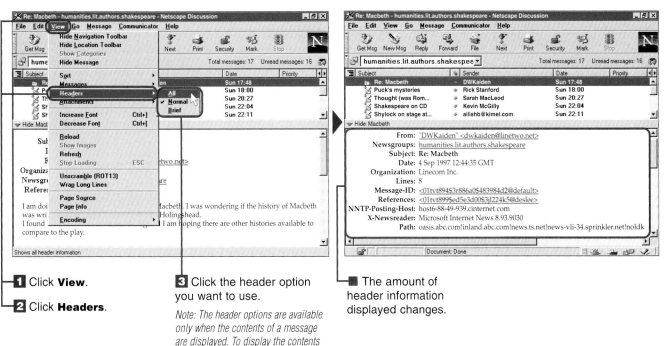

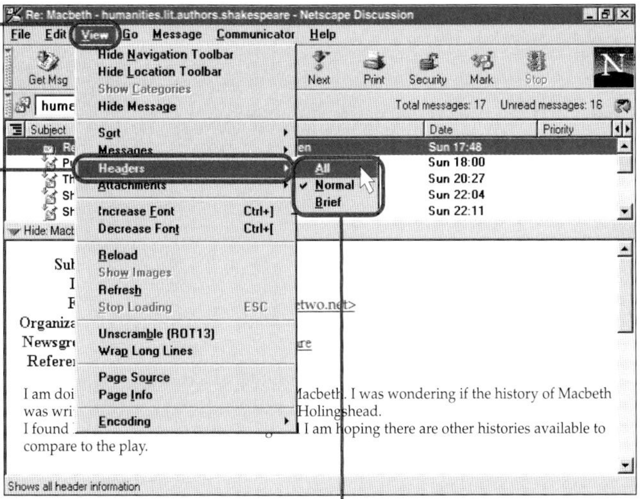

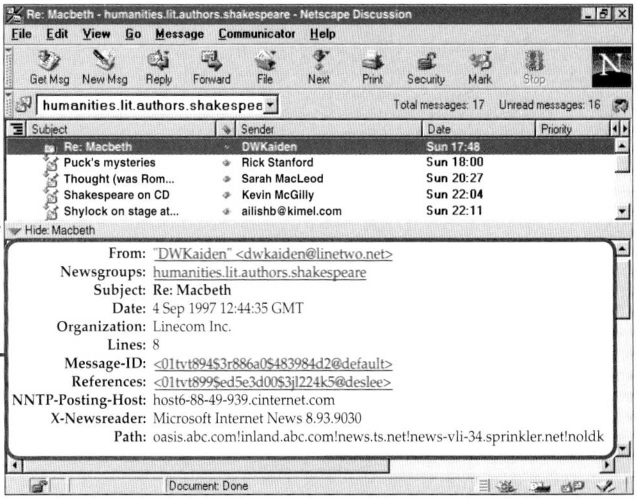

1. Click **View**.
2. Click **Headers**.
3. Click the header option you want to use.

Note: The header options are available only when the contents of a message are displayed. To display the contents of a message, refer to page 202.

■ The amount of header information displayed changes.

READ A MESSAGE

You can read the messages in a discussion group to learn the opinions and ideas of thousands of people around the world.

READ A MESSAGE

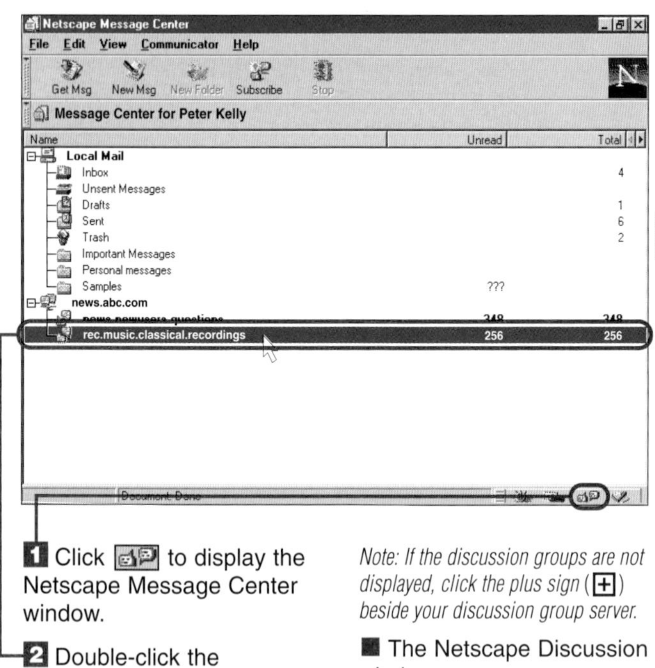

1 Click [icon] to display the Netscape Message Center window.

2 Double-click the discussion group containing the messages you want to read.

Note: If the discussion groups are not displayed, click the plus sign (⊞) beside your discussion group server.

■ The Netscape Discussion window appears.

■ This area displays the name of the discussion group, the total number of messages and the number of unread messages in the group.

■ This area displays the messages in the discussion group. Messages you have not read display a red tack ([icon]) and appear in **bold** type.

? Why does a dialog box appear when I try to read the messages in some discussion groups?

A dialog box appears if the discussion group you selected contains more than 500 messages.

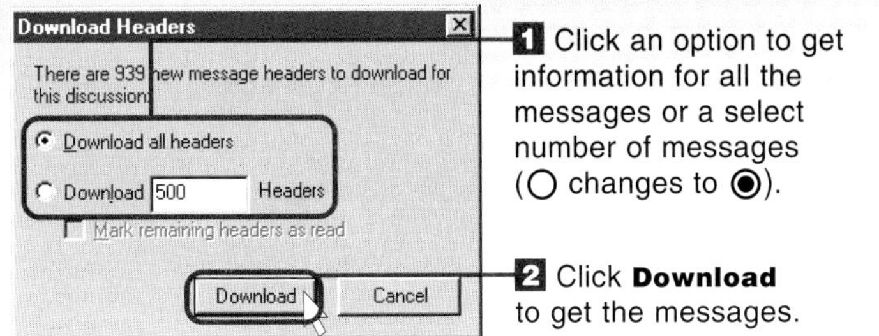

1 Click an option to get information for all the messages or a select number of messages (○ changes to ◉).

2 Click **Download** to get the messages.

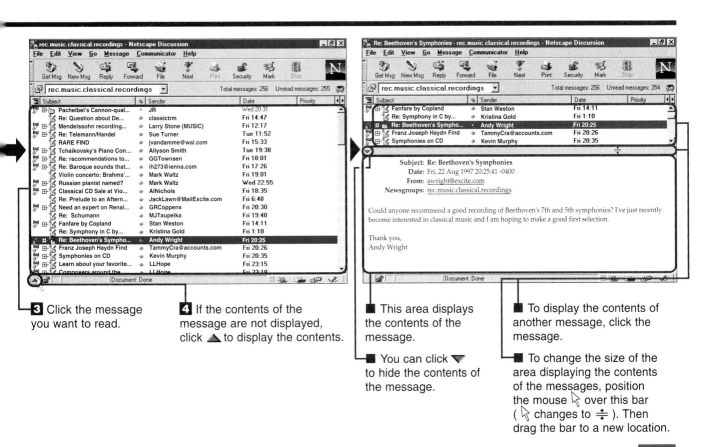

3 Click the message you want to read.

4 If the contents of the message are not displayed, click ▲ to display the contents.

■ This area displays the contents of the message.

■ You can click ▼ to hide the contents of the message.

■ To display the contents of another message, click the message.

■ To change the size of the area displaying the contents of the messages, position the mouse over this bar (changes to). Then drag the bar to a new location.

FILE A MESSAGE

You can place a copy of an interesting discussion group message in a folder. Filing a message allows you to review the message when you are not connected to the Internet.

You can create personalized folders to store discussion group messages. For more information, refer to page 124.

FILE A MESSAGE

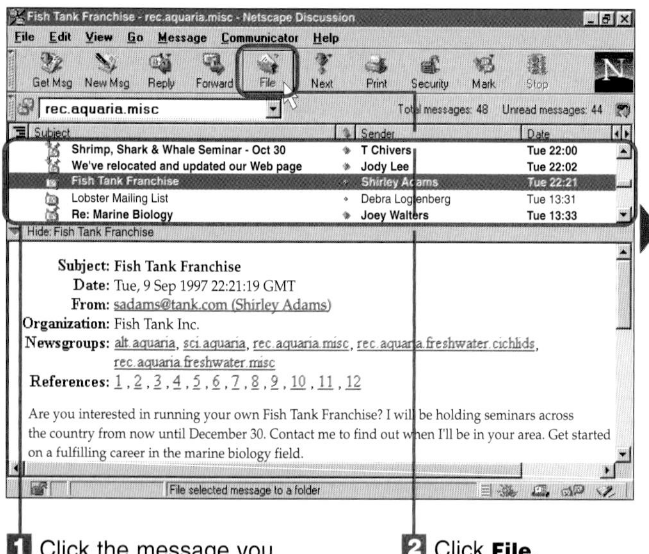

1 Click the message you want to place in a folder.

Note: To display the messages in a discussion group, refer to page 200.

2 Click **File**.

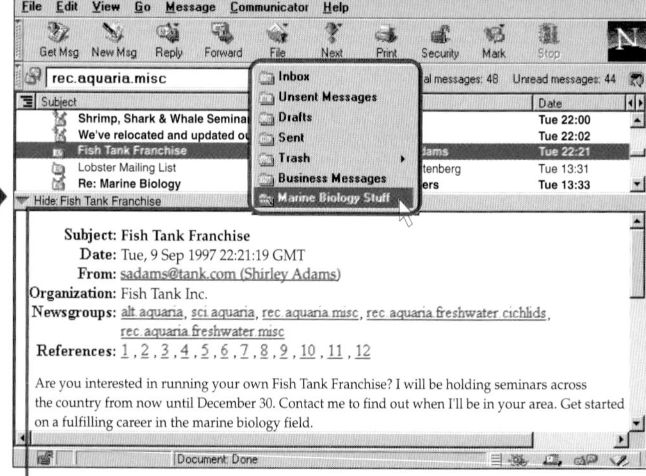

3 Click the folder you want to store the message.

■ Collabra places a copy of the message in the folder you selected.

Note: To display the messages in other folders, refer to page 122.

SORT MESSAGES

You can sort the messages in a discussion group so you can more easily find messages of interest.

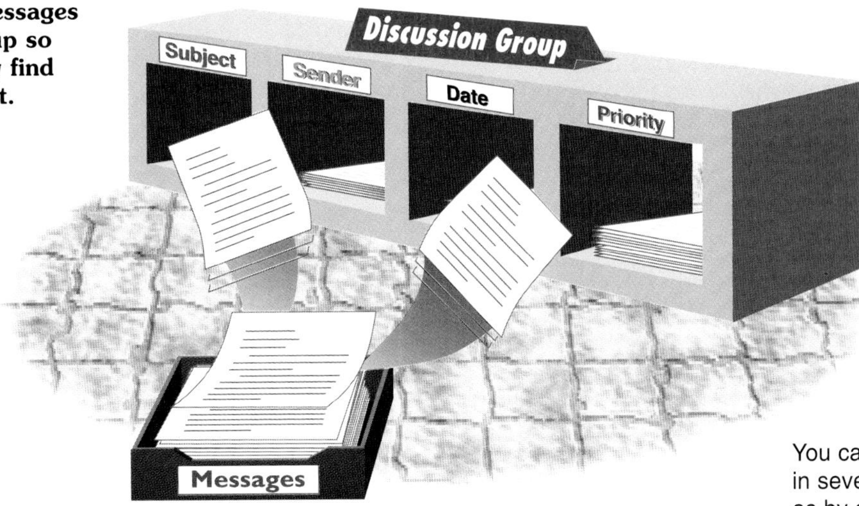

You can sort messages in several ways, such as by subject, sender, date or priority.

SORT MESSAGES

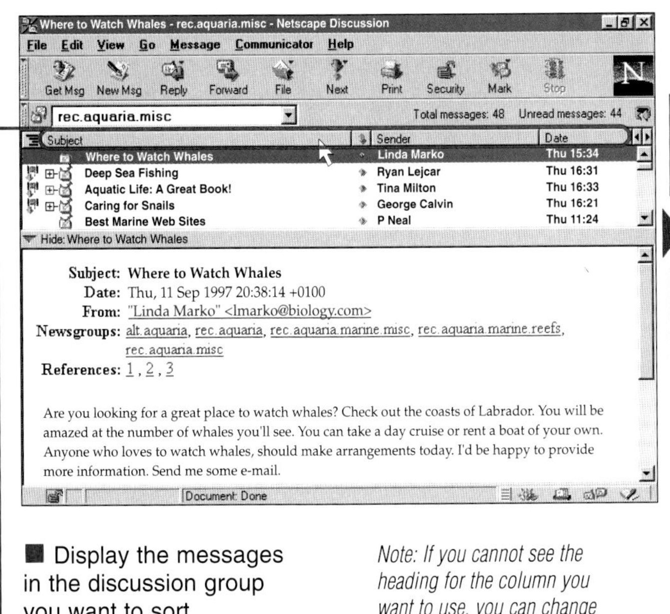

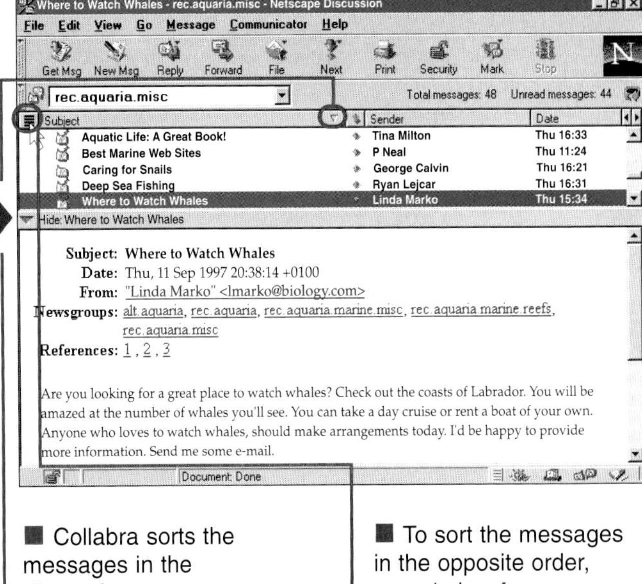

■ Display the messages in the discussion group you want to sort.

1 Click the heading for the column you want to use to sort the messages.

Note: If you cannot see the heading for the column you want to use, you can change the width of the columns to display the heading. To change the width of columns, refer to page 112.

■ Collabra sorts the messages in the discussion group.

■ A small arrow (▽) appears in the heading of the column you used to sort the messages.

■ To sort the messages in the opposite order, repeat step **1**.

■ You can click ☰ to return the messages to their original sort order.

MARK MESSAGES AS READ

You can mark discussion group messages as read. This allows you to de-emphasize messages you are not interested in.

MARK MESSAGES AS READ

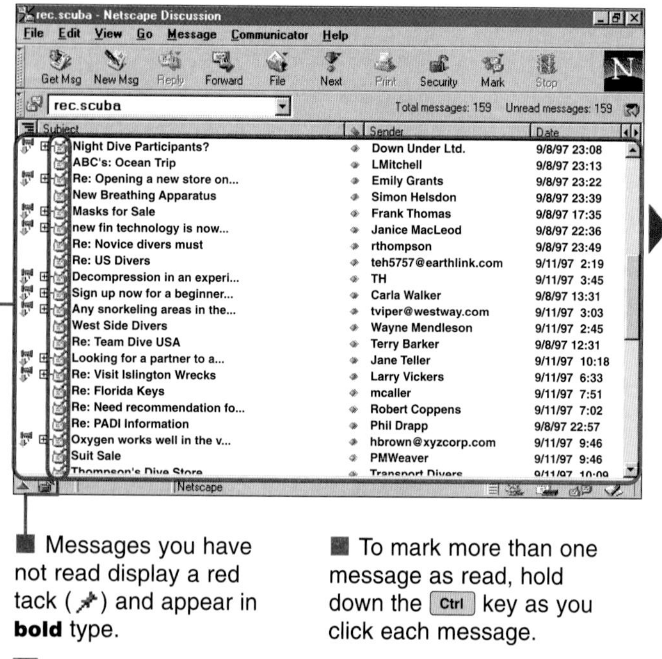

■ Messages you have not read display a red tack (📌) and appear in **bold** type.

1 Click a message you want to mark as read.

■ To mark more than one message as read, hold down the Ctrl key as you click each message.

Note: You do not have to select messages if you want to mark them by Date.

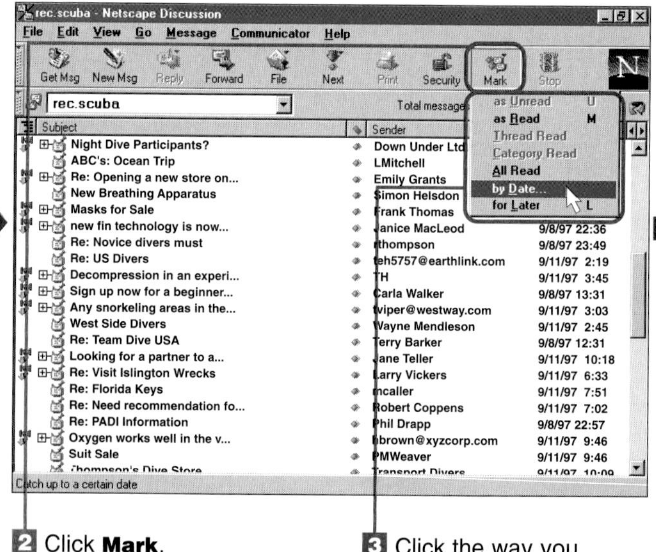

2 Click **Mark**.

3 Click the way you want to mark the message as read.

? How can I mark discussion group messages?

as Unread

Mark messages as unread.

as Read

Mark messages as read.

All Read

Mark all messages as read.

by Date

Mark all messages before a specific date as read.

Thread Read

Mark every message in a thread as read. A thread is a group of related messages.

Category Read

Mark every message in a category as read. Categories are folders within a discussion group found on company intranets.

for Later

Mark messages temporarily as read. When you return to the discussion group, the messages will appear as unread.

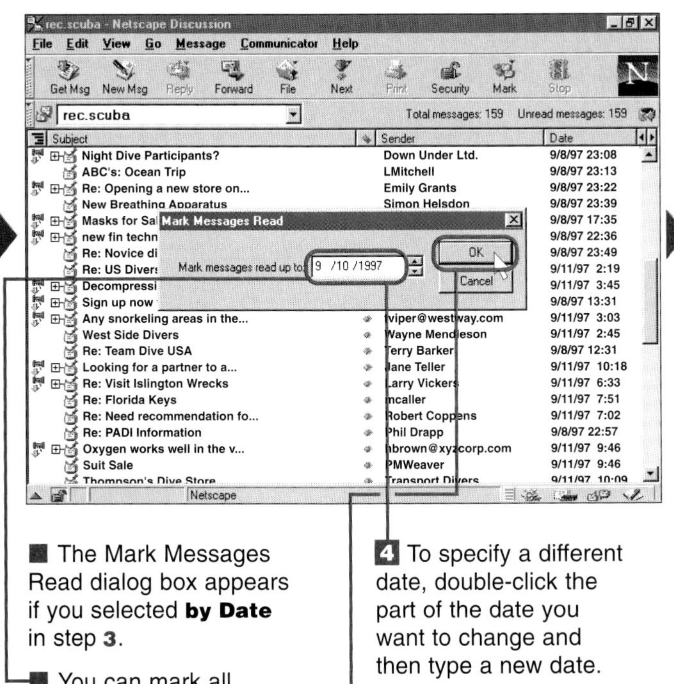

■ The Mark Messages Read dialog box appears if you selected **by Date** in step **3**.

■ You can mark all messages as read up to the date displayed in this area.

4 To specify a different date, double-click the part of the date you want to change and then type a new date.

5 Click **OK** to confirm the date.

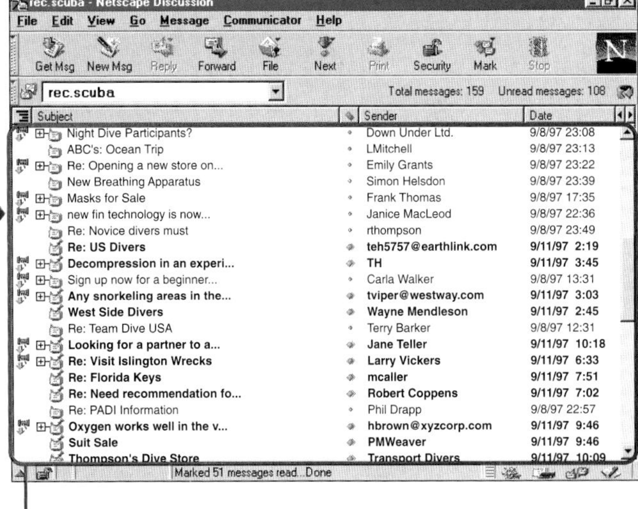

■ The messages you specified are marked as read. Read messages do not display a red tack (📌) and appear in regular type.

PRINT A MESSAGE

You can produce a paper copy of a discussion group message you find interesting.

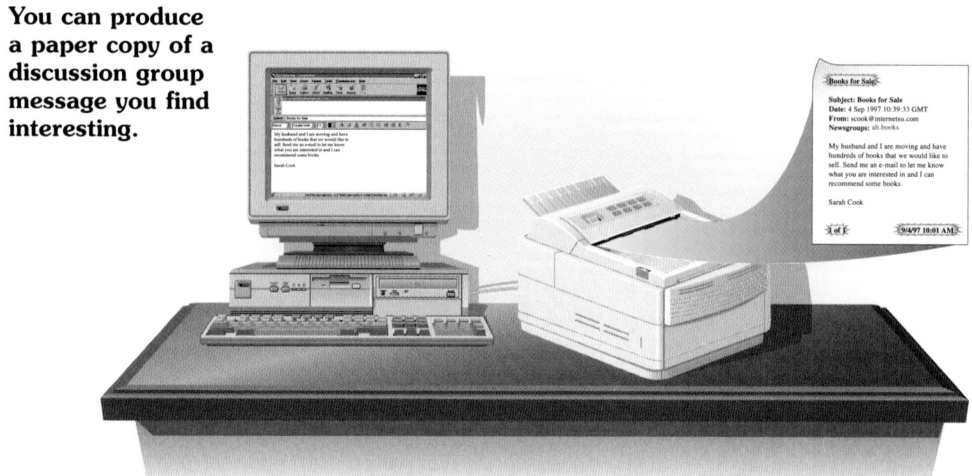

The subject prints at the top of the page. The page number, total number of pages and current date and time print at the bottom of the page.

PRINT A MESSAGE

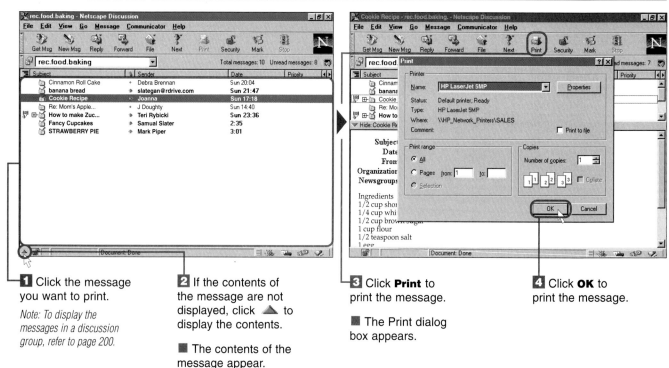

1 Click the message you want to print.

Note: To display the messages in a discussion group, refer to page 200.

2 If the contents of the message are not displayed, click ▲ to display the contents.

■ The contents of the message appear.

3 Click **Print** to print the message.

■ The Print dialog box appears.

4 Click **OK** to print the message.

FORWARD A MESSAGE

If a message in a discussion group contains information that would be of interest to a friend or colleague, you can send them the message with your comments.

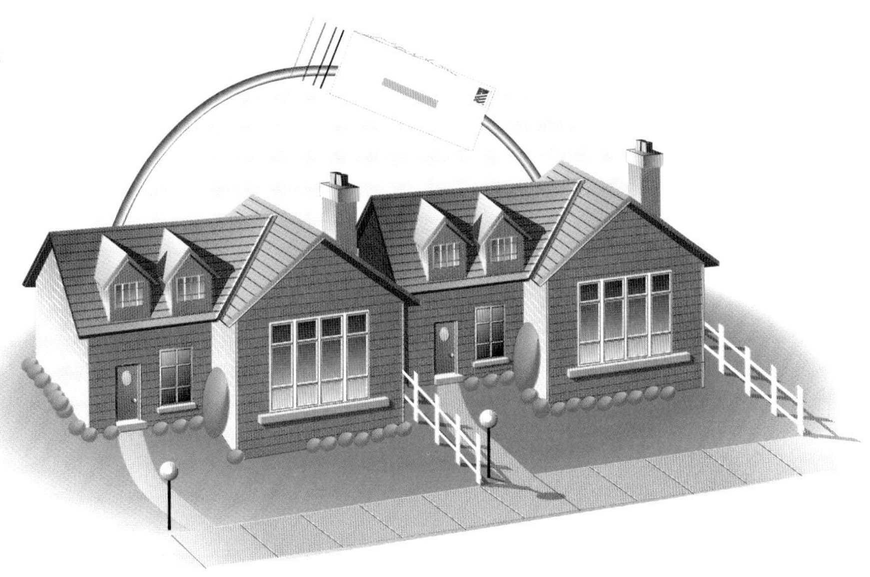

FORWARD A MESSAGE

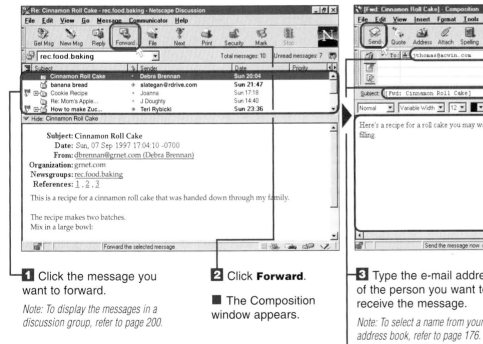

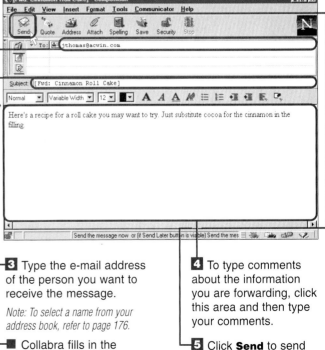

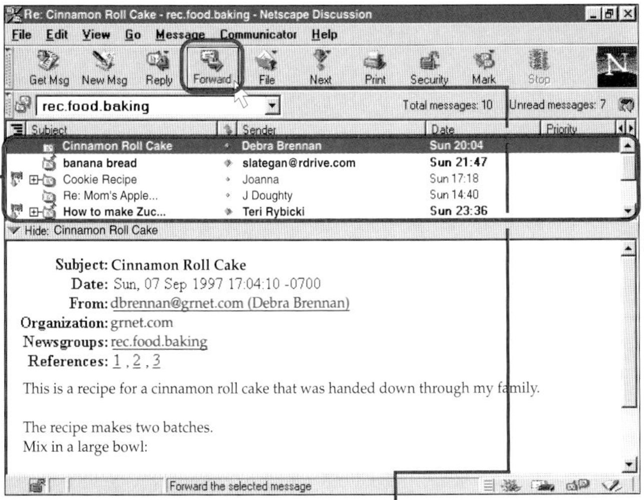

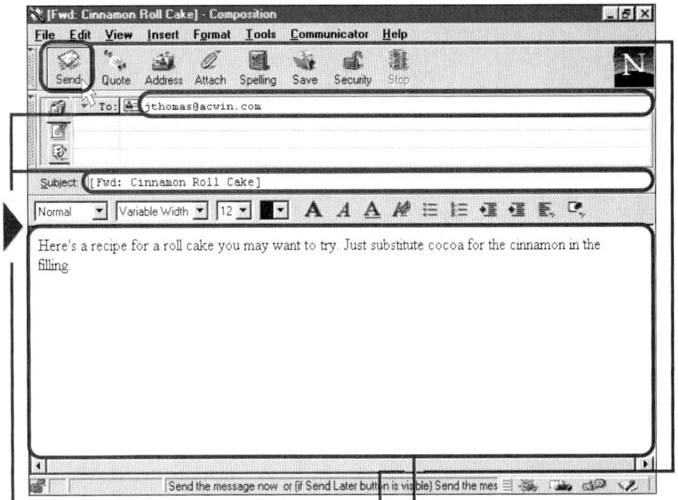

1 Click the message you want to forward.

Note: To display the messages in a discussion group, refer to page 200.

2 Click **Forward**.

■ The Composition window appears.

3 Type the e-mail address of the person you want to receive the message.

Note: To select a name from your address book, refer to page 176.

■ Collabra fills in the subject for you.

4 To type comments about the information you are forwarding, click this area and then type your comments.

5 Click **Send** to send the message.

REPLY TO A MESSAGE

You can reply to a message in a discussion group to answer a question, express an opinion or offer additional information.

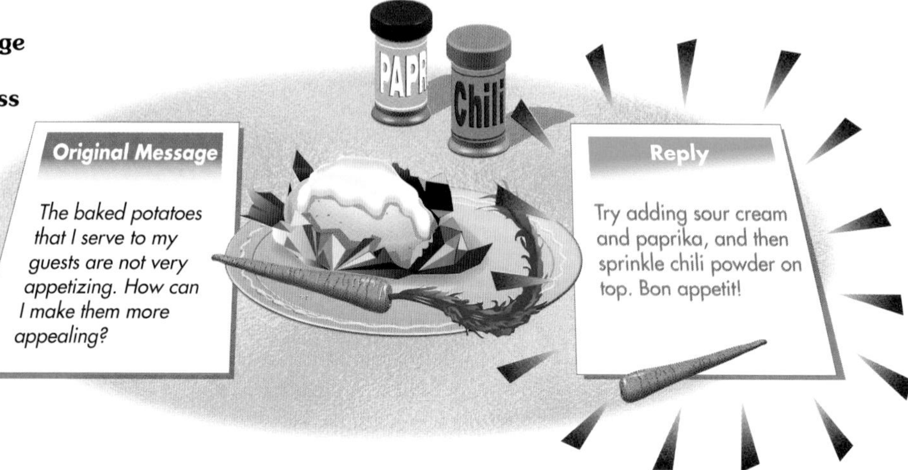

Original Message
The baked potatoes that I serve to my guests are not very appetizing. How can I make them more appealing?
Reply
Try adding sour cream and paprika, and then sprinkle chili powder on top. Bon appetit!
PAPR
Chili

Reply to a message only when you have something important to say. A reply such as "Me too" or "I agree" is not very informative.

REPLY TO A MESSAGE

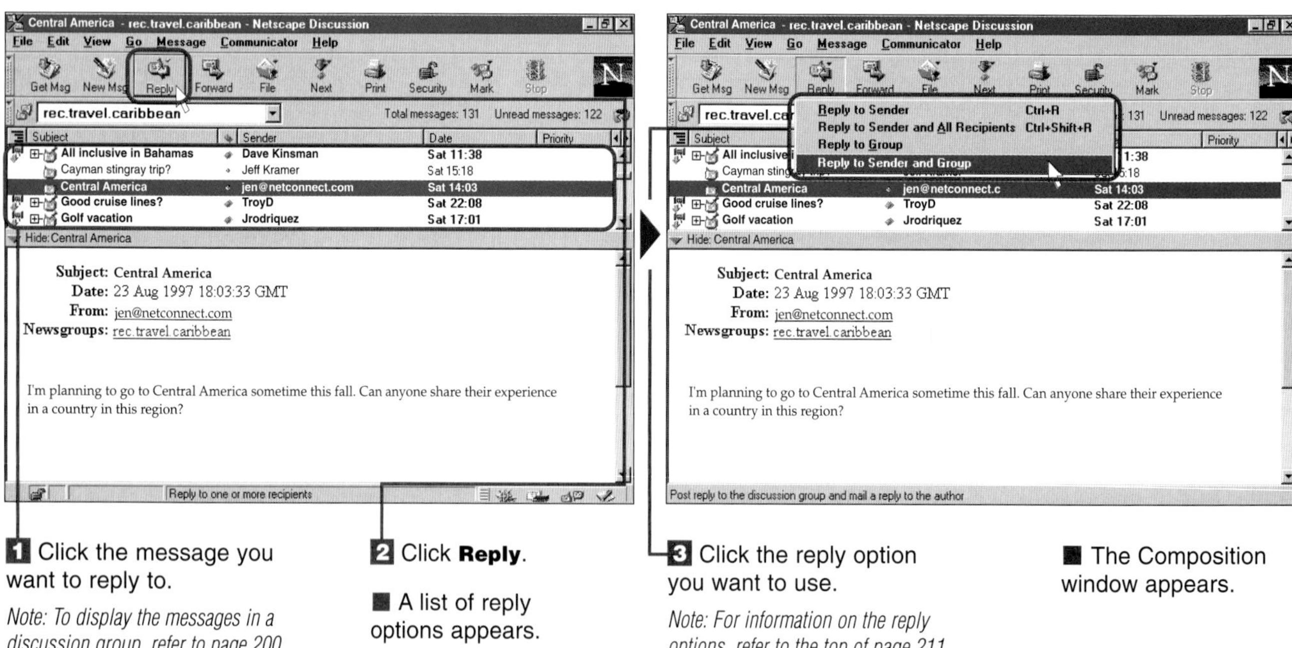

1 Click the message you want to reply to.

Note: To display the messages in a discussion group, refer to page 200.

2 Click **Reply**.

■ A list of reply options appears.

3 Click the reply option you want to use.

Note: For information on the reply options, refer to the top of page 211.

■ The Composition window appears.

Who can I send a reply to?

Reply to Sender

Sends a private message to the author of the original message.

Reply to Group

Sends a message to the discussion group for everyone to read.

Reply to Sender and All Recipients

Sends a private message to the author of the original message and to each person who received the message.

Reply to Sender and Group

Sends a message to the author of the original message and to the discussion group.

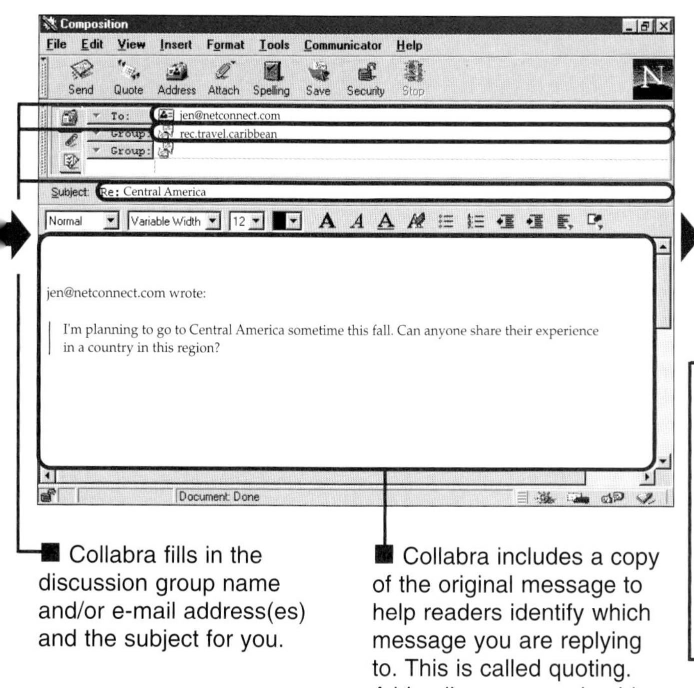

■ Collabra fills in the discussion group name and/or e-mail address(es) and the subject for you.

■ Collabra includes a copy of the original message to help readers identify which message you are replying to. This is called quoting. A blue line appears beside the quoted text.

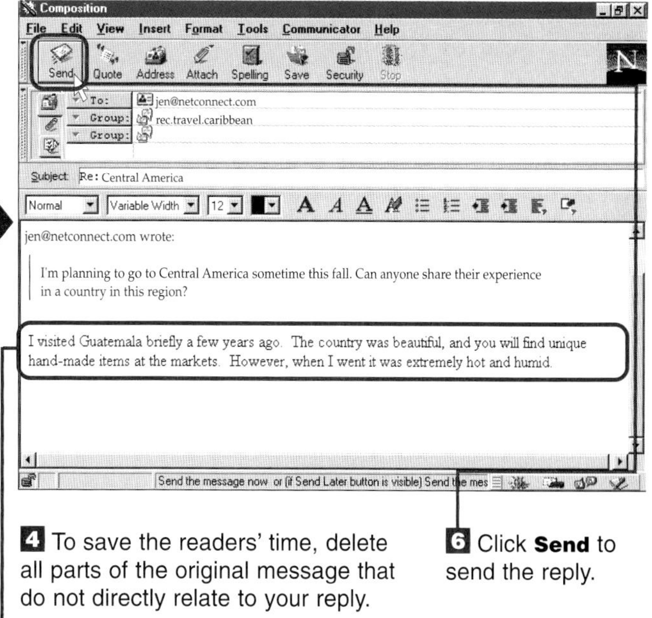

4 To save the readers' time, delete all parts of the original message that do not directly relate to your reply.

5 To add your comments to the message, click the area where you want the reply to appear and then type your reply.

6 Click **Send** to send the reply.

CREATE A NEW MESSAGE

You can send a new message to a discussion group to ask a question or express your opinion.

I am starting Yoga next week and I was wondering what I should wear to class. Also, is there anything that I should bring?
Thanks,
Katie Johnson

When sending a new message to a discussion group, keep in mind that thousands of people around the world may read the message.

If you want to practice sending a message, send a message to the misc.test discussion group. Do not send practice messages to other groups.

CREATE A NEW MESSAGE

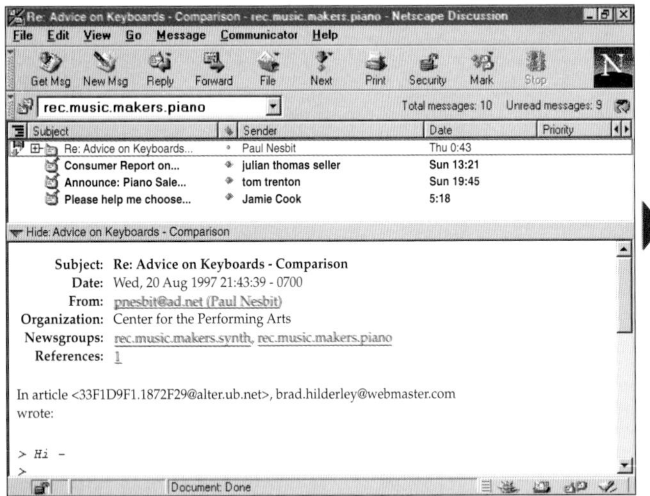

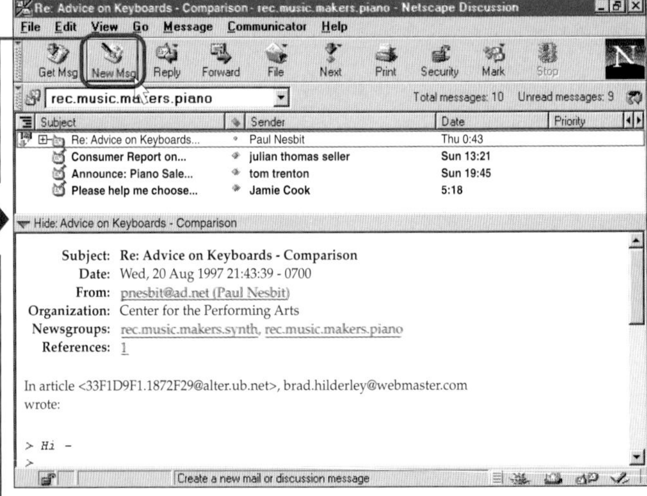

1 Display the messages in the discussion group you want to send a message to.

Note: To display the messages in a discussion group, refer to page 200.

2 Click **New Msg** to create a new message.

■ The Composition window appears.

?

Should I read the messages in a discussion group before sending a new message?

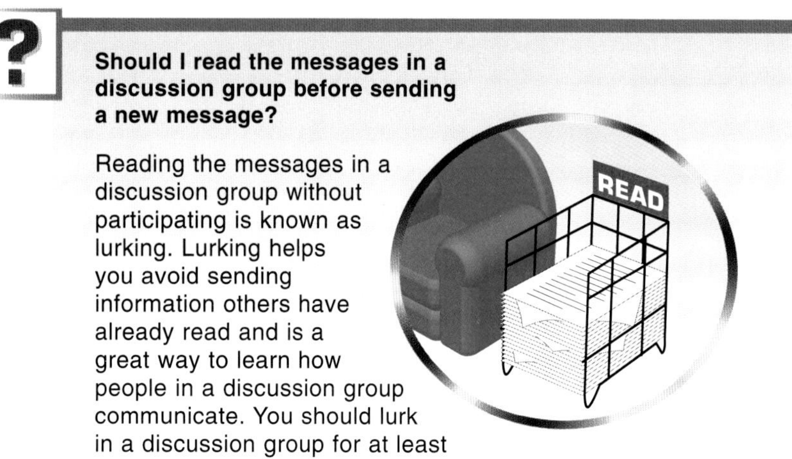

Reading the messages in a discussion group without participating is known as lurking. Lurking helps you avoid sending information others have already read and is a great way to learn how people in a discussion group communicate. You should lurk in a discussion group for at least one week before sending a new message.

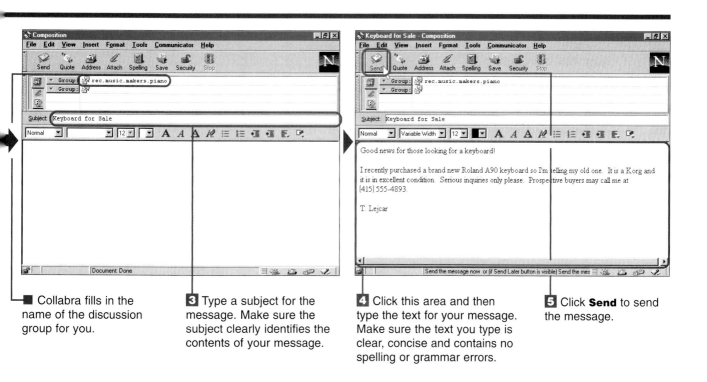

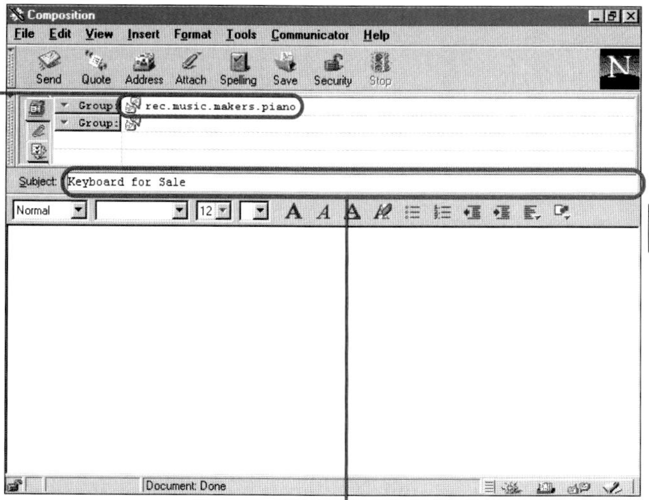

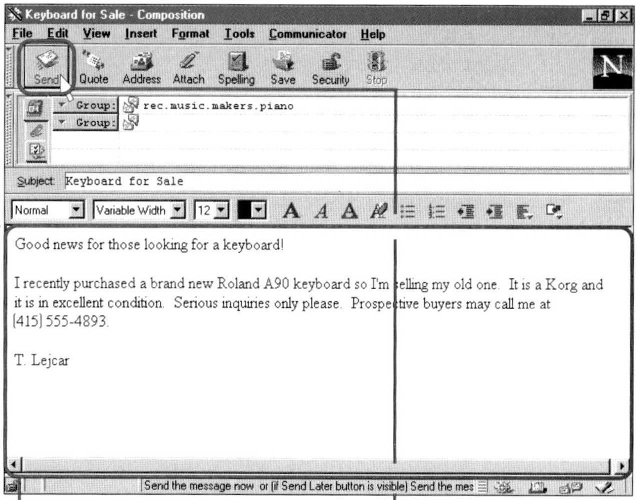

■ Collabra fills in the name of the discussion group for you.

3 Type a subject for the message. Make sure the subject clearly identifies the contents of your message.

4 Click this area and then type the text for your message. Make sure the text you type is clear, concise and contains no spelling or grammar errors.

5 Click **Send** to send the message.

CHECK SPELLING

You can use the Spelling feature to find and correct all the spelling errors in a message you are about to send to a discussion group.

CHECK SPELLING

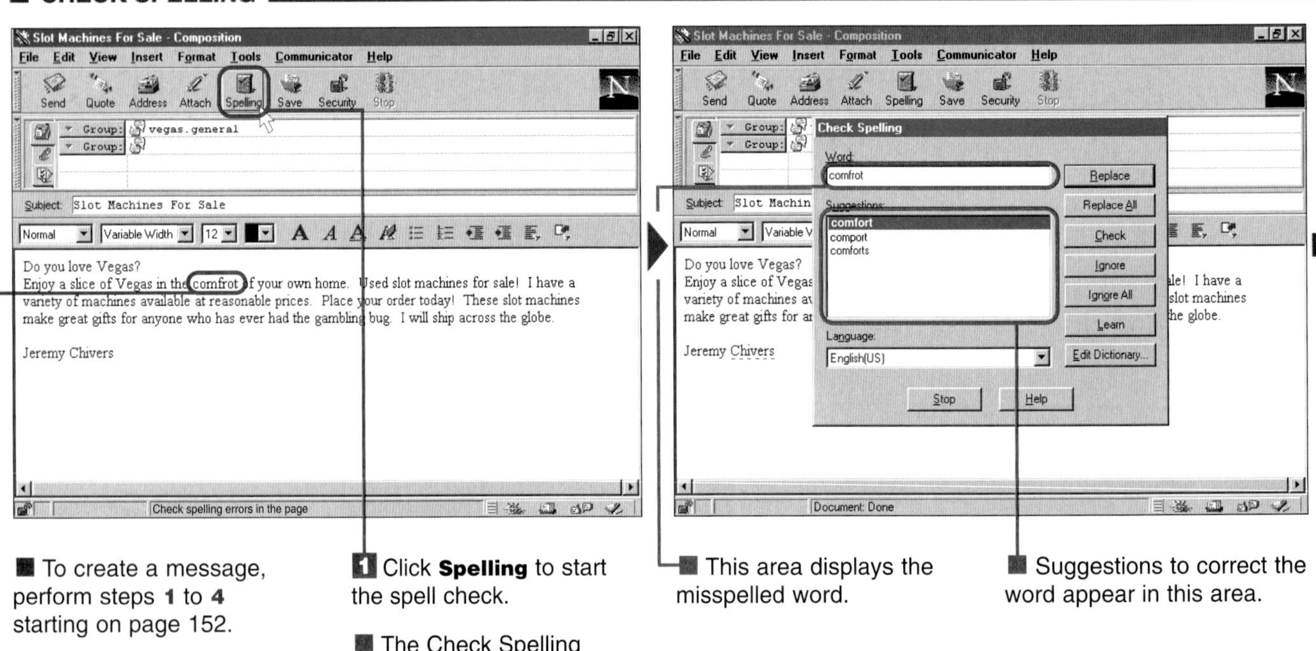

■ To create a message, perform steps **1** to **4** starting on page 152.

■ In this example, the spelling of **comfort** was changed to **comfrot**.

1 Click **Spelling** to start the spell check.

■ The Check Spelling dialog box appears.

■ This area displays the misspelled word.

■ Suggestions to correct the word appear in this area.

? Are there other types of errors I should check for before sending a message to a discussion group?

Thousands of people around the world may read a message you send to a discussion group. Before sending a message, reread the message to make sure the text is clear, concise and contains no grammar errors. Also make sure your message will not be misinterpreted. For example, not all readers will realize a statement is meant to be sarcastic.

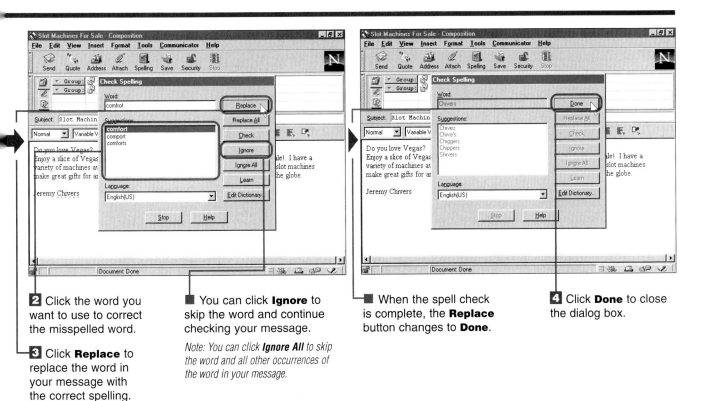

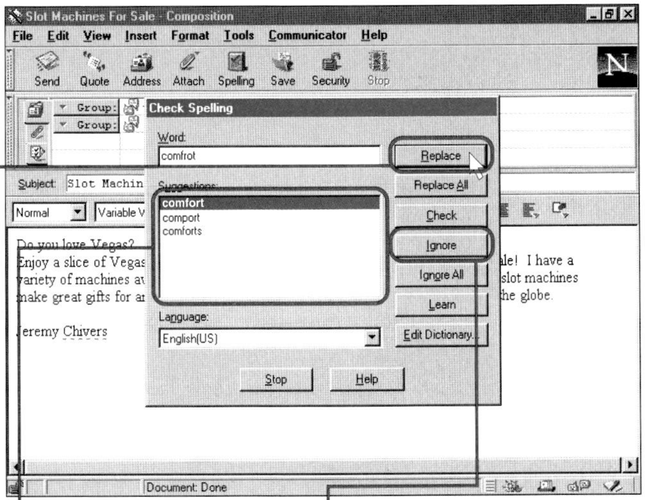

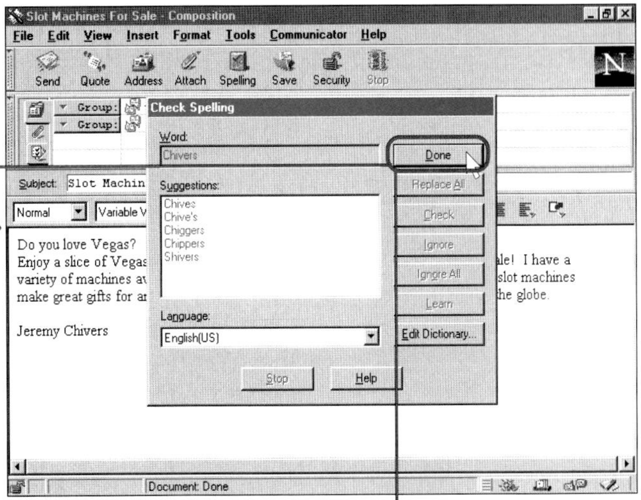

2 Click the word you want to use to correct the misspelled word.

3 Click **Replace** to replace the word in your message with the correct spelling.

■ You can click **Ignore** to skip the word and continue checking your message.

*Note: You can click **Ignore All** to skip the word and all other occurrences of the word in your message.*

■ When the spell check is complete, the **Replace** button changes to **Done**.

4 Click **Done** to close the dialog box.

WATCH THREADS

You can choose to watch messages in a particular thread. Watching threads helps you keep track of messages on topics that interest you.

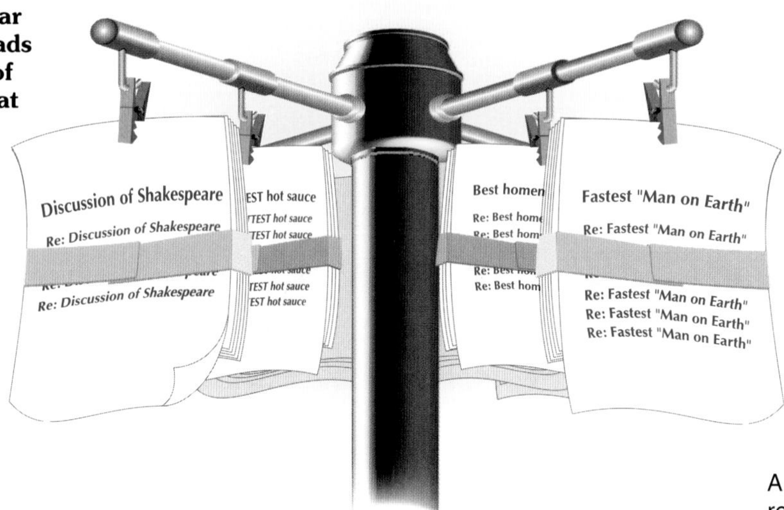

A thread is a group of related messages.

WATCH THREADS

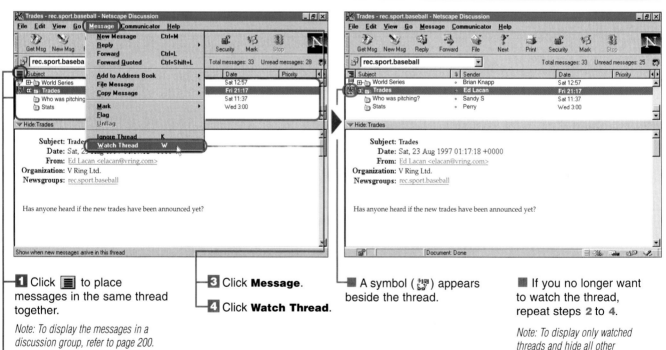

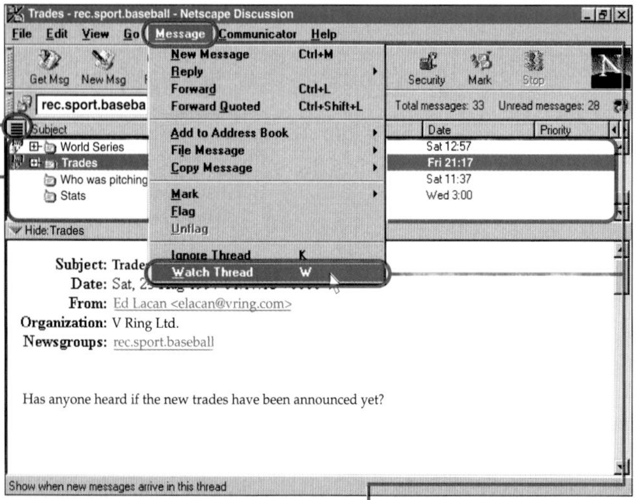

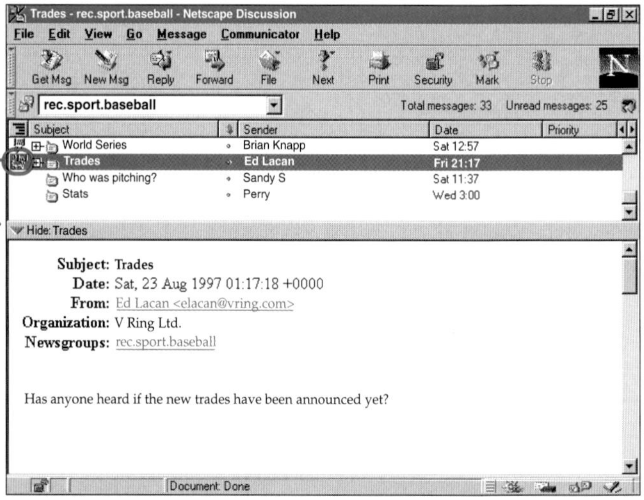

1 Click ▤ to place messages in the same thread together.

Note: To display the messages in a discussion group, refer to page 200.

2 Click a message in the thread you want to watch.

3 Click **Message**.

4 Click **Watch Thread**.

■ A symbol ( ) appears beside the thread.

■ If you no longer want to watch the thread, repeat steps **2** to **4**.

Note: To display only watched threads and hide all other messages, refer to page 218.

IGNORE THREADS

You can choose to ignore messages in a particular thread that does not interest you. An ignored message and all related messages will no longer appear on your screen.

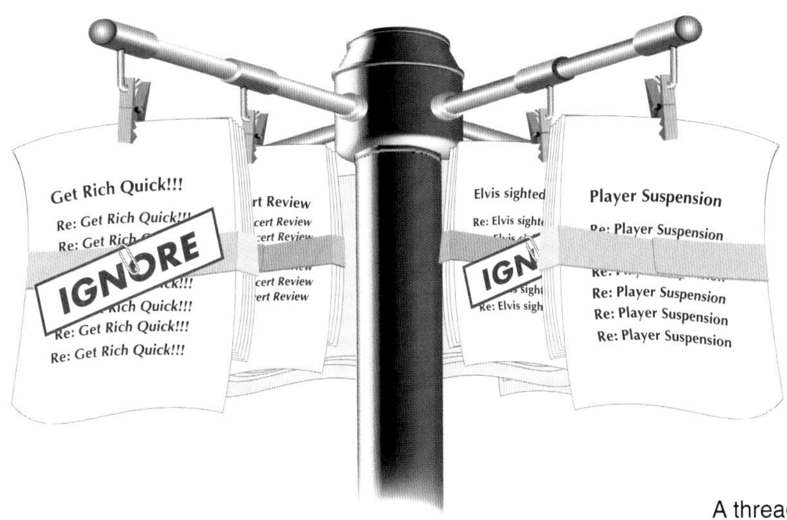

A thread is a group of related messages.

IGNORE THREADS

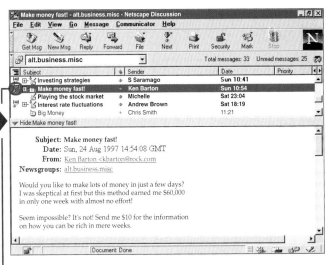

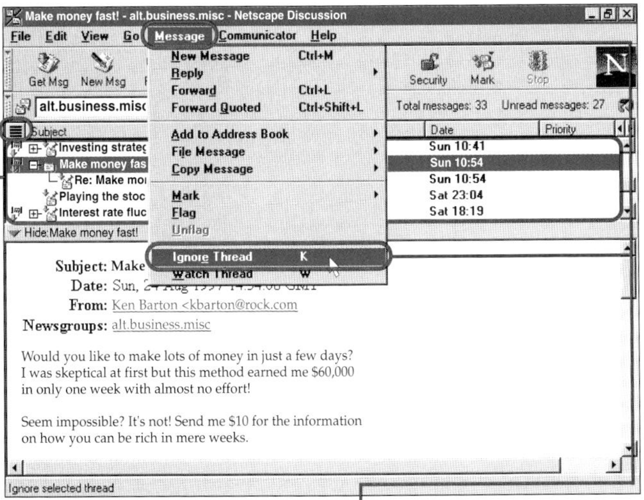

■1 Click ☰ to place messages in the same thread together.

Note: To display the messages in a discussion group, refer to page 200.

■2 Click a message in the thread you want to ignore.

■3 Click **Message**.

■4 Click **Ignore Thread**.

■ A symbol ( ) appears beside the thread.

■ The next time you display the messages in the discussion group, the message you selected and all related messages will not appear.

Note: To display ignored messages, refer to page 219.

CHANGE DISPLAY OF MESSAGES

You can change which messages appear on your screen so you can focus on messages of interest.

CHANGE DISPLAY OF MESSAGES

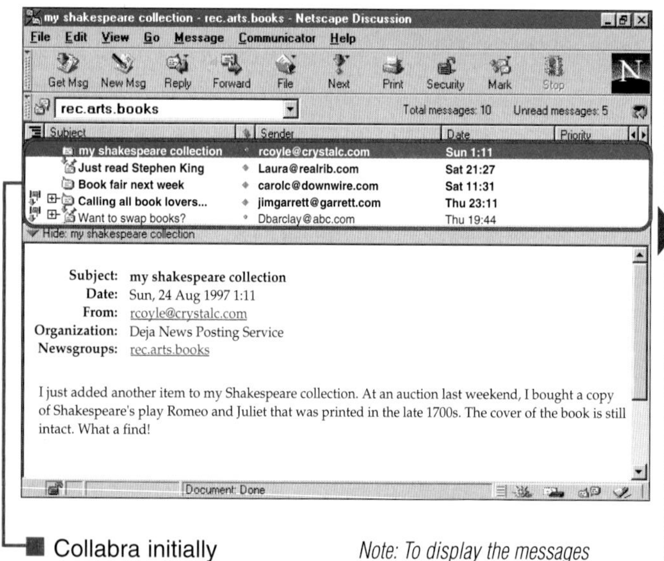

■ Collabra initially displays all the messages in a discussion group.

Note: To display the messages in a discussion group, refer to page 200.

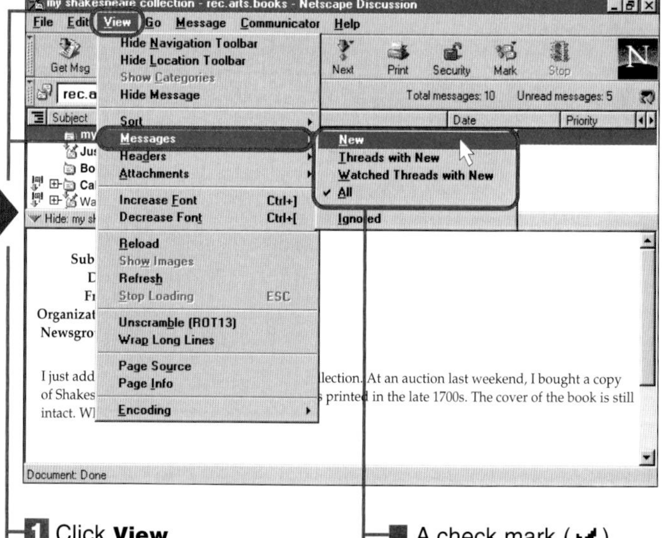

1 Click **View**.

2 Click **Messages** to change which messages appear on your screen.

■ A check mark (✔) appears beside the messages that are currently displayed.

3 Click the messages you want to display on your screen.

Which messages can I display on my screen?

New

Show only messages you have not read.

Watched Threads with New

Show only watched threads with messages you have not read.

Threads with New

Show only threads with messages you have not read. A thread is a group of related messages.

All

Show all messages.

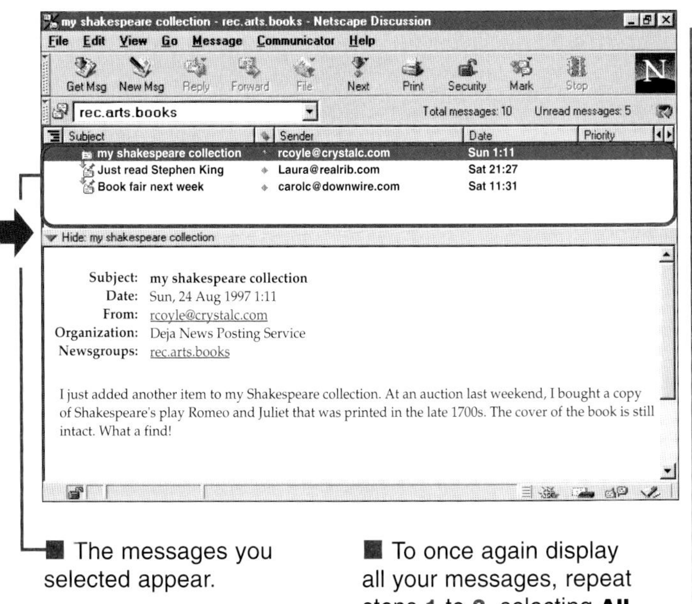

■ The messages you selected appear.

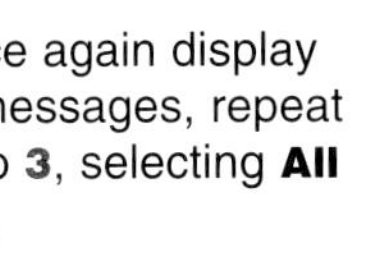

■ To once again display all your messages, repeat steps **1** to **3**, selecting **All** in step **3**.

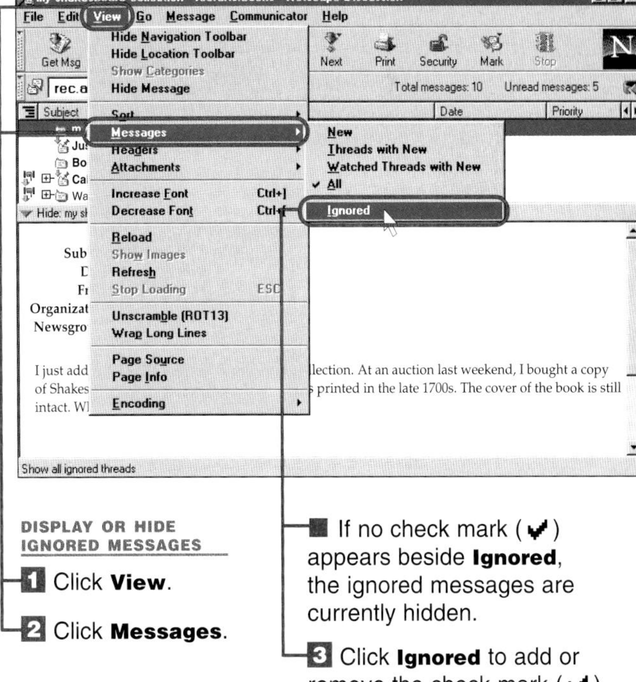

DISPLAY OR HIDE IGNORED MESSAGES

1. Click **View**.
2. Click **Messages**.

■ If no check mark (✔) appears beside **Ignored**, the ignored messages are currently hidden.

3. Click **Ignored** to add or remove the check mark (✔).

Note: The Ignored option is only available if all messages are currently displayed.

Financial News
Monday, September 29, 1997
50 cents
President promises tax cut
BY KELLEIGH WING
ABC Inc. Posts
Quarterly Results
Stocks Up!
CNNfn
the financial network
markets
u.s. stock markets
world markets
currencies
interest rates
commodities
tech stocks
bridge news
video updates
lipper report
CNN home page
markets
dow
s&p
nasdaq
time span
day
month
3 mo.
year
7920
7885
7850
7815
7780
9:30
10:30
11:30
12:30
1:30
2:30
3:30
7860.5
+38.08
dow
today
Tech stocks to set tempo?
stocks to watch
Spyglass (SPYG) 9.19 +0.16
Lycos (LCOS) 33.75
configure
techs
S&P 500: 934.26, +5.21
S+P
ADS

CHAPTER 8

Using Netcaster

Would you like to have Netcaster automatically deliver information of interest to your computer? This chapter teaches you how to add and update channels, change channel properties and much more.

Netcaster automatically delivers information of interest to your computer. You do not have to search the Web for information.

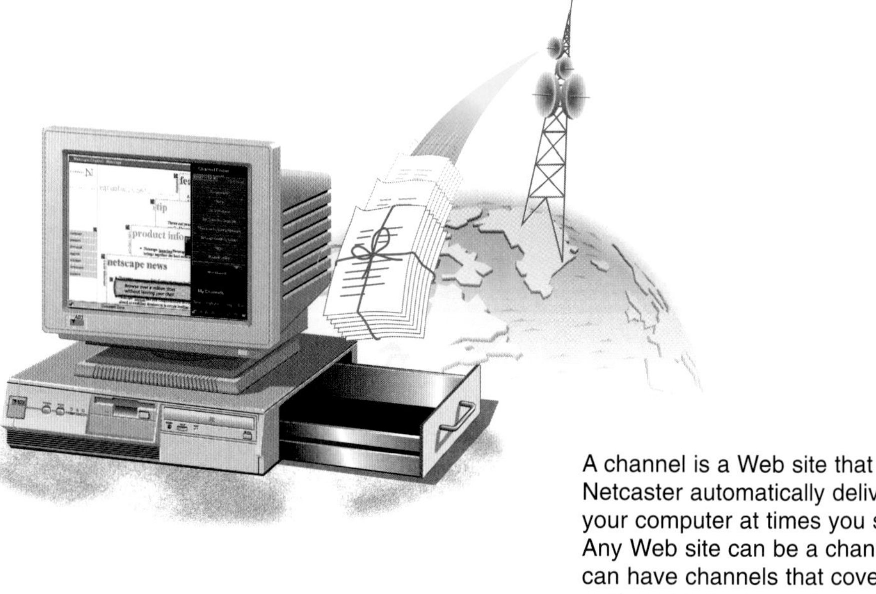

A channel is a Web site that Netcaster automatically delivers to your computer at times you specify. Any Web site can be a channel. You can have channels that cover topics such as home decorations, movies, music, news, stocks or travel.

START NETSCAPE NETCASTER

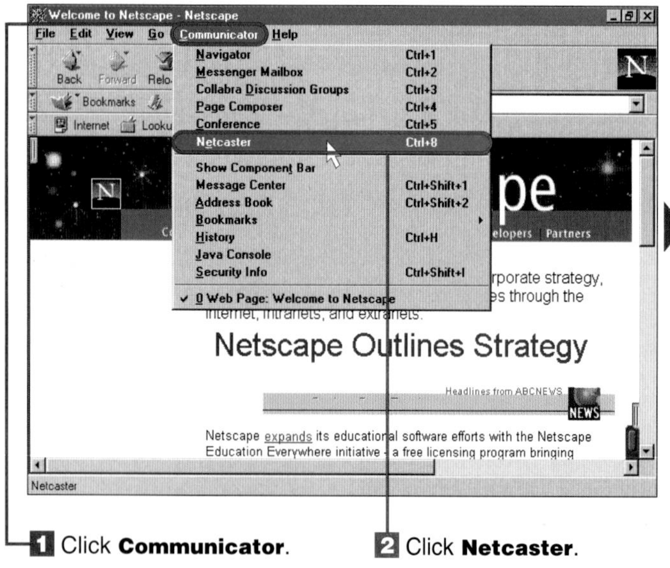

1 Click **Communicator**.

2 Click **Netcaster**.

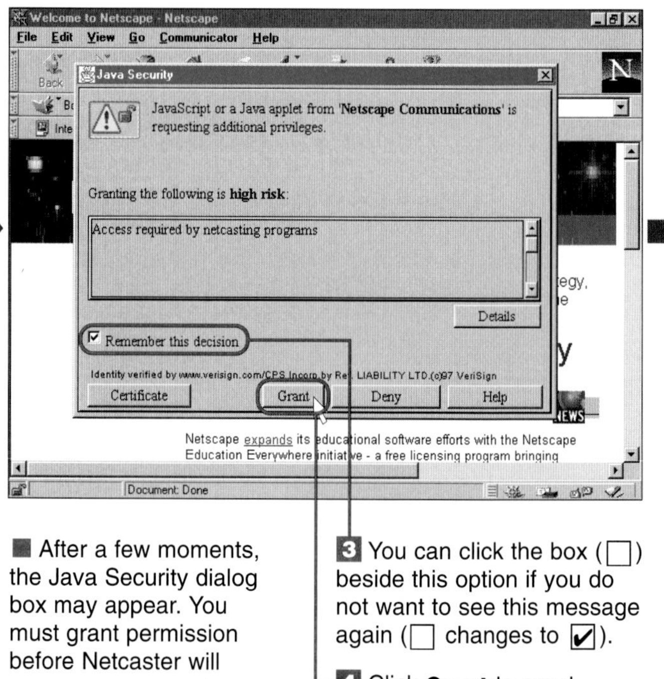

■ After a few moments, the Java Security dialog box may appear. You must grant permission before Netcaster will run on your computer.

3 You can click the box (☐) beside this option if you do not want to see this message again (☐ changes to ☑).

4 Click **Grant** to grant permission.

What is push technology?

Netcaster uses push technology to send or "push" information you request to your computer. Instead of you searching the Web for information, Netcaster checks the Internet at regular intervals and pushes the most current information to your computer. Push technology is also called netcasting or webcasting.

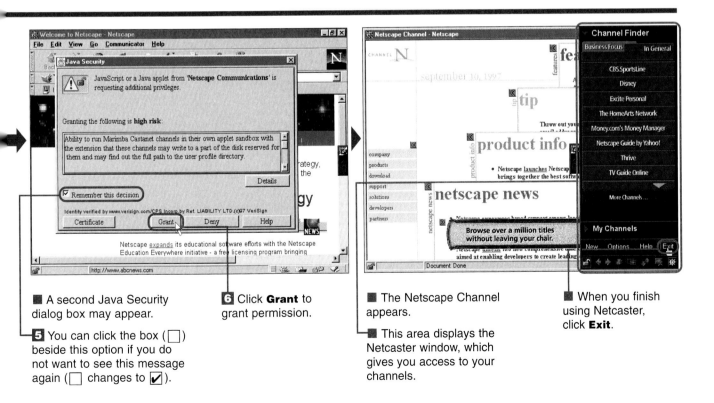

■ A second Java Security dialog box may appear.

5 You can click the box (☐) beside this option if you do not want to see this message again (☐ changes to ☑).

6 Click **Grant** to grant permission.

■ The Netscape Channel appears.

■ This area displays the Netcaster window, which gives you access to your channels.

■ When you finish using Netcaster, click **Exit**.

HIDE OR DISPLAY THE NETCASTER WINDOW

The Netcaster window allows you to access and work with your channels. You can hide the Netcaster window to provide more screen area for viewing a channel.

HIDE OR DISPLAY THE NETCASTER WINDOW

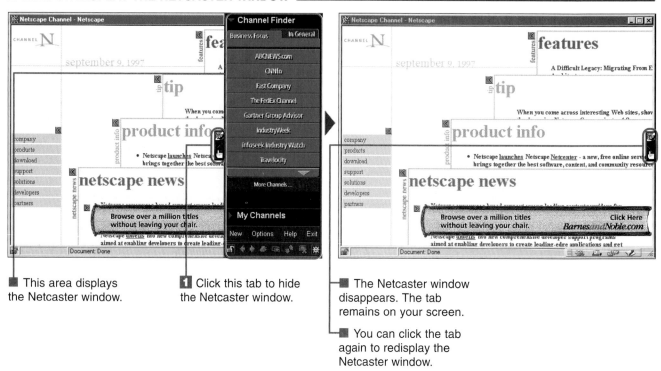

■ This area displays the Netcaster window.

1 Click this tab to hide the Netcaster window.

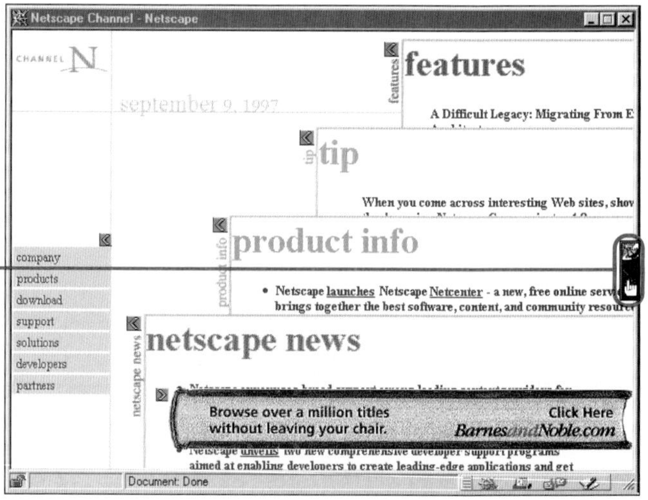

■ The Netcaster window disappears. The tab remains on your screen.

■ You can click the tab again to redisplay the Netcaster window.

DISPLAY THE MY CHANNELS LIST

The My Channels list displays all the channels you have added to Netcaster. These channels are stored on your computer and are updated automatically. You can quickly access any of these channels.

To add a channel, refer to page 228.

DISPLAY THE MY CHANNELS LIST

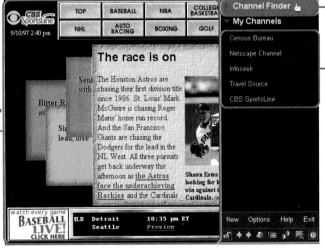

■ When you first start Netcaster, this area displays the Channel Finder list.

1 Click **My Channels** to display a list of channels you have added.

■ A list of your channels appears.

2 Click the channel you want to view.

Note: Netcaster automatically added the Netscape Channel for you.

■ The channel appears.

Note: The Netcaster window may disappear.

■ You can click **Channel Finder** to return to the Channel Finder list.

USING THE CHANNEL FINDER

The Channel Finder displays a list of interesting channels you can choose from. The channels come from various categories such as lifestyles, news, sports and personal finance.

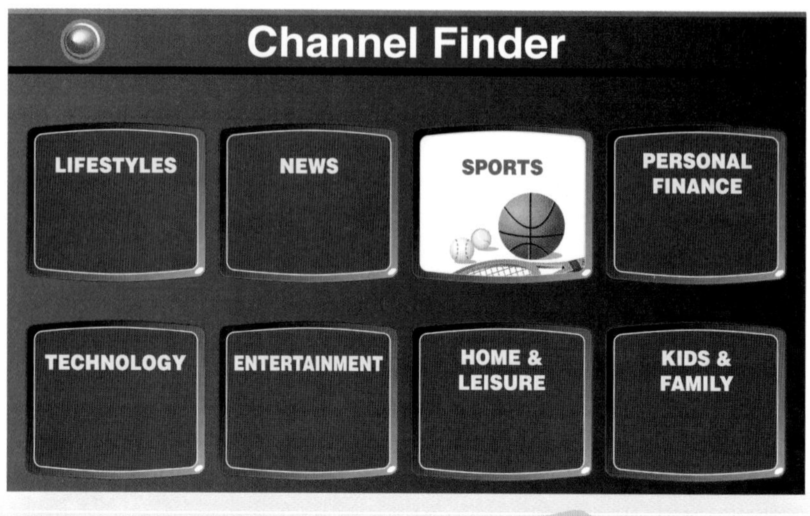

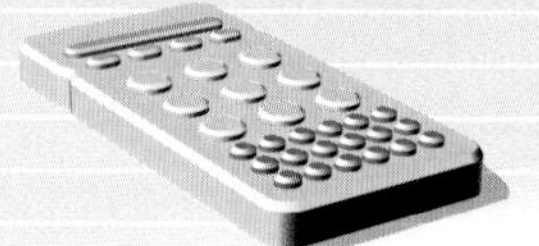

USING THE CHANNEL FINDER

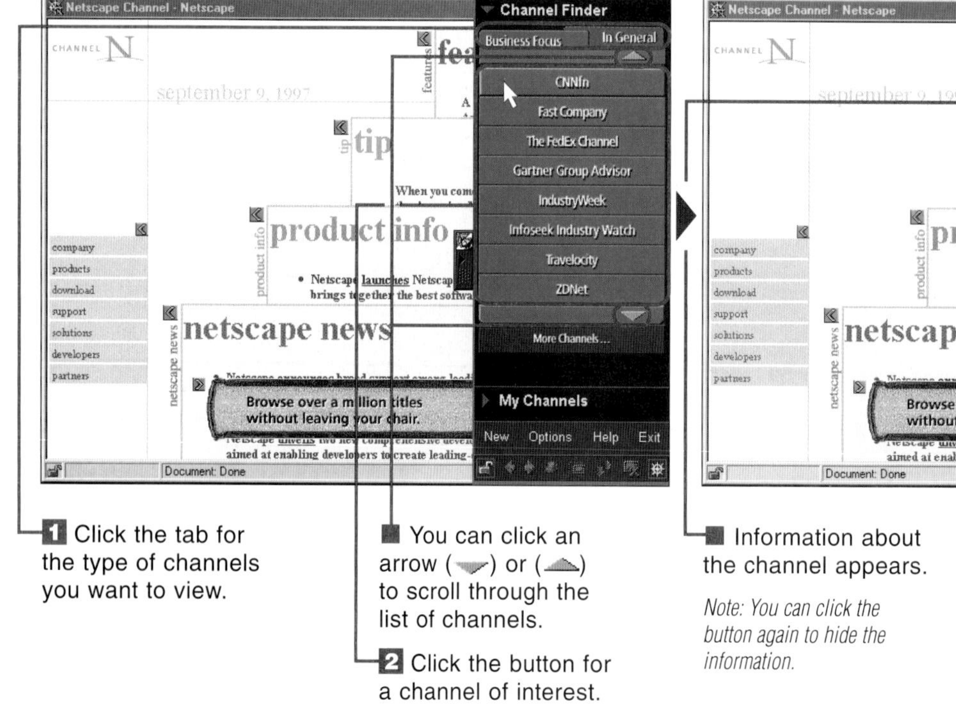

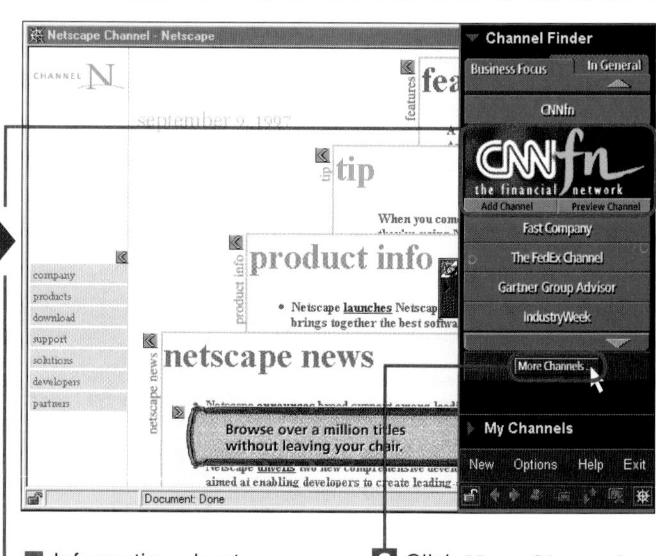

1 Click the tab for the type of channels you want to view.

■ You can click an arrow (▼) or (▲) to scroll through the list of channels.

2 Click the button for a channel of interest.

■ Information about the channel appears.

Note: You can click the button again to hide the information.

3 Click **More Channels** to see more channels that are available.

■ After a few moments, the Channel Finder window appears.

Do the channels in the Channel Finder update automatically?

The channels in the Channel Finder do not update automatically. The Channel Finder shows you some of the channels that are available.

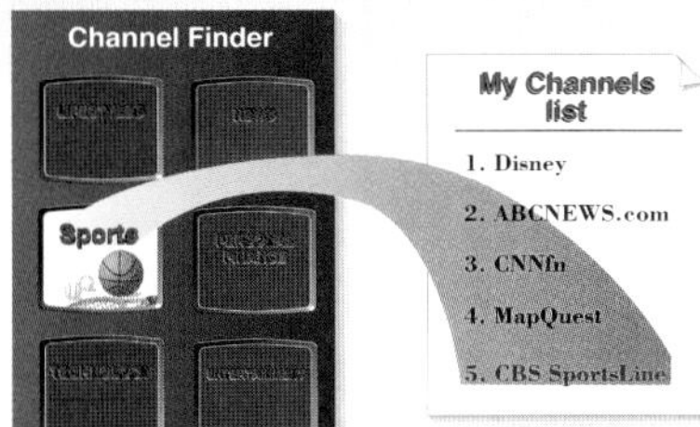

You need to add a channel to the My Channels list if you want the channel to update automatically. To add a channel, refer to page 228.

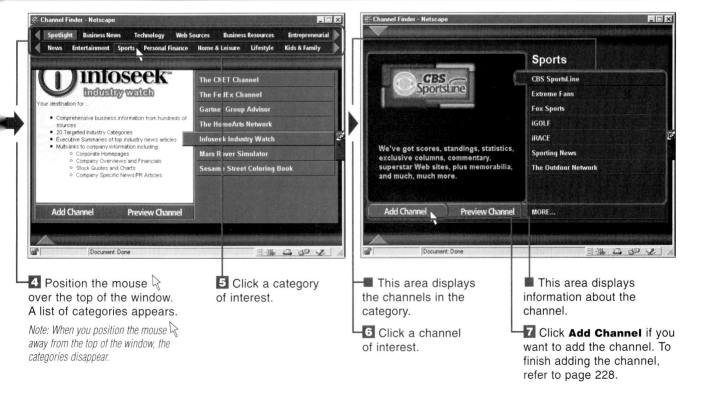

4 Position the mouse over the top of the window. A list of categories appears.

Note: When you position the mouse away from the top of the window, the categories disappear.

5 Click a category of interest.

■ This area displays the channels in the category.

6 Click a channel of interest.

■ This area displays information about the channel.

7 Click **Add Channel** if you want to add the channel. To finish adding the channel, refer to page 228.

ADD A CHANNEL

You can add a channel you want Netcaster to deliver automatically to your computer. Netcaster can automatically update a channel at intervals such as once a week or every hour so you can always see the most current information.

When you add a channel, Netcaster transfers the contents of the site and stores the information on your computer. Since the information is stored on your computer, you can view the channel when you are not connected to the Internet.

ADD A CHANNEL

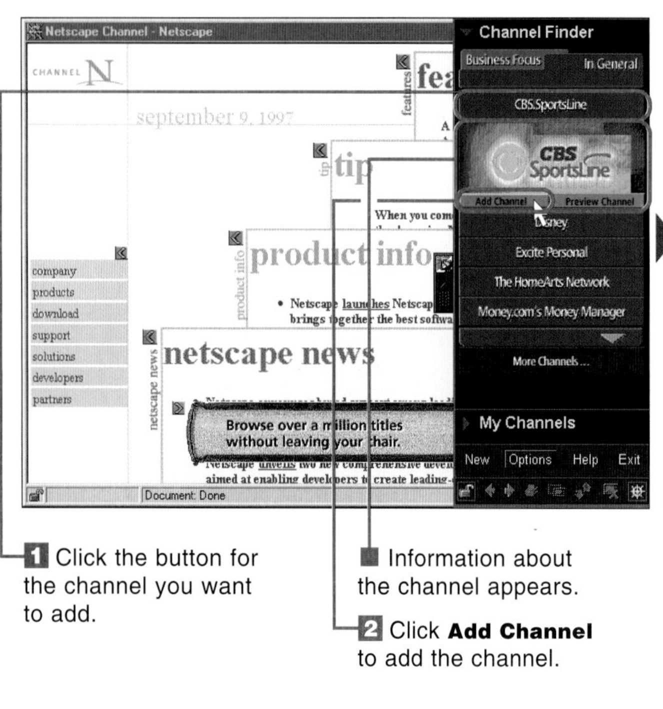

1 Click the button for the channel you want to add.

■ Information about the channel appears.

2 Click **Add Channel** to add the channel.

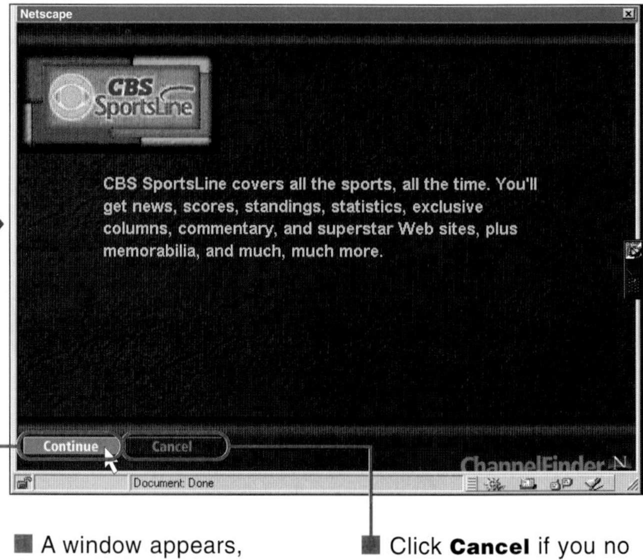

■ A window appears, displaying more information about the channel.

3 Click **Continue** to add the channel.

■ Click **Cancel** if you no longer want to add the channel.

■ The Channel Properties dialog box appears.

Note: You may be asked to register with Netscape. For information, refer to the top of page 229.

Do I have to register with Netscape to add channels?

The first time you add a channel, you must register with Netscape. Membership is free and you only have to register once.

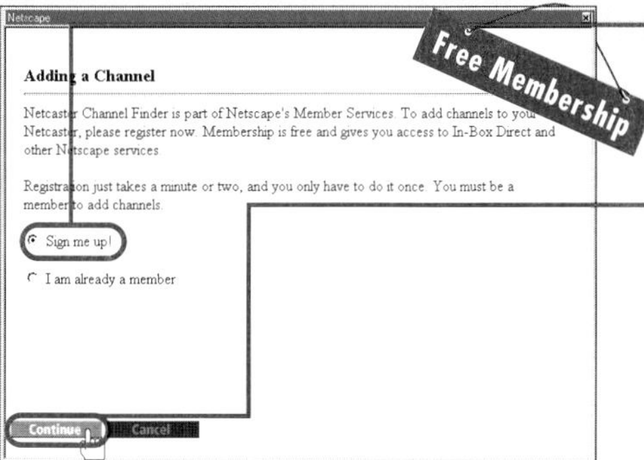

1 Click the circle (○) beside **Sign me up!** to register with Netscape (○ changes to ◉).

2 Click **Continue** and then follow the instructions on your screen.

*Note: If this window appears after you have registered, click the circle (○) beside **I am already a member** and follow the instructions on your screen.*

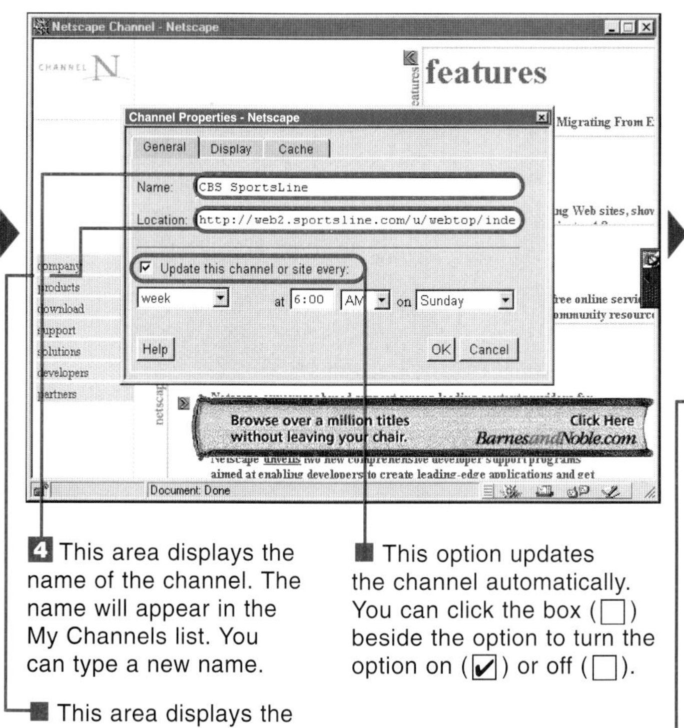

4 This area displays the name of the channel. The name will appear in the My Channels list. You can type a new name.

■ This area displays the location of the channel.

■ This option updates the channel automatically. You can click the box (☐) beside the option to turn the option on (☑) or off (☐).

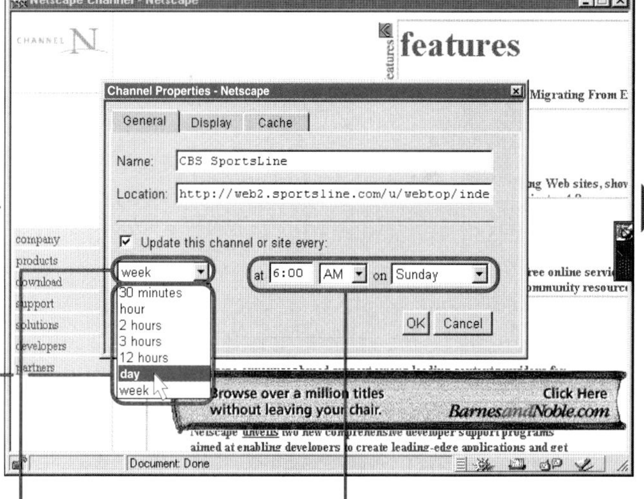

5 Click this area to specify how often you want to update the channel with new information from the Web.

6 Click how often you want to update the channel.

■ If you chose to update the channel every day or week, this area shows exactly when Netcaster will update the channel. You can change this information.

ADD A CHANNEL

When you add a channel, you can choose to display the channel in a Navigator window or as a webtop.

Navigator window

webtop

A webtop fills the entire screen and acts as a temporary replacement for your Windows desktop.

ADD A CHANNEL (CONTINUED)

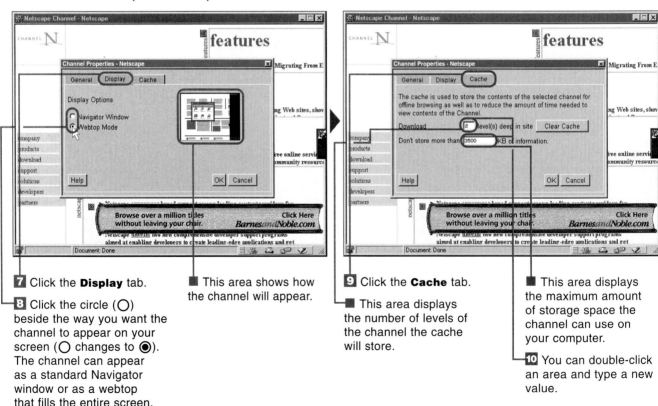

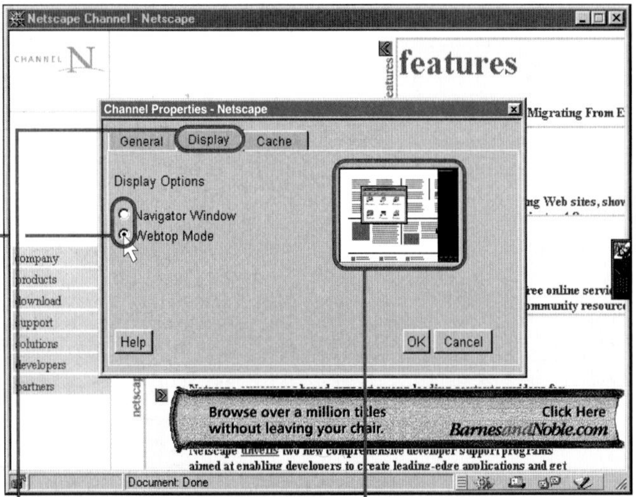

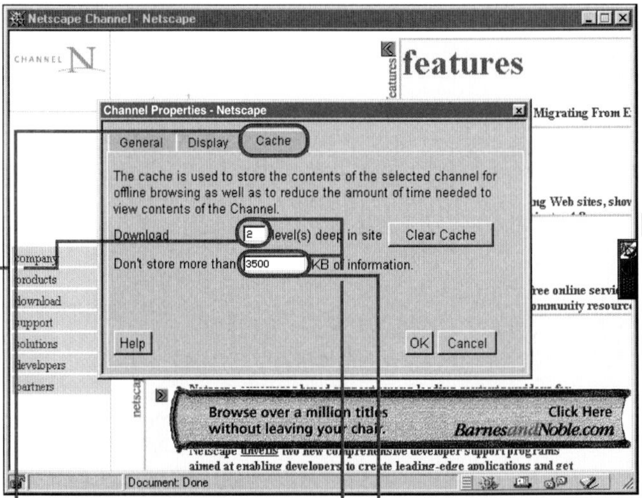

7 Click the **Display** tab.

8 Click the circle (○) beside the way you want the channel to appear on your screen (○ changes to ◉). The channel can appear as a standard Navigator window or as a webtop that fills the entire screen.

■ This area shows how the channel will appear.

9 Click the **Cache** tab.

■ This area displays the number of levels of the channel the cache will store.

■ This area displays the maximum amount of storage space the channel can use on your computer.

10 You can double-click an area and type a new value.

?

What is the cache?

The cache stores the contents of a channel on your computer. A larger cache allows you to view more of a channel's contents when you are not connected to the Internet.

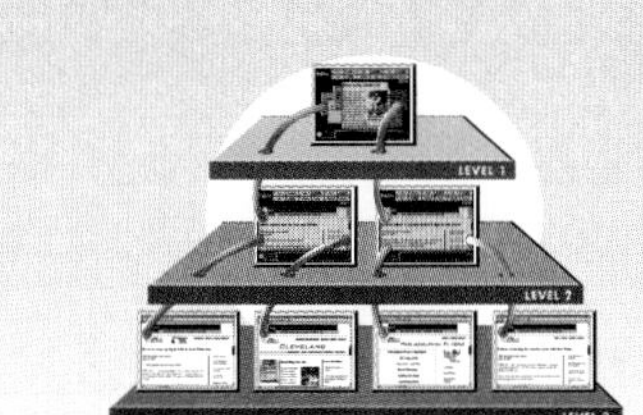

Levels deep

The number of levels of the channel the cache will store. The first level consists of the main page. The second level consists of the pages the main page links to, and so on.

Size in kilobytes (KB)

The maximum amount of storage space the channel can use on your computer.

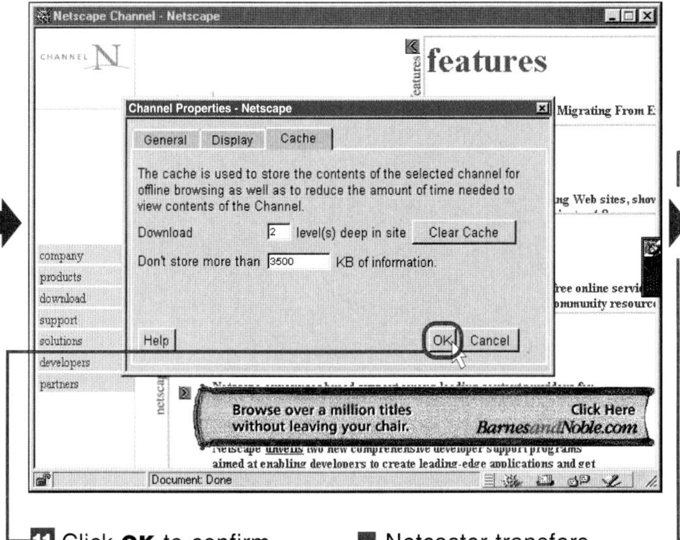

11 Click **OK** to confirm all the information you entered.

■ Netcaster transfers the channel to your computer.

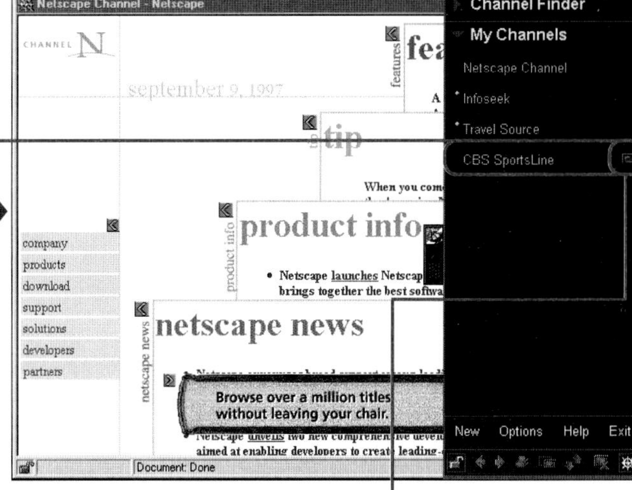

■ The channel appears in the My Channels list.

Note: To display the My Channels list, refer to page 225.

■ An icon (■) appears beside a channel you chose to display as a webtop.

ADD A CHANNEL MANUALLY

You can add any Web site to the My Channels list. Netcaster will transfer and then store the information on your computer so you can quickly access the channel at any time.

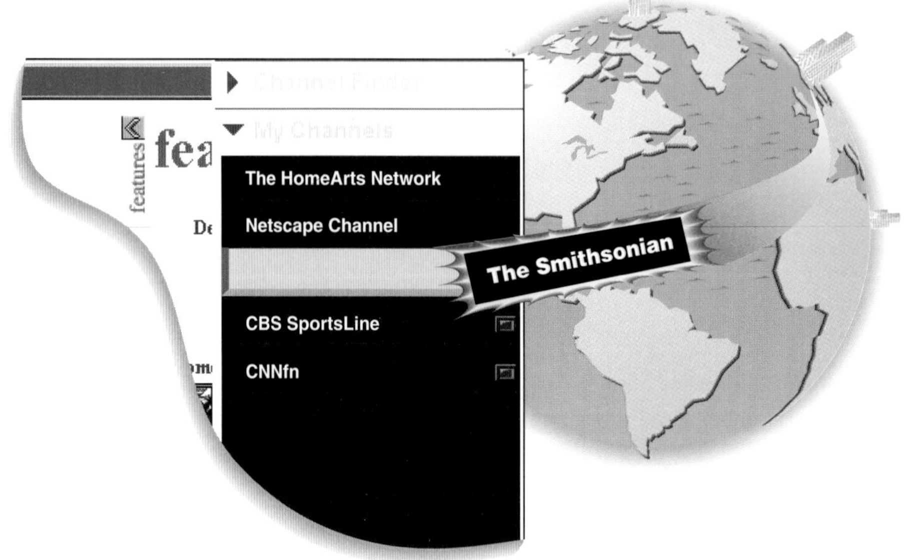

ADD A CHANNEL MANUALLY

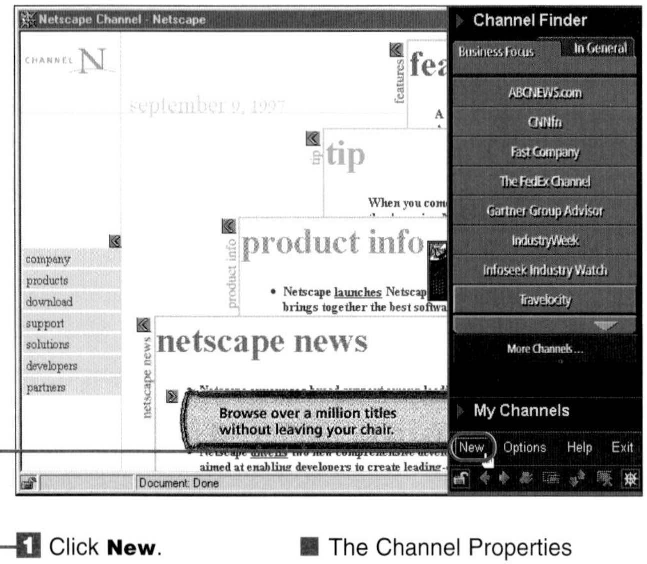

1 Click **New**.

■ The Channel Properties dialog box appears.

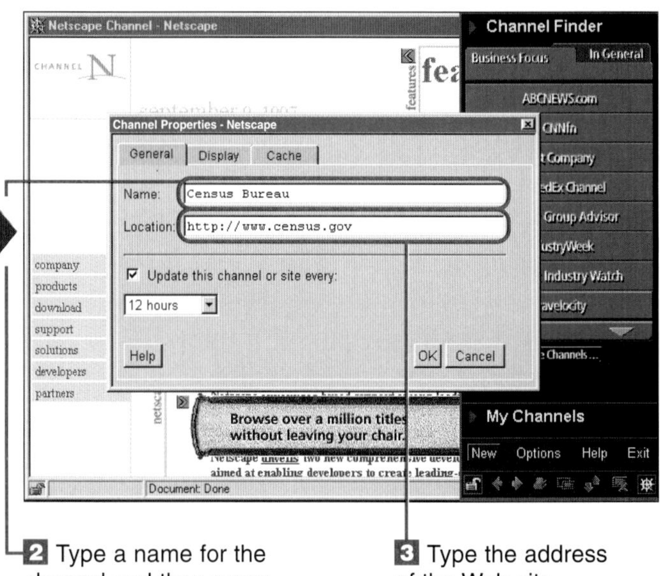

2 Type a name for the channel and then press the Tab key. The name will appear in the My Channels list.

3 Type the address of the Web site.

4 Set the properties for the new channel by performing steps **4** to **11** starting on page 229.

You can immediately update a channel in the My Channels list to view the current information.

When you update a channel, Netcaster transfers the contents of the site and then stores the information on your computer. You can then disconnect from the Internet and browse through the information as if you were still connected.

UPDATE A CHANNEL MANUALLY

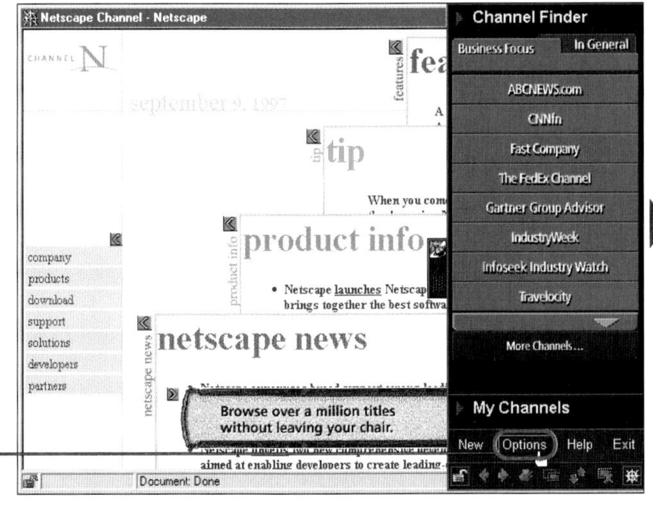

1 Click **Options**.

■ The Options dialog box appears.

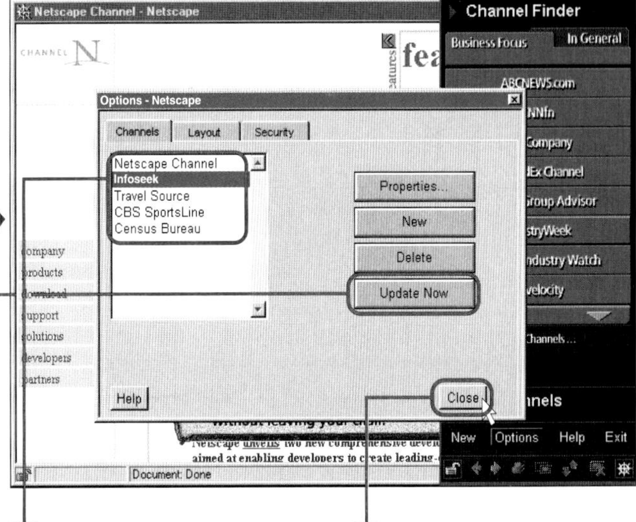

2 Click the channel you want to update.

3 Click **Update Now**.

4 Click **Close** to close the dialog box.

■ In the My Channels list, a red bar moves below the channel name while the channel updates.

Note: To display the My Channels list, refer to page 225.

CHANGE CHANNEL PROPERTIES

After you add a channel to the My Channels list, you can change the properties of the channel. For example, you may want to change how often the channel updates.

CHANGE CHANNEL PROPERTIES

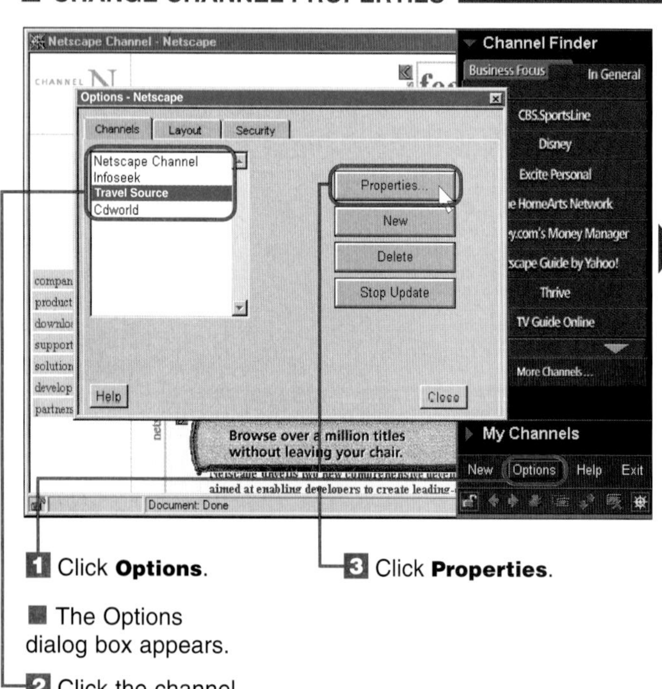

1 Click **Options**.

■ The Options dialog box appears.

2 Click the channel you want to change.

3 Click **Properties**.

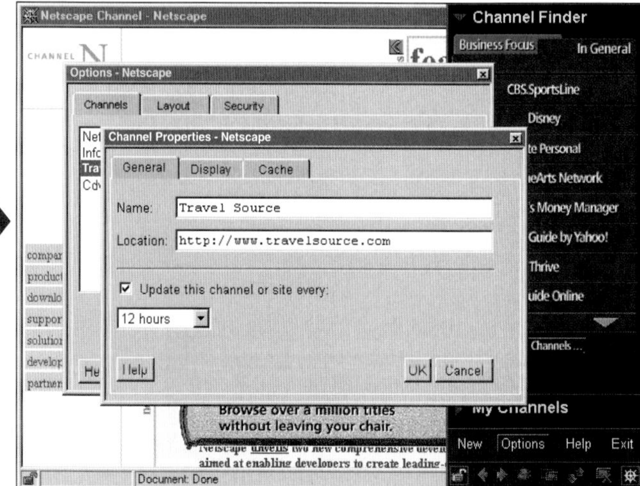

■ The Channel Properties dialog box appears.

■ You can now change the properties of the channel. Refer to steps **4** to **11** starting on page 229 for more information.

DELETE A CHANNEL

You can delete a channel you no longer want to use.

DELETE A CHANNEL

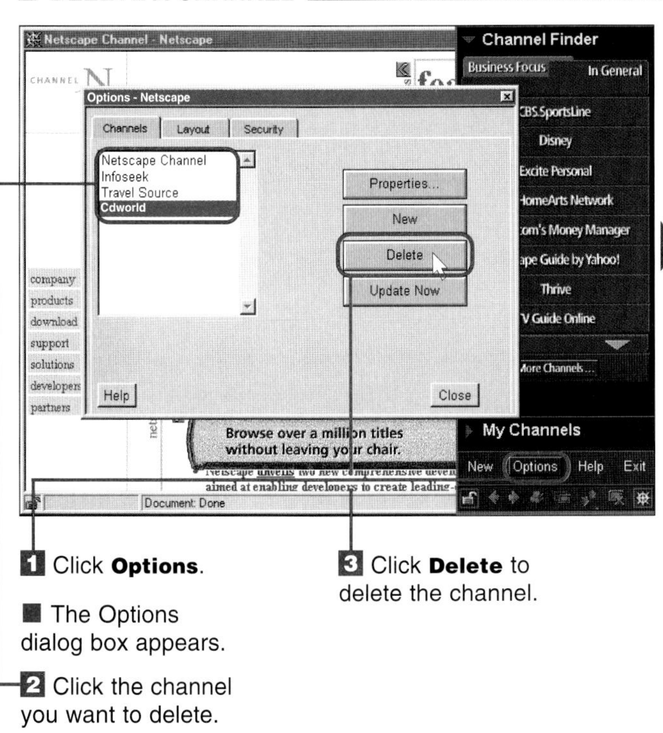

1 Click **Options**.

■ The Options dialog box appears.

2 Click the channel you want to delete.

3 Click **Delete** to delete the channel.

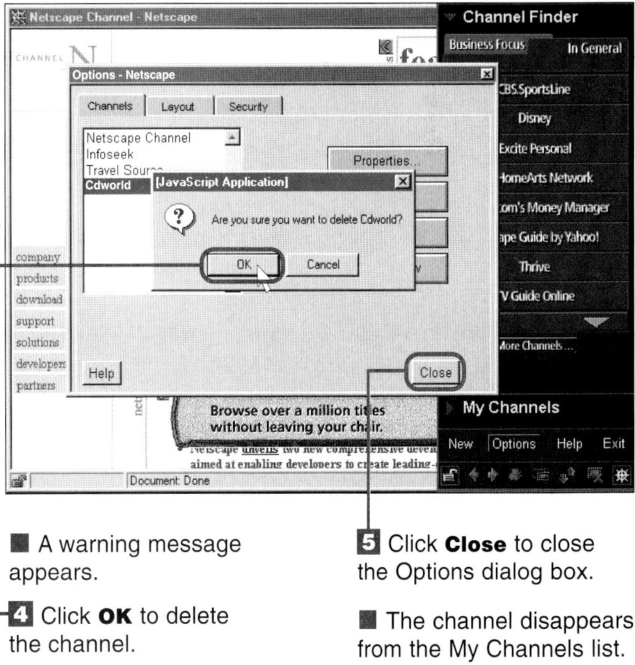

■ A warning message appears.

4 Click **OK** to delete the channel.

5 Click **Close** to close the Options dialog box.

■ The channel disappears from the My Channels list.

Note: To display the My Channels list, refer to page 225.

WORK WITH A WEBTOP

After you select links on a webtop, you can move back and forth through the pages you have viewed.

FLIP BETWEEN WEBTOP PAGES

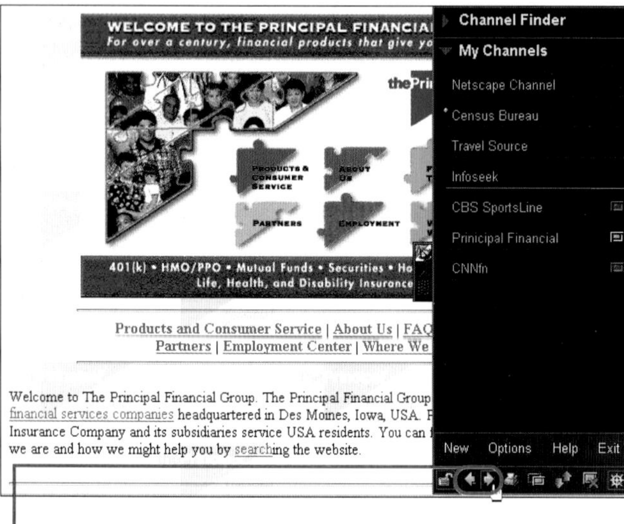

1 Click a button to go to the previous (◀) or next (▶) page on the webtop.

You can produce a paper copy of the webtop displayed on your screen.

PRINT THE WEBTOP

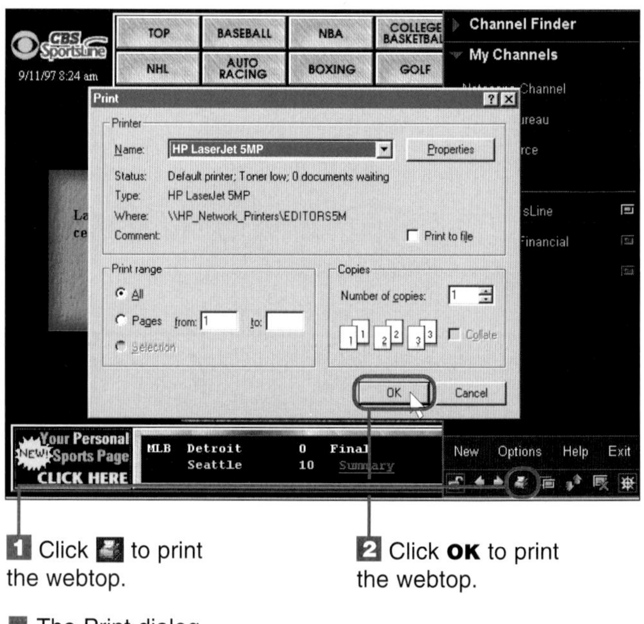

1 Click 🖨 to print the webtop.

■ The Print dialog box appears.

2 Click **OK** to print the webtop.

You can show or hide the webtop at any time. Hiding the webtop allows you to view the items on your desktop.

SHOW OR HIDE THE WEBTOP

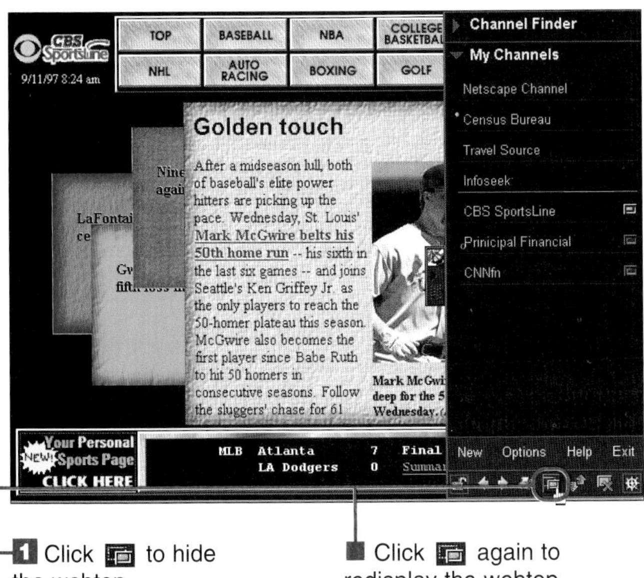

1 Click [icon] to hide the webtop.

■ Click [icon] again to redisplay the webtop.

When you have several windows open, you can place other windows in front of the webtop so you can accomplish other tasks. You can redisplay the webtop at any time.

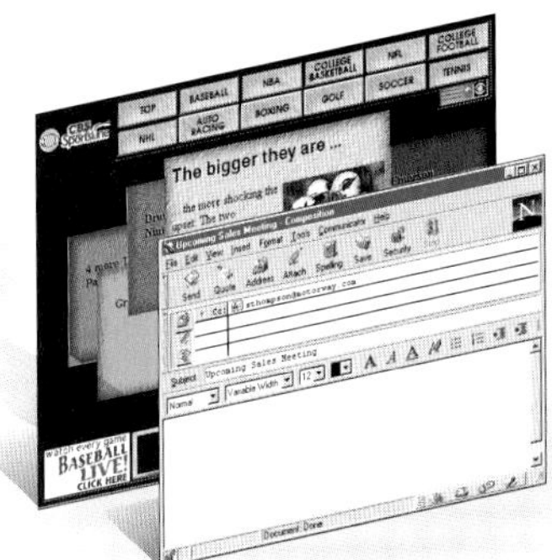

SEND WEBTOP TO THE BACK OR FRONT

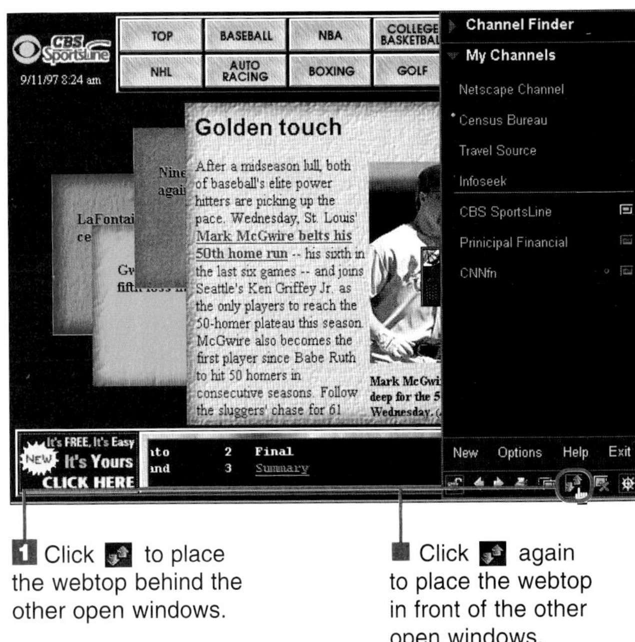

1 Click [icon] to place the webtop behind the other open windows.

■ Click [icon] again to place the webtop in front of the other open windows.

CHANGE NETCASTER OPTIONS

You can customize Netcaster to suit your needs.

You can choose to display the Netcaster window on the left or right side of your screen. You can also have the Netcaster window automatically disappear when you select a channel.

■ Netcaster window

CHANGE NETCASTER OPTIONS

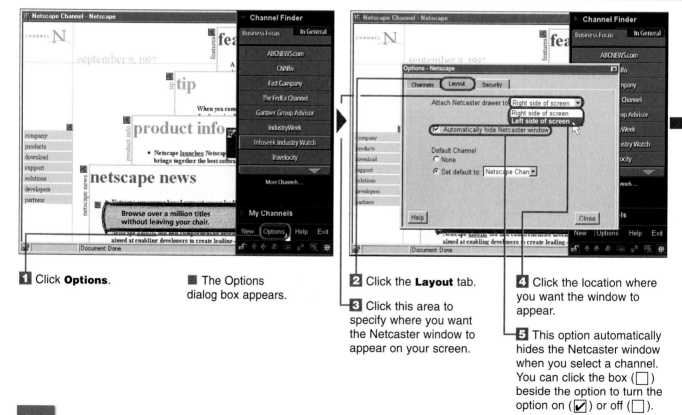

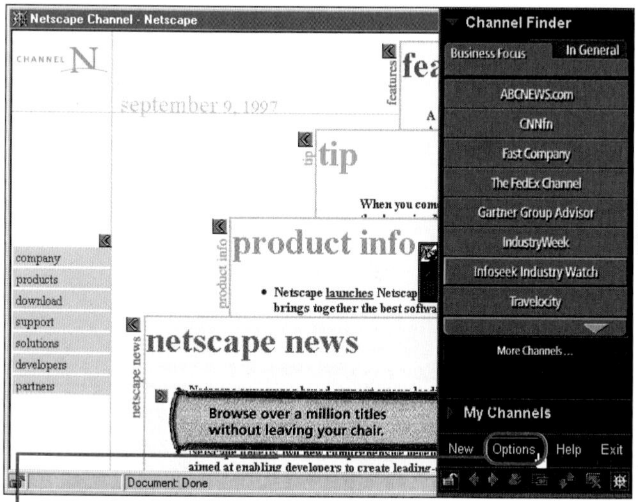

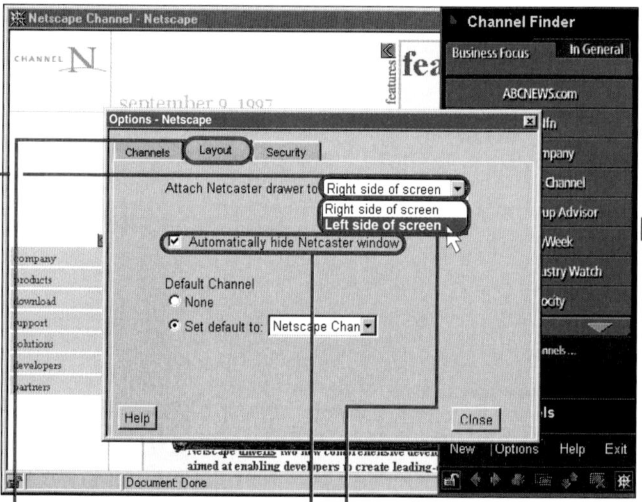

1 Click **Options**.

■ The Options dialog box appears.

2 Click the **Layout** tab.

3 Click this area to specify where you want the Netcaster window to appear on your screen.

4 Click the location where you want the window to appear.

5 This option automatically hides the Netcaster window when you select a channel. You can click the box (□) beside the option to turn the option on (☑) or off (□).

?

Which channel can I have automatically appear each time I start Netcaster?

You can have any channel from the My Channels list automatically appear each time you start Netcaster. This can save you time if you always view the same channel.

Note: To add a channel to the My Channels list, refer to page 228.

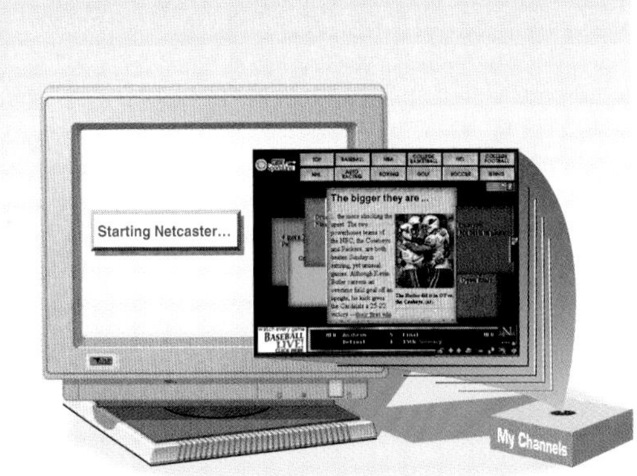

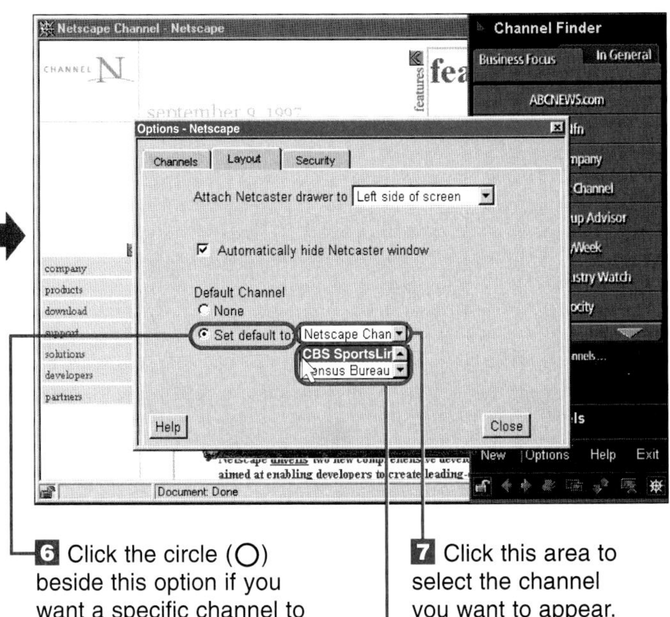

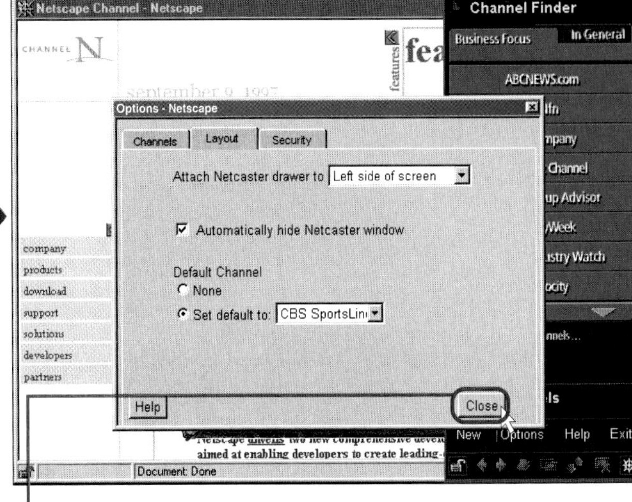

6 Click the circle (○) beside this option if you want a specific channel to automatically appear each time you start Netcaster (○ changes to ◉).

*Note: Click the circle (○) beside **None** if you do not want a channel to appear (○ changes to ◉).*

7 Click this area to select the channel you want to appear.

8 Click the channel you want to appear.

9 Click **Close** to close the dialog box.

Text
Sailing Ships
Sailing

CHAPTER 9

Create Your Own Web Pages

Do you want to create your own Web pages? Find out how Netscape Composer can help you design and publish your own Web pages in this chapter.

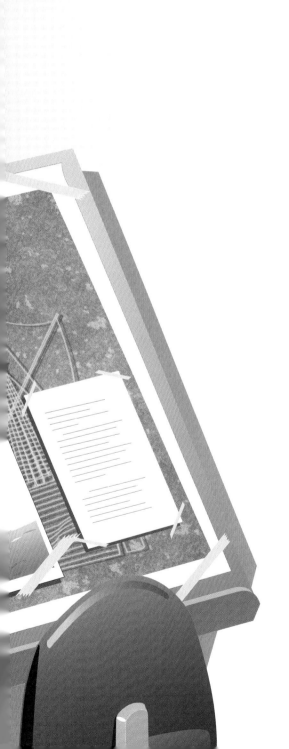

INTRODUCTION TO NETSCAPE COMPOSER

Netscape Composer allows you to create and edit Web pages. You can place pages you create on the Web so people around the world can view your information.

You can also place Web pages you create on a corporate intranet. An intranet is a small version of the Internet within a company or organization.

REASONS FOR PUBLISHING WEB PAGES

Personal

Many people use the Web to share information about a topic that interests them. You can create Web pages to display information about your favorite celebrity or hobby, show your favorite pictures, promote a club you belong to or present a résumé to potential employers.

Commercial

A company can place pages on the Web to provide the public with information about the company. Companies use Web pages to keep the public informed about new products, interesting news and job openings available within the company. Many companies allow readers to use their Web pages to place orders for products and services.

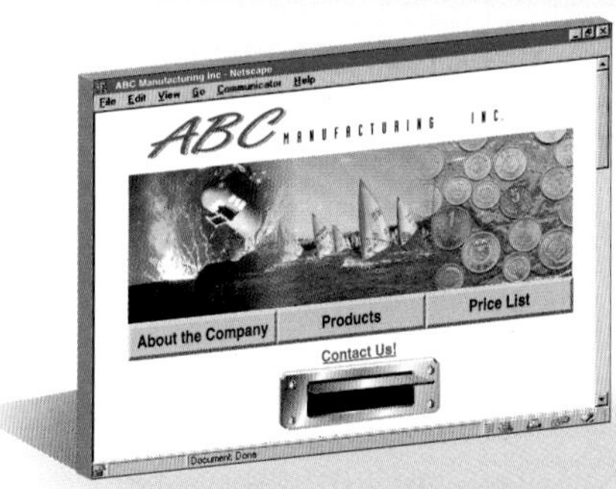

START NETSCAPE COMPOSER

You can start Netscape Composer to create your own Web pages. When you start Netscape Composer, a blank document appears.

START NETSCAPE COMPOSER

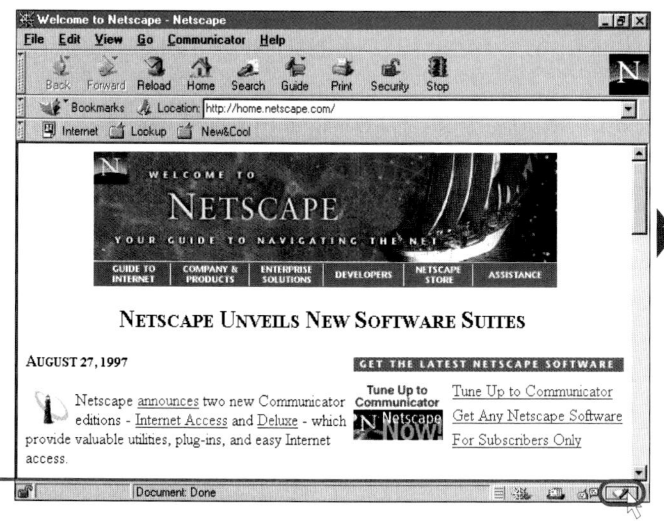

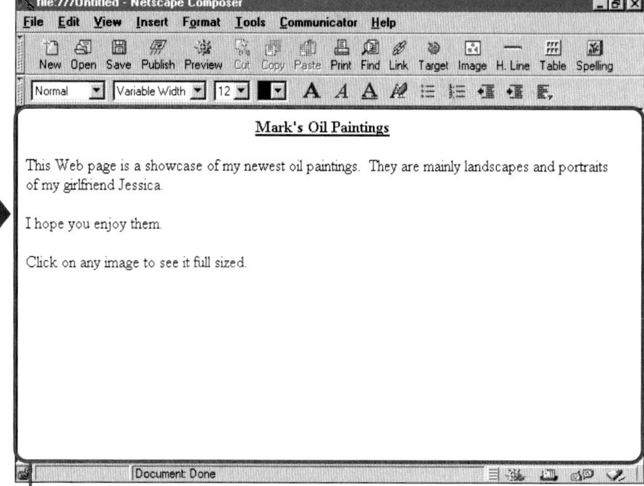

1 Click [icon] to start Netscape Composer.

■ The Netscape Composer window appears.

2 Type the text you want to appear on your Web page.

■ Press the Enter key only when you want to start a new line or paragraph.

SAVE A WEB PAGE

You should save a Web page you create to store the page for future use. This lets you later review and update the page.

SAVE A WEB PAGE

1 Click **Save** to save the Web page displayed on your screen.

■ The Save As dialog box appears.

Note: If you previously saved the Web page, the Save As dialog box will not appear since you have already named the page.

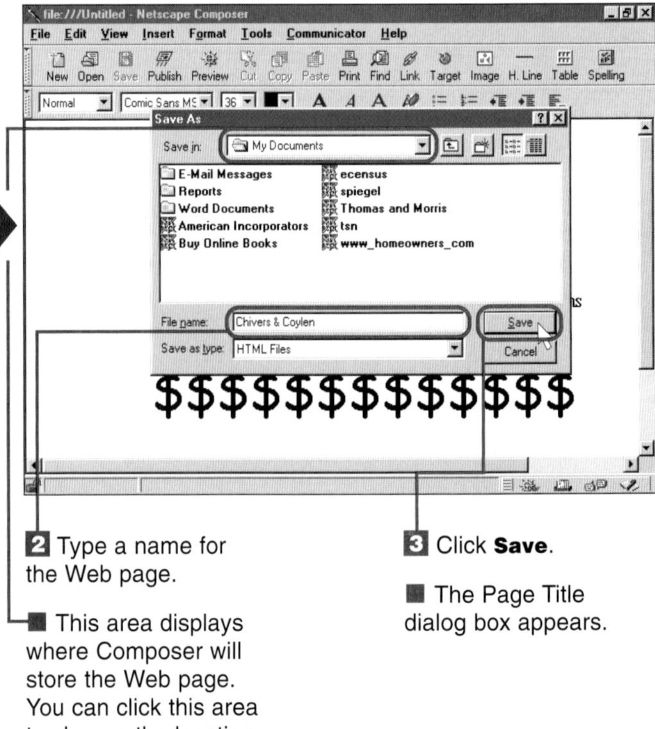

2 Type a name for the Web page.

■ This area displays where Composer will store the Web page. You can click this area to change the location.

3 Click **Save**.

■ The Page Title dialog box appears.

What is the difference between the file name and title of a Web page?

File Name

The file name is the name given to a saved Web page. If you plan to publish your Web page on a Web server, you may need to give your Web page a certain name. Check with your system administrator or Internet service provider.

Title

The title describes the information on a page and appears at the top of the screen when you view the page in a Web browser.

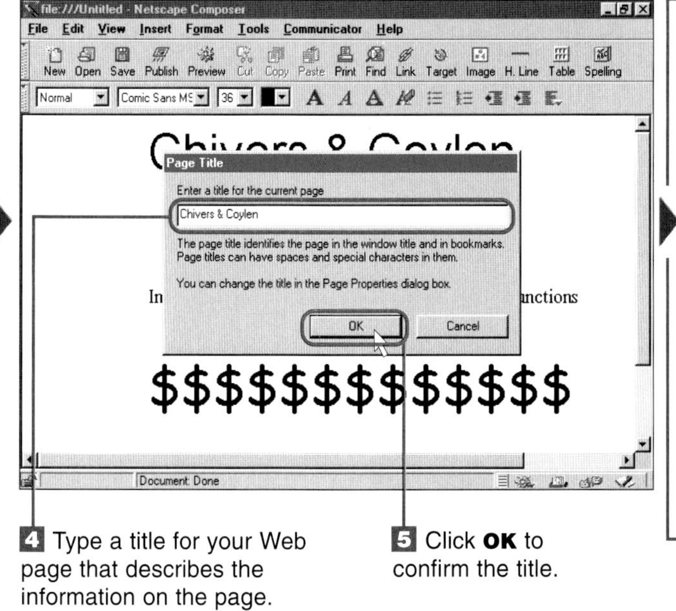

4 Type a title for your Web page that describes the information on the page.

5 Click **OK** to confirm the title.

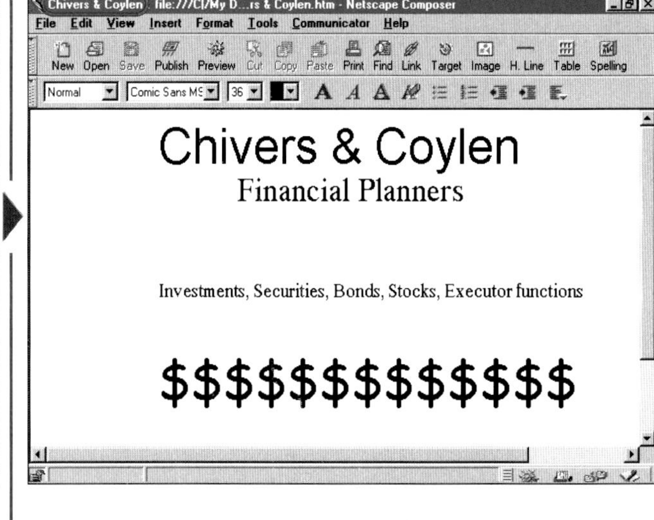

■ This area displays the title of the Web page.

■ After you save a Web page, Composer will automatically save the page every 10 minutes.

BOLD, ITALICIZE OR UNDERLINE TEXT

You can bold, italicize or underline text to emphasize information on your Web page.

BOLD, ITALICIZE OR UNDERLINE TEXT

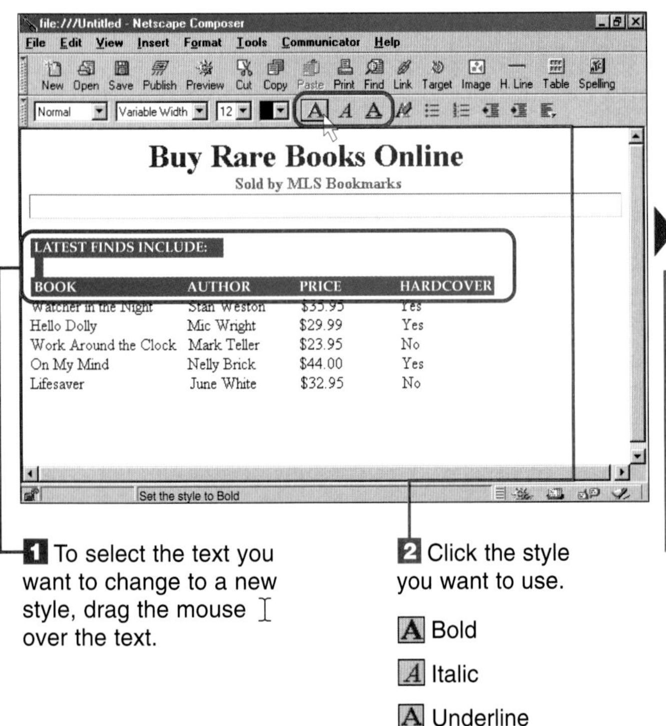

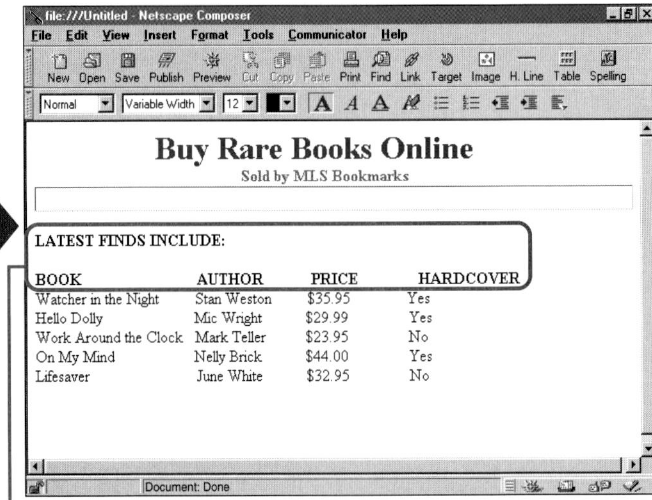

1 To select the text you want to change to a new style, drag the mouse I over the text.

2 Click the style you want to use.

A Bold

A Italic

A Underline

■ The text you selected appears in the new style.

■ To deselect text, click outside the selected area.

■ To remove a bold, italic or underline style, repeat steps **1** and **2**.

CHANGE TEXT COLOR

You can change the color of text on your Web page.

Some people set up their Web browser to always display text on Web pages in a specific color. The colors you choose for the text on your Web page may not look the same on some computers.

CHANGE TEXT COLOR

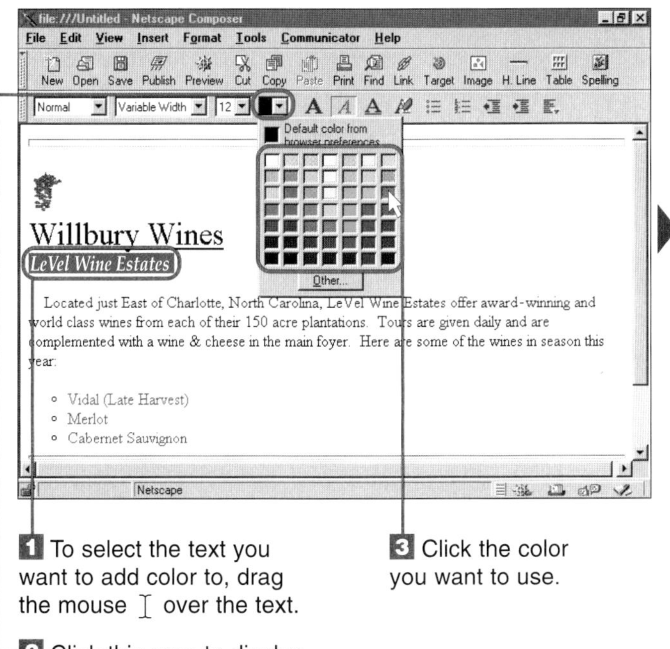

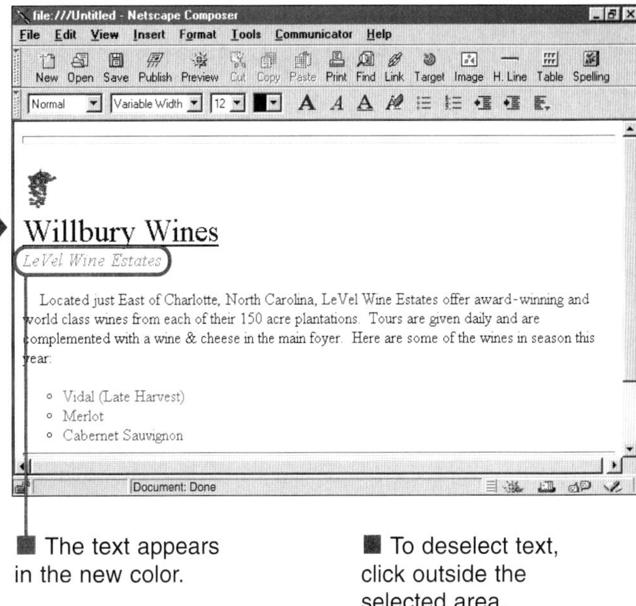

1 To select the text you want to add color to, drag the mouse I over the text.

2 Click this area to display the colors you can use.

3 Click the color you want to use.

■ The text appears in the new color.

■ To deselect text, click outside the selected area.

CHANGE FONT

You can make your Web page look more attractive by changing the design of the text.

CHANGE FONT

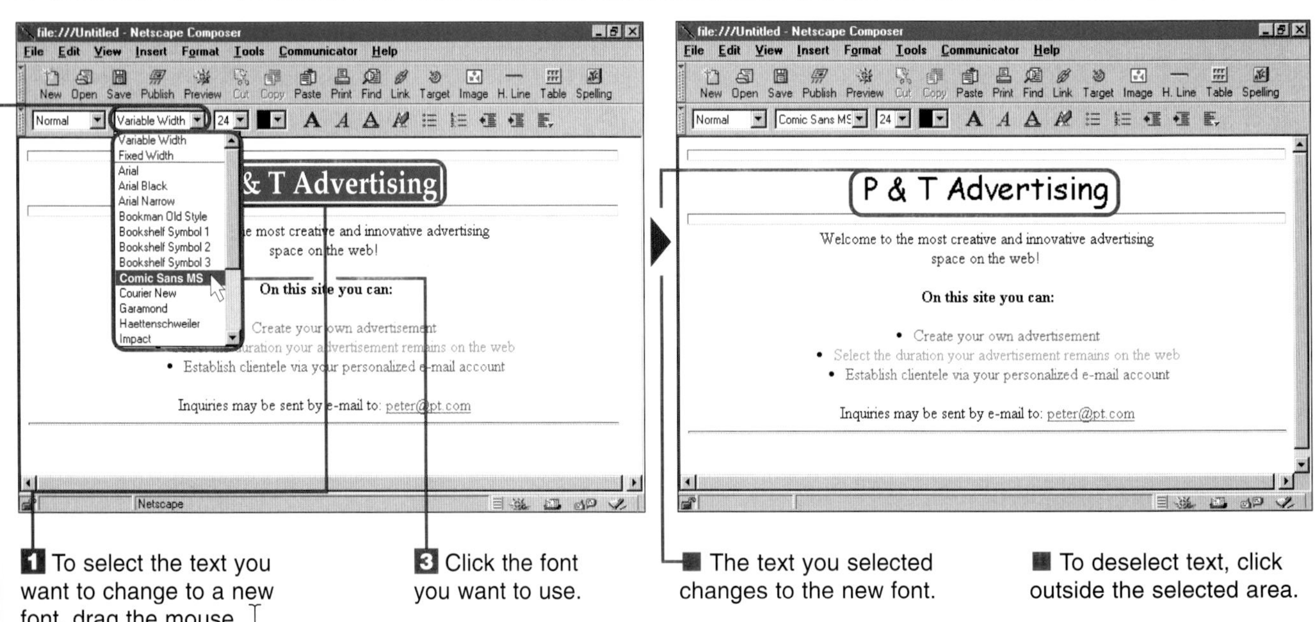

1 To select the text you want to change to a new font, drag the mouse over the text.

2 Click this area to display a list of the available fonts.

3 Click the font you want to use.

■ The text you selected changes to the new font.

■ To deselect text, click outside the selected area.

CHANGE FONT SIZE

You can increase or decrease the size of text on your Web page.

A larger font size makes information easier to read. A smaller font size lets you fit more information on a single screen.

CHANGE FONT SIZE

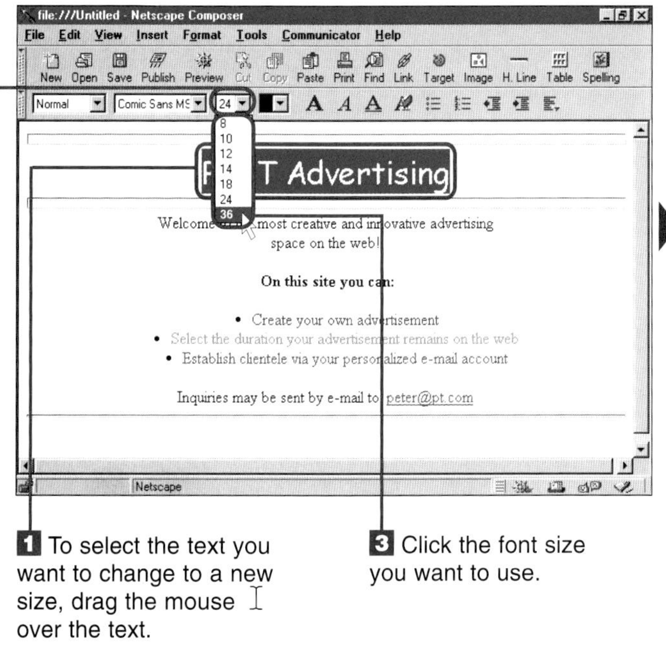

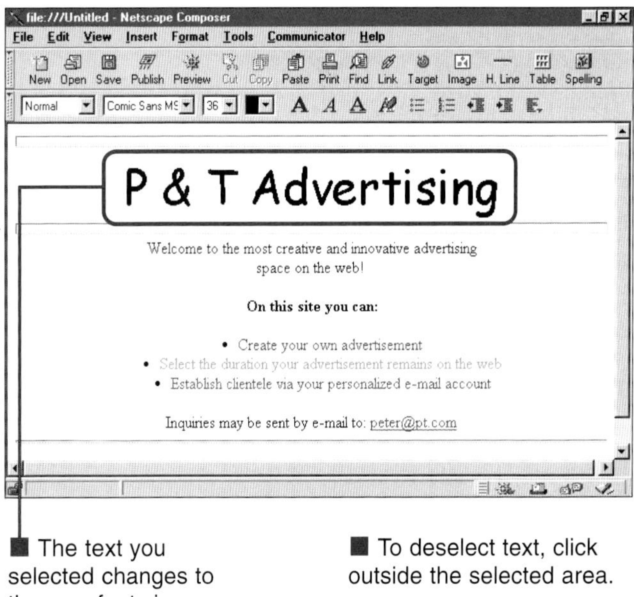

1. To select the text you want to change to a new size, drag the mouse over the text.
2. Click this area to display a list of the available font sizes.
3. Click the font size you want to use.

■ The text you selected changes to the new font size.

■ To deselect text, click outside the selected area.

CHANGE TEXT ALIGNMENT

You can enhance the appearance of your Web page by aligning text in different ways.

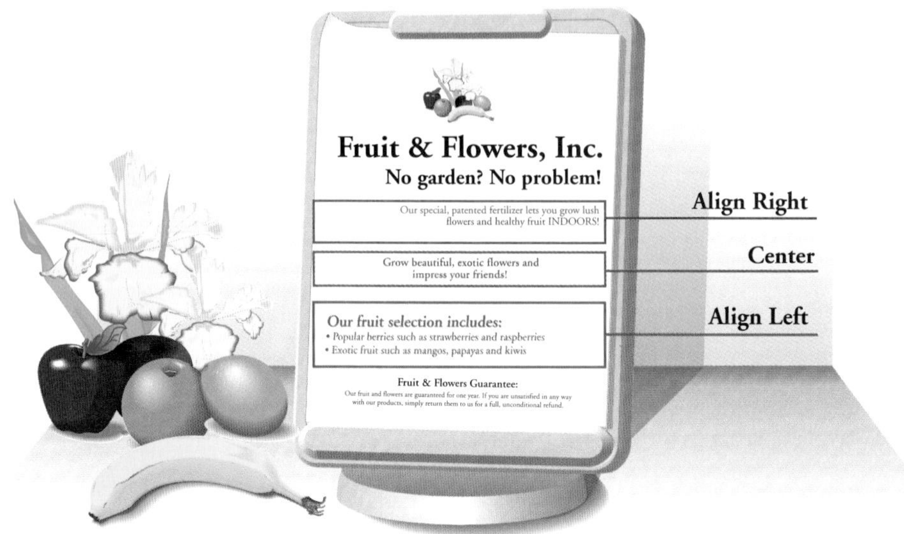

CHANGE TEXT ALIGNMENT

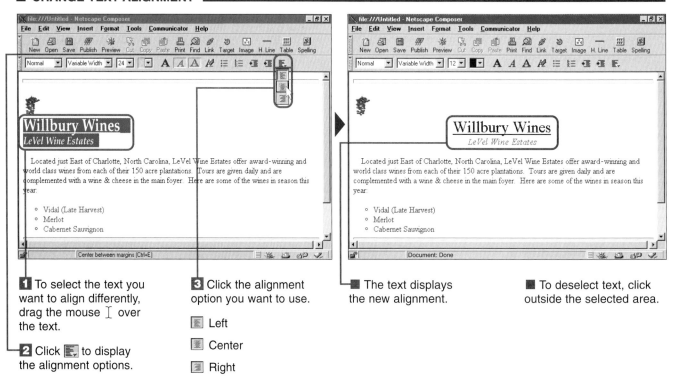

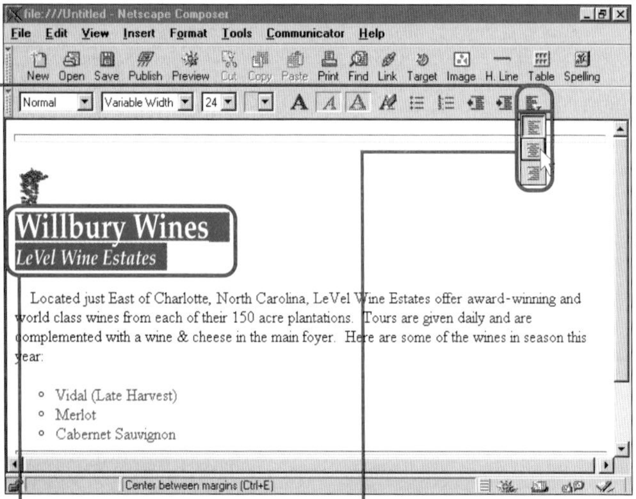

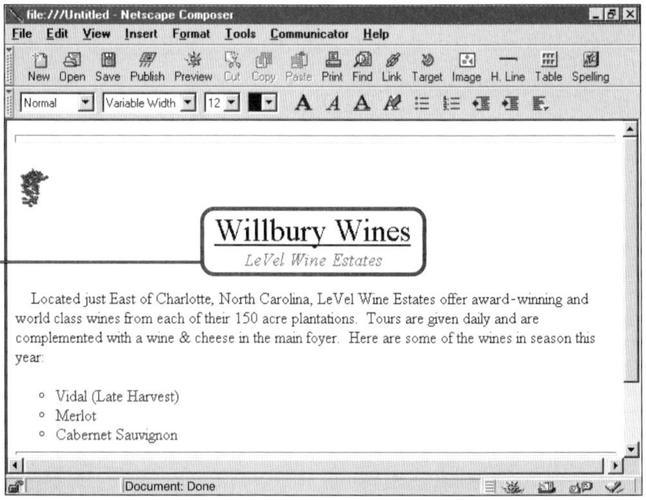

1 To select the text you want to align differently, drag the mouse I over the text.

2 Click ☰ to display the alignment options.

3 Click the alignment option you want to use.

☰ Left

☰ Center

☰ Right

■ The text displays the new alignment.

■ To deselect text, click outside the selected area.

You can use the Indent feature to set off paragraphs in your Web page.

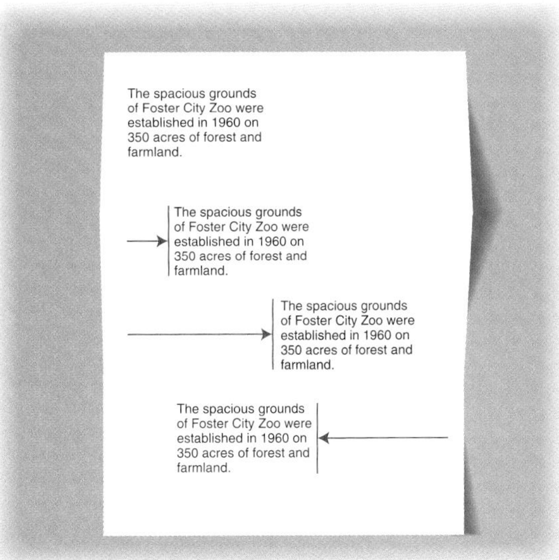

INDENT TEXT

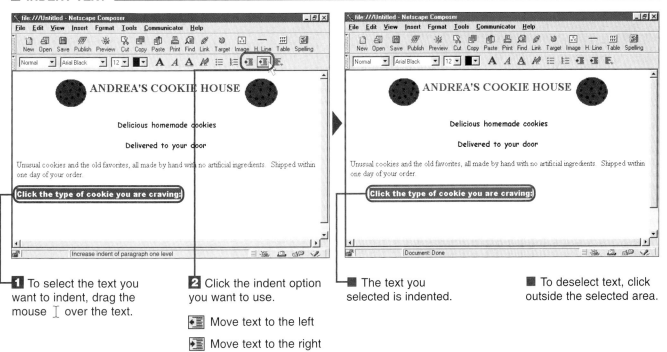

1 To select the text you want to indent, drag the mouse I over the text.

2 Click the indent option you want to use.

- Move text to the left
- Move text to the right

■ The text you selected is indented.

■ To deselect text, click outside the selected area.

CREATE A LIST

You can separate items in a list by beginning each item with a bullet or number.

Bullets are useful for items in no particular order, such as a checklist. Numbers are useful for items in a specific order, such as a set of instructions.

CREATE A LIST

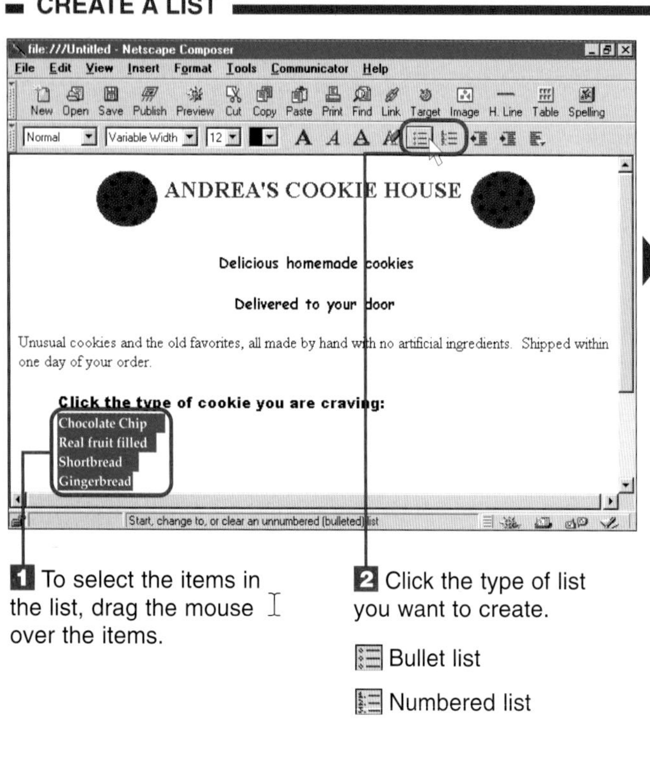

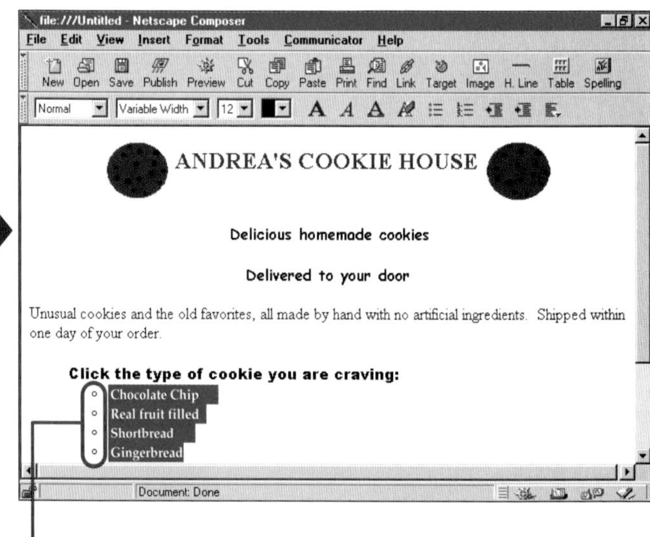

1 To select the items in the list, drag the mouse over the items.

2 Click the type of list you want to create.

Bullet list

Numbered list

■ A bullet (∘) or number sign (#) appears in front of each item in the list. When you display the Web page in a browser, the browser will replace the number signs (#) with numbers.

■ To deselect text, click outside the selected area.

■ To remove bullets or numbers from a list, repeat steps **1** and **2**.

ADD A HORIZONTAL LINE

You can place a line across your Web page to visually separate sections of the page.

ADD A HORIZONTAL LINE

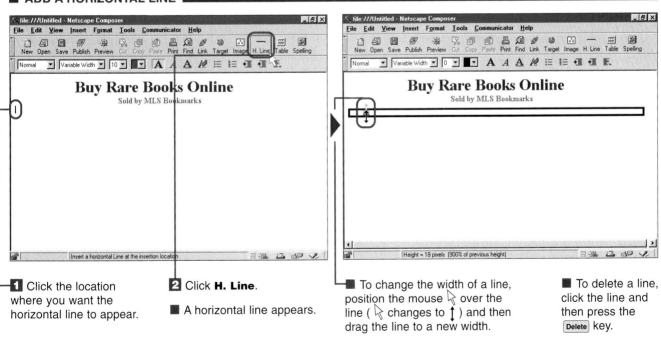

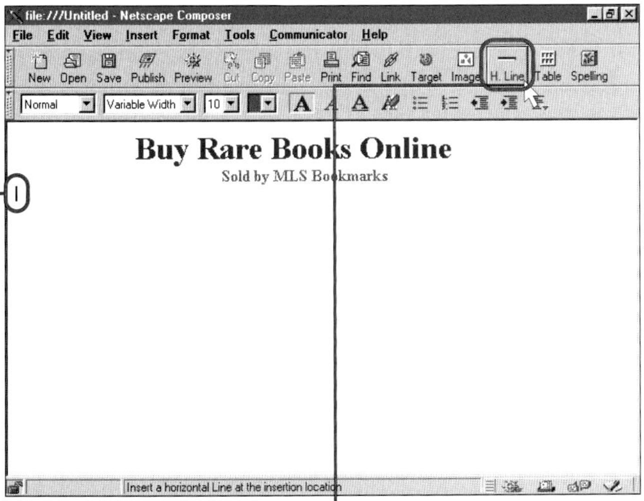

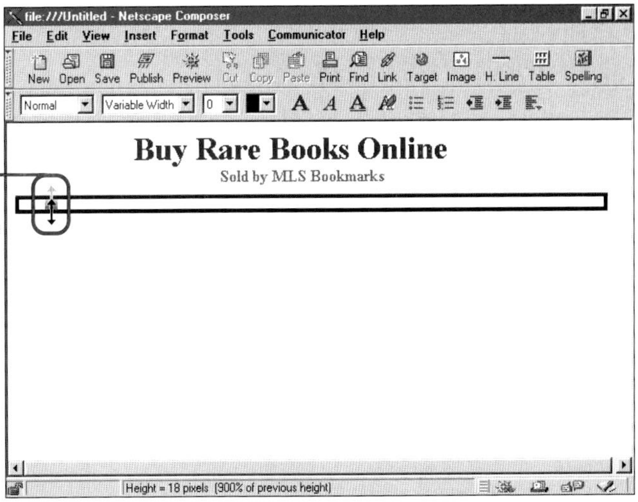

1 Click the location where you want the horizontal line to appear.

2 Click **H. Line**.

■ A horizontal line appears.

■ To change the width of a line, position the mouse over the line (changes to ↕) and then drag the line to a new width.

■ To delete a line, click the line and then press the Delete key.

CHECK SPELLING

You can use the Spelling feature to find and correct all the spelling errors in a Web page you created.

Composer compares every word in your Web page to words in its own dictionary. If a word does not exist in the dictionary, Composer considers the word misspelled.

CHECK SPELLING

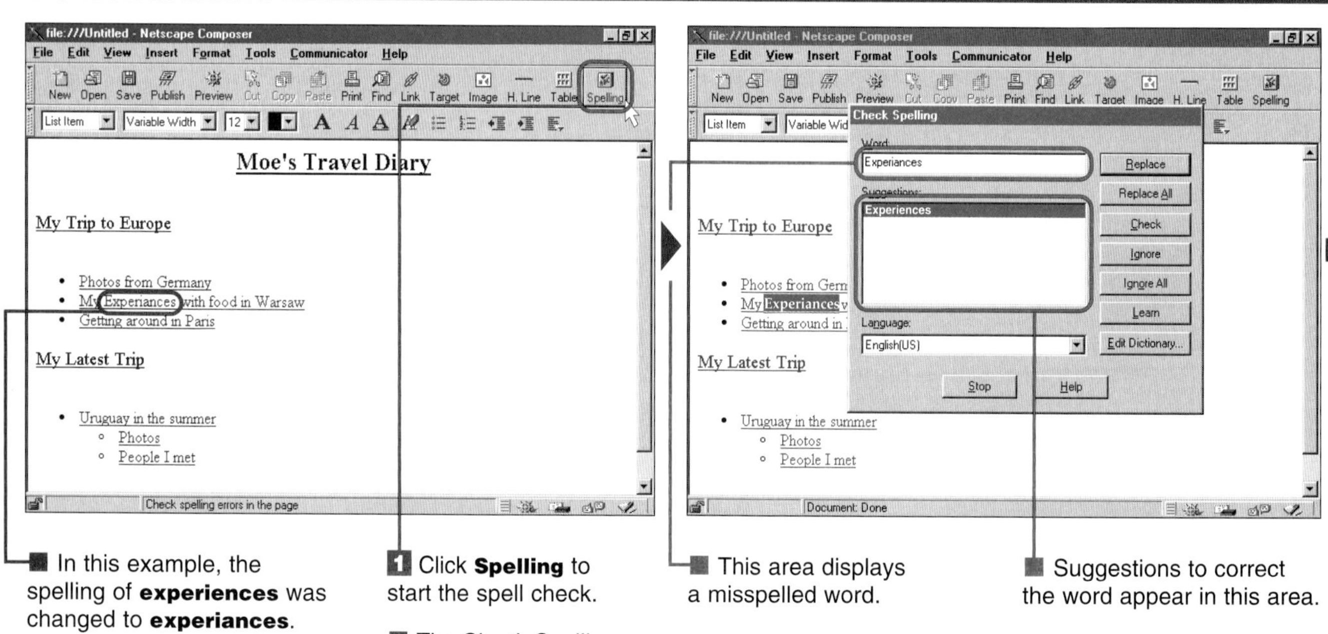

■ In this example, the spelling of **experiences** was changed to **experiances**.

1 Click **Spelling** to start the spell check.

■ The Check Spelling dialog box appears.

■ This area displays a misspelled word.

■ Suggestions to correct the word appear in this area.

?

Will Composer find all the spelling errors in my Web page?

Composer will find all misspelled words in your Web page but will not find a correctly spelled word used in the wrong context. You must review your Web page carefully to find this type of error.

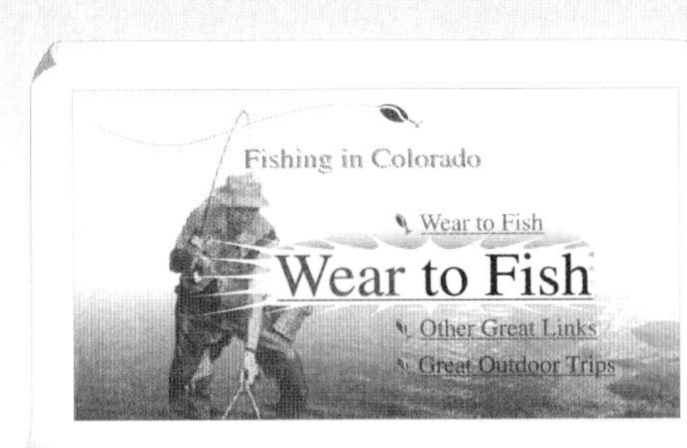

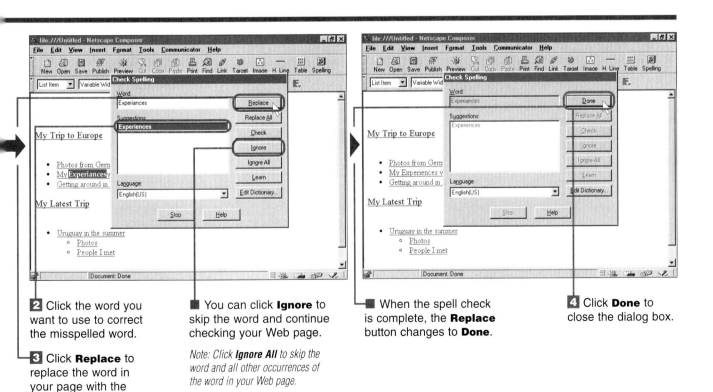

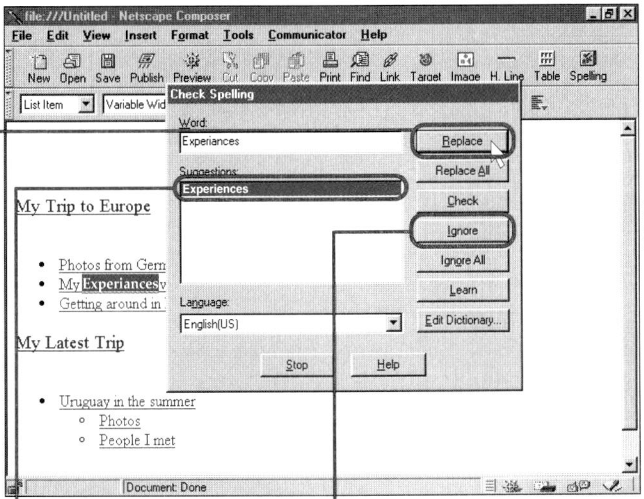

2 Click the word you want to use to correct the misspelled word.

3 Click **Replace** to replace the word in your page with the correct spelling.

■ You can click **Ignore** to skip the word and continue checking your Web page.

*Note: Click **Ignore All** to skip the word and all other occurrences of the word in your Web page.*

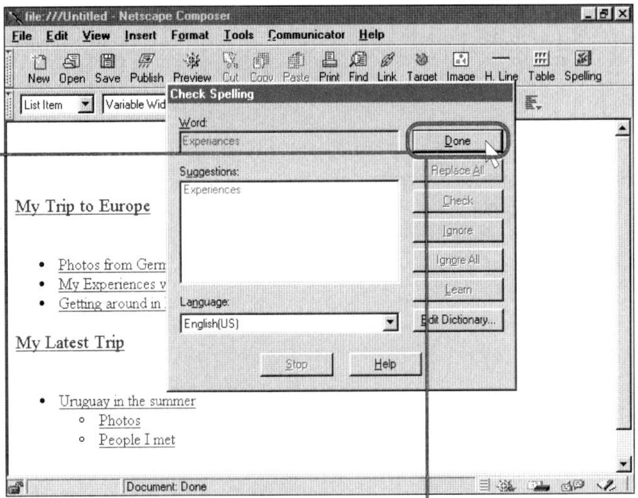

■ When the spell check is complete, the **Replace** button changes to **Done**.

4 Click **Done** to close the dialog box.

OPEN A WEB PAGE

You can open a Web page you created so you can review and make changes to the page.

OPEN A WEB PAGE

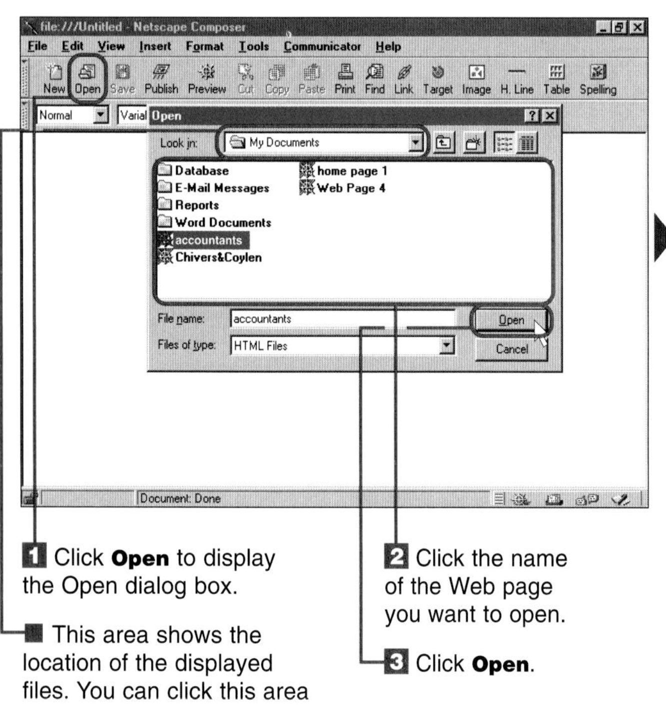

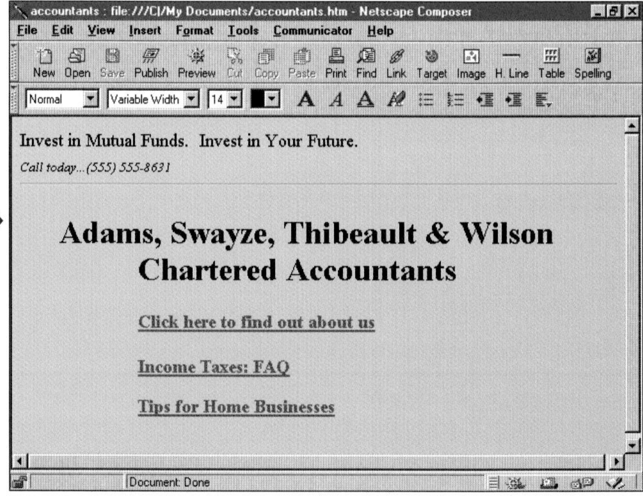

1 Click **Open** to display the Open dialog box.

■ This area shows the location of the displayed files. You can click this area to change the location.

2 Click the name of the Web page you want to open.

3 Click **Open**.

■ The Web page appears on your screen.

VIEW WEB PAGE IN BROWSER

You can see how your Web page will appear when viewed in a browser window. This allows you to see how your page will look when viewed by other people on the Web.

VIEW WEB PAGE IN BROWSER

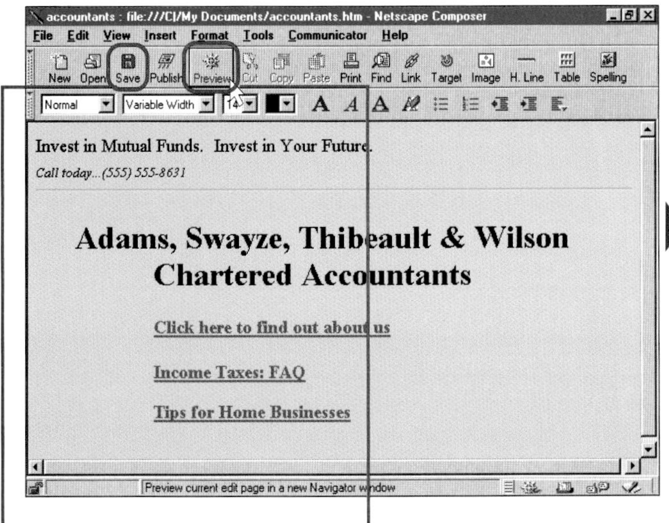

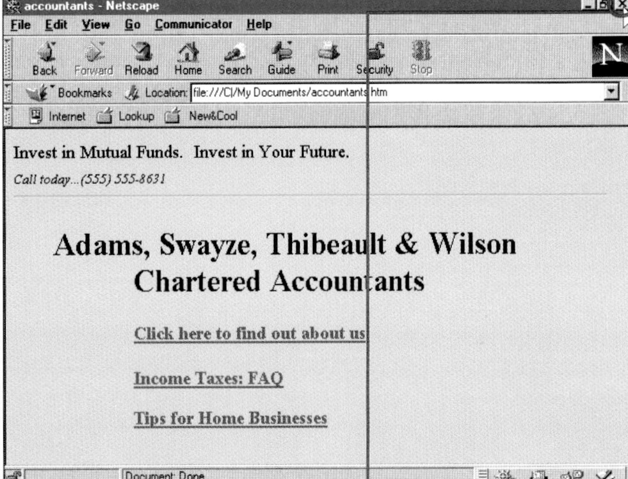

1 Click **Save** to save the Web page before viewing the page in the browser window.

Note: For information on saving a Web page, refer to page 244.

2 Click **Preview** to view the Web page in the browser window.

■ The Web page appears in the browser window.

3 Click ☒ to close the browser window when you finish reviewing the Web page.

You can add images to your Web pages to make the pages more interesting and attractive.

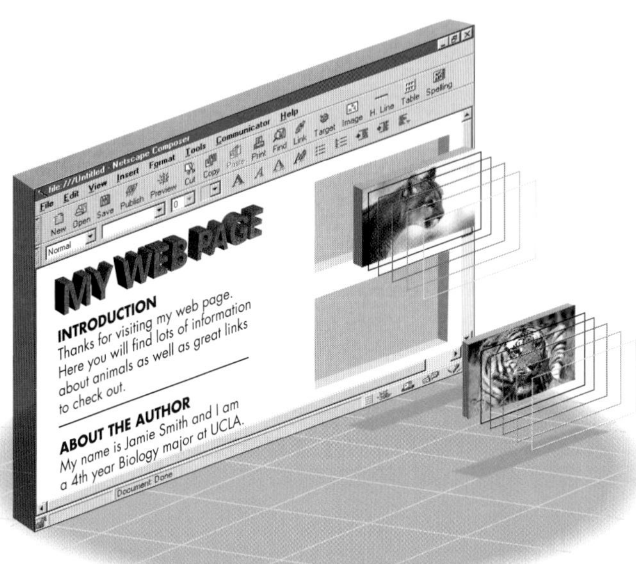

When adding images to your Web pages, try to use images with the .gif or .jpg extension, since these are the most common types of images on the Web.

INSERT AN IMAGE

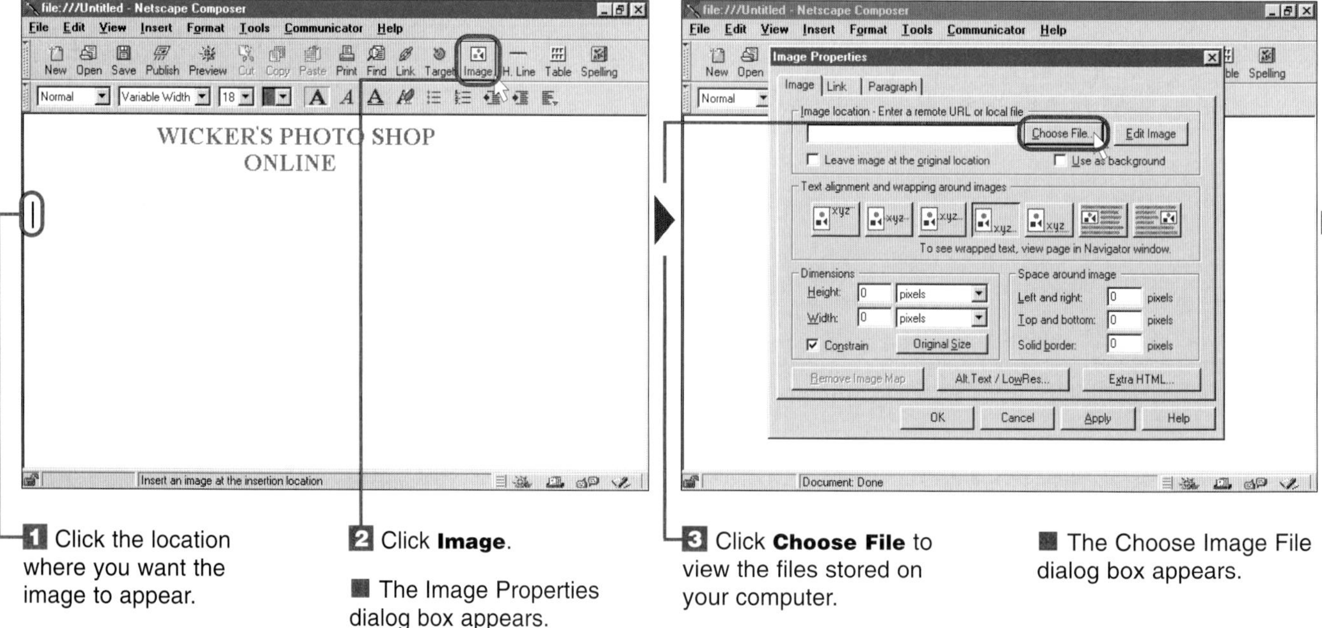

1 Click the location where you want the image to appear.

2 Click **Image**.

■ The Image Properties dialog box appears.

3 Click **Choose File** to view the files stored on your computer.

■ The Choose Image File dialog box appears.

?

Where can I get images to use in my Web pages?

Many pages on the Web offer images you can use for free. You can buy a collection of ready-made images, called clip art, at most computer stores or use a scanner to scan images into your computer.

You can also use a drawing program to create your own images. Make sure you have permission to use any images you do not create yourself.

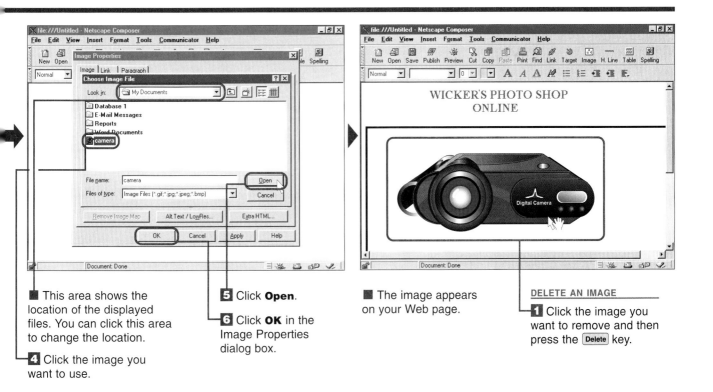

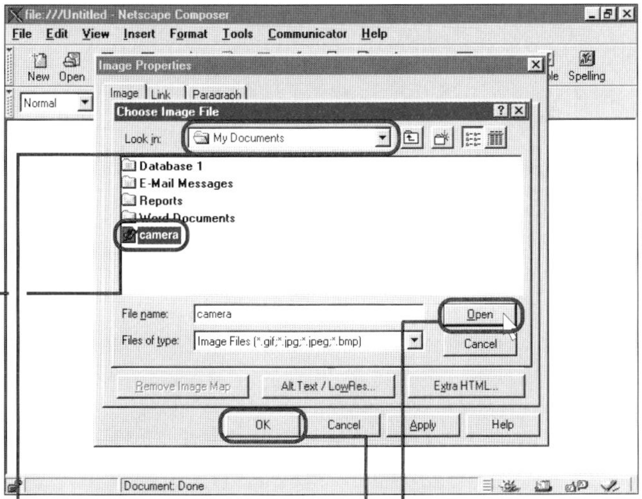

■ This area shows the location of the displayed files. You can click this area to change the location.

4 Click the image you want to use.

5 Click **Open**.

6 Click **OK** in the Image Properties dialog box.

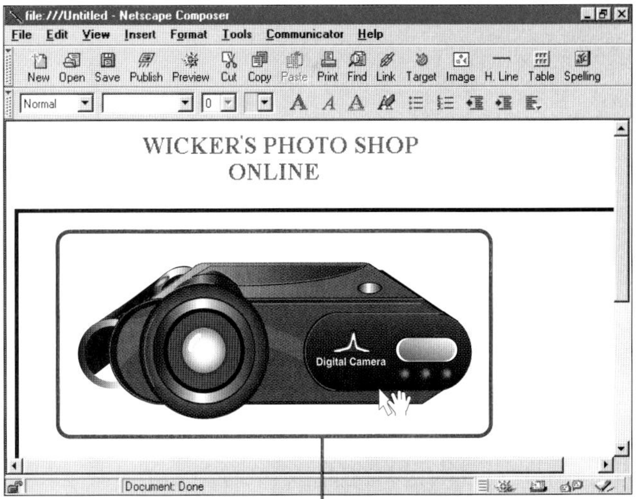

■ The image appears on your Web page.

DELETE AN IMAGE

1 Click the image you want to remove and then press the Delete key.

ADD A BACKGROUND IMAGE

You can have a small image repeat to fill an entire Web page. This can add an interesting background texture to your page.

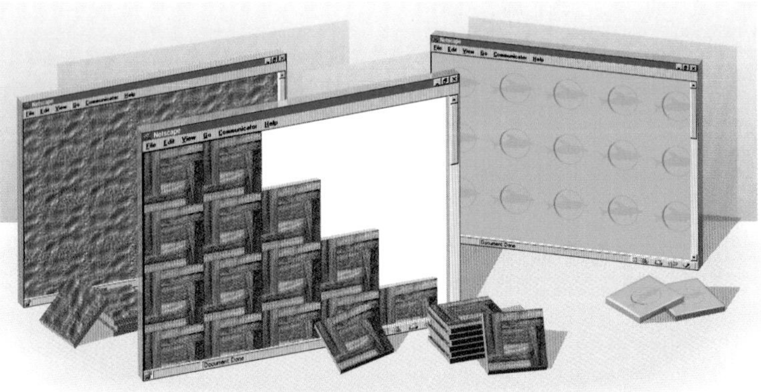

You can get background images at the following Web sites:

www.netscape.com/assist/net_sites/bg/backgrounds.html

www.ECNet.Net/users/gas52r0/Jay/backgrounds/back.htm

www.ender-design.com/rg/backidx.html

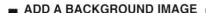

ADD A BACKGROUND IMAGE

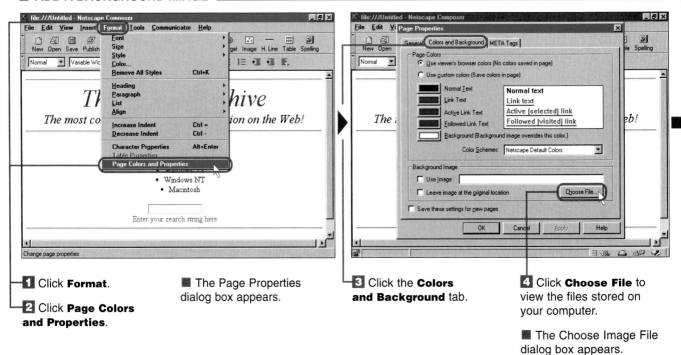

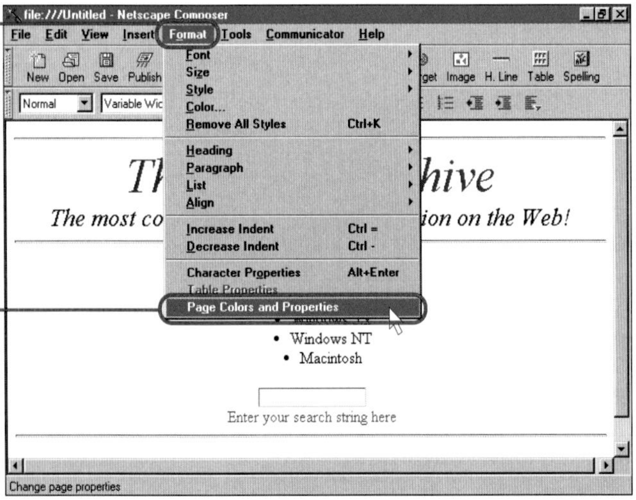

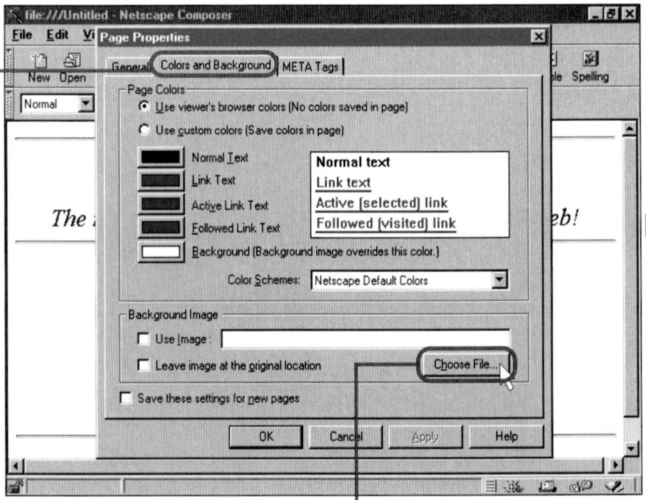

1 Click **Format**.

2 Click **Page Colors and Properties**.

The Page Properties dialog box appears.

3 Click the **Colors and Background** tab.

4 Click **Choose File** to view the files stored on your computer.

The Choose Image File dialog box appears.

Can I add a solid color to the background of my Web page?

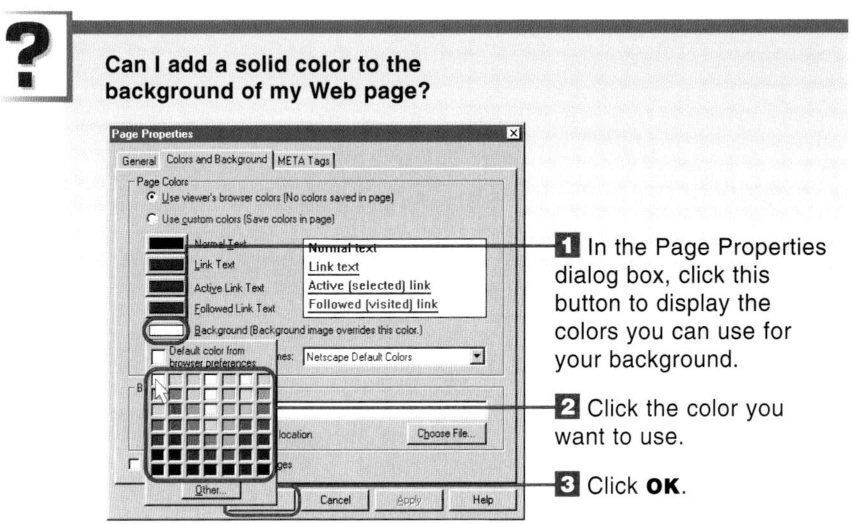

1 In the Page Properties dialog box, click this button to display the colors you can use for your background.

2 Click the color you want to use.

3 Click **OK**.

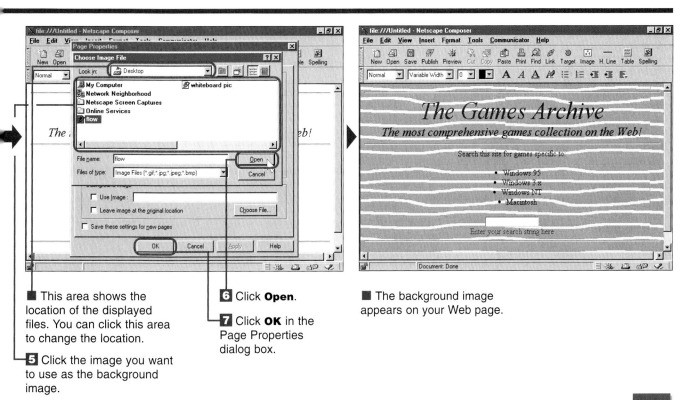

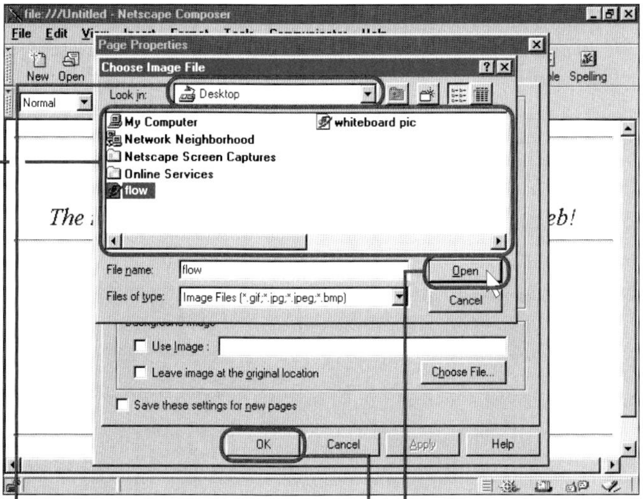

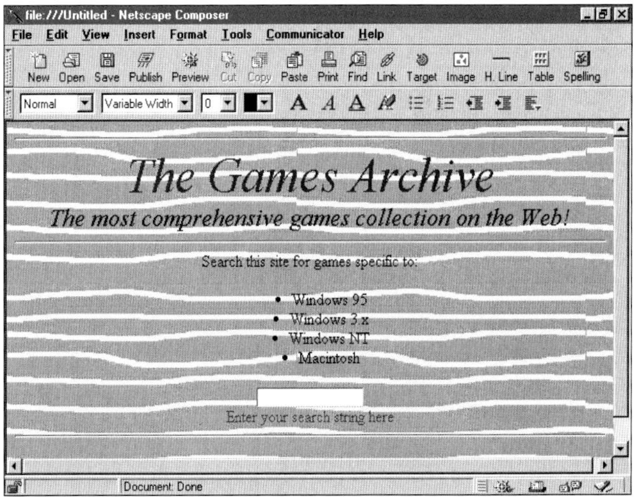

■ This area shows the location of the displayed files. You can click this area to change the location.

5 Click the image you want to use as the background image.

6 Click **Open**.

7 Click **OK** in the Page Properties dialog box.

■ The background image appears on your Web page.

CREATE A LINK

You can create a link to connect a word or phrase in your Web page to another Web page. When you select the word or phrase, the other Web page appears.

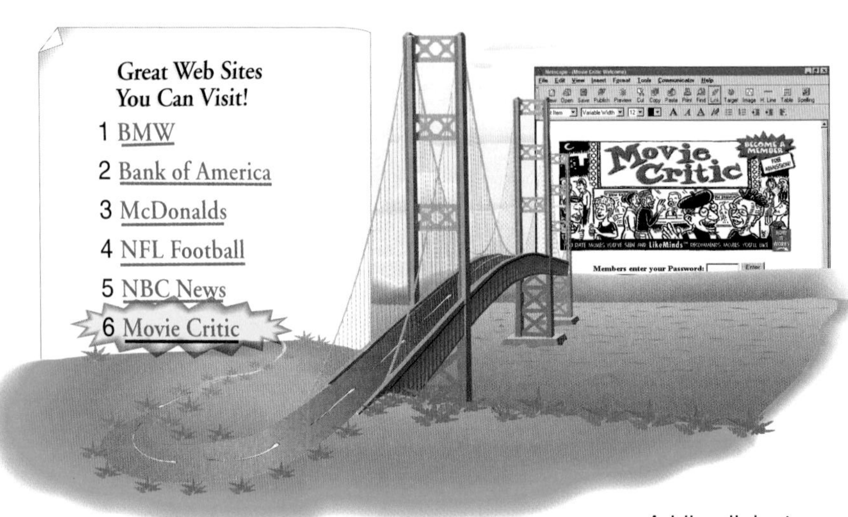

Adding links to your Web page gives readers quick access to Web pages that relate to your document.

CREATE A LINK

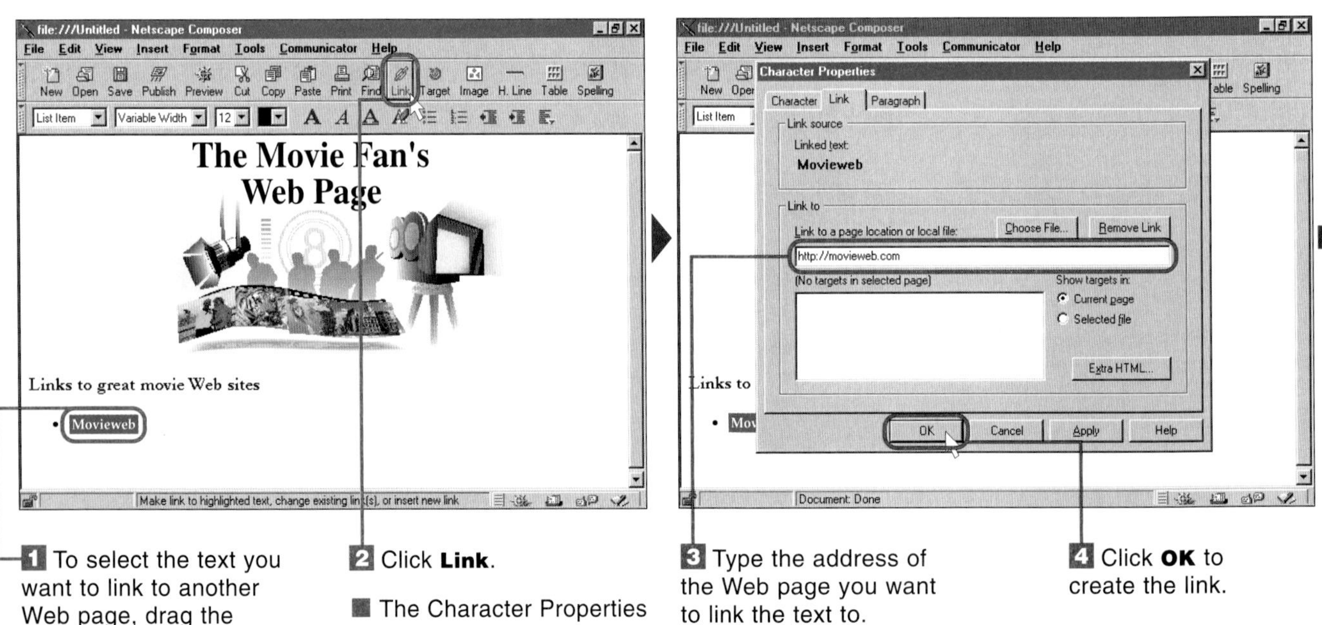

1 To select the text you want to link to another Web page, drag the mouse I over the text.

2 Click **Link**.

■ The Character Properties dialog box appears.

3 Type the address of the Web page you want to link the text to.

4 Click **OK** to create the link.

?

What information can I use as a link?

You can use any information on your Web page as a link. Make sure the information you choose clearly indicates where the link will take the reader. Avoid using the phrase "click here," since this phrase is not very informative.

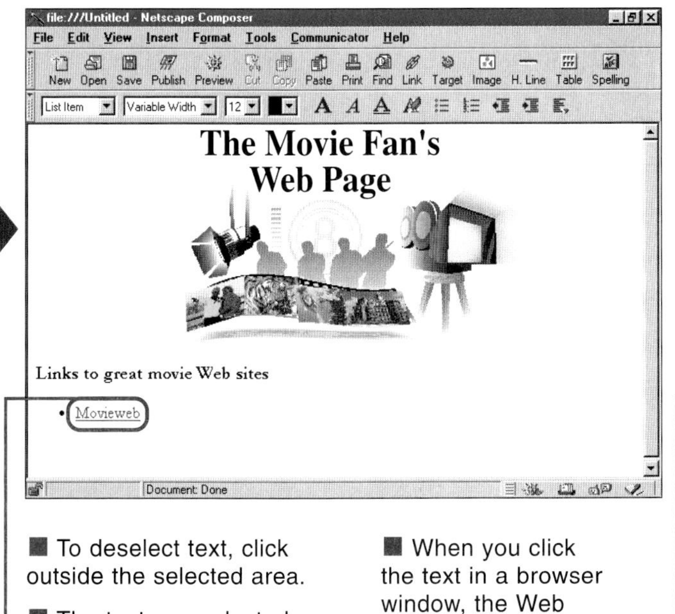

■ To deselect text, click outside the selected area.

■ The text you selected appears as a link. Links appear underlined and in color.

■ When you click the text in a browser window, the Web page connected to the link will appear.

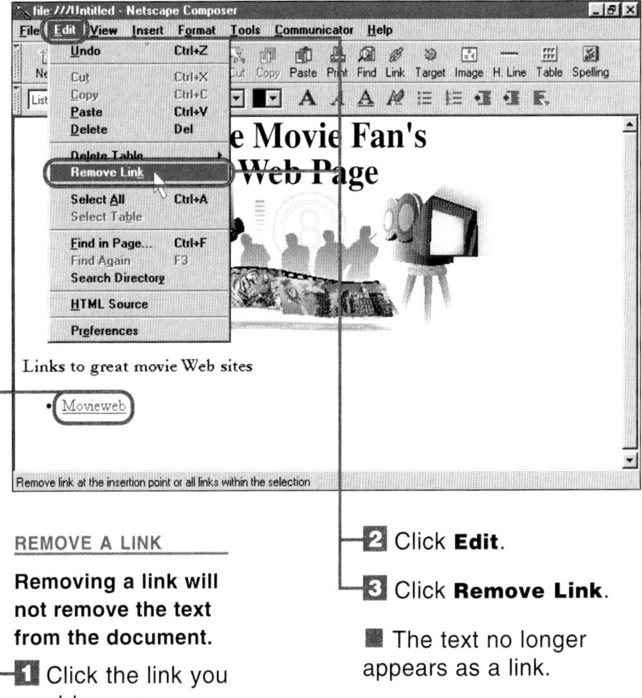

REMOVE A LINK

Removing a link will not remove the text from the document.

1 Click the link you want to remove.

2 Click **Edit**.

3 Click **Remove Link**.

■ The text no longer appears as a link.

CREATE A LINK TO ANOTHER SECTION OF A WEB PAGE

You can create links that quickly take you to other sections of a long Web page. This saves people from having to scroll all the way through the page to find an area of interest.

CREATE A LINK TO ANOTHER SECTION OF A WEB PAGE

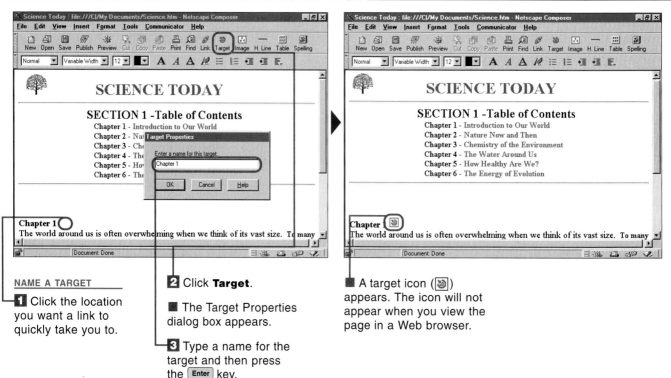

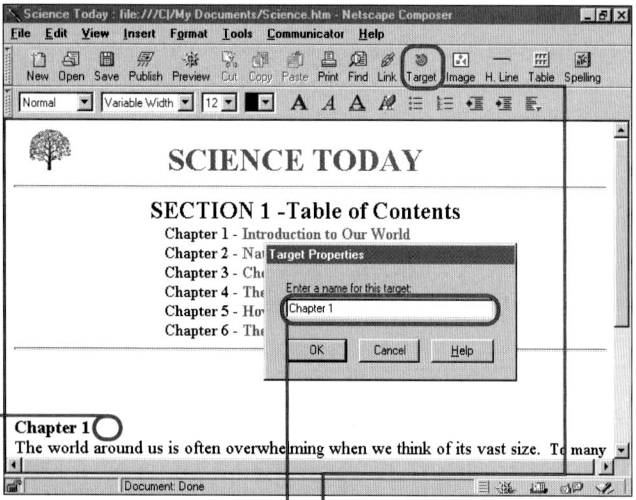

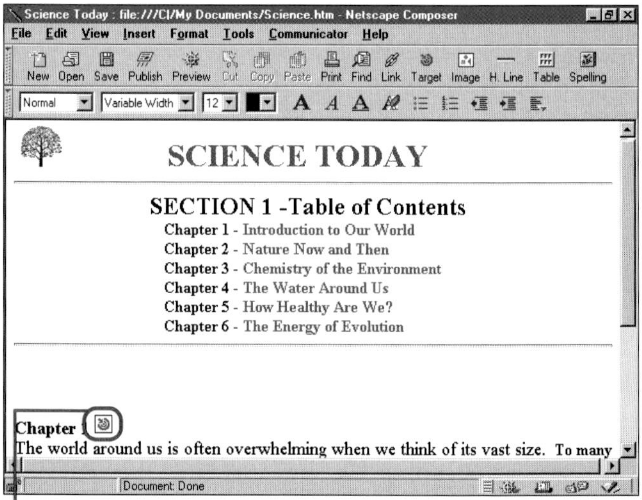

NAME A TARGET

1 Click the location you want a link to quickly take you to.

2 Click **Target**.

■ The Target Properties dialog box appears.

3 Type a name for the target and then press the Enter key.

■ A target icon ( ) appears. The icon will not appear when you view the page in a Web browser.

? When would I create a link to another section of a Web page?

You can place a link at the bottom of a Web page that takes you back to the top of the page.

You can create a table of contents that lists the material discussed on the Web page. Selecting a link from the table of contents will take you to the appropriate section of the Web page.

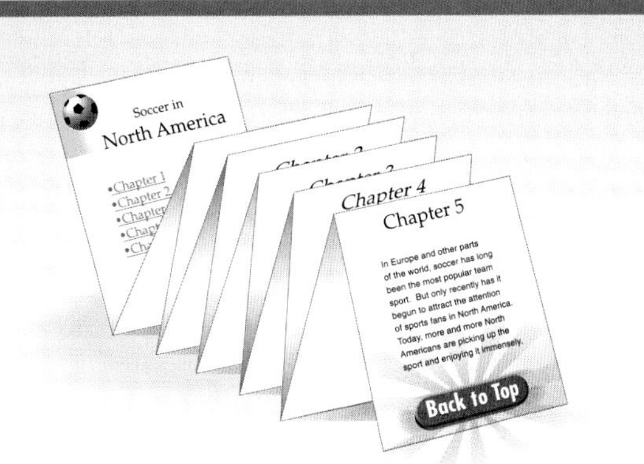

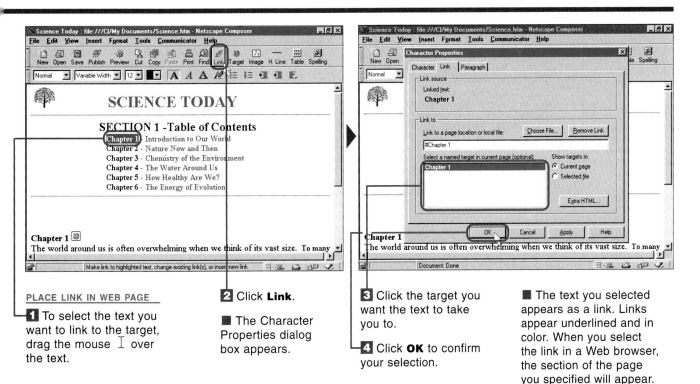

PLACE LINK IN WEB PAGE

1 To select the text you want to link to the target, drag the mouse over the text.

2 Click **Link**.

■ The Character Properties dialog box appears.

3 Click the target you want the text to take you to.

4 Click **OK** to confirm your selection.

■ The text you selected appears as a link. Links appear underlined and in color. When you select the link in a Web browser, the section of the page you specified will appear.

USING A TEMPLATE OR WIZARD

You can save time by using a template or the Page Wizard to create your own Web page.

USING A TEMPLATE OR WIZARD

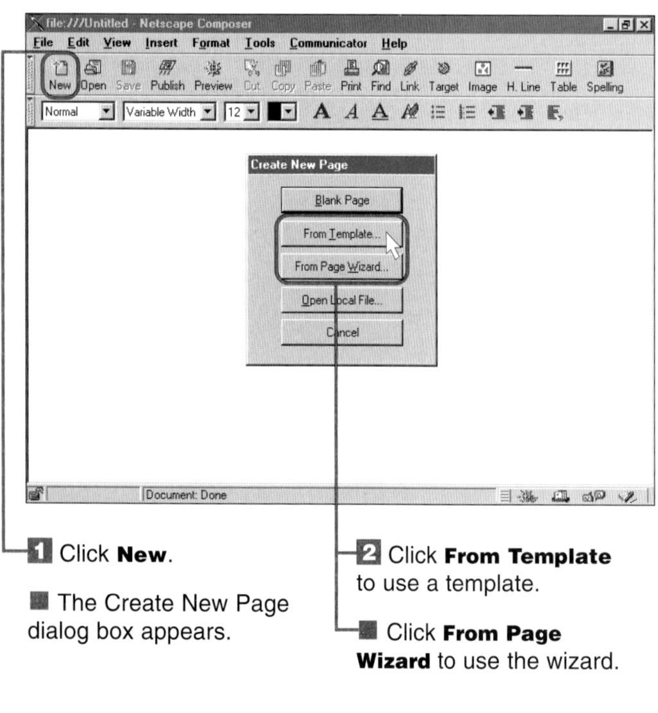

1 Click **New**.

■ The Create New Page dialog box appears.

2 Click **From Template** to use a template.

■ Click **From Page Wizard** to use the wizard.

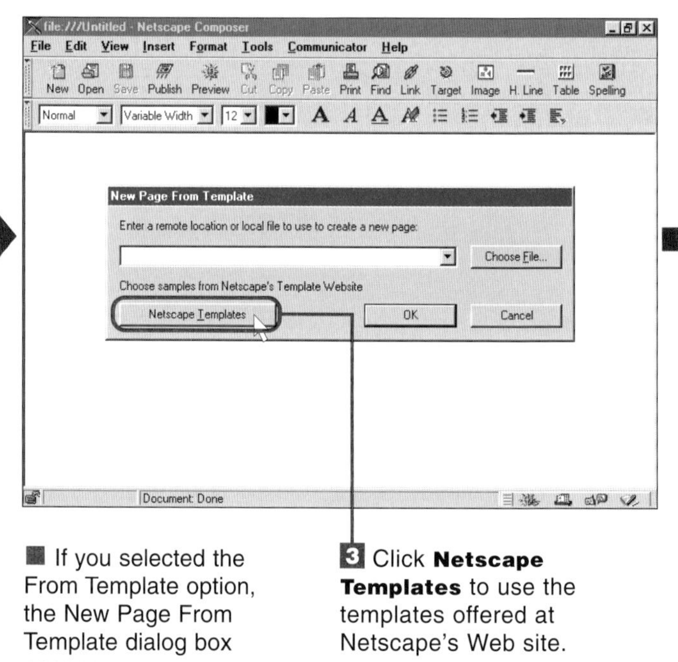

■ If you selected the From Template option, the New Page From Template dialog box appears.

3 Click **Netscape Templates** to use the templates offered at Netscape's Web site.

What is the difference between a template and the Page Wizard?

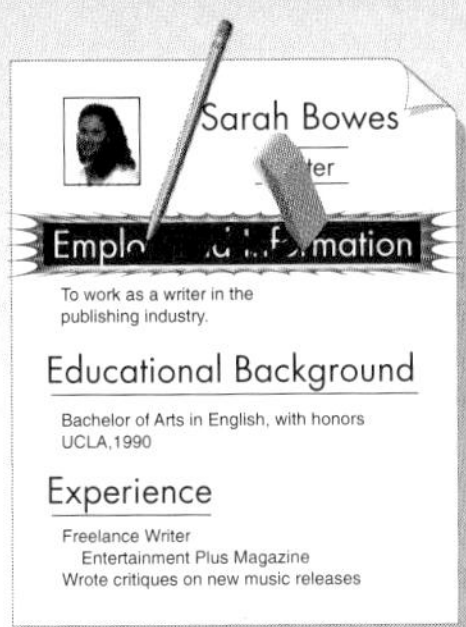

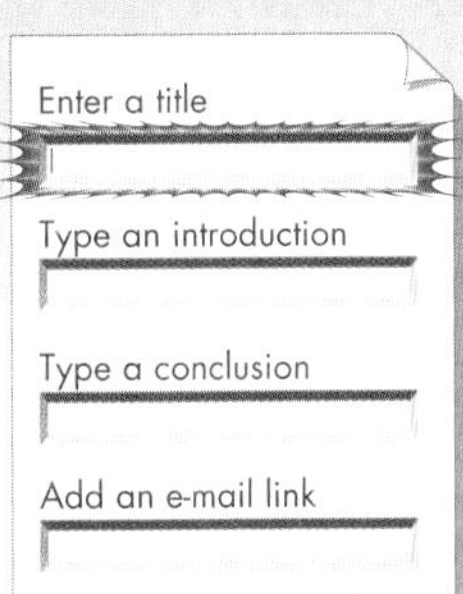

Template

A template provides the basic framework so you can concentrate on the content of your Web page. The templates offered by Netscape include the personal, company, department and product templates.

Page Wizard

The Page Wizard allows you to create a Web page step-by-step. You can determine the appearance and content of your Web page by specifying options such as a title, links and the text color.

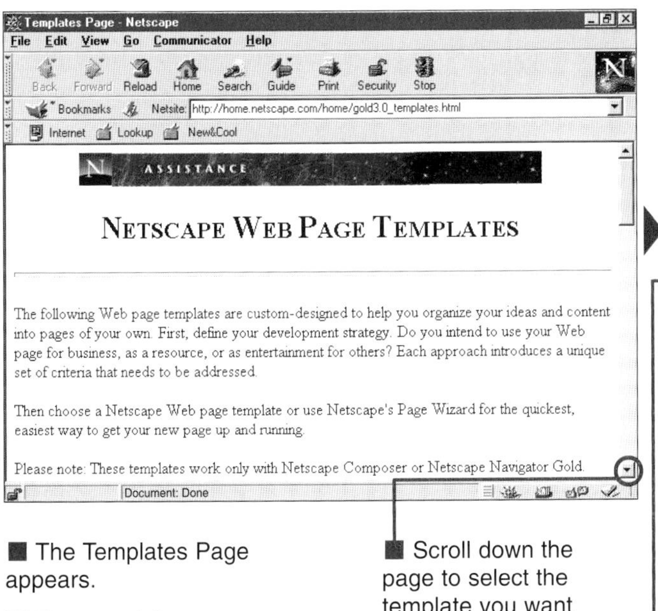

Netscape Page Wizard - Netscape
File Edit View Go Communicator Help
Back Forward Reload Home Search Guide Print Security Stop
Bookmarks Netsite: http://home.netscape.com/home/gold4.0_wizard.html
Internet Lookup New&Cool
ASSISTANCE
NETSCAPE PAGE WIZARD
The Netscape Page Wizard makes it easy to create a great Web page. When you click the Start button below, simple instructions will appear in the frame to the left. Just click on a feature, then choose from the options that appear in the frame below. Watch this window to see your page develop as you make your selections. After
Document: Done

■ The Templates Page appears.

■ The top of the page provides information about templates. The bottom of the page lists the templates you can choose from.

■ Scroll down the page to select the template you want to use.

■ If you selected the From Page Wizard option, the Netscape Page Wizard appears.

■ This area describes the wizard. You can scroll through this area to learn about the wizard.

■ Scroll down the page to locate the **START** button. Click **START** when you are ready to create your Web page and then follow the instructions on your screen.

PUBLISH A WEB PAGE

When you finish creating your Web page, you can transfer the page to a Web server. Once the Web page is on the server, your page will be available to everyone on the Web.

PUBLISH A WEB PAGE

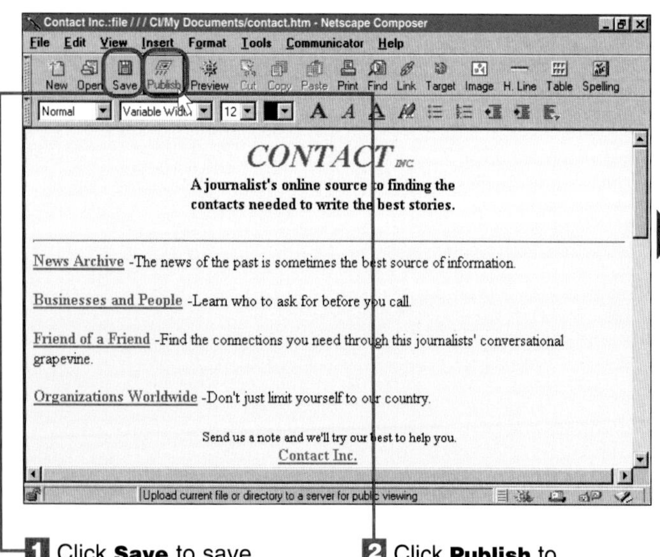

1 Click **Save** to save the Web page displayed on your screen before publishing the page.

Note: For information on saving a Web page, refer to page 244.

2 Click **Publish** to publish the Web page.

■ The Publish dialog box appears.

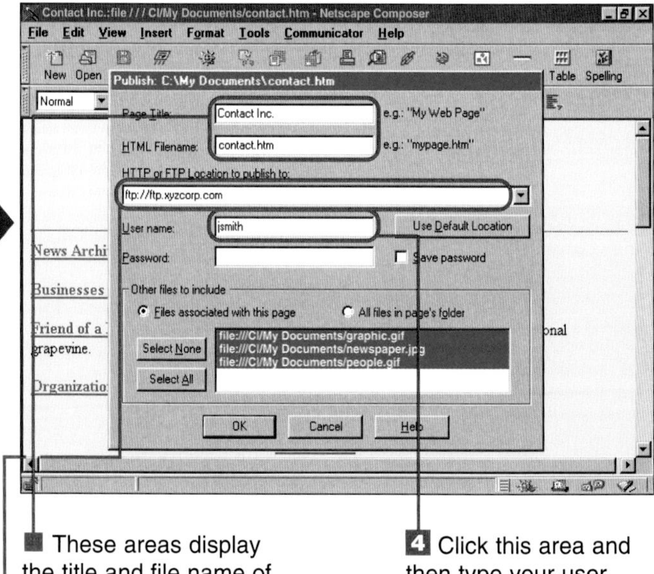

■ These areas display the title and file name of the Web page.

3 Click this area and then type the location where the Web server will store your Web page.

4 Click this area and then type your user name.

Note: You may need to ask your system administrator or Internet service provider for the information you need to enter.

Where can I publish my Web page?

The company that gives you access to the Internet usually offers space on its Web server where you can publish your Web page. There are also places on the Internet that will publish your Web page for free, such as GeoCities (www.geocities.com).

You can also publish a Web page you create on a corporate intranet. An intranet is a small version of the Internet within a company or organization. Ask your system administrator for details.

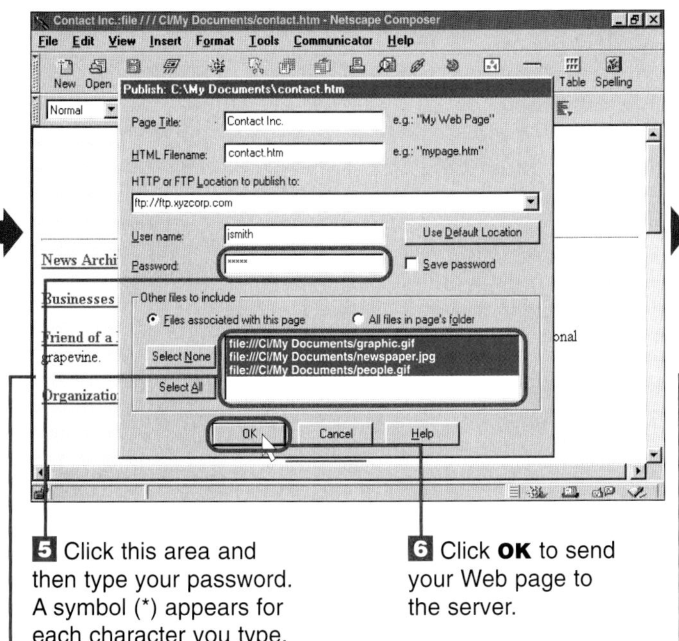

5 Click this area and then type your password. A symbol (*) appears for each character you type.

■ This area displays the location of each image file the Web page displays. The image files will transfer to the Web server along with your Web page.

6 Click **OK** to send your Web page to the server.

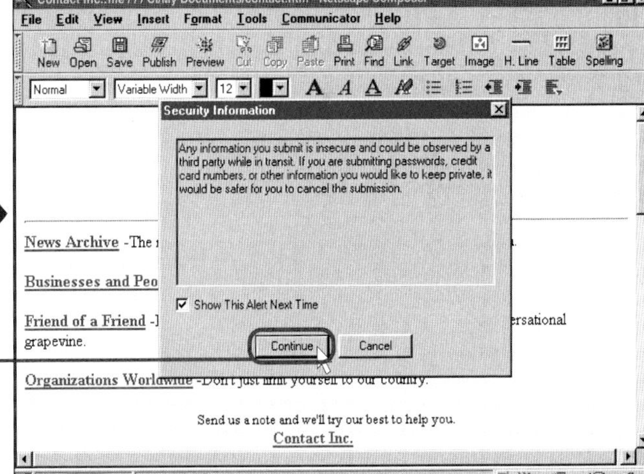

■ The Security Information dialog box appears, warning that the information you are sending could be read by other people.

7 Click **Continue** to send your Web page.

■ A message will appear to tell you the Web page was successfully sent. Click **OK** to close the dialog box.

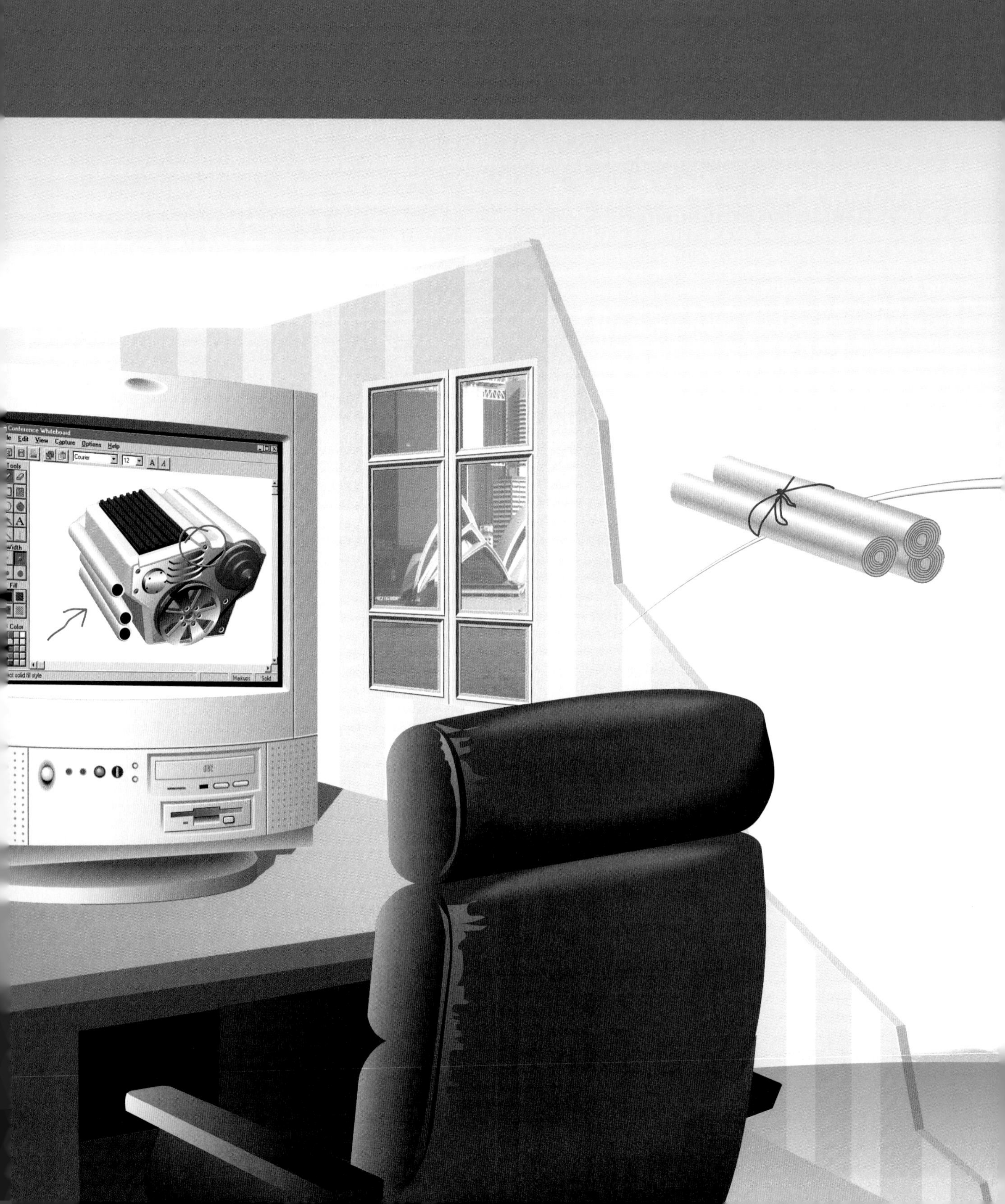

Conference Whiteboard
Edit View Capture Options Help
Courier
12
Tools
Width
Fill
Color
Markups
Solid

CHAPTER 10

Using Conference

Are you ready to begin using Conference to chat, exchange files and browse the Web with another person? This chapter shows you how.

START AND SET UP NETSCAPE CONFERENCE

Netscape Conference allows you to communicate with another person on the Internet. You can chat with another person, exchange files, browse the Web together and work on the same document.

START AND SET UP NETSCAPE CONFERENCE

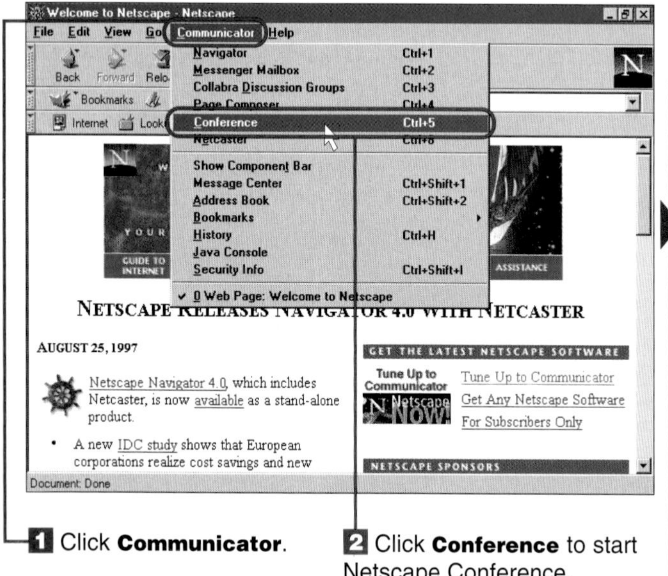

1 Click **Communicator**.

2 Click **Conference** to start Netscape Conference.

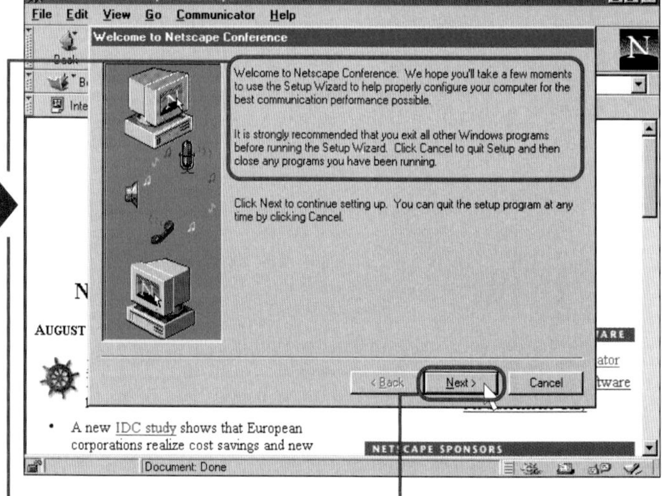

■ The Setup Wizard appears the first time you start Conference.

■ This area introduces you to Conference and recommends that you exit all other Windows programs before continuing.

3 Click **Next** to continue.

?

Will the Setup Wizard appear the next time I start Conference?

No, the wizard only appears the first time you start Conference. The next time you start the program, the Netscape Conference window appears, allowing you to immediately start a conference with another person.

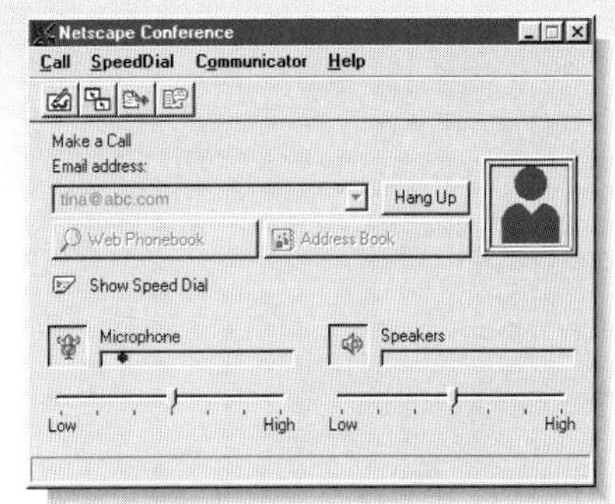

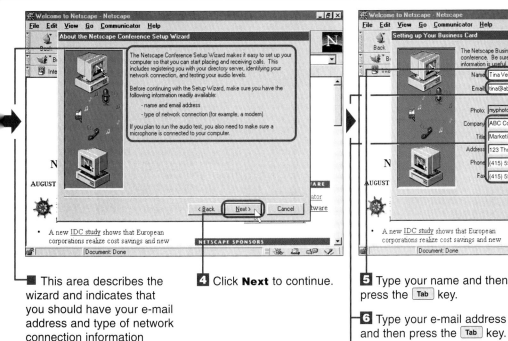

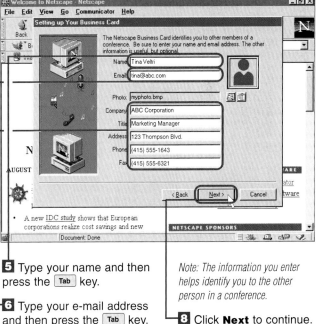

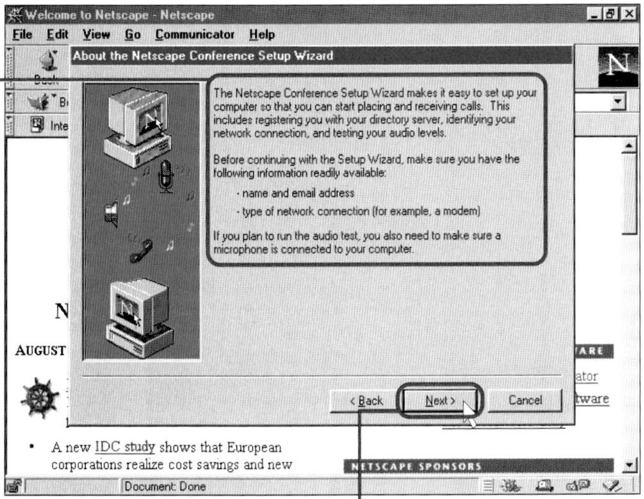

■ This area describes the wizard and indicates that you should have your e-mail address and type of network connection information available before continuing.

4 Click **Next** to continue.

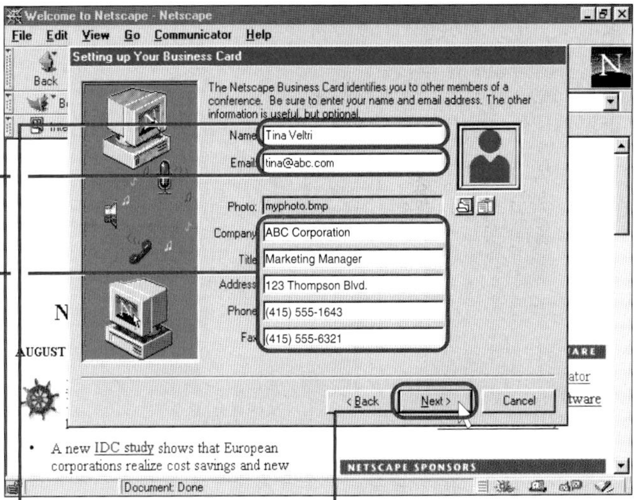

5 Type your name and then press the Tab key.

6 Type your e-mail address and then press the Tab key.

7 To add information to any of these areas, click the area and then type the information. This information is optional.

Note: The information you enter helps identify you to the other person in a conference.

8 Click **Next** to continue.

CONTINUED

START AND SET UP NETSCAPE CONFERENCE

When you are using Conference, you can have your name appear on the Internet to help other people find and contact you.

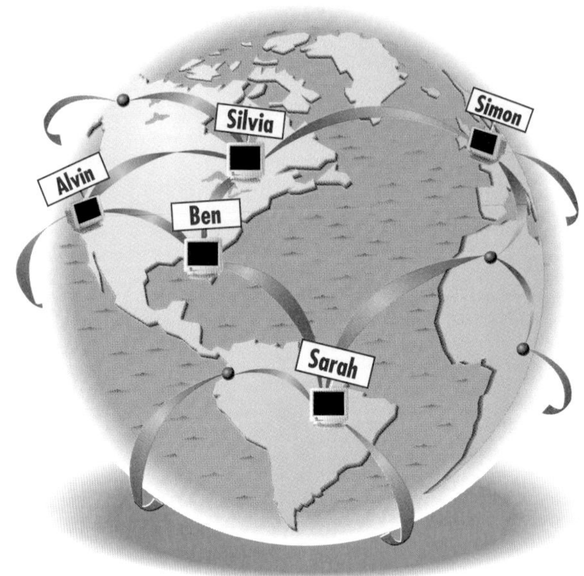

Your name only appears on the Internet when you are connected to the Internet and have Conference open.

START AND SET UP NETSCAPE CONFERENCE (CONTINUED)

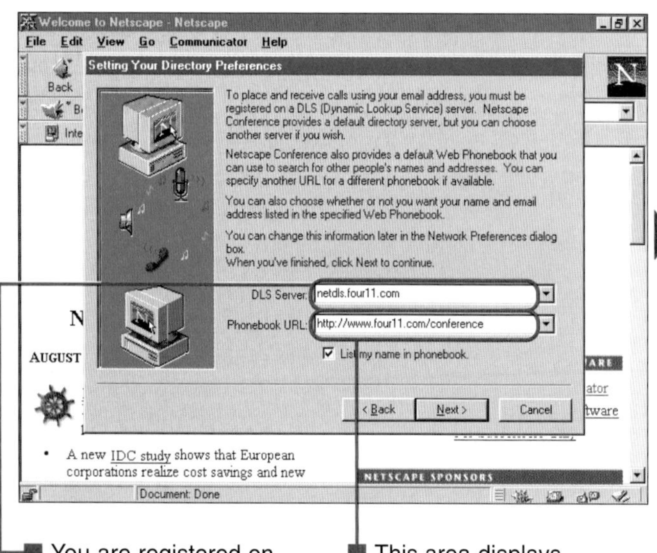

■ You are registered on the DLS server displayed in this area. The server allows you to make and receive calls using your e-mail address.

■ This area displays the location of the Web Phonebook you can use to search for people you want to start a conference with.

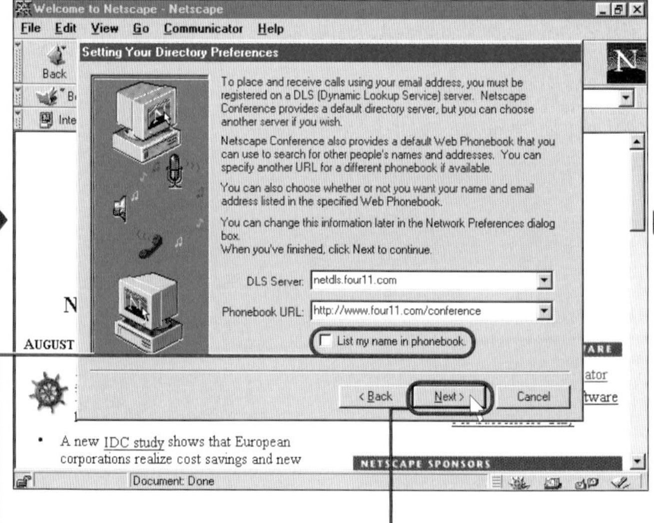

■ This option places your name in the Web Phonebook on the Internet. Click this option if you do not want your name to appear on the Internet (☑ changes to ☐).

9 Click **Next** to continue.

?

What equipment do I need if I want to hear sound when using Conference?

You need a sound card and speakers to hear sound. You need a microphone to talk during a conference.

A full-duplex sound card lets two people talk at the same time, like a telephone. A half-duplex sound card lets only one person talk at a time, like a CB radio.

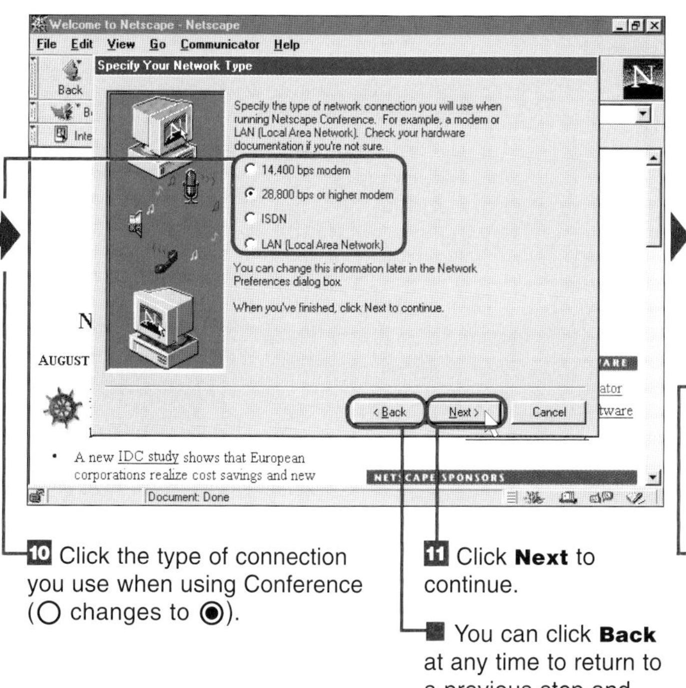

10 Click the type of connection you use when using Conference (○ changes to ◉).

11 Click **Next** to continue.

■ You can click **Back** at any time to return to a previous step and change your answers.

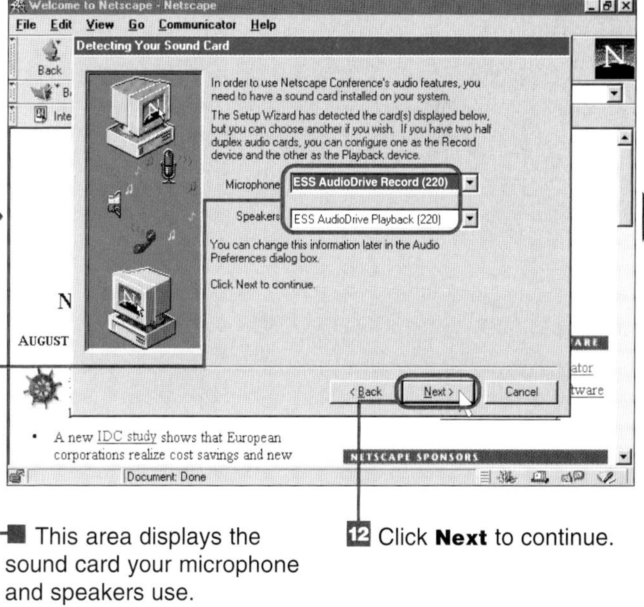

■ This area displays the sound card your microphone and speakers use.

12 Click **Next** to continue.

CONTINUED

START AND SET UP NETSCAPE CONFERENCE

You may need to adjust the audio levels to reduce background noise when talking over the Internet.

You need a microphone attached to your computer to test the audio levels.

START AND SET UP NETSCAPE CONFERENCE (CONTINUED)

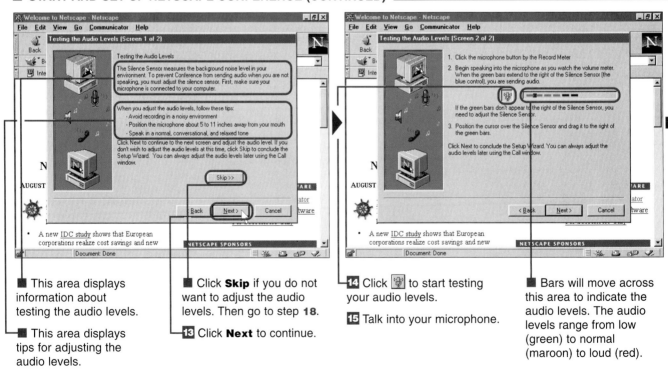

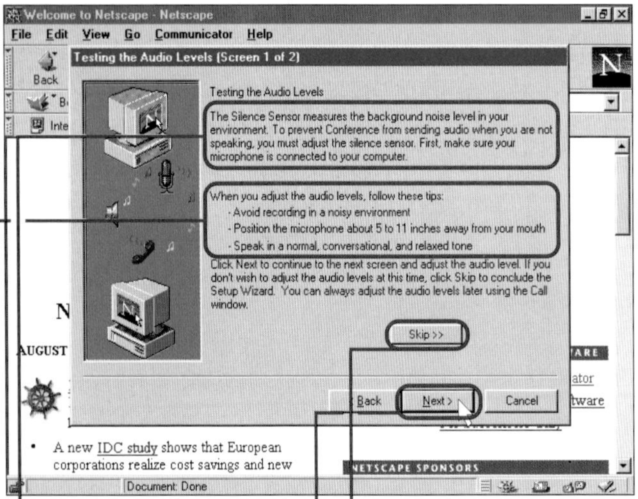

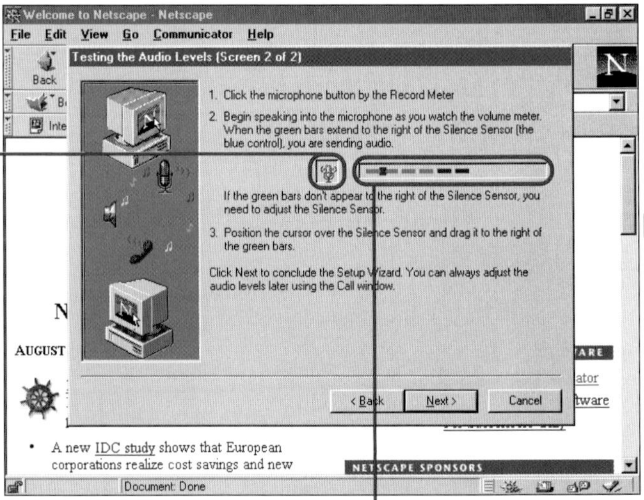

■ This area displays information about testing the audio levels.

■ This area displays tips for adjusting the audio levels.

■ Click **Skip** if you do not want to adjust the audio levels. Then go to step **18**.

13 Click **Next** to continue.

14 Click [microphone icon] to start testing your audio levels.

15 Talk into your microphone.

■ Bars will move across this area to indicate the audio levels. The audio levels range from low (green) to normal (maroon) to loud (red).

?

Can I use Conference with my company's intranet?

You can use Conference with your company's intranet to communicate with your colleagues. An intranet is a small version of the Internet inside a company or organization.

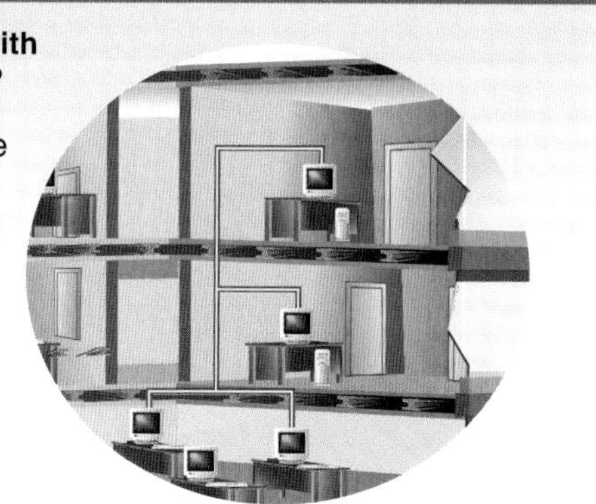

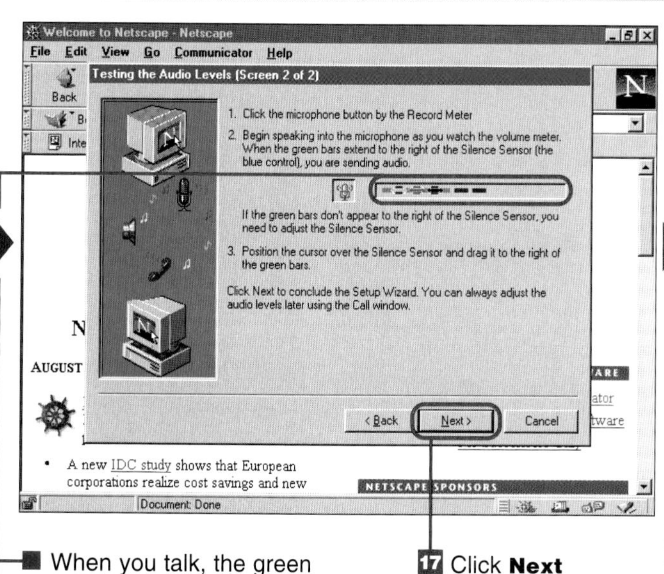

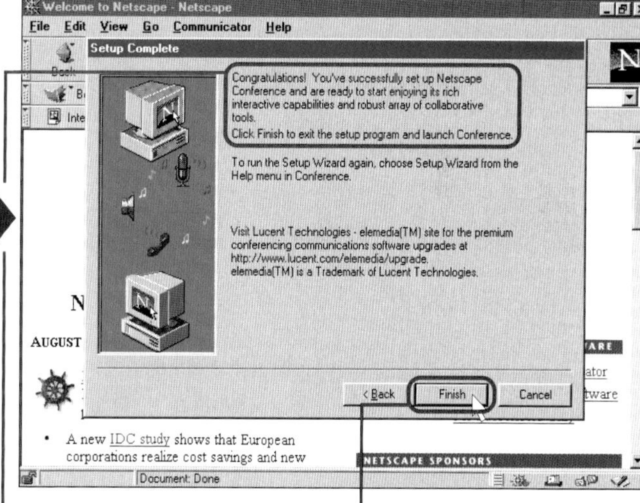

■ When you talk, the green bars should extend past the blue control. Other people will only hear the sound that goes past the blue control.

16 To move the blue control (■), position the mouse over the control (changes to ⟷) and then drag the control to a new location.

17 Click **Next** to continue.

■ This area indicates that you have successfully set up Conference and you can begin using the program.

18 Click **Finish** to exit the Setup Wizard.

■ The Netscape Conference window appears.

MAKE A CALL

You can make a call to contact another person on the Internet you want to communicate with. Once contacted, you can chat, exchange files, browse the Web together and more.

The person you want to call must have Conference open on their computer.

MAKE A CALL

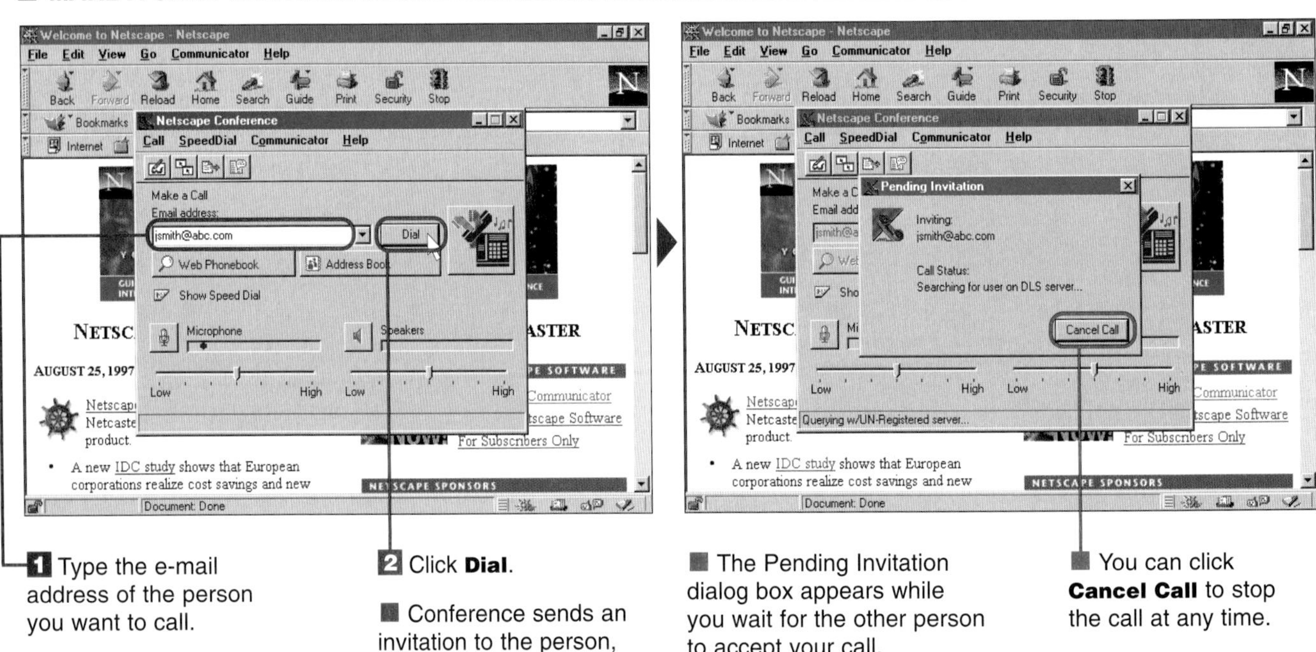

1 Type the e-mail address of the person you want to call.

2 Click **Dial**.

■ Conference sends an invitation to the person, asking if they want to accept your call.

■ The Pending Invitation dialog box appears while you wait for the other person to accept your call.

■ You can click **Cancel Call** to stop the call at any time.

? How can I find someone to call?

You can display a list of people on the Internet that you can call.

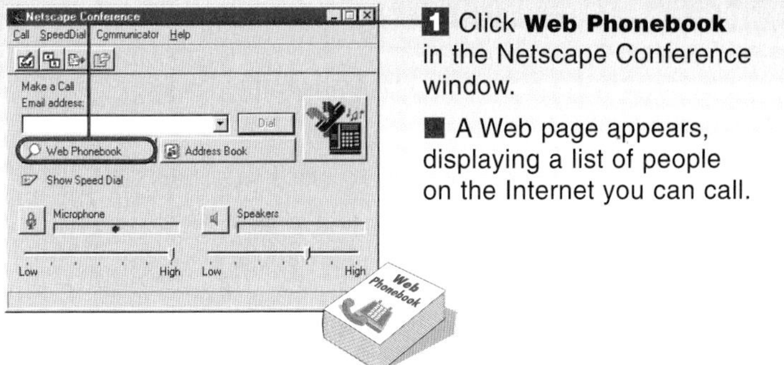

1 Click **Web Phonebook** in the Netscape Conference window.

■ A Web page appears, displaying a list of people on the Internet you can call.

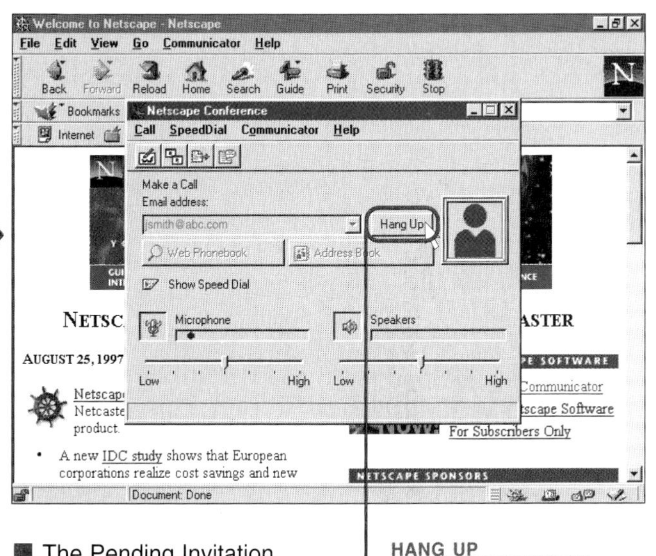

■ The Pending Invitation dialog box disappears when the person accepts your call. You can now start communicating with the other person.

HANG UP

1 Click **Hang Up** when you are finished with a call.

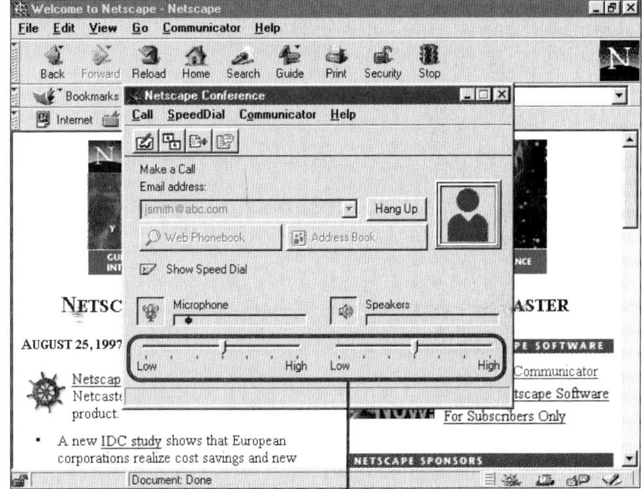

TALK OVER THE INTERNET

■ If you and the other person both have a microphone and speakers, you can talk to each other over the Internet without paying any long-distance charges.

■ To adjust the microphone sensitivity or speaker volume, position the mouse over the appropriate slider. Then drag the slider to a new location.

You can exchange typed messages with a person on the Internet. A message you send will instantly appear on the other person's computer.

CHAT

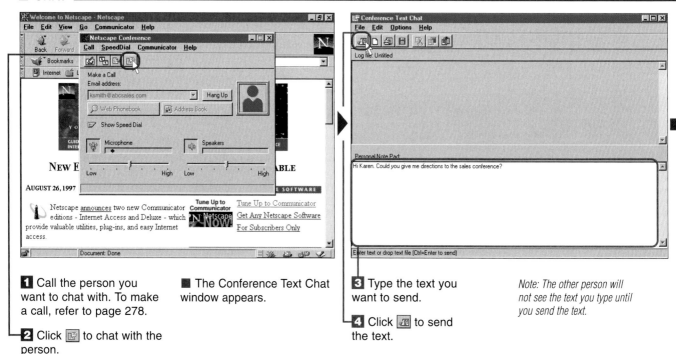

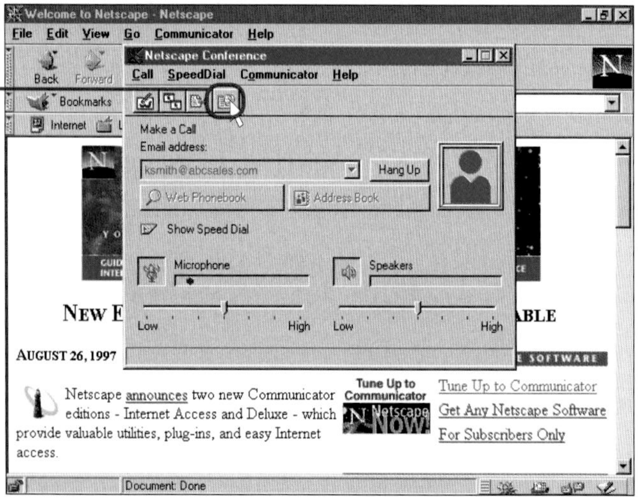

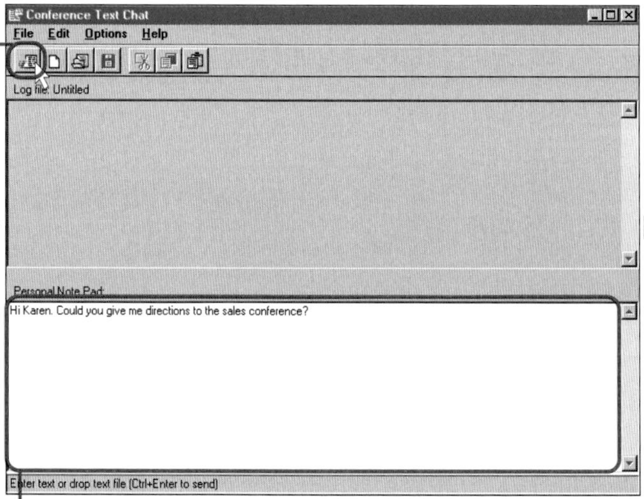

1 Call the person you want to chat with. To make a call, refer to page 278.

2 Click [icon] to chat with the person.

■ The Conference Text Chat window appears.

3 Type the text you want to send.

4 Click [icon] to send the text.

Note: The other person will not see the text you type until you send the text.

? Can I display information about the person I am communicating with?

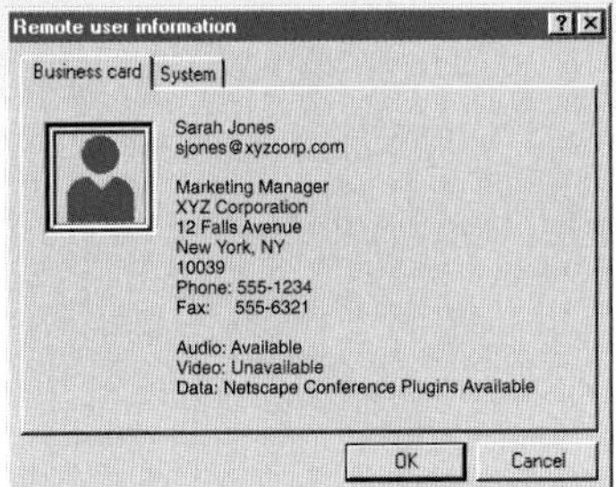

1 Click in the **Netscape Conference** window to display information about the other person.

■ The other person can also display information about you. The information that appears is the same information you entered when you set up Conference.

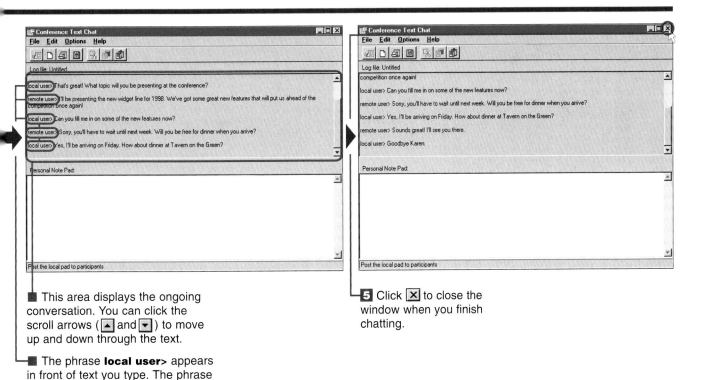

■ This area displays the ongoing conversation. You can click the scroll arrows (▲ and ▼) to move up and down through the text.

■ The phrase **local user>** appears in front of text you type. The phrase **remote user>** appears in front of text the other person types.

5 Click ☒ to close the window when you finish chatting.

EXCHANGE FILES

You can easily exchange files with another person on the Internet. You can instantly transfer important and interesting documents to colleagues, friends and family members.

You can transfer any type of file, such as a text document, picture, sound or video.

SEND FILES

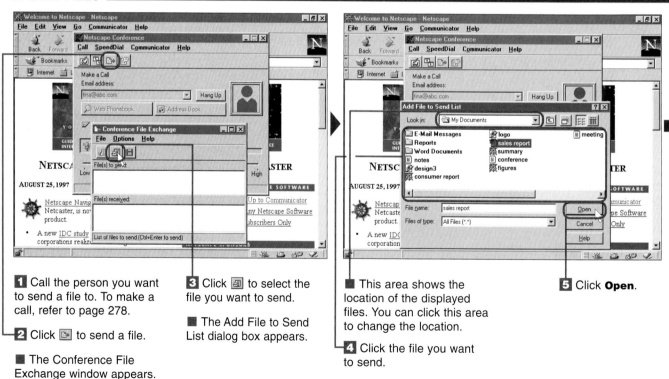

1 Call the person you want to send a file to. To make a call, refer to page 278.

2 Click to send a file.

■ The Conference File Exchange window appears.

3 Click to select the file you want to send.

■ The Add File to Send List dialog box appears.

■ This area shows the location of the displayed files. You can click this area to change the location.

4 Click the file you want to send.

5 Click **Open**.

How do I save a file that I receive?

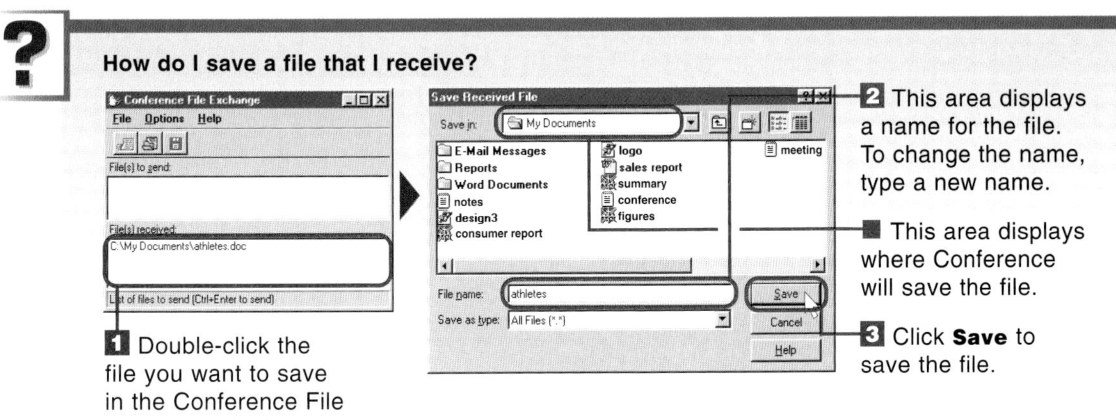

1 Double-click the file you want to save in the Conference File Exchange window.

2 This area displays a name for the file. To change the name, type a new name.

■ This area displays where Conference will save the file.

3 Click **Save** to save the file.

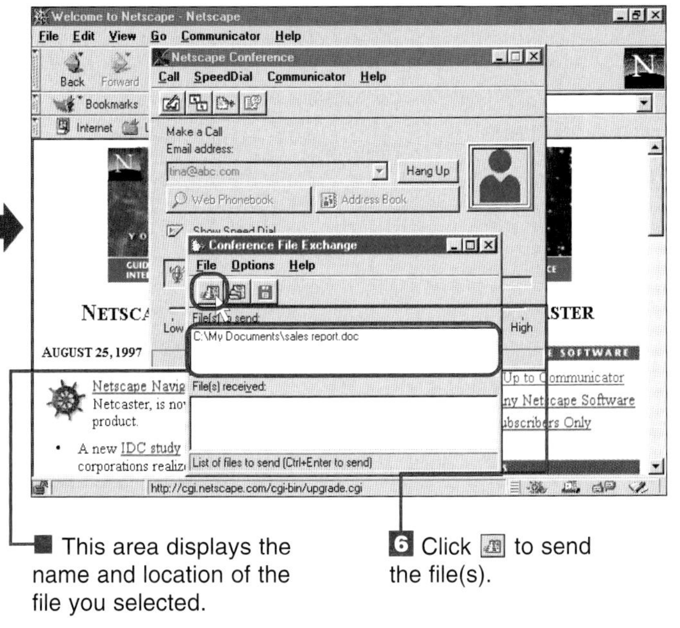

■ This area displays the name and location of the file you selected.

6 Click [icon] to send the file(s).

■ You can repeat steps **3** to **5** to send additional files.

RECEIVE FILES

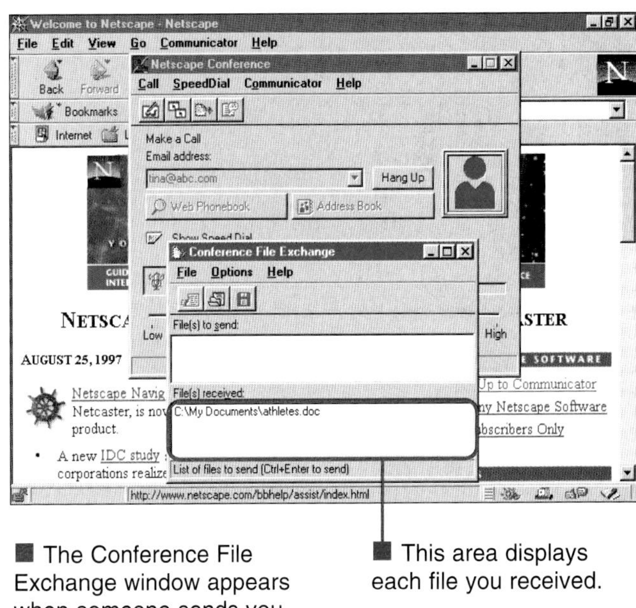

■ The Conference File Exchange window appears when someone sends you a file.

■ This area displays each file you received.

USING THE WHITEBOARD

You can work on a Whiteboard with another person on the Internet. You can draw and make changes to images on the Whiteboard that will instantly appear on the other person's computer.

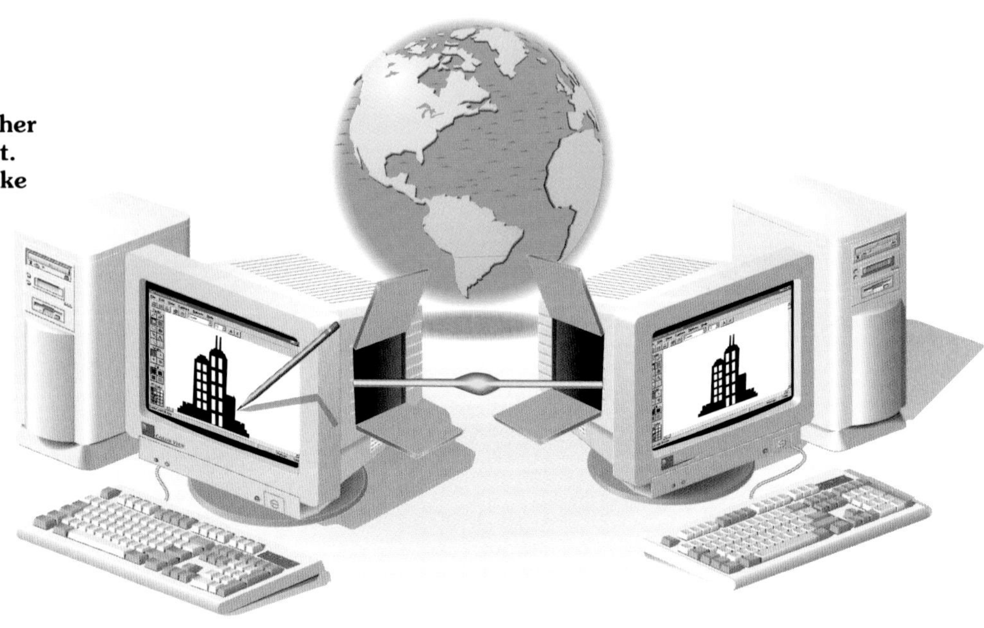

USING THE WHITEBOARD

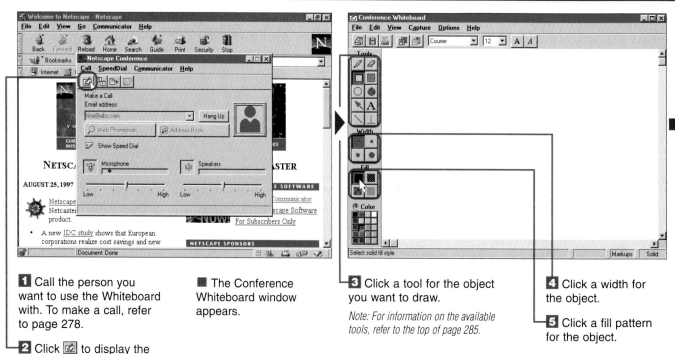

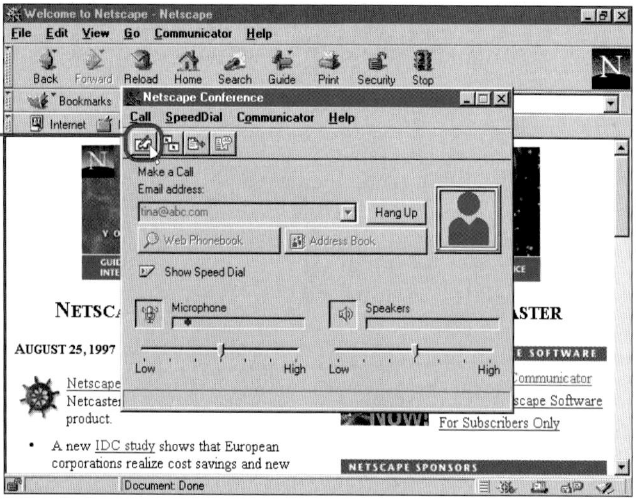

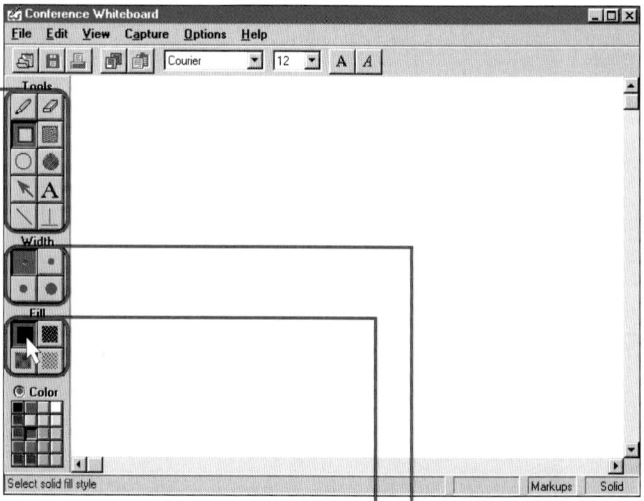

1 Call the person you want to use the Whiteboard with. To make a call, refer to page 278.

2 Click [Whiteboard button] to display the Whiteboard.

■ The Conference Whiteboard window appears.

3 Click a tool for the object you want to draw.

Note: For information on the available tools, refer to the top of page 285.

4 Click a width for the object.

5 Click a fill pattern for the object.

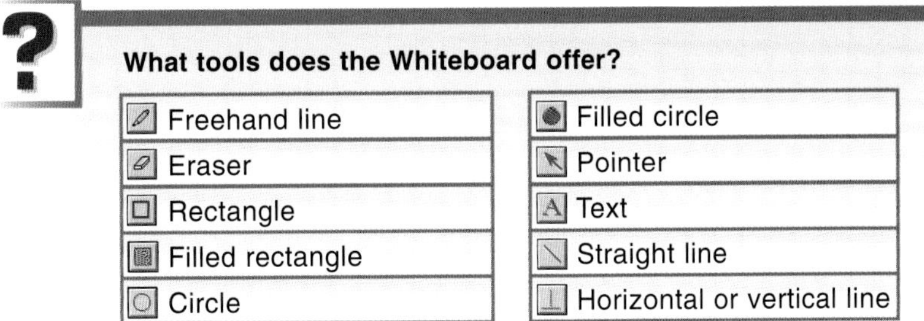

What tools does the Whiteboard offer?

Freehand line	Filled circle
Eraser	Pointer
Rectangle	Text
Filled rectangle	Straight line
Circle	Horizontal or vertical line

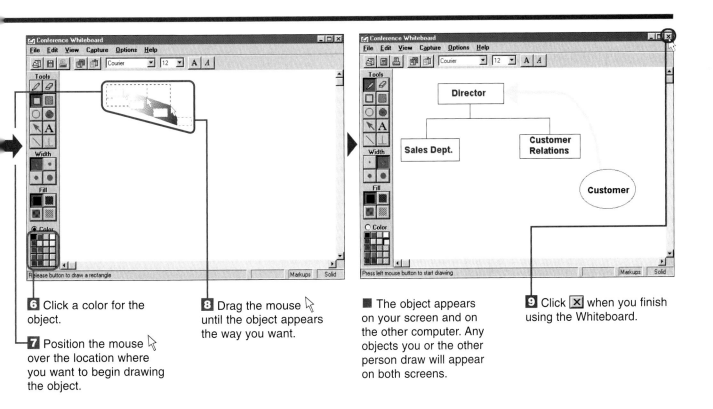

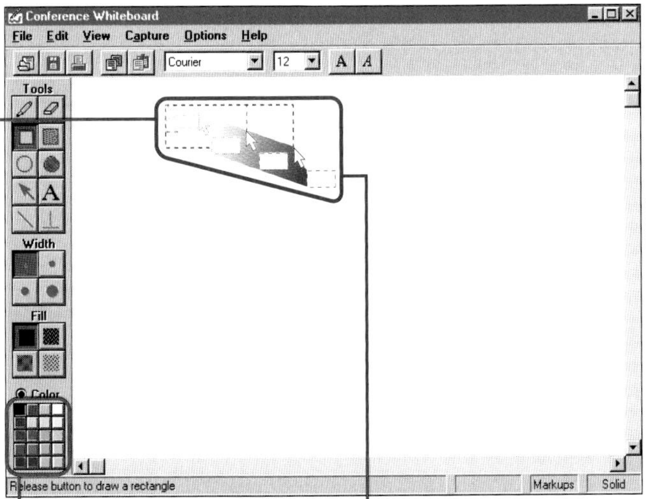

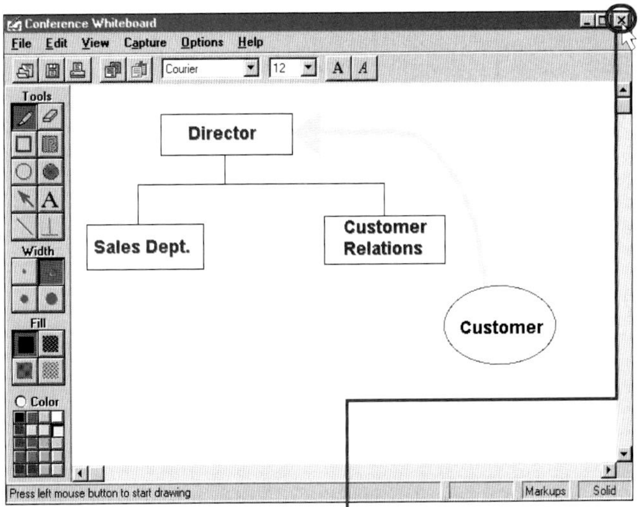

6 Click a color for the object.

7 Position the mouse over the location where you want to begin drawing the object.

8 Drag the mouse until the object appears the way you want.

■ The object appears on your screen and on the other computer. Any objects you or the other person draw will appear on both screens.

9 Click ☒ when you finish using the Whiteboard.

BROWSE THE WEB TOGETHER

While you browse through pages on the Web, you can have another person's computer display the same pages.

Browsing the Web with another person is useful for training purposes, such as showing a new employee at another office how to browse through information on the Web.

BROWSE THE WEB TOGETHER

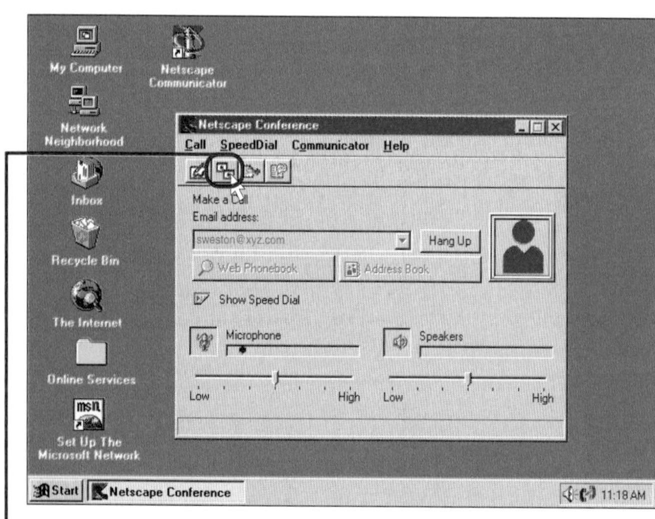

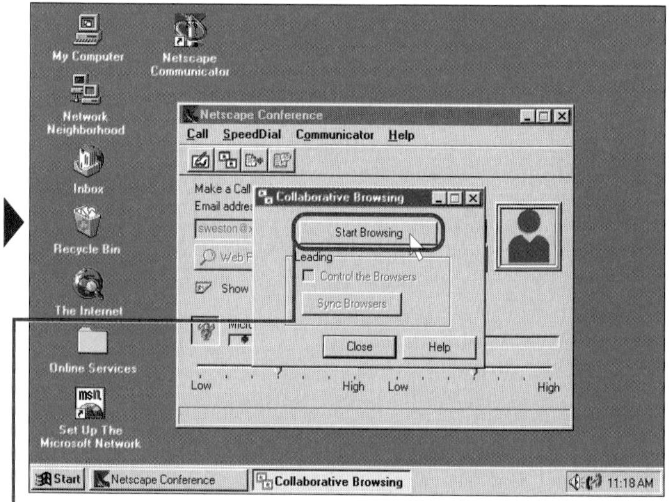

1 Call the person you want to browse the Web with. To make a call, refer to page 278.

2 Click ▣ to browse the Web with the other person.

■ The Collaborative Browsing window appears.

3 Click **Start Browsing** to begin browsing the Web.

■ Conference sends an invitation to the other person, asking if they want to browse the Web with you.

How do I take control of which Web pages appear?

One person always leads the browsing session, while the other person follows.

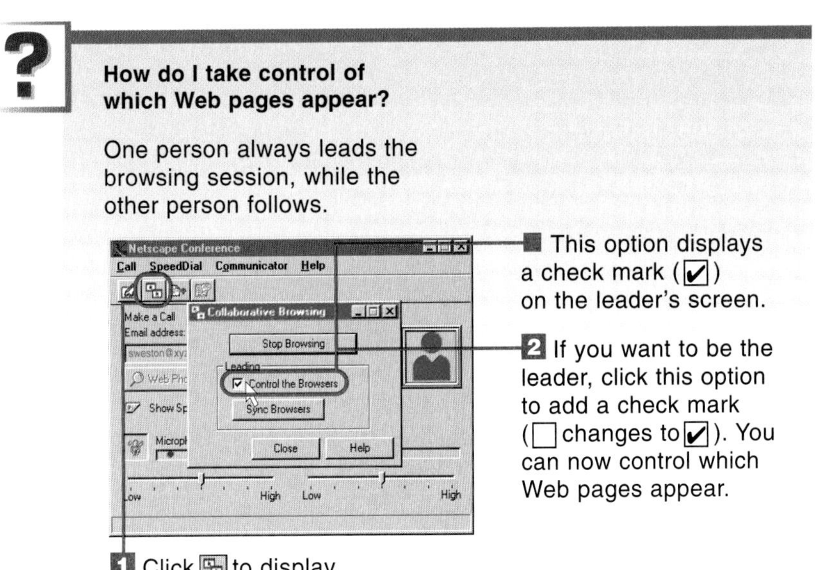

■ This option displays a check mark (☑) on the leader's screen.

2 If you want to be the leader, click this option to add a check mark (☐ changes to ☑). You can now control which Web pages appear.

1 Click ▣ to display the Collaborative Browsing window.

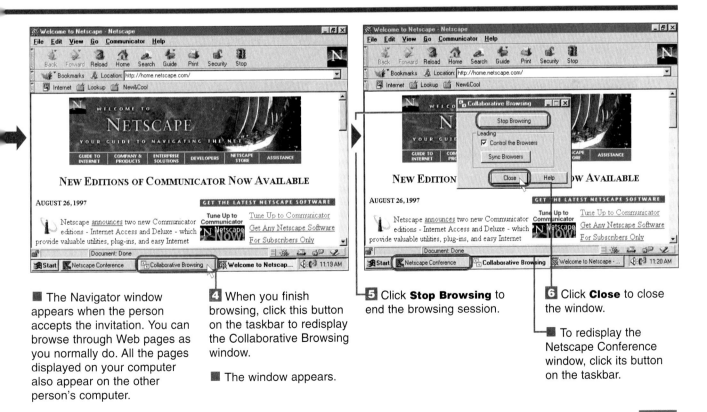

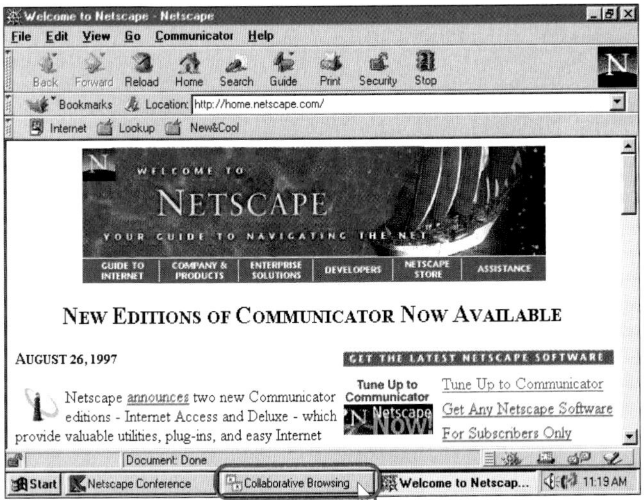

■ The Navigator window appears when the person accepts the invitation. You can browse through Web pages as you normally do. All the pages displayed on your computer also appear on the other person's computer.

4 When you finish browsing, click this button on the taskbar to redisplay the Collaborative Browsing window.

■ The window appears.

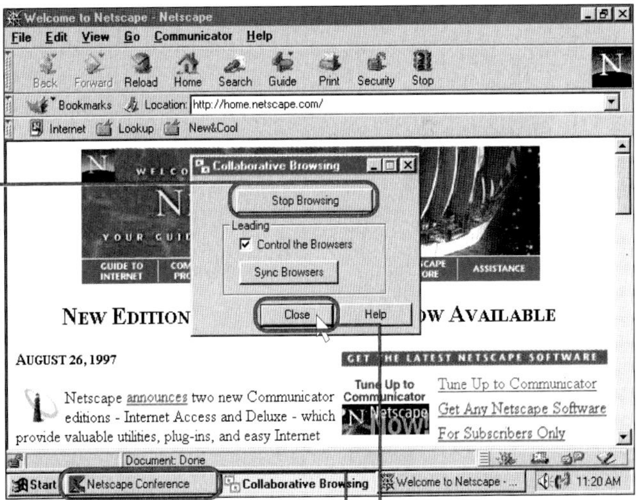

5 Click **Stop Browsing** to end the browsing session.

6 Click **Close** to close the window.

■ To redisplay the Netscape Conference window, click its button on the taskbar.

PLANET EARTH HOME PAGE

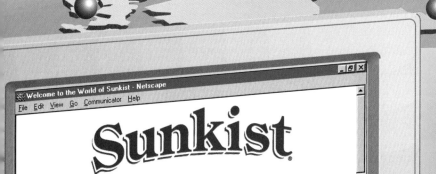

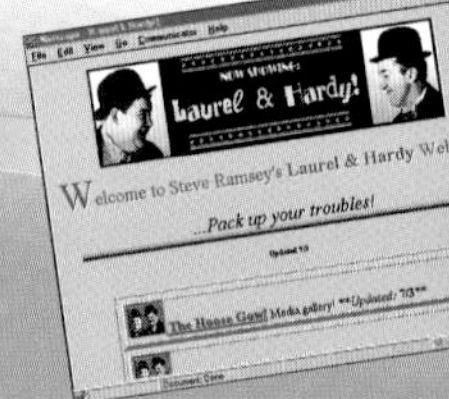

Laurel & Hardy!
Welcome to Steve Ramsey's Laurel & Hardy Web
Pack up your troubles!

Welcome to the World of Sunkist - Netscape
File Edit View Go Communicator Help
Sunkist

Sunkist
100 Years of Quality
About Sunkist
JUST

CH 01 02 03 04 05 06 07 08 09

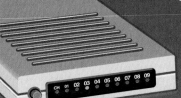

CHAPTER 11

Cool Web Sites

Looking for examples of impressive Web pages? Check out the Web sites in this chapter.

CNNfn

URL www.cnnfn.com

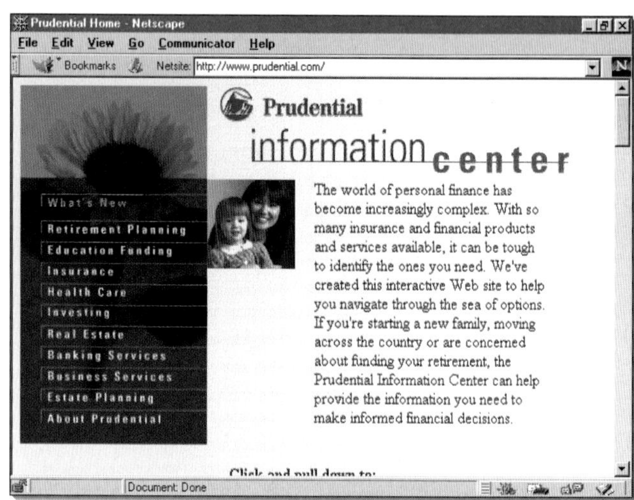

Prudential Insurance

URL www.prudential.com

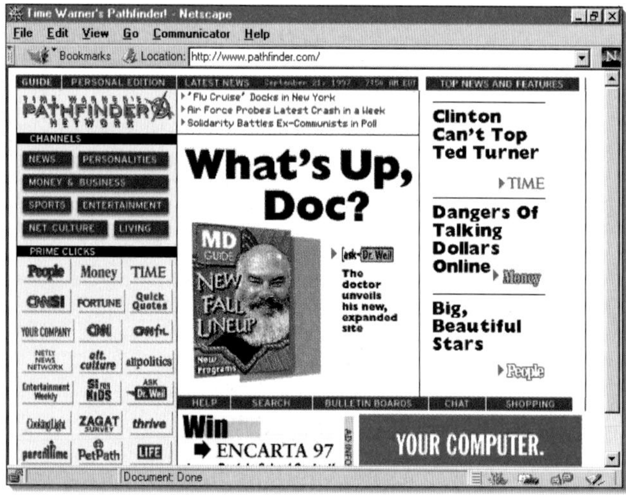

Time Warner's Pathfinder Network

URL www.pathfinder.com

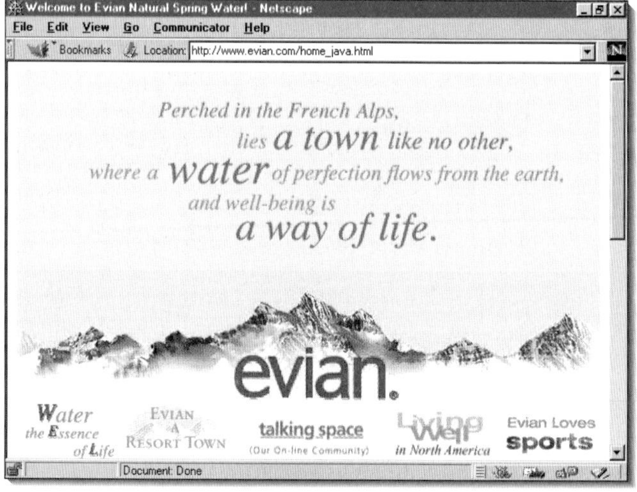

Evian

URL www.evian.com

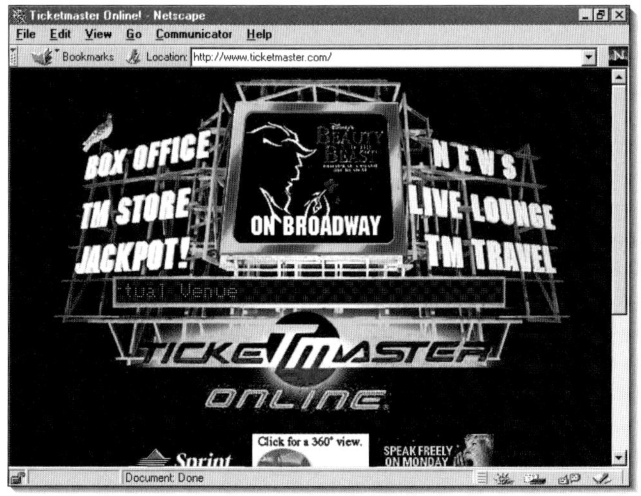

Ticketmaster
URL www.ticketmaster.com

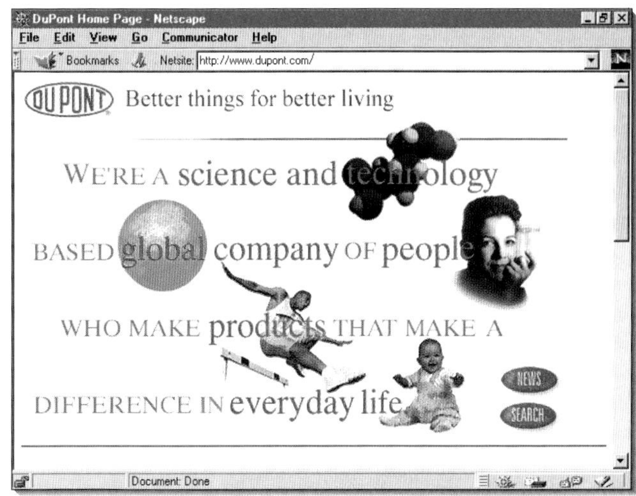

DuPont Company
URL www.dupont.com

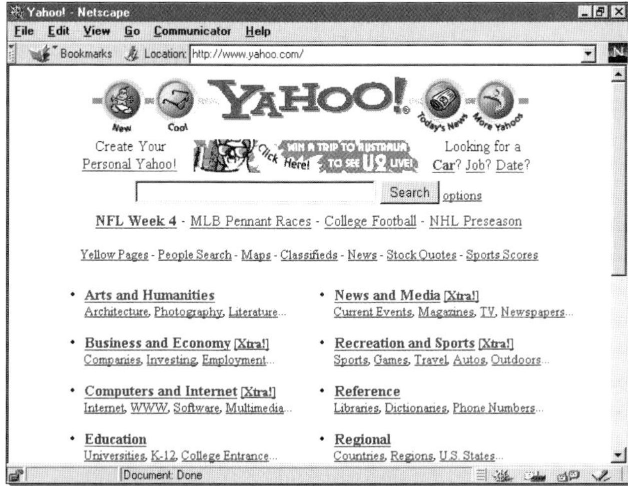

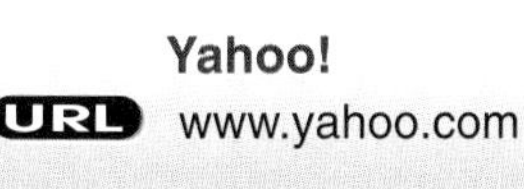
Yahoo!
URL www.yahoo.com

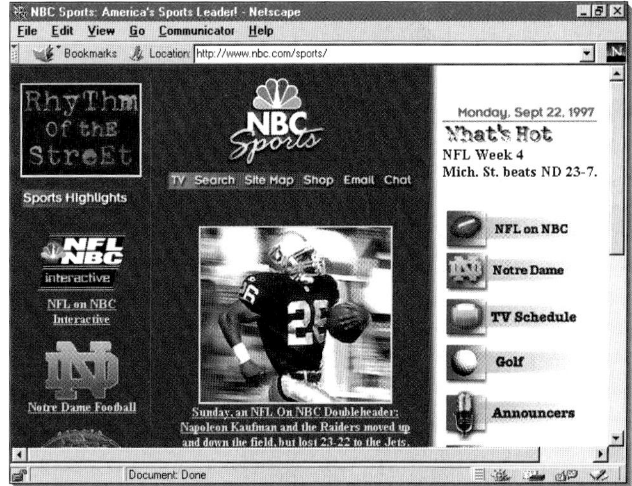

NBC Sports
URL www.nbc.com/sports

USA TODAY Online
URL www.usatoday.com

Smithsonian Institution

URL www.si.edu

Maytag Appliances
URL www.maytag.com

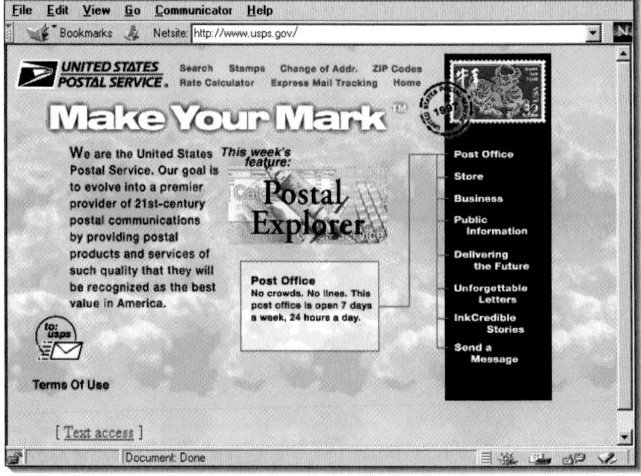

United States Postal Service
URL www.usps.gov

Greenpeace International

URL www.greenpeace.org

Milk

URL www.whymilk.com

Sunkist

URL www.sunkist.com

Minolta

URL www.minolta.com

Discovery Channel Online
URL www.discovery.com

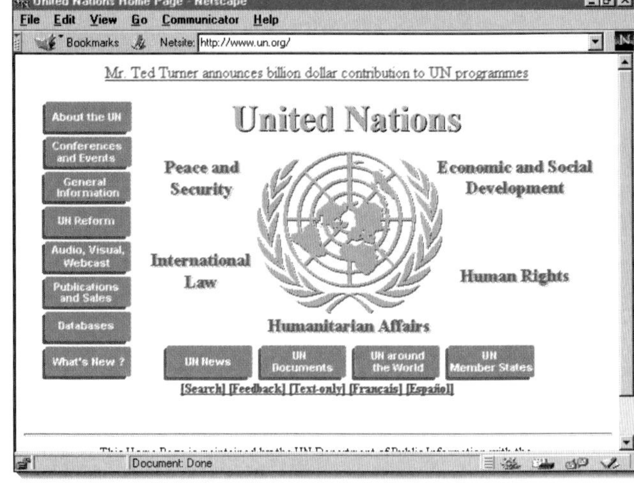

United Nations
URL www.un.org

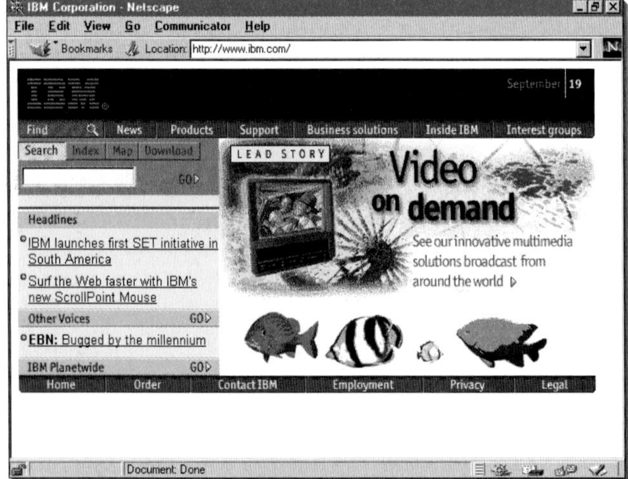

IBM
URL www.ibm.com

American Stock Exchange
URL www.amex.com

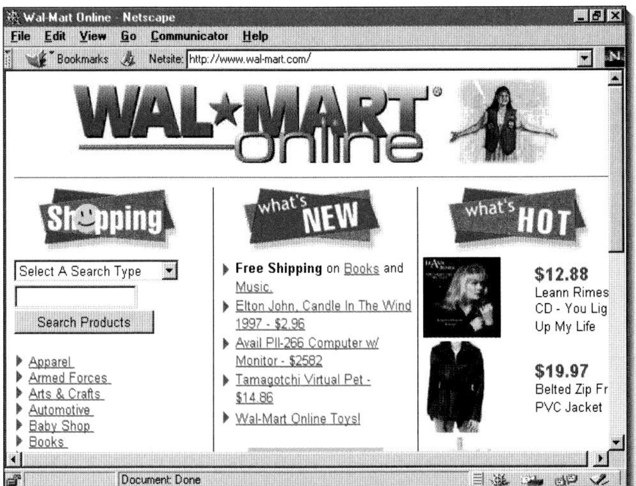

Wal-Mart Online

URL www.wal-mart.com

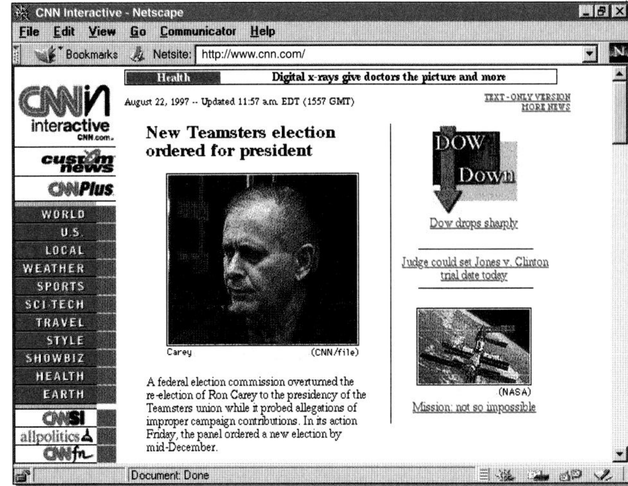

CNN

URL www.cnn.com

FAO Schwarz

URL www.faoschwarz.com

Best Western International

URL www.bestwestern.com

Spiegel
URL www.spiegel.com

jcrew
URL www.jcrew.com

Campbell's Soup
URL www.campbellsoup.com

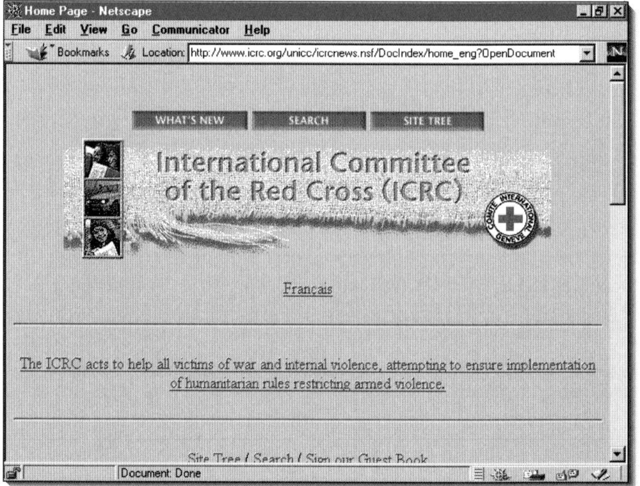

International Committee of the Red Cross
URL www.icrc.org

Trimark Pictures
URL www.trimarkpictures.com

New Balance Cyberpark
URL www.newbalance.com

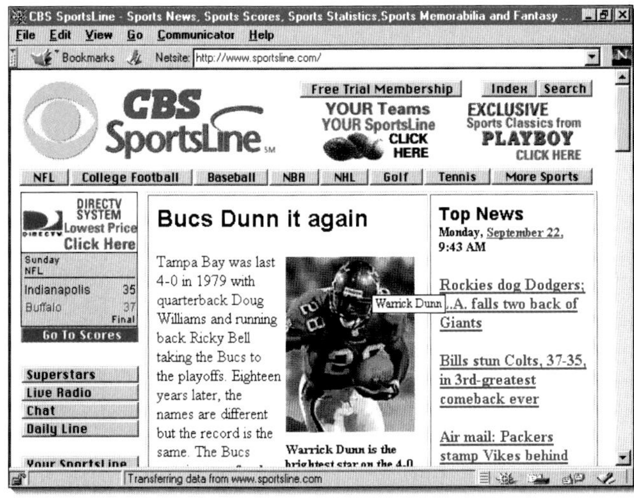

CBS SportsLine
URL www.sportsline.com

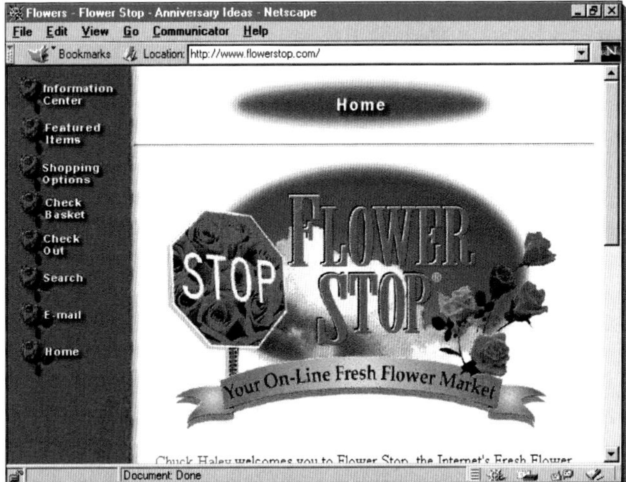

Flower Stop
URL www.flowerstop.com

INDEX

A

B

C

D

F

G

H

I

N

Y